LEWIS & CLARK

AND THE

INDIAN COUNTRY

LEWIS & CLARK

AND THE

INDIAN COUNTRY

The Native American Perspective

EDITED BY

Frederick E. Hoxie
and Jay T. Nelson

PUBLISHED FOR THE NEWBERRY LIBRARY

UNIVERSITY OF ILLINOIS PRESS

URBANA AND CHICAGO

Library of Congress Cataloging-in-Publication Data
Lewis and Clark and the Indian country : the Native American
perspective / edited by Frederick E. Hoxie and Jay T. Nelson.
p.   cm.
Based on an exhibition that opened in Oct. 2004 at
the Newberry Library, Chicago, Ill.
Includes bibliographical references and index.
ISBN-13 978-0-252-03266-0 (cloth : alk. paper)
ISBN-10 0-252-03266-7 (cloth : alk. paper)
ISBN-13 978-0-252-07485-1 (pbk. : alk. paper)
ISBN-10 0-252-07485-8 (pbk. : alk. paper)
1. Lewis and Clark Expedition (1804–1806)—Exhibitions.
2. Lewis and Clark Expedition (1804–1806)—Influence—Exhibitions.
3. Lewis, Meriwether, 1774–1809—Relations with Indians—Exhibitions.
4. Clark, William, 1770–1838—Relations with Indians—Exhibitions.
5. Culture conflict—West (U.S.)—History—19th century—Exhibitions.
6. West (U.S.)—Race relations—History—19th century—Exhibitions.
7. Indians of North America—West (U.S.)—Social life and customs—
     19th century—Exhibitions.
8. Indians of North America—West (U.S.)—Social life and customs—
     20th century—Exhibitions.
9. West (U.S.)—Description and travel—Exhibitions.
10. United States—Territorial expansion—Exhibitions.
I. Hoxie, Frederick E., 1947– II. Nelson, Jay T.
F592.7.L496   2007
917.804'2—dc22   2007015798

CONTENTS

———•◆•———

INTRODUCTION

What Can We Learn from a Bicentennial?
Frederick E. Hoxie

In May 1804, Meriwether Lewis and William Clark, two young army captains from Virginia, embarked from their camp near St. Louis on a journey up the Missouri River. Their mission was to travel to the source of the Missouri and then to pass beyond it to the Pacific Ocean. According to their commander in chief, President Thomas Jefferson, the purpose of this trip was to explore "the most direct and practicable water communication across the continent for the purposes of commerce." Central to that commerce in 1804 were the hundreds of Native communities whose homelands would be traversed by these soldiers and their detachment of some two-dozen men. Because the United States had recently obtained from France title to the vague territory called "Louisiana," which stretched from the Mississippi River to the Rocky Mountains, the president also instructed his men to inform the Indian people they met along the way that "henceforward" the Americans would "become their fathers and friends." The president hoped the commanders would learn "at what places and times we must establish stores of goods among them, to exchange for their peltries." The commanders were largely successful; in fall 1806 they, and most of their men, returned to St. Louis.[1]

The arrival of the year 2004—the two hundredth anniversary of the expedition's beginning—set off an outburst of commemorative activities. The onset of this celebration exerted an almost gravitational pull on the American

1

public, as well as on history students from all ages and levels of expertise. Tourists, television crews, school groups—and even reenactors—set off up the Missouri in imitation of the original expedition. Countless others sat at home taking in the films and videos, reading newly published books, and watching the news reports of this western activity. This irresistible pull was triggered by a phenomenon that has become a hallmark of popular culture in modern America: the bicentennial.

Perhaps it dates from 1976. The commemoration of the two hundredth anniversary of the Declaration of Independence appears to have initiated the combination of media coverage, historical reenactment, self-congratulation, and absorption in the minute details of the past that Americans have come to recognize as the bicentennial phenomenon. Arriving on the heels of a divisive decade and defeat in a foreign war, the "Bicentennial of the Revolution" gave Americans something to celebrate together. Its chief sponsors were state and federal governments, corporations, and the tourist industry. The success of the 1976 bicentennial inspired subsequent celebrations of other major events from the late eighteenth century: the bicentennial of the Northwest Ordinance was quickly followed by the bicentennial of the U.S. Constitution and the bicentennial of the U.S. Congress (whose current members couldn't pass up that opportunity for speechmaking).

Soon creative Americans developed variations on this bicentennial theme: the centennial of the Statue of Liberty, the centennial of Wilbur and Orville Wright's flight, and the quincentennial of the Columbus voyages. In 1989 and 1990 five western states celebrated their centennials, and, as the 1990s got underway, Americans presented yet another celebratory innovation: they began commemorating the major events of World War II. The most highly celebrated of these in the United States and Western Europe was D-day, June 6, 1944, when the Allied forces landed in France to begin dislodging the Germans from northwestern Europe. This was an ideal event for it allowed the Americans in particular to celebrate their own heroism and sacrifice while neatly avoiding the inclusion of the Russians, World War II allies who spent 1944 incurring far higher casualties as they rolled the Nazis back along the eastern front. D-day was celebrated first in an event featuring an eloquent speech by Ronald Reagan in 1984 (the fortieth anniversary), then by a similar effort from Bill Clinton (the fiftieth), and finally in 2004 by a French-sponsored extravaganza that briefly overcame divisions among the former allies. The new millennium has brought the centennial of the automobile, the promise of centennials of World War I, and, for our children and grandchildren, the bicentennials of the Alamo and the Civil War, and, no doubt, the centennial of D-day. The list is endless.

The tone of these proliferating commemorations is typically set by reverent nods to the past and booster-style celebrations of the present. The spirit of celebration often overcomes the reality of the historic event. As one Boston wag observed during the bicentennial of the American Revolution in 1976, when Queen Elizabeth's royal yacht docked in that city as part of her triumphal tour of the United States: "the British lost the revolution but they are winning the Bicentennial!" As that comment suggests, grand historic commemorations present the American public with opportunities to revisit history and to remember the past with a positive—and commercially beneficial—spirit. The actual historical reality of the event being celebrated can fade into the background as politicians preen for the cameras and visitors' bureaus line up cut-rate hotel rooms for the tourists. Encouraged perhaps by the increasingly powerful national media industries (particularly television, with its voracious appetite for attractive and soporific content), the public has come to accept commemorations as public spectacles in which self-congratulation takes precedence over doubt or regret. Let us forget the Constitution's endorsement of slavery or the fact that the Statue of Liberty's "golden door" was open only to Europeans or that D-day may not have been the turning point of World War II. Let us turn instead to noble words carved in granite, the manicured lawns of the Normandy cemetery, or the marble columns of Congress. Commemorations have not been a time for ambiguity or difficult questions. They teach instead that the anniversary recalls something wonderful in the past that has made possible something even more wonderful in the present. Americans witness these commemorations as they witness the conclusion of an epic television special: hardship and sadness have been resolved and the heroes—or their descendants—have found their way to the promised land. The music rises and viewers marvel at the fireworks bursting in the night sky. Almost by definition, fiftieth anniversaries, centennials, and bicentennials exude a positive and nonreflective spin.

But what is wrong with that? After all, public commemorations are not seminars. They are staged for people to see and to participate in, and the words and music that accompany them are logically organized to build the gate. The television shows, books, and exhibits—most financed with private funds—require viewers and participants. The success of the commemoration is measured by participation; it doesn't get a grade for accuracy or intellectual ambition. And perhaps there is nothing wrong with that. But one must recognize that when organizers of commemorations assemble large groups of people, either in person or electronically, they know that the safest way to proceed is to avoid complexity.

The best way to keep things simple while delivering something meaty and historical enough to attract an audience is to focus on a set of noncontroversial details: George Washington's wooden teeth, the condition of the Constitution's parchment, the mechanism of muskets, or the rigging on Columbus's flagship. In the public arena, grand events are usually remembered through such tiny facts. As with other aspects of this "bicentennial phenomenon," we can see vivid evidence of the appeal of minutiae by looking back at the 1976 bicentennial. During that year television viewers were fed a regular diet of "Bicentennial Minutes." These well-produced sixty-second spots ran throughout the year, focusing on individuals or on incidents that could be cast as instructive tidbits of information about the Revolution. It was a wonderful way to work in women, African Americans, and others who are generally ignored in commemorations. But the effect was to surround viewers with an array of disconnected "trees" that could not communicate the meaning—or the questions surrounding—the "forest" of the Revolution. Inspired by the Bicentennial Minutes, subsequent celebrations have involved similar presentations of little human stories, clever objects, replicas of historic ships, costumes, and, of course, reenactments. To provide politicians with a spirit-boosting occasion for speaking out in support of New York's recovery from the attacks of September 11, 2001, members of Congress even reenacted the time when the national legislature met in New York City. And note that reenactments have become a generally popular form of historical commemoration—from Civil War soldiers, to homesteaders, to combatants gathering in 2006 to celebrate the two hundred fiftieth anniversary of the Seven Years' War. These events (particularly when they are filmed in closeup, in documentary style) allow people to "be there," imitating the lives of original participants. In a wonderful example of these "authentic" celebrations' overcoming history, Wyoming's state centennial involved the reenactment of a nineteenth-century wagon train (even though most Wyoming homesteaders arrived by rail). The reenactors were "there" in a past that had not existed.[2]

How does this brief review of the history of commemorations help us better understand the Lewis and Clark bicentennial? First, it suggests that national commemorations like the one that began in 2004 are, almost by definition, celebrations of tiny events and obscure details: the technology of Lewis's air gun, the fate of Clark's slave York, the American explorers' indecision on the upper reaches of the Missouri (which way did the main course run and which stream was the tributary?), or Clark's willingness to dance with his Indian hosts. By focusing on physical hardships, technological inventions, and little stories of grace under pressure, bicentennial celebrants introduce the public to something historical without undermining the event's positive tone and commercial potential. By thinking only about these two-dozen men and their boats, tourists could believe that the journey, while difficult, was, at some level, "fun" and worth retracing by car or, vicariously, by videotape or book. Small events encourage local pride and can persuade vacationers from Atlanta and Baltimore to visit Great Falls instead of Paris. Whether they are filmmakers, museum directors, or tourism officials, Lewis and Clark bicentennial organizers have been largely determined to focus on small, human events, to emphasize dramatic (but not bloody) encounters, and to keep the tone positive.

Second, deeper discussions of complex events or difficult issues are typically reduced to examinations of individual character traits. Thomas Jefferson: patriot, or duplicitous slave owner? Meriwether Lewis: courageous captain or manic depressive? Sekakawea: patient guide or abused captive? This tendency to focus on individuals suggests that uncomfortable themes and tragic events are probably traceable to personal quirks or failings rather than to deeper problems with the Americans' immediate goals or long-term objectives. It seems that there is an inverse relationship between the size of historical commemorations and the level of their accompanying historical imagination. The greater the celebration, the smaller the questions being asked about it. Great events are recalled with great celebrations, but too often those celebrations reduce public discussion of great events to sophisticated games of Trivial Pursuit.

Students of the Lewis and Clark expedition can reflect on the recent history of American commemorations as they observe the celebrations surrounding the expedition's bicentennial. For example, examining the January 18, 2004, edition of the *Chicago Tribune,* the careful reader will find the journey described in a headline as "An American Odyssey . . . America's Greatest Adventure Story." Odysseus, this reader will recall, traveled a long and circuitous route home from the Trojan war, facing monsters, sirens, and other threats along the way. The warrior's heroism in the face of this danger lay at the heart of Homer's adventure story. This powerful image suggests the American soldiers in the "Corps of Discovery" experienced something similar: a small but brave band's perilous journey through torment and temptation. This theme is echoed and refined in the opening panels of Lewis and Clark: The National Bicentennial

Exhibition, which opened in St. Louis in 2004 before spending the next two years moving to Philadelphia, Denver, Portland, and Washington, D.C.[3]

An exhibit panel showing text identified as a "Wishram Prophecy" (who are the Wishrams?) tells visitors, "One old man . . . dreamt; he saw strange people, they spoke to him and showed him everything. He said: 'Soon all sorts of strange things will come.'" A companion panel quotes President Jefferson, who wrote, "Possessing a chosen country, with room enough for our descendants to the one hundredth and one thousandth generation, what more is necessary to make us a happy and prosperous people?" While not threatening, the disembodied voice of the Wishram placed alongside that of the third president seems to confirm the central message of the *Tribune* headline: in this historic event we will identify with the travelers and sympathize with the hardships they endured. The payoff, of course, is that the journey helped our heroes to "possess" this country and contribute to the future of a "happy and prosperous people."

To be fair, the National Bicentennial Exhibition contains a great deal of information about Native Americans; they are not always as mysterious as the "Wishrams" quoted in the opening panel. But the Native peoples in the exhibit are not really actors in the story; they are part of the "cultural landscape" through which the heroes traveled. The exhibit, organizers declare, "will compare the assumptions of Lewis and Clark and the Indian peoples they were among." The historical significance of this comparison is not made clear.

It is unlikely that most readers of the *Chicago Tribune* or visitors to the National Bicentennial Exhibition will explore the complexity and the meaning of the Lewis and Clark journey or call into question the image of the American soldiers in the Corps of Discovery as nineteenth-century versions of Odysseus. Readers of this book will. The purpose of the documents and commentaries assembled here is to lead readers into a territory most bicentennials have declared off-limits: the vast and complex "Indian country" that surrounded the travelers as they moved up the Missouri and on to the Pacific. What is more, this book presents documents and first-person accounts that are stories not generally welcome in celebratory events such as the National Bicentennial Exhibition: tales of suspicion and fear, stories of the expedition's long-term impact on the territory it explored, and testimonies of survival and cultural pride from contemporary Indian people. Finally, this volume brings together essays and references designed to inspire further research and reflection on the meaning of the Lewis and Clark expedition. The purpose of these materials is not to demonize the explorers or to denigrate their achievements, but to place them in a broad and multifaceted historical context that will allow serious students of history the opportunity to reflect on the deeper meaning of the expedition, both for the past and for the future.

There is nothing wrong with celebrating the journey of Lewis and Clark or with praising their courage. But there is something wrong with reducing to a mythic odyssey a complex series of events involving widely divergent American cultural traditions. All the actors in this story were Americans; all participated in the creation of the American democracy that so vividly surrounds the commemoration of these events. To ignore or marginalize the Native American historical actors in this story serves neither history nor the cause of our democracy.

But what will broadening the scope of our examination contribute, either to history or to democracy? That question is best answered by referring to three facts about the expedition that most Americans do not know.

First, the Corps of Discovery was not the first party of Euro-Americans to travel the Upper Missouri. From their base in Illinois, several French traders had traveled as far as modern North Dakota in the 1740s and 1750s. Following the Seven Years' War, free traders—most notably the Englishman David Thompson—followed the Saskatchewan River west from Lake Winnipeg. Thompson first reached modern Alberta in 1792 and established fur-trade outposts throughout what is now the Canadian side of the northern Rockies before identifying the source of the Columbia River in 1807 and following that river to the sea. When the Corps of Discovery reached the Mandan villages near modern Bismarck, North Dakota, they found French Canadian traders well established there and learned that furs from the Missouri were flowing north to rivers that ran east and led ultimately to the warehouses of Montreal.

The second piece of information rarely understood by celebrants of the expedition's bicentennial is that rather than forming a hostile barrier to the Americans' explorations, Indians were vital allies on the trail. The odyssey image is wrong. In fact, the image is not only inaccurate, it distorts the expedition's history. It is clear from the journals of the expedition as well as from an analysis of the history of the travelers' journey that there were several moments in the two-year trip when Indians provided critical assistance and saved the Americans from certain death. It is not an overstatement to declare that without that Indian assistance, the Americans would have died or been forced to turn back. Three brief examples:

- The corps spent the winter of 1804–5 near the Mandan villages on the Upper Missouri. They did not have enough food for the winter. They traded metal tools for corn from the Mandans and Hidatsas.

- By the fall of 1805 the Americans had traveled from the Mandan villages to the eastern slope of the Rocky Mountains. Here they learned that their image of the Rockies based on their eastern experiences—of a range of mountains that could be traversed relatively quickly—was dangerously inaccurate. When they reached Lemhi Pass in what is now southern Idaho, for example, they saw not a valley leading to the sea but dozens of new mountain ranges. As September began, they found themselves headed north into the Bitterroot Valley. The Shoshones (also rendered as "Shoshonis" in some documents) had told them that a nearby trail would take them up a canyon to the west and eventually to westward-flowing rivers, but they did not know the trail's precise location or its length. The Americans' horses were clearly incapable of carrying them over the mountains. At that point the explorers encountered a group of Salish hunters who exchanged twelve "elegant" mounts for a group of the expedition's played-out ponies and pointed them in the right direction. These were the horses that carried them over the Lolo Trail and to tributaries of the Columbia River.

- Despite these mounts, weather caught up with the party as it worked its way down the westward slopes. On September 16 they awoke and found themselves covered with snow. Clark was dispatched to travel ahead in search of help and food. Four days later he stumbled upon a party of Nez Perce families gathering roots. Again, Native hospitality saved the day. The Nez Perces exchanged horses for canoes and refilled the party's food stores.

Another "fact" overlooked today is that the expedition to the Pacific was not a benign scientific enterprise. Funded by Congress and sent forth by the man who had pulled off the Louisiana Purchase, the mission had serious geopolitical goals. The Americans were to learn about the Indians along their route, Jefferson had written, because "the commerce . . . which may be carried on with them renders [it] important." In addition to inserting the interests of the United States into the rapidly expanding fur trade of the Great Plains and the Pacific Coast, Jefferson was eager to ratify America's claim to the newly purchased Louisiana Territory. The president was putting American "boots on the ground," and while the explorers said nothing explicit about American control when they met Indian leaders or Canadian fur traders, they would brook no opposition to their mission. The clearest picture of their tolerance level came on the journey home.

The trip west—from the spring of 1804 to the fall of 1805—was all diplomacy: presents and flags for the Mandans and a salary for Toussaint Charbonneau, the French Canadian (Northwest Company) trader who was living with the Mandans but was willing to change his loyalty for American gold. Speeches and more flags for the Shoshones and the Salish horse traders. The same for the Nez Perces and the Chinooks along the Columbia who guided the Americans to the sea. The tone of the expedition changed during the winter of 1805–6. The American soldiers were appalled at the prices local Chinook people charged for provisions and worried that local leaders seemed uninterested in forging alliances with the United States. This meant that unease reached a climax in the spring when the captains decided they were justified in stealing a Chinook canoe because the price the local chief had demanded was too high. Indians were always treacherous, Lewis argued. A few months later Lewis acted again on this belief in Native treachery. Encountering a small party of young Blackfeet men north of the Missouri in what is now western Montana, Lewis delivered a bold speech indicating the Americans had recently made alliances with the tribe's enemies. The Americans spent the night camped with the Blackfeet. But frightened by the explorers' bravado—or simply acting to fulfill the obligations of young men in a warrior society—members of the Blackfeet group rose early the next morning and attempted to steal some of the Americans' guns and horses. In the ensuing scuffle two Blackfeet were killed, one by Lewis. But more revealing of the explorers' feelings was what happened in the immediate aftermath of the skirmish. Captain Lewis gathered up the weapons and shields dropped by the fleeing young men and burned them. He then took a Jefferson peace medal and hung it around the neck of one of the dead men.

These insights are not particularly new. They reflect a generation of new scholarship focused on the American West prior to the Lewis and Clark expedition and to the Native American communities who called this place their home. Prominent among the works of this generation are James Ronda's *Lewis and Clark among the Indians* and Colin Calloway's *One Vast Winter Count*, but also included with them would be the writings of W. Raymond Wood and Gary Moulton.[4] The contributions of these authors will be clear in the materials and commentaries contained in this volume. Just as important as this new scholarship, however, is the process of reflecting on the ways in which it alters the traditional—and the bicentennial—view of the Corps of Discovery. A key element in this reflection and reeducation concerning the expedition has also been conversations with Native American educators.

In the fall of 2001, thanks to support from the National Endowment for the Humanities and an invitation from the Newberry Library to explore the possibility of an exhibition that would incorporate new scholarship on Lewis and Clark, I assembled a group of four Native American consultants—each representing a major tribe encountered by the American explorers—to consider the idea. My plan was to focus on the Lewis and Clark expedition's relationship to Native Americans and, if possible, to develop the program collaboratively with my four consultants. The group consisted of a tribal museum director, the founder and principal of a language immersion school on a reservation, a curator at a tribal museum, and a National Park Service historian with long experience interpreting the history of his and surrounding tribes. I had circulated an outline to the group in advance of our meeting and was excited to hear their reactions.

My outline focused on a number of famous events in which the explorers interacted closely with Indian people—the winter in the Mandan villages, the explorers' relationship with the French Canadian Charbonneau and his Shoshone "wife" Sekakawea, and the winter at Fort Clatsop on the Oregon coast. I wanted to explore the importance of Indians to the expedition and to point out how relations between tribes and explorers had deteriorated steadily from the high point among the Mandans to the violent encounter with the Blackfeet during the return in 1806. Like lots of non-Indian "organizers" in this kind of situation, I opened the meeting with a long description of my ideas.

The four consultants were extremely polite. I knew they liked the general idea of the exhibit, but as they began to respond to my presentation I grew apprehensive. The first consultant talked about tribal languages. Like many communities, his has seen a decline in the number of native speakers of the tribal language over the past century. He worried that place names, historical figures, religious stories, and ceremonial knowledge would be lost as the language slipped away. He also took enormous pride in the growth of a new language program and the spread of concern for language within his community.

The second consultant spoke of the importance of tribal museums and cultural centers. She noted that no institutions have a primary commitment to the preservation of tribal stories and local material culture except tribal museums. Without such institutions, she added, a tribe's cultural resources—precious, incapable of duplication or imitation, and vital to the community's future—would be lost.

The third consultant spoke at length about the preservation of sacred lands and environmental resources. He reported that even tourism—which he, like other tribal officials, hoped would increase during the coming bicentennial—endangered community lands and resources because it opened them to overuse and permanent damage. Important places, special places, would not simply endure because they were made of stone or timber; they needed people to understand them and care for them, both now and into the future. Educating people about the significance of the Native American landscape was for him far more important than new techniques for policing tribal property.

Finally, the fourth consultant spoke about tribal histories. "You know," he said, "our communities functioned for centuries without social welfare agencies, homes for the elderly, and police departments. Our families and our villages were all of those things. Our people don't understand that; they are forgetting both our past and the community values that have kept us together for thousands of years."

When the fourth consultant finished speaking I asked if we could take a break. We chatted over coffee but I felt totally confused. We had gathered to talk about a Lewis and Clark exhibit. I had outlined the script for an exhibit about Lewis and Clark and the Indians. They had that outline in their hands. But their "advice" consisted of speeches on contemporary issues: tribal languages, cultural centers, sacred lands, and tribal histories. I sympathized with their problems, but what did their concerns have to do with Lewis and Clark and my effort to bring new academic scholarship before the public? When we reassembled, I could think of only one question: Is anyone interested in an exhibit on Lewis and Clark?

Well, of course, they all said. "But you have talked about everything *but* Lewis and Clark," I replied. Then someone made the connection: Lewis and Clark began the process that led to this situation. The explorers didn't cause the current problems but their vague appreciation of the Indian country through which they traveled passed on to those who came behind them. The issues of language loss, culture change, economic dislocation, and the disruption of community social traditions were products of their communities' relationship with the United States, a relationship that began with Lewis and Clark. Stated more pointedly: Lewis and Clark represented a moment in a two-century-long struggle over native culture and community sovereignty.

For these four Native Americans, the Lewis and Clark expedition was not an event lost in the past that needed to be recovered and described as an academic exercise—as a source of either celebration or regret. It was, rather, part of a historical process that was ongoing and whose effects could be witnessed in their home communities today.

My conversation with these four consultants suggested two additional themes in my reformulation of the expedition and its meaning two hundred years later. First, it was clear that the Lewis and Clark expedition could not be understood as a discrete event that began in 1804 and ended in 1806. I had been correct to reject the idea that the journey was an "odyssey," but it was also important to look both before and after the first years of the nineteenth century. The expedition's effects multiplied in the nineteenth century and are apparent today in both the Indian and the non-Indian communities of the West.

Second, an analysis of Lewis and Clark's relationship to Indian people requires setting aside the notion that the expansion of the United States to the Pacific was in some way a "natural or "inevitable" process. It was clear from my conversations with the tribal educators that Lewis and Clark inaugurated a diplomatic, military, cultural, and economic struggle over the future of this sector of North America. This struggle continues and, even with decades of reconciliation and the current bicentennial celebration, it is likely to mark the culture of this region for decades to come. Moreover, the ultimate outcome of this struggle over the sovereignty and identity of North America is not clear.

As I reflected on those two lessons I learned a third: the four consultants who spoke to me that day did not dismiss my ambition to mount an exhibit on Lewis and Clark. They could have done that by sending me an e-mail from home: "No thanks! Lewis and Clark is about *you*, white boy, not about *us*." They had come to Chicago to hear my ideas and they had come to talk about language survival, about the work of cultural centers, about successful programs to protect sacred lands and resources, and to deliver the message that Native families still functioned and tribal values still endured. (A fifth consultant would soon join the team and she would be no less committed to presenting information on the role of tribal arts in both traditional cultures and contemporary tribal communities.) These educators were telling me something very important: Lewis and Clark and their expedition did not mark the "end of history." In fact, by enabling me to widen the lens through which I viewed the Lewis and Clark expedition, these extraordinary consultants were telling me that a new chapter in the history of the region *could begin only if we looked back honestly at the expedition and its consequences.* I came to believe that this bicentennial might be a moment of opportunity that might truly energize and teach important lessons; it did not have to be simply a snapshot of a moment of imminent destruction and loss. So I came to believe that in commemorating the Lewis and Clark expedition, we need not say "something new" about Lewis and Clark. As welcome as new research is, we didn't have to persuade ourselves that the commemoration required us to uncover sensational new details about the private lives of the explorers or their colleagues. It also wouldn't require that the public memorize some "revisionist" interpretation of the voyage. What was crucial instead was to allow ourselves—and to invite others—to do something that is hard to convey in a Bicentennial Minute or even a documentary or exhibition: we needed to encourage people to reflect about the meaning of what we know about the expedition and to consider that knowledge in the context of a continental struggle over sovereignty and cultural power. To accomplish that reflection, it is essential that students of history appreciate the events of two hundred years ago from the perspective of Native Americans. If this bicentennial were to escape the gravitational pull of the modern bicentennial movement, it would be because individuals made the effort to imagine the linkages between the Native communities of the twenty-first century and their ancestors who had already lived on this continent for ten thousand years when the spearpoint of U.S. power reached their doorsteps two centuries ago.

The reward for this effort was a moment of reconciliation that brought together communities that began to be broken apart in 1805. The starting point for that process is the establishment of a new perspective from which to view the past. Establishing that perspective was the principal objective of Lewis and Clark and the Indian Country, the exhibit that ultimately emerged from the conversations that began in 2001. Supported by the National Endowment for the Humanities, the National Park Service, the University of Illinois, and the Newberry Library, the exhibit introduced visitors to the Indian country as it existed on the eve of the American expedition, traced the Corps of Discovery through several key encounters with Native peoples, and offered a portrait of both the consequences of American expansion and life in the Indian country today. The exhibit opened in October 2004 for a four-month run that was punctuated by lectures, performances, and seminars. This book replicates and deepens the intellectual content of the original exhibit.

The table of contents for this book duplicates the organization of the exhibit. In that sense, readers of this book will have the opportunity to "tour" an exhibit without having to travel or wait in line. The materials here also provide background information and deeper analysis than is possible in a museum exhibit. These materials were selected and edited to make it easy to "browse" through the topics and move to parts of the story that readers find most interesting. Each section of the book begins with a brief introduction enabling readers to understand the topic at hand in the context of the larger project of rethinking and reimagining the history of the expedition.

The first five chapters present an overview of the Indian country that lay west of St. Louis in 1804. Rather than reverting to a textbook summary of tribes and cultural practices, however, the section focuses on aspects of the region that made it distinctive, both culturally and politically. The section introduces readers to Indian ideas about creation and the environment and to the fundamental values that motivated Native people in their relations with each other as well as with outsiders.

Chapters 6 through 12 offer a cross-cultural portrait of the American expedition. This section begins with a discussion of what people in the United States and Europe knew about the Indian country in 1804 and proceeds to six snapshots of encounters between the travelers and their hosts. Excerpts from journals kept by the commanders and by several of the enlisted men offer fascinating descriptions of encounters where both visitors and Natives struggled to understand one another and to decide how best to respond to the unexpected people suddenly sitting across from them.

"A New Nation Comes to the Indian Country" replicates the third section of the Newberry exhibit. In six brief chapters it presents some of the key forces that enabled the United States to extend its sovereignty over the Indian country and allows readers to glimpse some of the consequences of this process of conquest and expansion. The chapters in this section keep the focus on several communities that first hosted Lewis and Clark and, when possible, identifies how specific individuals who befriended the Americans were later disappointed by them or their government.

In "The Indian Country Today," documents and commentaries organized as chapters 19 through 23 give readers a parting glimpse of Native peoples along the Lewis and Clark trail in the twentieth century. As in previous sections—and as is obligatory in an museum exhibit—this portrait avoids broad overviews, concentrating instead on specific communities. As a consequence, readers will learn about the importance of salmon restoration to plateau peoples on the western slope of the Rockies, language restoration among the Blackfeet, educational reform in reservation tribal colleges, and environmental protection among the Nez Perces. These serve as illustrations and examples of the enduring strength and distinctiveness of the people who still claim the Indian country as their home.

Finally, the book closes with an eloquent series of reflections offered by the exhibit's Native American consultants and the preeminent historian of the Lewis and Clark expedition, James P. Ronda. Based on a lecture delivered in Chicago in conjunction with the exhibit, Ronda's essay looks back at the bicentennial celebrations and describes some of the central lessons of both the journey and its history.

Lewis and Clark and the Indian Country, in either book or exhibit form, would not have been possible without its principal sponsors: the National Endowment for the Humanities, the National Park Service, the University of Illinois, and the Newberry Library. Willis G. Regier, director of the University of Illinois Press, first suggested the idea of a book that would replicate and deepen the message and analysis contained in the exhibit; without his invitation this book would not exist. In addition, this volume has benefited from the efforts of Joan Catapano, editor-in-chief at the Press; Kerry Wynn, Stacy Schlegel, Brian Ingrassia, and Ian Hartman, research assistants at the University of Illinois at Urbana-Champaign; and Jordan Hinderyckx, research assistant at the Newberry Library; and from the support of James Grossman, vice president for research and education at the Newberry Library; Brian Hosmer, director of the library's D'Arcy McNickle Center for American Indian History; and Rob Galler, the center's associate director during the planning stages of the project.

Finally, whatever is of value here was inspired by the wisdom and patience of the five Native American community consultants who worked with us on the exhibit: Frederick Baker, from Fort Berthold, North Dakota; Pat Courtney Gold, from Scapoose, Oregon; Otis Half Moon, from both the Nez Perce and the National Park Service "tribes"; Darrell Robes Kipp, of the Piegan Institute on the Blackfeet Reservation in Montana; and Marjorie Waheneka, curator at the Tamástslikt Cultural Institute serving the Cayuse, Umatilla, and Walla Walla peoples in eastern Oregon. We are grateful to Loretta Fowler, Jacki Thompson Rand, and James P. Ronda for their advice and assistance in planning the exhibit.

We dedicate this book to the memory of Marjorie Waheneka's son, Alexius Minthorn (Suh-Pul-Its-A-Kee), a promising young man whose tragic loss has saddened our team and inspired us to redouble our efforts to build a stronger, more inclusive world.

Notes

1. For Thomas Jefferson's instructions, here and in ensuing paragraphs, see Thomas Jefferson, *Writings* (New York: Library of America, 1984), 1126–32.

2. For discussions of American bicentennial behavior, see John Bodnar, *Remaking America: Public Memory, Commemoration, and Patriotism in the Twentieth Century* (Princeton: Princeton University Press, 1992); and Lyn Spillman, *Nation and Com-*

memoration: Creating National Identities in the United States and Australia (New York: Cambridge University Press, 1997).

3. There is an excellent Web site about the exhibit at http://www.lewisandclarkexhibit .org, accessed February 21, 2007.

4. See James P. Ronda, *Lewis and Clark among the Indians,* rev. ed. (Lincoln: University of Nebraska Press, 2002); Colin G. Calloway, *One Vast Winter Count: The Native American West before Lewis and Clark* (Lincoln: University of Nebraska Press, 2003). See also W. Raymond Wood and Thomas D. Thiessen, eds., *Early Fur Trade on the Northern Plains: Canadian Traders among the Mandan and Hidatsa Indians, 1738–1808* (Norman: University of Oklahoma Press, 1985); and Gary E. Moulton, ed., *The Journals of the Lewis and Clark Expedition,* 10 vols. (Lincoln: University of Nebraska Press, 1983–2000).

PART 1

---◆---

THE INDIAN COUNTRY

The Native American people the Corps of Discovery encountered on its two-and-a-half-year round-trip journey to the Pacific belonged to well-established communities that made their living by combining farming, fishing, and hunting techniques in a variety of ways. Despite the diversity of these communities, they followed similar cultural traditions. Centuries of life in North America had shaped a stable system of community relationships and encouraged a common set of values. Among these were a deep respect for the earth's creators, a keen sense of the environment and its products, a social ethic based on generosity and gift-giving, a conviction that men and women could contribute equally to the common good, and dependence on a vast network of trade and diplomatic relations. While not a country in the European sense, the region the Americans traversed two centuries ago was bound together by common values and customs.

CHAPTER ONE

The Arrival of Horses Accelerates Trade and Cultural Change

John C. Ewers, an anthropologist from the Smithsonian Institution, was among the first scholars to study the historical development of Native American culture in the centuries preceding sustained contact with Europeans. Drawing on both archaeology and historical documents, Ewers demonstrated that Plains Indians inhabited a dynamic historical environment and that they were quick to capitalize on the advantages offered by a powerful new animal, the horse. The acquisition of horses by Indians across western North America had profound consequences in many areas of life.

THE ACQUISITION OF THE HORSE
John C. Ewers

Clark Wissler (1927, p. 154) has named the period 1540 to 1880 in the history of the Indian tribes of the Great Plains "the Horse Culture period." This period can be defined more accurately and meaningfully in cultural than in temporal terms. Among all the tribes of the area it began much later than 1540. With some tribes it ended before 1880. Yet for each Plains Indian tribe the Horse Culture Period spanned the years between the acquisition and first use of horses and the extermination of the economically important buffalo in the region in which that tribe lived.

Anthropologists and historians have been intrigued by the problem of the diffusion of the European horse among the Plains Indians. It is well known that many tribes began to acquire horses before their first recorded contacts

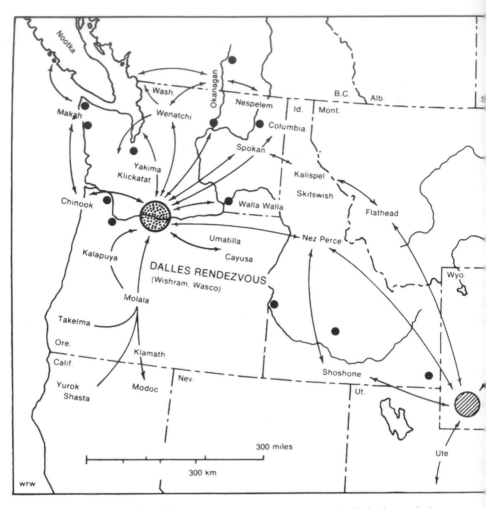

This map by Raymond Wood illustrates the trade connections that linked population centers in the Indian country before regular contacts were established with Europeans and other outsiders. Large circles represent major trade centers; smaller circles represent minor trading points. Courtesy the Newberry Library, Chicago (Ayer oE78 G73 A57, p. 101).

with white men. Paucity of documentation has given rise to much speculation as to the sources of the horses diffused to these tribes, the date when the first Plains Indians acquired horses, the rate of diffusion from tribe to tribe, and the conditions under which the spread took place.

The three Blackfoot tribes of the northwestern Plains, the Piegan, Blood, and North Blackfoot, were among those tribes that possessed horses when

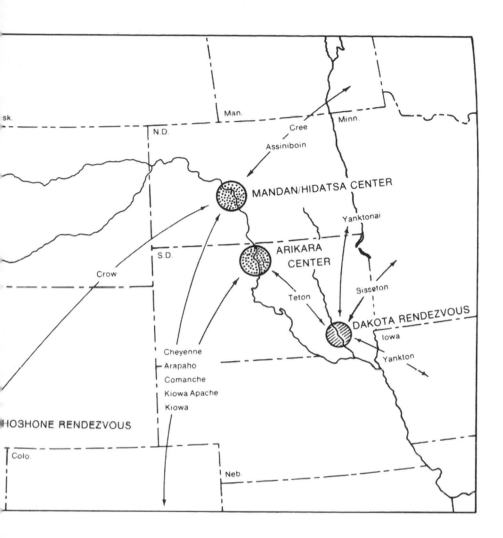

first met by literate white men. To view their acquisition in proper historical and cultural perspective it is necessary to consider the larger problem of the diffusion of horses to the northern Plains and Plateau tribes. Critical study of this problem dates from Wissler's paper, entitled, "The Influence of the Horse in the Development of Plains Culture," published in the *American Anthropologist* (Wissler, 1914). That stimulating, pioneer effort encouraged further study of the problem. Of the more recent contributions two papers by Francis Haines (1938, a and b), based to a considerable extent upon data unavailable to Wissler a quarter of a century earlier, have been most influential in revising the thinking of students of this problem.

The Northward Spread of Horses:
Sources of the Horses of the Plains Indians

Haines' major contributions were to point out that the Plains Indians acquired their first horses from a different source and at a considerably later date than Wissler had considered probable. Wissler gave credence to the theory that the first horses obtained by Plains Indians were animals lost or abandoned by the Spanish exploring expeditions led by De Soto and Coronado in 1541 (Wissler, 1914, pp. 9–10). The historian Walter P. Webb, in "The Great Plains," an important regional history published 17 years later, acknowledged his debt to Wissler in his acceptance of this theory (Webb, 1931, p. 57). However, another historian, Morris Bishop, who had made a critical study of early Spanish explorations, termed this theory, "a pretty legend" (Bishop, 1933, p. 31). Haines virtually laid the old theory to rest. After a careful review of the evidence he concluded that "the chances of strays from the horse herds of either De Soto or Coronado having furnished the horses of the Plains Indians is so remote that it should be discarded" (Haines, 1938a, p. 117).

This conclusion has been supported by more recent scholarship. John R. Swanton, who has been a thorough student of the De Soto Expedition over a period of years, concurred in Haines' interpretation of the De Soto evidence (Swanton, 1939, pp. 170–171). Arthur S. Aiton, in publishing Coronado's Compostela muster roll, commented significantly, "Five hundred and fifty-eight horses, two of them mares, are accounted for in the muster. The presence and separate listing of only two mares suggests that we may have been credulous in the belief that stray horses from the Coronado expedition stocked the western plains with their first horses." Furthermore, he found no record of the loss of either mare during Coronado's expedition to the Plains (Aiton, 1939, pp. 556–70). Herbert E. Bolton, profound student of early Spanish explorations in the Southwest, has pointed out that even though Coronado may have taken some mares to the Plains which had not been listed in the Compostela roll, the biological possibility of strays from this expedition having stocked the Plains with Spanish horses was slight. He also noted the lack of any mention of encounters with stray horses or mounted Indians in the accounts of Spanish expeditions to the Great Plains in the later years of the 16th and early years of the 17th century (Bolton, 1949, pp. 68–69, 400).

Exploring the alternatives, Haines found that the early 17th-century Spanish stock-raising settlements of the Southwest, particularly those in the neighborhood of Santa Fe, furnished "just the items necessary to encourage the adoption of horses by the Indians to the east—friendly contact through trade, ample supply of horses, and examples of the advantages of the new servants" (Haines, 1938a, p. 117).

Dating the Northward Spread of Horses among the Indians

Different concepts of the sources of the horses of the Plains Indians led to very different interpretations of the rate of their diffusion among these tribes. Wissler's assumption that horses were available to the Plains Indians as early as 1541, caused him to consider it possible that they might have spread northward during the remainder of that century so rapidly that they could have reached the Crow and Blackfoot on the headwaters of the Missouri as early as 1600 (Wissler, 1914, p. 10). Haines, however, found "the available evidence indicates that the Plains Indians began acquiring horses some time after 1600, the center of distribution being Santa Fe. This development proceeded rather slowly; none of the tribes becoming horse Indians before 1630, and probably not until 1650" (Haines, 1938a, p. 117). The logical and historical soundness of Haines' position has been acknowledged by more recent students of the problem (Wyman, 1945, pp. 53–55; Mishkin, 1940, pp. 5–6; Denhardt, 1947, p. 103. Acceptance of this position is also implied in Bolton, 1949, p. 400).

In tracing the northward spread of horses from the Southwest to the Plains and Plateau tribes we must acknowledge the meagerness of the historical data bearing on this movement. Wissler logically assumed that "those to get to them first would be the Ute, Comanche, Apache, Kiowa and Caddo" (Wissler, 1914, p. 2). If we exclude the Comanche, this assumption seems to be in accord with more recent findings. Horses were first diffused northward and eastward to those tribes on the periphery of the Spanish settlements of the Southwest. Marvin Opler found in Southern Ute traditions a suggestion that those Indians acquired horses from the Spanish "probably around 1640" (Linton, 1940, pp. 156–157, 171). Spanish records, dated 1659, reported Apache raids on the ranch stock of the settlements which continued into the next decade. The Apache carried off as many as 300 head of livestock in a single raid. At the same time the Apache engaged in an intermittent exchange of slaves for horses with the Pueblo Indians (Scholes, 1937, pp. 150, 163, 398–399). The French explorer La Salle heard that the Gattacka (Kiowa-Apache) and Manrhoat (Kiowa) were trading horses to the Wichita or Pawnee in 1682. He believed the animals had been stolen from the Spaniards of New Mexico (Margry, 1876–86, vol. 2, pp. 201–202). In 1690, Tonti found the Cadodaquis on Red River in possession of about 30 horses, which the Indians called cavalis, an apparent derivation from the Spanish "caballos." While among the Naouadiché, another Caddoan tribe, farther south, he found horses "very common," stating "there is not a cabin which has not four or five" (Cox, 1905, pp. 44–50).

Data on the spread of the horse northward over the Plains in the late years of the 17th century are sparse. In 1680, Oto Indians who visited La Salle at Fort Crèvecoeur (near present Peoria, Ill.) brought with them a piebald horse taken from some Spaniards they had killed (Pease and Werner, 1934a, p. 4). Deliette reported that prior to 1700 the Pawnee and Wichita obtained branded Spanish horses "of which they make use sometimes to pursue the buffalo in the hunt" (Pease and Werner, 1934b, p. 388). In the summer of 1700, Father Gabriel Marest included Missouri, Kansa, and Ponca, along with the Pawnee and Wichita, as possessors of Spanish horses (Garraghan, 1927, p. 312). These brief references suggest that by the end of the century most and probably all Plains Indian tribes living south of the Platte River had gained familiarity with horses. Nevertheless, testimony, of the French explorers La Harpe, Du Tisne, and Bourgmont (Margry, 1876–86, vol. 6) in the first quarter of the 18th century indicates that horses still were scarce among the tribes living eastward of the Apache and northward of the Caddo.

In 1705, the Comanche, an offshoot of the Wyoming Shoshoni, first were seen on the New Mexican frontier. In company with linguistically related Ute, they came to beg for peace, but on their departure stole horses from the settlements (Thomas, 1935, p. 105). In succeeding years they launched repeated bold attacks upon New Mexico, riding off with horses and with goods intended by the Spanish for trade with the Apache living northeastward of the Rio Grande Pueblos. Comanche thefts were extended to the Apache villages as well. Specific mention was made in Spanish records of one raid in which 3 Comanch and Ute Indians ran off 20 horses and a colt from an Apache rancheria in 1719. At that very time Governor Valverde was leading a punitive expedition against the troublesome Comanche (ibid., pp. 105–109, 122).

Plains tribes northeast of the Black Hills were met by white traders before they acquired horses. When La Vérendrye accompanied an Assiniboin trading party to the Mandan villages on the Missouri in 1738, those Assiniboin had no horses. La Vérendrye made no mention of any horses among the Mandan. However, he was told that the Arikara, northernmost of the Caddoan-speaking peoples, living south of the Mandan on the Missouri, owned horses, as did nomadic tribes living southwestward toward and beyond the Black Hills (La Vérendrye, 1927, pp. 108, 337). Two Frenchmen, left by La Vérendrye at the

Mandan villages through the summer of 1739, witnessed the visit of horse-using tribes to the Mandan for trading purposes (ibid., pp. 366–368). These tribes cannot be identified with certainty. However, the two Frenchmen learned that they feared the "Snake" Indians. Therefore, it seems improbable these people were Shoshoni or their Comanche kinsmen. They may have been the Kiowa and Kiowa Apache, who were mentioned by La Salle as actively engaged in the northward diffusion of horses a half century earlier, and who were known to have traded horses to the horticultural peoples on the Missouri in later years.

In 1741, La Vérendrye's son took two horses with him on his return from the Mandan villages (ibid., p. 108, 387). This event seems to have marked the beginning of the trade in horses from nomadic tribes southwest of the Missouri, through the Mandan to the peoples north and east of them. Hendry (1907, pp. 334–335) traveled with an Assiniboin trading party in 1754, which employed horses for packing but not for riding. Twelve years later the elder Henry (1809, pp. 275–89) saw horses in some numbers among the Assiniboin and mentioned their use in mounted warfare. Umfreville reported (in 1789) "it is but lately that they [horses] have become common among the Nehethawa [Cree] Indians" (Umfreville, 1790, p. 189). The French trader Jacques d'Eglise, in 1792, saw horses equipped with Mexican saddles and bridles among the Mandan in the first description of that tribe after the visits of the La Vérendryes a half century earlier (Nasitir, 1927, p. 58). It is most probable that a trickle of trade in Spanish horses through the Mandan to the Assiniboin and Plains Cree existed throughout the last half of the 18th century.

The third quarter of the century witnessed a rapid expansion of the horse frontier among tribes living to the eastward of the Missouri. In 1768 Carver (1838, p. 188) found no horses among the Dakota of the Upper Mississippi, and placed the frontier of horse-using tribes some distance to the westward of them. Yet by 1773 Peter Pond saw Spanish horses among the Sauk on the Wisconsin River. Two years later he observed that the Yankton Dakota had "a Grate Number of Horses" which they used for hunting buffalo and carrying baggage (Pond, 1908, pp. 335, 353). Since the Yankton probably obtained their horses from the Teton, Hyde's 1760 estimate of the date of Teton Dakota acquisition of horses appears reasonable (Hyde, 1937, pp. 16, 18, 68). According to Teton tradition, they acquired their first horses from the Arikara on the Missouri. It was probably during the third quarter of the 18th century that the Cheyenne began to acquire horses also (Jablow, 1951, p. 10).

At the close of the 18th century the Red River marked the northeastern boundary of Plains Indian horse culture. In 1798, David Thompson noted that the Ojibwa east of that river had no horses (Thompson, 1916, p. 246). Two years thereafter Alexander Henry the younger purchased two horses from visiting Indians who lived on the Assiniboin River to the west, and commented significantly, "Those were the first and only two horses we had on Red river; the Saulteurs had none, but always used canoes" (Henry and Thompson, 1897, vol. 1, p. 47). In January, 1806, Zebulon Pike observed that traders at the Northwest Company post on Lac de Sable, near the Mississippi, had "horses they procured from Red river of the Indians" (Pike, 1810, p. 60). In the summer of that year Henry encountered nine lodges of canoe-using Ojibwa at the forks of Scratching River in present southeastern Manitoba, hunting buffalo. They owned some horses and were planning to go to the Missouri to purchase more (Henry and Thompson, 1897, vol. 1, p. 286). These were the Plains Ojibwa in process of transition from woodland canoemen to Plains Indian horsemen.

By 1805 horses had also been diffused far to the northwest in larger numbers. The Lewis and Clark Expedition established the first recorded white contact with the Plateau tribes in 1805–06. On their return from the Pacific coast they were able to purchase four horses from Skilloot Indians at the Dalles, paying twice as much for them as they had paid for horses obtained from Shoshoni and Flathead on their outward journey (Coues, 1893, vol. 2, pp. 954–955). As they moved eastward they found horses more plentiful, indicating that the Dalles was near the northwestern limit of horse diffusion at that time. Lewis and Clark were impressed with the large numbers of horses owned by many Plateau tribes. Yet the Lemhi Shoshoni told them of related peoples living to the southwest of them (probably Ute) "where horses are much more abundant than they are here" (Coues, 1893, vol. 2, p. 569). The explorers found Spanish riding gear and branded mules among the Shoshoni. They believed these animals came from the Spanish settlements, which the Indians reported to be but 8 to 10 days' journey southward (Coues, 1893, vol. 2, p. 559; Ordway, 1916, p. 268).

Northern Shoshoni tradition claims that their kinsmen, the Comanche, furnished them their first horses (Clark, 1885, p. 338; Shimkin, 1938, p. 415). If we may credit this tradition, it seems possible these Shoshoni may have begun to acquire horses a few years after Comanche raids were launched on the New Mexican settlements in 1705. It is probably, too, that the Ute of western Colorado served as intermediaries through whom Spanish horses passed northward to the Shoshoni during the 18th century (Steward, 1938, p. 201). However, these movements cannot be historically documented.

Nevertheless, the sizable herds of horses seen among the Lemhi Shoshoni and their neighbors by Lewis and Clark in 1805, presuppose an extended period of horse diffusion on a considerable scale toward the Northwest prior to that date. Haines (1938b, p. 435) has postulated a route of diffusion west of the Continental Divide from Santa Fe to the Snake River by way of the headwaters of the Colorado, the Grand, and Green Rivers. This was the most direct route to the Northwest from New Mexico. We may note, also, that it passed through the country of Shoshonean tribes offering a peaceful highway for Comanche and Ute such as was unavailable on the western Plains, infested as that region was with hostile Apache and Kiowa. There was little incentive to divert horses westward from that route, as the Great Basin afforded inadequate pasturage for horses.

Through the Northern Shoshoni, horses were distributed to the Plateau tribes. Tribal traditions of the Flathead and Nez Percé credit the Shoshoni with furnishing them their first mounts (Turney-High, 1937, p. 106; Haines, 1939, p. 19). The Coeur d'Alene, Pend d'Orielle, Kalispel, Spokan, Colville, and Cayuse tribes of the Northwestern Plateau obtained their first horses either directly from the Shoshoni or indirectly from tribes previously supplied by Shoshoni (Teit, 1930, p. 351). Although a Crow tradition recorded by Bradley (1923, p. 298) refers to their acquisition of horses from the Nez Percé, it seems more probable that the first horses obtained by the Crow came from the Comanche (Morgan, MS., bk. 9, p. 12).

The Process of Diffusion

Previous writers have been more concerned with the historical problem of *when* the Plains Indians obtained horses than with the cultural problem of *how* horses were diffused. Certainly the paucity of 18th century documentation sheds little light on the diffusion process. However, when we add to this documentation the information in the literature of the first decade of the 19th century, we find much that is helpful in seeking an explanation of this process.

At the beginning of the 19th century two main routes for the diffusion of horses to the tribes of the northern Plains were observable. One route led from the Upper Yellowstone eastward to the Hidatsa and Mandan villages on the Missouri. The Crow Indians of the Middle Yellowstone served as intermediaries in a flourishing trade in horses and mules, securing large numbers of these animals from the Flathead, Shoshoni, and probably also the Nez Percé on the Upper Yellowstone in exchange for objects of European manufacture. At the Mandan and Hidatsa villages they disposed of some of these horses and mules, at double their purchase value, in exchange for the European-made objects desired for their own use and eagerly sought by the far-off Flathead and Shoshoni. Thus tribes of the Upper Yellowstone and Plateau began to receive supplies of knives, axes, brass kettles, metal awls, bracelets of iron and brass, a few buttons worn as hair ornaments, some long metal lance heads, arrowheads of iron and brass, and a few fusils of Northwest Company trade type, before their first direct contacts with white traders in their own territories. Thus also, horn bows and possibly other products of the western Indians reached the village tribes on the Missouri, and bridle bits and trade blankets of Spanish origin arrived at the Mandan and Hidatsa villages by a long and circuitous route. On their summer trading visits to the Mandan and Hidatsa the Crow also exchanged products of the chase (dried meat, robes, leggings, shirts, and skin lodges) for corn, pumpkins, and tobacco of the villagers. In 1805, the Northwest Company trader Larocque, the first white man to spend a season with the Crow, reported that this trade was well-organized (Larocque, 1910, pp. 22, 64, 66, 71–72). This trade was also noted by Lewis and Clark (Coues, 1893, vol. 1, pp. 198–199; vol. 2, pp. 398–399), Mackenzie (1889, p. 346), and Tableau (1939, pp. 160–161).

We cannot be sure how long this trade was in existence before the opening of the 19th century. However, the experienced fur trader Robert Meldrum, who probably knew the Crow Indians better than any other white man of his time, told Lewis Henry Morgan that when he first went among the Crow (1827) old people of that tribe told him they "saw the first horses ever brought into their country," and that they obtained these horses from the Comanche. Morgan estimated, "This would make it about 100 years ago that they first obtained the horse," i.e., ca. 1762 (Morgan, MS., bk. 9, p. 122). Denig (1953, p. 19) and Bradley (1896, p. 179) independently dated the separation of the Crow from the Hidatsa about the year 1776 or a few years earlier. It is probably that the Crow Indians did not become actively engaged in this trade until they had acquired enough horses to make it practical for them to leave the Hidatsa and become nomadic hunters.

The other major route by which horses were diffused northward to the tribes of the northern Plains at the beginning of the 19th century I assume to have been an older one, and probably the route followed by the Comanche themselves in supplying the Crow with their first horses. It led from the Spanish settlements of New Mexico and Texas to the vicinity of the Black Hills in South Dakota via the western High Plains, thence eastward and northeastward to the Arikara, Hidatsa, and Mandan villages on the Missouri. The important middlemen in this trade at the beginning of the 19th century were the nomadic Kiowa, Kiowa-Apache, Comanche, Arapaho, and Cheyenne.

Antoine Tabeau, a French trader from St. Louis, who was among the Arikara in 1803–4, was told that prior to that time the Arikara were accustomed to transport tobacco, maize, and goods of European manufacture "to the foot of the Black Hills" where they met the Kiowa, Kiowa-Apache, Comanche, Arapaho, and Cheyenne in a trading fair. There they secured dressed deerskins, porcupine-quill-decorated shirts of antelopeskin, moccasins, quantities of dried meat, and prairie turnip flour in exchange for their wares. Coincident with that trade was the barter of European firearms for horses, which Tabeau described: "The horse is the most important article of their trade with the Ricaras. Most frequently it is given as a present: but, according to their manner, that is to say, it is recalled when the tender in exchange does not please. This is an understood restriction. This present is paid ordinarily with a gun, a hundred charges of powder and balls, a knife and other trifles" (Tabeau, 1939, p. 158). Tabeau was told that the nomadic traders obtained their horses directly from the Spaniards at "St. Antonio or Santa Fe," either buying them at low prices or stealing them, at their discretion (ibid., pp. 154–158).

Lewis and Clark made brief mention of Kiowa, Kiowa-Apache, and possibly some Comanche as wandering tribes who "raise a great number of horses, which they barter to the Ricaras, Mandans &c. for articles of European manufactory" (Coues, 1893, vol. 1, pp. 58–59). In the summer of 1806, Henry accompanied the Hidatsa on a visit to the Cheyenne to trade guns and ammunition (then scarce among the Cheyenne) for fine horses (Henry and Thompson, 1897, vol. 1, pp. 367–393).

Although this north-south trade route may have been employed for the northward diffusion of horses for several decades before the west-east trade route (previously described) was opened, it is most probably that the Arapaho and Cheyenne were not involved in it as intermediaries before their abandonment of the sedentary horticultural life in favor of a nomadic existence. Cheyenne conversion to nomadism probably began no earlier than 1750, and some villages of that tribe clung to the horticultural life until after 1790 (Strong, 1940, pp. 359, 371; Trudeau, 1921, pp. 165–167). According to Arapaho tradition that tribe also made the transition from sedentary to nomadic life (Elkin, 1940, p. 207). Presumably Arapaho conversion to nomadism did not long antedate that of the Cheyenne. Of the nomadic tribes actively engaged in supplying horses to the village tribes on the Missouri by the northward route in 1804, this leaves only the Kiowa-Apache, Kiowa, and Comanche as probable initiators of this trade. Since the Comanche are credited with supplying horses to their kinsmen, the Northern Shoshoni, in the 18th century, it is most probably that the Kiowa-Apache and Kiowa played more important roles in the early trade in horses with the village tribes of the Missouri.

The Arikara, Mandan, and Hidatsa villages served as foci for the further diffusion of horses to the tribes dwelling east and north of that river at the beginning of the 19th century. In late summer the nomadic Teton Dakota obtained horses, mules, corn, beans, pumpkins, and tobacco from the Arikara in exchange for products and byproducts of the hunt and European trade goods. Each spring the Teton met their Dakota relatives, the Yankton, Yanktonai, and Eastern Dakota at a great trading fair on the James River in present South Dakota, where they bartered some of the horses received from the Arikara, together with buffaloskin lodges, buffalo robes, and shirts and leggings of antelopeskin, with other Dakota tribes for the materials of the latter's country (walnut bows and red stone pipes are specifically mentioned), and European manufactured goods (guns and kettles are named) which those tribes obtained from white traders on the St. Peters (Minnesota) and Des Moines Rivers. Tabeau (1939, pp. 121, 131) reported that this Sioux trading fair sometimes attracted as many as 1,000 to 1,200 tents, housing about 3,000 men bearing arms. Lewis and Clark made repeated mention of this trade (Coues, 1893, vol. 1, pp. 95, 99, 100, 144, 217). They regarded it of special significance because it made the powerful Teton Dakota independent of white traders on the Missouri and hostile to the extension of the trade from St. Louis up the Missouri which would serve only to place deadly firearms in the hands of their enemies.

From the Mandan and Hidatsa villages horses passed to the Assiniboin, Plains Cree, and Plains Ojibwa of northern North Dakota and southern Canada. The actual trading took place at the villages of the horticultural tribes, during periodic visits from the nomadic ones. Trudeau, in 1796, told of the Assiniboin obtaining horses, corn, and tobacco from the Mandan and Hidatsa for guns and other merchandise (Trudeau, 1921, p. 173). Tabeau (1939, p. 161) and Lewis and Clark (Coues, 1893, vol. 1, p. 195) referred to the exchange of horses and agricultural products of the Mandan and Hidatsa for the "merchandise" (arms and ammunition were named) of the Assiniboin and Plains Cree.

The Mandan and Hidatsa also served as bases for the horse supply of white traders operating in the country north and east of them. Lewis and Clark's statement that Mr. Henderson of the Hudson's Bay Company came to the Hidatsa villages in December 1804, with tobacco, beads, and other merchandise to trade for furs, and "a few guns which are to be exchanged for horses" is significant of the preferred position given to both guns and horses in this trade (Coues, 1893, vol. 1, p. 207).

On the map I have summarized graphically the foregoing data on trade routes employed in the diffusion of horses northward to the majority of the Plains Indian tribes dwelling north of the Platte River at the beginning of the 19th century.

A study of this map in conjunction with the preceding text seems to justify some conclusions relative to the pattern of diffusion.

First, I am impressed with the fact that the trade in horses on the Northern Plains at that time was almost without exception a trade between nomadic and horticultural peoples, and that this horse trade was coincident with the exchange of products of the hunt for agricultural produce on the part of these same tribes. This barter between hunting and gardening peoples enabled each group to supplement its own economy with the products of the other's labors. There was little incentive for trade between two horticultural tribes or between two hunting peoples, as neither possessed an abundance of desirable products which the other did not have. However, the natural environment of the western Plateau yielded wild foods and other natural resources which were not found on the Plains. Therefore, the nomadic Plateau tribes stood in much the same desirable trading relationship to the Plains Indian nomads as did the gardening peoples of the Plains. So we find that horses were diffused from the Flathead to the nomadic Crow, to the horticultural Hidatsa and Mandan, to the nomadic Assiniboin, Plains Cree, and Plains Ojibwa, with the same alternate rhythm as occurred in the northward progression of horses from the Spanish settlements to the nomadic Kiowa, Kiowa-Apache, Comanche, Arapaho, and Cheyenne, to the horticultural Arikara, to the nomadic Teton Dakota, to the horticultural Eastern Dakota.

There is good evidence that the pattern of trade in the respective products of their different economies between gardening and nomadic tribes was an old one in the Plains, and that it antedated the introduction of the horse into the area. Definite references to the trade of Plains Indians in pre-horse days reveal the pattern.

The Coronado expedition in 1541 observed that the nomadic Querechos and Teyas of the southwestern Plains ". . . follow the cows, hunting them and tanning the skins to take to the settlements in the winter to sell, since they go there to pass the winter, each company going to those which are nearest, some to the settlement of Cicuye, others toward Quivera, and others to the settlements situated in the direction of Florida. . . . They have no other settle-

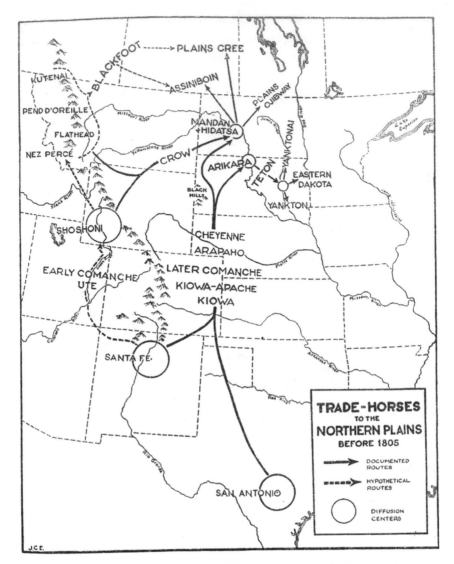

Following the Pueblo revolt in 1680, Spanish horses became available across the southern plains. During the eighteenth century these horses were gradually traded north on both sides of the Continental Divide. This map illustrates the trade routes that had been established by the time of the Lewis and Clark expedition. Courtesy the Newberry Library, Chicago (Ayer 301 .A5 v. 159, p. 11).

ment or location than comes from traveling around with the cows. . . . They exchange some cloaks with the natives of the river for corn" (Winship, 1896, pp. 527–528).

In the fall of 1599, Vicente de Saldivar Mendoca met a roving band of Plains Indians not far from the Canadian River ". . . coming from trading with the Picuries and Taos, populous pueblos of this New Mexico, where they sell meat, hides, tallow, suet, and salt in exchange for cotton blankets, potter, maize, and some small green stones which they use" (Bolton, 1916, p. 226).

The two Frenchmen left at the Mandan villages by La Vérendrye in 1739 reported the existence of a similar trade in words suggesting that it had been active for a period of years:

> . . . every year, in the beginning of June, there arrive at the great fort on the bank of the river of the Mandan, several savage tribes which use horses and carry on trade with them; that they bring dressed skins trimmed and ornamented with plumage and porcupine quills, painted in various colors, also white buffalo skins, and that the Mandan give them in exchange grain and beans, of which they have ample supply.
>
> Last spring two hundred lodges of them came; sometimes even more come; they are not all of the same tribe but some of them are only allies. (La Vérendrye, 1927, pp. 366–367)

Undoubtedly some of the articles received by the Mandan in this trade were passed along to the Assiniboin. In 1738, La Vérendrye himself had found that the Mandan offered not only grains and tobacco, but also colored buffalo robes, deerskins, and buckskins carefully dressed and ornamented with fur and feathers, painted feathers and furs, worked garters, headbands, and girdles to the Assiniboin in return for guns, powder, balls, axes, knives, kettles, and awls of European manufacture (ibid., pp. 323, 332). Horses do not appear to have been articles of trade at the Mandan villages at that time, but it is clear that the Assiniboin middlemen, operating far in advance of white traders, were offering to the Mandan firearms and ammunition as well as other trade goods obtained from Whites.

It is necessary to consider the diffusion of firearms to the Plains Indians as a factor related to and influencing the routes of trade followed in the northward diffusion of horses. If there was any possession as keenly sought by the historic Plains Indians as was the horse, it was the gun. As much as these Indians wanted the rapid mobility afforded by the horse, they sought the deadly firepower provided by the gun. Any tribe possessing either without the other was at a distinct disadvantage in opposition to an enemy owning both. British and French traders approaching the Plains from the north and east supplied guns to Indians. However, Spanish policy strictly prohibited the trading of firearms and ammunition to the natives. This placed those tribes in early contact with the British and French traders in an advantageous trading position. Having obtained firearms and ammunition directly from Europeans they were able to act as middlemen in bartering some of these highly desirable weapons with distant tribes that had as yet no direct contacts with white traders.

In the middle of the 18th century the village tribes of the Upper Missouri (Arikara, Mandan, and Hidatsa) were situated in a most admirable position for trading both to the northeast and the southwest. It was at those villages that the northeastward-moving frontier of the horse met the southwestward-moving frontier of the gun. Indians learned to equate guns and horses as standards of value, and a mutually profitable trade ensued by which the armed tribes of the Northeast secured mounts and the mounted tribes of the South and West secured firearms. Undoubtedly the demand for both firearms and horses far exceeded the supply. The need on the part of those Indians who received firearms for ammunition, which they could not make themselves, also helped to perpetuate this trade. At the beginning of the 19th century (as indicated by the data quoted from Tabeau) firearms still were the most desired articles sought in exchange for horses by those tribes which had access to considerable numbers of the latter, although canny horse traders then insisted that ammunition and some other articles be thrown into the scale to seal the bargain.

So it was that during the 18th century a trade in Spanish horses for French and British firearms grew up alongside the earlier pattern of exchange of products between horticultural and nomadic hunting tribes of the region. The trade in horses, therefore, appears to have been an historic elaboration of a prehistoric trade pattern among the Plains Indians.

Another aspect of this trade is worthy of note as a factor determining the direction of flow in the diffusion of horses. All other factors being equal, the nomadic tribes preferred to trade with horticultural peoples with whom they were closely related linguistically, if not biologically as well. Thus Crow traded primarily with Hidatsa, Teton with other Dakota groups, and Comanche and Ute with the Northern Shoshoni. It may well have been the attraction of European firearms that caused the Comanche to divert their trade to the unrelated horticultural peoples of the Missouri several decades after they had begun supplying horses to the Shoshoni.

Recently Denhardt has made a further significant observation: "...that the natives obtained their original horses, and always by far the greatest number, from the Spaniards or neighboring tribes and not from the wild herds. The Indians had mounts by the time the wild herds dotted the plains, and always preferred domesticated animals to the mestenos. Mustangs were hard to catch, and once caught, harder to tame" (Denhardt, 1947, pp. 103–104).

Certainly the lack of references to the capture of wild horses by the Indians of the northern Plains in the literature prior to 1800, serves to support this observation and to suggest that the wild herds furnished a negligible source of horses for those tribes prior to that time.

But what of theft as a factor in the northward spread of horses? Certainly a considerable number of the horses that reached the northern tribes prior to 1800 were animals stolen from Spanish, Pueblo, or Apache settlements by intermediary nomads. It is also true that intertribal theft of horses among the northern tribes occurred prior to that time. Nevertheless, and some native traditions to the contrary, it is hardly credible that any northern tribes obtained their *first* horses by stealing the mounts of neighboring tribes who had acquired horses at a somewhat earlier date. I believe peaceful contact was a necessary condition of initial horse diffusion, in order that some members of the pedestrian tribe might learn to overcome their initial fear of horses and learn to ride and manage those lively animals. The pre-existing pattern of trade furnished the most important medium of peaceful contacts and of initial diffusion of horses. The fact that such trade supplied inadequate numbers of horses to meet the needs of Indians who had gained some knowledge of handling them and a realization of the superiority of their use over foot travel and transport of camp equipment, encouraged intertribal theft. Actually there need not have been any prolonged interval between a tribe's first acquisition of horses and its initiation of horse-raiding operations. Some tribes may have begun raiding for horses within a decade after they acquired their first animals by peaceful means.

References
Aiton, Arthur S. 1939. "Coronado's Muster Roll." *American Historical Review* 44 (no. 3): 556–70.
Bishop, Morris. 1933. *The Odyssey of Cabeca de Vaca.* Reprint, Westport, Conn.: Greenwood, 1971.
Bolton, Herbert, ed. 1916. "Spanish Exploration in the Southwest, 1542–1706." In *Original Narratives of Early American History.* New York: Scribner.
———. 1949. *Coronado, Knight of the Pueblos.* Reprint, Albuquerque: University of New Mexico Press, 1964.

Bradley, James H. 1896–1923. "The Bradley Manuscript in the Montana Historical Society Library." *Montana Historical Society Contributions.* Helena, Montana.

Carver, Jonathan. 1838. *Travel through the Interior Parts of North America, in the Years 1766, 1767, and 1768.* Charleston: Samuel Etheridge.

Clark, Capt. W. P. 1885. *The Indian Sign Language.* Philadelphia: W. R. Hamersly.

Coues, Elliott, ed. 1893. *History of the Expedition under the Command of Lewis and Clark.* 4 vols. New York: Francis P. Harper.

Cox, Isaac Joslin, ed. 1905. *The Journeys of Réne Robert Cavelier, Sieur de La Salle.* 2 vols. New York: A. S. Barnes.

Denhardt, Robert M. 1947. *The Horse of the Americas.* Norman: University of Oklahoma Press.

Denig, Edwin T. 1953. *Of the Crow Nation.* Edited by John C. Ewers. Anthropological Paper 33, *Bureau of American Ethnology Bulletin* 151.

Elkin, Henry. 1940. "The Northern Arapaho of Wyoming." In *Acculturation in Seven American Indian Tribes,* edited by Ralph Linton. New York: D. Appleton.

Garraghan, Gilbert J. 1927. "Emergence of the Missouri Valley in History." *Illinois Catholic Historical Review* 9 (no. 4): 312.

Haines, Francis. 1938a. "Where Did the Plains Indians Get Their Horses?" *American Anthropologist* n.s., 40 (no. 1): 117.

———. 1938b. "The Northern Spread of Horses among the Plains Indians." *American Anthropologist* n.s., 40 (no. 3): 435.

———. 1939. *Red Eagles of the Northwest.* Los Angeles.

Hendry, Anthony. 1907. "York Factory to Blackfeet Country." In *The Journal of Anthony Hendry, 1754–1755,* edited by Lawrence J. Burpee. *Trans. Royal Society of Canada* ser. 3, 1, sect. 2, 275–89.

Henry, Alexander. 1809. *Travels and Adventures in Canada, and the Indian Territories, between the Years 1760 and 1776.* New York.

Henry, Alexander, and David Thompson. 1897. *New Light on the Early History of the Greater Northwest.* Edited by Elliott Coues. 3 vols. New York.

Hyde, George. 1937. *Red Cloud's Folk: A History of the Oglala Sioux Indians.* Norman, Okla.

Jablow, Joseph. 1951. "The Cheyenne in Plains Indian Trade Relations, 1795–1840." *Monographs of the American Ethnological Society* 19, 10. New York.

Larocque, François. 1910. *Journal of Larocque from Assiniboine to the Yellowstone, 1805.* Publications of the Canadian Archives 3.

La Vérendrye, P. G. V. 1927. *Journals and Letters of Pierre Gaultier de Varennes de la Vérendrye and His Sons.* Edited by Lawrence J. Burpee. Publications of the Champlain Society 16. Toronto.

Linton, Ralph, ed. 1940. *Acculturation in Seven Indian Tribes.* New York: D. Appleton.

Mackenzie, Charles. 1889. "The Missouri Indians." In L. R. Masson, *Les bourgeois de la compagnie du Nord-Ouest,* vol. 1. Quebec: De l'imprimerie generale.

Margry, Pierre. 1876–1886. "Découvertes et etablissements des français dans l'ouest et dans le sud de l'Amérique Septentrionale (1614–1754)." *Memoires et documents originaux recueillis et publés par Pierre Margry.* 6 vols. Paris: D. Jouaust.

Mishkin, Bernard. 1940. "Rank and Warfare among the Plains Indians." *Monographs of the American Ethnological Society 3.* New York.

Morgan, Lewis Henry. MS. "Journal of a Trip up the Missouri River on the Steamboat Shreveport (Spread Eagle) in 1862." Rush Rhees Library, University of Rochester.

Nasitir, Abraham P. 1927. "Spanish Exploration of the Upper Missouri." *Missouri Valley Historical Review* 14 (no. 1): 57–71.

Ordway, John. 1916. *Sergeant John Ordway's Journal.* Edited by Milo Quaife. Madison: Wisconsin State Historical Society.

Pease, T. C., and R. C. Werner, eds. 1934a. *La Salle in the Illinois Country, 1860.* Collections of the Illinois State Historical Society Library 23. French Series 1. Springfield, Ill.

———, eds. 1934b. *Memoir of De Gannes Concerning the Illinois Country.* Collections of the Illinois State Historical Society Library 23. French Series 1. Springfield, Ill.

Pike, Zebulon M. 1810. *An Account of Expeditions to the Sources of the Mississippi, and through the Western Parts of Louisiana.* Philadelphia.

Pond, Peter. 1908. "Journal of Peter Pond." Vol. 18. Collection of Wisconsin State Historical Society.

Scholes, F. V. 1937. "Troublous Times in New Mexico, 1659–1670." *New Mexico Historical Review* 12:150–63, 398–99.

Shimkin, D. B. 1938. "Wind River Shoshone Geography." *American Anthropologist,* n.s., 40 (no. 3): 413–15.

Steward, Julian H. 1938. "Basin-Plateau Aboriginal Sociopolitical Groups." *Bureau of American Ethnology Bulletin* 120.

Strong, W. Duncan. 1940 "From History to Prehistory in the Northern Great Plains." *Smithsonian Miscellaneous Collections* 100:353–94.

Swanton, John R. 1939. "The Survival of Horses Brought to North America by De Soto." *American Anthropologist,* n.s., 41 (no. 1): 170–71.

Tabeau, Pierre-Antoine. 1939. *Tabeau's Narrative of Loisel's Expedition to the Upper Missouri.* Edited by Annie Heloise Abel. Norman: University of Oklahoma Press.

Teit, James. 1930. "Salishan Tribes of the Western Plateau." Edited by Franz Boas. *45th Annual Report, Bureau of American Ethnology,* 1927–1928, 23–396.

Thomas, Alfred B. 1935. *After Coronado: Spanish Exploration Northeast of New Mexico, 1697–1727.* Norman: University of Oklahoma Press.

Thompson, David. 1916. *David Thompson's Narrative of His Explorations in Western America, 1784–1812.* Edited by J. B. Tyrell. Champlain Society Publication 12. Toronto.

Trudeau, Jean-Baptiste. 1921. "Description of the Upper Missouri." Edited by Annie Heloise Abel. *Mississippi Valley Historical Review* 8:149–79.

Turney-High, Harry H. Holbert. 1937. *The Flathead Indians of Montana.* Memoirs of the American Anthropological Association 48. Menasha, Wisc.

Umfreville, Edward. 1790. *The Present State of Hudson's Bay*. London: Charles Stalker.

Webb, Walter Prescott. 1931. *The Great Plains*. Boston: Ginn.

Winship, George Parker. 1896. "The Coronado Expedition, 1540–1542." *14th Annual Report, Bureau of American Ethnology*, 1892–1893, part 1, 329–613.

Wissler, Clark. 1914. "The Influence of the Horse in the Development of Plains Culture." *American Anthropologist*, n.s., 16, part 1: 1–25.

———. 1927. *North American Indians of the Plains*. Handbook Series 1, 3d ed. New York: American Museum of Natural History.

Wyman, Walker D. 1945. *The Wild Horse of the West*. Caldwell, Idaho: Caxton.

From "The Acquisition of the Horse," in John Ewers, *The Horse in Blackfoot Culture*, Bureau of American Ethnology Bulletin 159 (Washington, D.C.: Government Printing Office, 1955), 1–15.

CHAPTER TWO

A Brilliant Plan for Living: Creators

Even though European diseases had penetrated and disrupted the Indian country by 1800, the Native communities in the Missouri and Columbia River regions survived and remained prosperous. Organized into villages and bands, the people lived well by exploiting the abundant resources around them and trading for items they lacked. Trading partners and allies were also sources of songs, stories, and new insights into the spirit world. Gatherings with strangers in the Indian country often inspired celebrations marked by dancing, oratory, and even intermarriage. This pattern of community organization and inter-group exchange produced brilliant plans for living. The communities of the Indian country generated loyalty without coercion and lived by a moral code that was inclusive and generous rather than judgmental and self-serving.

The people of the Indian country communicated their values best through stories of creation and tales of the spirit world. This oral literature was passed from elders to young people and provided vivid lessons regarding the values they believed were essential for community well-being. Among the most important stories were those that told of the origins of the world and of individual communities.

For the people of the Indian country, "creation" was not a distant or solitary event. They believed the world was the product of many creative acts involving many spiritual forces, which continued to affect their lives. Creation was a complex and ongoing process. Elders explained that the cosmic forces that made the world lived above and beneath it. They told of spirit beings who affected the weather, the hunt, and the size of the harvest. The forces of creation were present in every aspect of life, offering help and demanding respect.

LEGEND OF POÏA
Walter McClintock

The Blackfeet story of Feather Woman and Morning Star underscores the intimate relationship between human beings and the natural world. There are many versions of this story of Feather Woman's marriage to Morning Star, but they all retain the core elements of an ancient tale: a young girl travels to the heavens to marry Morning Star but is returned to earth after she disobeys him. Their son—Poïa—grows up on earth but eventually travels to the sky to make peace with his father and obtain wisdom he can bring back to earth. Poïa forged a powerful and enduring bond between Blackfeet people and the forces of the cosmos. An easterner and a graduate of Yale College, Walter McClintock (1870–1949) first visited the Blackfeet in 1896 while working for the National Forest Service. He remained among them for many years and produced a number of popular books about their traditional culture. He collected this story from an elder named Brings Down the Sun in the first decade of the twentieth century. McClintock presented the story as an extended quotation from his consultant.

"There are two bright stars that sometimes rise together, just before the sun comes up, Morning Star and Young Morning Star or Star Boy (referring to the conjunction of the planets Venus and Jupiter before daybreak). I will tell you the story of these two Morning Stars, as it was related to me by my father, having been handed down to him through many generations."

"We know not when the Sun-dance had its origin. It was long ago, when the Blackfeet used dogs for beasts of burden instead of horses; when they stretched the legs and bodies of their dogs on sticks to make them large, and when they used stones instead of wooden pegs to hold down their lodges. In those days, during the moon of flowers (early summer), our people were camped near the mountains. It was a cloudless night and a warm wind blew over the prairie. Two young girls were sleeping in the long grass outside the lodge. Before daybreak, the eldest sister, So-at-sa-ki (Feather Woman), awoke. The Morning Star was just rising from the prairie. He was very beautiful, shining through the clear air of early morning. She lay gazing at this wonderful star, until he seemed very close to her, and she imagined that he was her lover. Finally she awoke her sister, exclaiming, 'Look at the Morning Star! He is beautiful and must be very wise. Many of the young men have wanted to marry me, but I love only the Morning Star.' When the leaves were turning yellow (autumn), So-at-sa-ki became very unhappy, finding herself with child. She was a pure maiden, although not knowing the father of her child. When the people discovered her secret, they taunted and ridiculed her, until she wanted to die. One day while the geese were flying southward, So-at-sa-ki went alone to the river for water. As she was returning home, she beheld a young man standing before her in the trail. She modestly turned aside to pass, but he put forth his hand, as if to detain her, and she said angrily, 'Stand aside! None of the young men have ever before dared to stop me.' He replied, 'I am the Morning Star. One night, during the moon of flowers, I beheld you sleeping in the open and loved you. I have now come to ask you to return with me to the sky, to the lodge of my father, the Sun, where we will live together, and you will have no more trouble.'

"Then So-at-sa-ki remembered the night in spring, when she slept outside the lodge, and now realised that Morning Star was her husband. She saw in his hair a yellow plume, and in his hand a juniper branch with a spider web hanging from one end. He was tall and straight and his hair was long and shining. His beautiful clothes were of soft-tanned skins, and from them came a fragrance of pine and sweet grass. So-at-sa-ki replied hesitatingly, 'I must first say farewell to my father and mother.' But Morning Star allowed her to speak to no one. Fastening the feather in her hair and giving her the juniper branch to hold, he directed her to shut her eyes. She held the upper strand of the spider web in her hand and placed her feet upon the lower one. When he told her to open her eyes, she was in the sky. They were standing together before a large lodge. Morning Star said, 'This is the home of my father and mother, the Sun and the Moon,' and bade her enter. It was day-time and the Sun was away on his long journey, but the Moon was at home. Morning Star addressed his mother saying, 'One night I beheld this girl sleeping on the prairie. I loved her and she is now my wife.' The Moon welcomed So-at-sa-ki to their home. In the evening, when the Sun Chief came home, he also gladly received her. The Moon clothed So-at-sa-ki in a soft-tanned buckskin dress, trimmed with elk-teeth. She also presented her with wristlets of elk-teeth and an elk-skin robe, decorated with the sacred paint, saying, 'I give you these because you have married our son.' So-at-sa-ki lived happily in the sky with Morning Star, and learned many wonderful things. When her child was born, they called him Star Boy. The Moon then gave So-at-sa-ki a root digger, saying, 'This should be used only by pure women. You can dig all kinds of roots with it, but I warn you not to dig up the large turnip growing near the home of the Spider Man. You have now a child and it would bring unhappiness to us all.'

"Everywhere So-at-sa-ki went, she carried her baby and the root digger. She often saw the large turnip, but was afraid to touch it. One day, while pass-ing the wonderful turnip, she thought of the mysterious warning of the Moon, and became curious to see what might be underneath. Laying her baby on the ground, she dug until her root digger stuck fast. Two large cranes came flying from the east. So-at-sa-ki besought them to help her. Thrice she called in vain, but upon the fourth call, they circled and lighted beside her. The chief crane sat upon one side of the turnip and his wife on the other. He took hold of the turnip with his long sharp bill, and moved it backwards and forwards, singing the medicine song,

'This root is sacred. Wherever I dig, my roots are sacred.'

"He repeated this song to the north, south, east and west. After the fourth song he pulled up the turnip. So-at-sa-ki looked through the hole and beheld the earth. Although she had not known it, the turnip had filled the same hole, through which Morning Star had brought her into the sky. Looking down, she saw the camp of the Blackfeet, where she had lived. She sat for a long while gazing at the old familiar scenes. The young men were playing games. The women were tanning hides and making lodges, gathering berries on the hills, and crossing the meadows to the river for water. When she turned to go home, she was crying, for she felt lonely, and longed to be back again upon the green prairies with her own people. When So-at-sa-ki arrived at the lodge, Morning Star and his mother were waiting. As soon as Morning Star looked at his wife, he exclaimed, 'You have dug up the sacred turnip!' When she did not reply, the Moon said, 'I warned you not to dig up the turnip, because I love Star Boy and do not wish to part with him.' Nothing more was said, because it was day-time and the great Sun Chief was still away on his long journey. In the evening, when he entered the lodge, he exclaimed, 'What is the matter with my daughter? She looks sad and must be in trouble.' So-at-sa-ki replied, 'Yes, I am homesick, because I have to-day looked down upon my people.' Then the Sun Chief was angry and said to Morning Star, 'If she has disobeyed, you must send her home.' The Moon interceded for So-at-sa-ki, but the Sun answered, 'She can no longer be happy with us. It is better for her to return to her own people.' Morning Star led So-at-sa-ki to the home of the Spider Man, whose web had drawn her up to the sky. He placed on her head the sacred Medicine Bonnet, which is worn only by pure women. He laid Star Boy on her breast, and wrapping them both in the elk-skin robe, bade her farewell, saying, 'We will let you down into the centre of the Indian camp and the people will behold you as you come from the sky.' The Spider Man then carefully let them down through the hole to the earth.

"It was an evening in midsummer, during the moon when the berries are ripe, when So-at-sa-ki was let down from the sky. Many of the people were outside their lodges, when suddenly they beheld a bright light in the northern sky. They saw it pass across the heavens and watched, until it sank to the ground. When the Indians reached the place, where the star had fallen, they saw a strange looking bundle. When the elk-skin cover was opened, they found a woman and her child. So-at-sa-ki was recognised by her parents. She returned to their lodge and lived with them, but never was happy. She used to go with Star Boy to the summit of a high ridge, where she sat and mourned for her husband. One night she remained alone upon the ridge. Before daybreak, when Morning Star arose from the plains, she begged him to take her back. Then he spoke to her, 'You disobeyed and therefore cannot return to the sky. Your sin is the cause of your sorrow and has brought trouble to you and your people.'

"Before So-at-sa-ki died, she told all these things to her father and mother, just as I now tell them to you. Star Boy's grandparents also died. Although born in the home of the Sun, he was very poor. He had no clothes, not even moccasins to wear. He was so timid and shy that he never played with other children. When the Blackfeet moved camp, he always followed barefoot, far behind the rest of the tribe. He feared to travel with the other people, because the other boys stoned and abused him. On his face was a mysterious scar, which became more marked and he grew older. He was ridiculed by everyone and in derision was called Poïa (Scarface).

"When Poïa became a young man, he loved a maiden of his own tribe. She was very beautiful and the daughter of a leading chief. Many of the young men wanted to marry her, but she refused them all. Poïa sent this maiden a present, with the message that he wanted to marry her, but she was proud and disdained his love. She scornfully told him, she would not accept him as her lover, until he would remove the scar from his face. Scarface was deeply grieved by the reply. He consulted with an old medicine woman, his only friend. She revealed to him, that the scar had been placed on his face by the Sun God, and that only the Sun himself could remove it. Poïa resolved to go to the home of the Sun God. The medicine woman made moccasins for him and gave him a supply of pemmican.

"Poïa journeyed alone across the plains and through the mountains, enduring many hardships and great dangers. Finally he came to the Big Water (Pacific Ocean). For three days and three nights he lay upon the shore, fasting and praying to the Sun God. On the evening of the fourth day, he beheld a bright trail leading across the water. He traveled this path until he drew near the home of the Sun, when he hid himself and waited. In the morning, the great Sun Chief came from his lodge, ready for his daily journey. He did not recognize Poïa. Angered at beholding a creature from the earth, he said to the Moon, his wife, 'I will kill him, for he comes from a good-for-nothing-race,' but she interceded and saved his life. Morning Star, their only son, a young man with a handsome face and beautifully dressed, came forth from the lodge. He brought with him dried sweet grass, which he burned as incense. He first placed Poïa in the sacred smoke, and then led him into the presence of his father and mother, the Sun and the Moon. Poïa related the story of his long journey, because of his rejection by the girl he loved. Morning Star then saw how sad and worn he looked. He felt sorry for him and promised to help him.

"Poïa lived in the lodge of the Sun and Moon with Morning Star. Once, when they were hunting together, Poïa killed seven enormous birds, which had threatened the life of Morning Star. He presented four of the dead birds to the Sun and three to the Moon. The Sun rejoiced, when he knew that the dangerous birds were killed, and the Moon felt so grateful, that she besought her husband to repay him. On the intercession of Morning Star, the Sun God consented to remove the scar. He also appointed Poïa as his messenger to the Blackfeet, promising, if they would give a festival (Sun-dance) in his honour, once every year, he would restore their sick to health. He taught Poïa the secrets of the Sun-dance, and instructed him in the prayers and songs to be used. He gave him two raven feathers to wear as a sign that he came from the Sun, and a robe of soft-tanned elk-skin, with the warning that it must be worn only by a virtuous woman. She can then give the Sun-dance and the sick will recover. Morning Star gave him a magic flute and a wonderful song, with which he would be able to charm the heart of the girl he loved.

"Poïa returned to the earth and the Blackfeet camp by the Wolf Trail (Milky Way), the short path to the earth. When he had fully instructed his people concerning the Sun-dance, the Sun God took him back to the sky with the girl he loved. When Poïa returned to the home of the Sun, the Sun God made him bright and beautiful, just like his father, Morning Star. In those days Morning Star and his son could be seen together in the east. Because Poïa appears first in the sky, the Blackfeet often mistake him for his father, and he is therefore sometimes called Poks-o-piks-o-aks, Mistake Morning Star.

"I remember," continued Brings-down-the-Sun, "when I was a young man, seeing these two bright stars rising, one after the other, before the Sun. Then, if we were going on a war, or hunting expedition, my father would awake me, saying, 'My son, I see the Morning Star and Young Morning Star in the sky above the prairie. Day will soon break and it is time we were started.' For many years these stars have traveled apart. I have also seen them together in the evening sky. They went down after the sun. This summer, Morning Star and Poïa are again travelling together. I see them in the eastern sky, rising together over the prairie before dawn. Poïa comes up first. His father, Morning Star, rises soon afterwards, and then his grandfather, the Sun.

"Morning Star was given to us as a sign to herald the coming of the Sun. When he appears above the horizon, we know a new day is about to dawn. Many medicine men have dreamed of the Sun, and of the Moon, but I have never yet heard of one so powerful as to dream of Morning Star, because he shows himself in the sky for such a short time.

"The 'Star that stands still' (North Star) is different from other stars, because it never moves. All the other stars walk round it. It is a hole in the sky, the same hole through which So-at-sa-ki was first drawn up to the sky and then let down again to earth. It is the hole, through which she gazed upon the earth, after digging up the forbidden turnip. Its light is the radiance from the home of the Sun God shining through. The half circle of stars to the east (Northern Crown) is the lodge of the Spider Man, and the five bright stars just beyond (in the constellation of Hercules) are his five fingers, with which he spun the web, upon which So-at-sa-ki was let down from the sky. Whenever you see the half-buried and overgrown circles, or clusters of stones upon the plains, marking the sites of Blackfeet camps in the ancient days, when they used stones to hold down the sides of their lodges, you will know why the half-circle of stars was called by our fathers, 'The Lodge of the Spider Man.'

"When So-at-sa-ki came back to earth from the lodge of the Sun, she brought with her the sacred Medicine Bonnet and dress trimmed with elk teeth, the Turnip Digger, Sweet Grass (incense), and the Prongs for lifting hot coals from the fire. Ever since those days, these sacred articles have been used in the Sun-dance by the woman who makes the vow. The Turnip Digger is always tied to the Medicine Case, containing the Medicine Bonnet, and it now hangs from the tripod behind my lodge."

From "Legend of Poïa," in Walter McClintock, *The Old North Trail: or, Life, Legends and Religion of the Blackfeet Indians* (London: Macmillan, 1910), 491–500.

THE CREATION OF THE NEZ PERCES
Archie Phinney

*Archie Phinney (1903–49), a linguist, graduated from the University of Kansas in
1926 and went on to study anthropology at Columbia University with Franz Boas.
Phinney was not able to complete his graduate work, however, and soon went to work
for the Bureau of Indian Affairs. He remained with the bureau for the rest of his
life. In the winter of 1929–30, Phinney collected this version of his tribe's origin story
from his mother, Wayi'låtpu.*

*In this story, Coyote discovered one day that a colossal monster had eaten "all the
people." In response, Coyote tricked the creature into eating him and then cut out its
heart. Coyote cut up the monster's body and tossed the pieces in four directions. Wherever a portion fell to the ground, a tribe of Indians sprang up. In the end, Coyote
washed his bloody hands and sprinkled the wash water across the valleys along the
Clearwater River in modern Idaho. The Nez Perces sprang into being about him and
Coyote declared, "You may be little people but you will be powerful." Coyote's actions
reminded Phinney and his relatives of their dependence on spirit beings like Coyote
and it underscored for them the fact that their homeland was also a place of creation.*

Coyote was building a fish-ladder, by tearing down the waterfall at Celilo, so
that salmon could go upstream for the people to catch. He was busily engaged
at this when someone shouted to him, "Why are you bothering with that? All
the people are gone; the monster has done for them."—"Well," said Coyote to
himself, "then I'll stop doing this, because I was doing it for the people, and
now I'll go along too."

From there he went along upstream, by the way of the Salmon River country.
Going along he stepped on the leg of a meadow-lark and broke it. The meadow-
lark in a temper shouted, *"limá, limá, limá,* what a chance of finding the
people you have, going along!" Coyote then asked, "My aunt! Please inform me,
afterwards I will make for you a leg of brush-wood." So the meadow-lark told
him, "Already all the people have been swallowed by the monster." Coyote then
replied, "Yes, that is where I, too, am going." From there he traveled on. Along
the way he took a good bath saying to himself, "Lest I make myself repulsive
to his taste," and then he dressed himself all up, "Lest he will vomit me up or
spit me out." There he tied himself with rope to three mountains. From there
he came along up and over ridges. Suddenly, behold, he saw a great head. He
quickly hid himself in the grass and gazed at it. Never before in his life had he
seen anything like it; never such a large thing—away off somewhere melting

into the horizon was its gigantic body. Now then Coyote shouted to him, "Oh Monster, we are going to inhale each other!" The big eyes of the monster roved around looking all over for Coyote but did not find him, because Coyote's body was painted with clay to achieve a perfect protective coloring in the grass. Coyote had on his back a pack consisting of five stone knives, some pure pitch, and a flint fire-making set. Presently Coyote shook the grass to and fro and shouted again, "Monster! we are going to inhale each other." Suddenly the monster saw the swaying grass and replied, "Oh you Coyote, you swallow me first then; you inhale first." Now Coyote tried. Powerfully and noisily he drew in his breath and the great monster just swayed and quivered. Then Coyote said, "Now you inhale me, for already you have swallowed all the people, so swallow me too lest I become lonely." Now the Monster inhaled like a mighty wind. He carried Coyote along just like that, but as Coyote went he left along the way great camas roots and great service berries, saying, "Here the people will find them and will be glad, for only a short time away is the coming of the human race." There he almost got caught on one of the ropes but he quickly cut it with his knife. Thus he dashed right into the monster's mouth.

From there he walked along down the throat of the monster. Along the way he saw bones scattered about and he thought to himself, "It is to be seen that many people have been dying." As he went along he saw some boys and he said to them, "Where is his heart? Come along and show me!" Then, as they were all going along, the bear rushed out furiously at him. "So!" Coyote said to him, "You make yourself ferocious only to me," and he kicked the bear on the nose. As they were going along the rattlesnake bristled at him in fury, "So! Only towards me you are vicious—we are nothing but dung." Then he kicked the rattlesnake on the head and flattened it out for him. Going on he met the brown bear who greeted him, "I see he (the monster) selected you for the last."—"So! I'd like to see you save your people (derogatory diatribe)." Thus all along the people hailed him and stopped him. He told the boys, "Pick up some wood." Here his erstwhile friend Fox hailed him from the side, "Such a dangerous fellow (the monster), what are you going to do to him?"—"So!" replied Coyote. "You too hurry along and look for wood." Presently Coyote arrived at the heart and he cut off slabs of fat and threw them to the people. "Imagine you being hungry under such conditions—grease your mouths with this." And now Coyote started a fire with his flint, and shortly smoke drifted up through the monster's nose, ears, eyes, and anus. Now the monster said, "Oh you Coyote, that's why I was afraid of you. Oh you Coyote, let me cast you out." And Coyote replied, "Yes, and later let it be said, 'He who was cast out is officiating in the distribution of salmon.'"—"Well then, go out through the nose." Coyote replied, "And will not they say the same?" And the monster said, "Well then, go out through the ears," to which Coyote replied, "And let it be said, 'Here is ear-wax officiating in the distribution of food.'"—"*Hn, hn, hn,* oh you Coyote! This is why I feared you; then go out through the anus," and Coyote replied, "And let people say, 'Faeces are officiating in the distribution of food.'" There was his fire still burning near the heart and now the monster began to writhe in pain and Coyote began cutting away on the heart, whereupon very shortly he broke the stone knife. Immediately he took another and in a short time this one also broke and Coyote said to all the people, "Gather up all the bones and carry them to the eyes, ears, mouth and anus; pile them up and when he falls dead kick all the bones outside." Then again with another knife he began cutting away at the heart. The third knife he broke and the fourth, leaving only one more. He told the people, "All right, get yourselves ready because as soon as he falls dead each one will go out of the opening most convenient. Take the old women and old men close to the openings so that they may get out easily." Now the heart hung by only a very small piece of muscle and Coyote was cutting away on it with his last stone knife. The monster's heart was still barely hanging when his last knife broke, whereupon Coyote threw himself on the heart and hung on just barely tearing it loose with his hands. In his death convulsions the monster opened all the openings of his body and now the people kicked the bones outside and went on out. Coyote, too, went on out. Here now the monster fell dead and now the anus began to close. But there was the muskrat still inside. Just as the anus closed he squeezed out, barely getting his body through but alas! his tail was caught; but he pulled and it was bare when he pulled out; all the tail-hair peeled right off. Coyote scolded him, "Now what were you doing; you had to think up something to do at the last moment. You're always behind in everything." Then he told the people, "Gather up all the bones and arrange them well." They did this, whereupon Coyote added, "Now we are going to carve the monster."

Coyote then smeared blood on his hands, sprinkled this blood on the bones, and suddenly there came to life again all those who had died while inside the monster. They carved the great monster and now Coyote began dealing out portions of the body to various parts of the country all over the land; toward the sunrise, toward the sunset, toward the warmth, toward the cold, and by that act destining and forenaming the various peoples; Coeur d'Alêne, Cayuse, Pend Oreilles, Flathead, Blackfeet, Crow, Sioux, et al. He consumed the entire body of the monster in this distribution to various lands far and wide. Nothing more remained of the great monster. And now Fox came up and said to Coyote, "What is the meaning of this, Coyote? You have distributed all of the body to far away lands but have given yourself nothing for this immediate locality." "Well," snorted Coyote, "and did you tell me that before? Why didn't you tell me that awhile ago before it was too late? I was engrossed to the exclusion of thinking. You should have told me that in the first place." And he turned to the people and said, "Bring me some water with which to wash my hands." They brought him water and he washed his hands and now with the bloody washwater he sprinkled the local regions saying, "You may be little people but you will be powerful. Even though you will be little because I have deprived you, nevertheless you will be very, very, manly. Only for a short time away is the coming of the human race."

*It should be understood that there is little agreement among Indians today regarding the distribution of the monster's body parts. The particular body part assigned to a territory is assumed to account for certain racial traits of its inhabitants, as for example, the scalp of the monster made for a people with an abundance of long beautiful hair.

Archie Phinney, *Nez Perce Texts*, Columbia Contributions to Anthropology (New York: Columbia University Press, 1934), 26–29. Reprinted with permission of the publisher.

FIRST CREATOR AND LONE MAN
Martha Beckwith

Martha Warren Beckwith (1871–1959), a professor at Vassar College and a celebrated expert on Native Hawaiian culture, traveled to the Fort Berthold reservation in 1929 at the request of her academic mentor, Franz Boas, to help save the stories of traditional Mandan and Hidatsa culture for future generations.

Written down by Arthur Mandan, a contemporary of Beckwith's, this story is based on the version Mandan learned as a child from his mother. It was preserved by a Catholic priest at the Fort Berthold agency. In this story, First Creator and Lone Man view the world covered with water and ask a duck where he gets his food. Learning that there is earth beneath the waters, First Creator and Lone Man ask the bird to bring some up to them. When they receive a ball of mud in their hands, they decide to use it to create the earth. The Mandan creation story does not end here. Lone Man and First Creator go on to create people and animals and to teach human beings how to behave toward each other and their creators. Throughout this process, the stories emphasize that all human beings were created through the joint efforts of animals and spiritual beings. Lone Man and First Creator teach that creation is a process that requires cooperation, sensitivity, and respect.

In the beginning the surface of the earth was all water and there was darkness. The First Creator and Lone Man were walking on the top of the waters and as they were walking along they happened to see a small object which seemed to have life and upon investigation they found it to be a small bird of the duck family—the kind that is very fond of diving.—"Well!" they said, "Let us ask this creature where it gets its subsistence. We don't see any kind of food on the waters and she must have something to keep her alive." So they asked her and she told them that she got her food in the bed of the waters. They asked her to show them a sample of the food. She told them she would be very glad to do so and at once she dived down to the bed of the waters and up she came with a small ball of sand. Upon seeing the sand they said, "Well! if this keeps the bird alive it must be good for other creatures also. Let us create land out of this substance and living creatures, and let us make the land productive that it may bear fruit for the subsistence of the creatures that we shall create. Let us choose therefore the directions where each shall begin." So Lone Man chose the northern part and the First Creator the southern, and they left a space between in the water, which is the Missouri river. Then, after agreeing to compare results, they began the creation.

The First Creator made broad valleys, hills, coulees with timber, mountain streams, springs, and, as creatures, the buffalo elk, black-tailed and white-tailed antelope, mountain sheep, and all other creatures useful to mankind for food and clothing. He made the valleys and coulees as shelter for the animals as well as for mankind. He set lakes far apart. Lone Man created for the most part level country with lakes and small streams and rivers far apart. The animals he made lived some of them in the water, like beaver, otter, and muskrat. Others were the cattle of many colors with long horns and long tails, moose, and other animals.

After all this was ended they met as agreed upon to compare their creations. First they inspected what Lone Man had created and then they went on to what First Creator had made, then they began to compare results. First Creator said, "The things you have created do not meet with my approval. The land is too level and affords no protection to man. Look at the land I have created. It contains all kinds of game, it has buttes and mountains by which man can mark his direction. Your land is so level that a man will easily lose his way for there are no high hills as sings to direct him. Look at the waters I have created,—the rivers, brooks, springs with running water always pure and refreshing for man and beast. In summer the springs are always cool, in winter they are always warm. The lakes you have made have most of them no outlet and hence become impure. The things I have made are far more useful to man. Look at the buffalo,—they are all black save here and there a white one so rare as to be prized. In winter their hair grows long and shaggy to combat the cold; in warm weather they shed their hair in order to endure the heat more comfortably. But look at the cattle you have created with long horns and tail, of all colors, and with hair so short and smooth that they cannot stand the cold!" Lone Man said, "These things I have created I thought were the very things most useful to man. I cannot very well change them now that they are once created. So let us make man use first the things that you have made until the supply is exhausted and then the generations to come shall utilize those things which I have created." So it was agreed between them and both blessed their creation and the two parted.

In the course of time Lone Man looked upon the creation and saw mankind multiplying and was pleased, but he also saw evil spirits that harmed mankind and he wanted to live among the men that he had created and be as one of them. He looked about among all nations and peoples to find a virgin to be his mother and discovered a very humble family consisting of a father, mother, and daughter. This virgin he chose to be his mother. So one morning when the young woman was roasting corn and eating it he thought this would be the proper time to enter into the young woman. So he changed himself into the corn and the young woman ate it and conceived the seed. In the course of time the parents noticed that she was with child and they questioned her, saying, "How is it, daughter, that you are with child when you have not known man? Have you concealed anything from us?" She answered, "As you say, I have known no man. All I know is that at the time when I ate roast corn I thought that I had conceived something, then I did not think of the matter again until I knew I was with child." So the parents knew that this must be a marvel since the child was not conceived through any man, and they questioned her no more.

In the course of time the child was born and he grew up like other children, but he showed unusual traits of purity and as he grew to manhood he despised all evil and never even married. Everything he did was to promote goodness. If a quarrel arose among the people he would pacify them with kind words. He loved the children and they followed him around wherever he went. Every morning he purified himself with incense, which fact goes to show that he was pure.

The people of the place where he was born were at that time Mandans. They were in the habit of going to an island in the ocean off the mouth of a river to gather *ma-tä-ba-ho*. For the journey they used a boat by the name of *I-di-he* (which means Self Going); all they had to do was to strike it on one side and tell it to go and it went. This boat carried twelve persons and no more; if more went in the boat it brought ill luck. On the way to the island they were accustomed to meet dangerous obstacles.

One day there was a party setting out for the island to get some *ma-tä-ba-ho* and everyone came to the shore to see them off and wish them good luck. The twelve men got into the boat and were about to strike the boat on the side for the start when Lone Man stepped into the boat, saying that he wanted to go too. The men in the boat as well as the people on the shore objected that he would bring ill luck, but he persisted in accompanying them and finally, seeing that they could not get rid of him, they proceeded on the journey.

Now on the way down the river, evil spirits that lived in the water came out to do them harm, but every time they came to the surface Lone Man would rebuke them and tell them to go back and never show themselves again. As they neared the mouth of the river, at one place the willows along the bank changed into young men who were really evil spirits and challenged the men in the boat to come ashore and wrestle with them. Lone Man accepted the challenge. Everyone with whom he wrestled he threw and killed until the wrestlers, seeing that they were beaten, took to their heels. Then he rebuked the willows, saying that he had made them all and they should not turn themselves into evil spirits any more. When they reached the ocean they were confronted by a great whirlpool, into which the men in the boat began to cast trinkets as a sacrifice in order to pacify it, but every time they threw in a trinket Lone Man would pick it up saying that he wanted it for himself. Meanwhile, in spite of all they could do, the whirlpool sucked them in closer. Then the men began to murmur against Lone Man and complain that he brought them ill luck and lament that they were to be sucked in by the whirlpool. Then Lone Man rebuked the whirlpool saying, "Do you not know that I am he who created you? Now I command you to be still." And immediately the waters became smooth. So they kept on the journey until they came to a part of the ocean where the waves were rough. Here the men again began to offer sacrifices to pacify the waves, but in spite of their prayers and offerings the waves grew even more violent. All this time Lone Man was picking up the offerings and the men were trying to persuade him not to do so, but he kept right on,—never stopped! By this time the boat was rocking pretty badly with the waves and the men began to murmur again and say that Lone Man was causing their death. Then he rebuked the waves, saying, "Peace, be still," and all at once the sea was still and calm and continued so for the rest of the trip.

Upon the island there were inhabitants under a chief named Ma-na-ge (perhaps water of some kind). On their arrival, the chief told the inhabitants of his village to prepare a big feast for the visitors at which he would order the visitors to eat all the food set before them and thus kill them. Lone Man foresaw that this would happen and on his way he plucked a bulrush and inserted it by way of his throat through his system. So when the feast was prepared and all were seated in a row with the food placed before them, he told the men each to eat a little from the dish as it passed from one man to the next until it reached Lone Man, when he would empty the whole contents of the dish into the bulrush, by which means it passed to the fourth strata of the earth. When all the food was gone, Lone Man looked about as if for more and said, "Well! I always heard that these people were very generous in feeding visitors. If this is all you have to offer I should hardly consider it a feast." All the people looked at the thirteen men and when they saw no signs of sickness they regarded them as mysterious.

Next Ma-na-ge asked the visitors if they wanted to smoke. Lone Man said, "Certainly! for we have heard what good tobacco you have." This pleased Ma-na-ge, for he thought he would surely kill the men by the effects of the tobacco. So he called for his pipe, which was as big as a pot. He filled the pipe and lighted it and handed it over to the men. Each took a few puffs until it came to Lone Man, who, instead of puffing out the smoke, drew it all down the bulrush to the fourth strata of the earth. So in no time the whole contents of the pipe was smoked. Then he said he had always heard that Ma-na-ge was accustomed to kill his visitors by smoking with them but if this was the pipe he used it was not even large enough to satisfy him. From that time on Ma-na-ge watched him pretty closely.

Now Lone Man was in disguise. The chief then asked his visitors for their bags to fill with the ma-tä ba-ho, as much as each man had strength to carry, and each produced his bag. Lone Man's was a small bag made of two buffalo hides sewed together, but they had to keep putting in to fill it. The chief watched them pretty closely by this time and thought, "If he gets away with that load he must be Lone Man!" So when the bag was filled, Lone Man took the bag by the left hand, slung it over his right shoulder and began to walk away. Then Ma-na-ge said, "Lone Man, do you think that we don't know you?" Said Lone Man as he walked away, "Perhaps you think that I am Lone Man!" Ma-na-ge said, "We shall come over to visit you on the fourth night after you reach home." By this he meant, in the fourth year.

When they reached home, Lone Man instructed his people how to perform ceremonies as to himself and appointed the men who were to perform them. He told them to clear a round space in the center of the village and to build a round barricade about it and to take four young cottonwood trees as a hoop. In the center of the barricade they were to set up a cedar and paint it with red earth and burn incense and offer sacrifices to the cedar. Lone Man said, "This cedar is my body which I leave with you as a protection from all harm, and this barricade will be a protection from the destruction of the water. For as Ma-na-ge said, they are coming to visit you. This shall be the sign of their coming. There will be a heavy fog for four days and four nights, then you may know that they are coming to destroy you. But it is nothing but water. When it comes, it will rise no higher than the first hoop next to the ground and when it can get no higher it will subside."

After he had instructed them in all the rites and ceremonies they should perform he said, "Now I am going to leave you,—I am going to the south—to other peoples—and shall come back again. But always remember that I leave with you my body." And he departed to the south. And after four years Ma-na-ge made his visit in the form of water and tried in every way to destroy the inhabitants of the village, but when he failed to rise higher than the first hoop he subsided.

"First Creator and Lone Man," in *Mandan-Hidatsa Myths and Ceremonies,* ed. Martha Beckwith (New York: American Folklore Society, 1938), 1–17.

OUR LANDS AND OUR HISTORY
Armand Minthorn

In this excerpt from an interview in 2002, Armand Minthorn of the Confederated Tribes of the Umatilla Reservation reflects on the meaning of creation stories for contemporary Native Americans. In Minthorn's view, stories both enhance the historical record and remind modern Indian people of their fundamental values.

We have oral histories today that go back ten thousand years. We know where this individual lived, we know how he lived, we know where he traveled, we know what he ate, and we know the kinds of traditions that he carried. There are no other people in the United States that have oral histories that go back 10,000 years.

Our traditions and our language have not changed. We have songs; we have customs, which are handed down generation to generation and because of that we have been able to maintain a way of life that has been carried for thousands of years. When we can go back and say this spot and this spot and this area were used at this time and by these people, that is what enables us to keep our past a part of our everyday life. All of that history is carried through our traditions and customs and language and religion and our foods. We are reminded every day of that past because we live it.

Rattlesnake Mountain is a sacred site for us. If you look at it today there's lines that go across the whole mountain, clear up to the top. My elders told me that a long time ago this mountain saved them. They said that there was a time when the rivers kept rising and rising and rising and the people kept going back and back and back, until they ended up on Rattlesnake Mountain. Anthropologists and archaeologists today call that time the Missoula floods, when the great ice dam near present-day Missoula, Montana, burst and sent out unimaginable quantities of water. It flooded the Columbia River. It is part of our oral history. Archaeologists tell us that this happened over 9,700 years ago. Our histories have a lot to do with the environment, and nature's elements, whether they'd be water, snow, rain, even heat and droughts. Those are the indicators that we use within our oral histories to help us gauge time.

Armand Minthorn, filmed interview by Sally Thompson, Tamástslikt Cultural Institute, Pendleton, Oregon, April 16, 2002.

CHAPTER THREE

A Brilliant Plan for Living: Gifts

People in the Indian country believed it was wise to show respect to the spiritual beings who gave them the world by constantly responding to life's blessings with presents and prayers of gratitude. Gifts from the creators—healthy children, good crops, a successful hunt—deserved gifts in return. In villages and hunting bands people organized their lives to mirror this mutual relationship. Elders also taught that generosity was an essential element of community life. Just as people expected prayers and gifts to spirit beings would sustain their good fortune, they also believed that gifts to relatives, neighbors, and friends would produce gifts in return, generating happiness and prosperity for all. Gifts made life possible; every gift demanded a gift in return.

RED STICK CEREMONY
Alfred W. Bowers

Many communities developed buffalo-calling rituals intended to bring the animals close to their villages. Among the Mandans, this ceremony recreated a story in which twelve buffalo bulls visited a young man who had gone out into the hills to fast and pray for assistance. The twelve buffalo bulls sang the young man a song that answered his prayers and each left him a red stick as he departed.

In the Mandan Buffalo Calling (Red Stick) Ceremony twelve older men line up holding red sticks to symbolize the life force brought to the village by the buffalo. They face young men accompanied by their wives, who wear only buffalo robes. In the course of the ceremony, the older men transfer the life force to the women through

*sexual intercourse. The women, in turn, pass this force on to the young men, thereby
ensuring the survival of the community.*

*Shocking to outsiders such as the American members of the Lewis and Clark
expedition, the buffalo-calling ritual was intended to welcome the buffalo to a village
and to establish close ties between this important animal and the human beings who
relied on them.*

The Red Stick Ceremony was a winter buffalo-calling rite of four nights' du-
ration and was held during the coldest part of the winter to bring the winter
herds near the village. The ceremony was given by some young man who
in his dream witnessed the ceremony given, heard the buffaloes singing the
sacred song, or saw the ceremonial objects arranged in their proper place in
his lodge.

Standing Bear, last bundle-owner before the disappearance of the buffaloes,
purchased the bundle from his father and mother but, having no children, sold
the bundle from his father and mother to Iron Eyes, who was not a relative.
The bundle consisted of a buffalo robe representing First Pretty Woman and
twelve flat boards painted red, with vestigial buffalo hoofs attached. One end
was tapered to provide a handhold. There were a large wooden pipe, an owl,
two hide rattles, a painted robe, and sage in the bundle.

There was only one song belonging to the ceremony, and it referred to the
information given by the twelve winter buffalo bulls who appeared during a
blizzard and sang:

The one first woman pretty
Has eaten most of you.

The ceremony was based on a dramatization of the exploits of Corn Silk,
who brought back a little girl to the Mandan Village. Each night the occupants
of one earth lodge would disappear until the village became alarmed. The old
men met to seek a solution to the mysterious disappearance of their people.
One young man volunteered to fast in an effort to get advice from the spirits
as to the cause of the misfortune to these households. A blizzard came in from
the north, and twelve buffalo bulls, each carrying a red stick to which buffalo
vestigial hoofs, lungs, heart, and windpipe were tied, drifted along with the
wind until they reached the foot of the hill where the young man was fasting.
They sang a song which mentioned the name of the young girl who was the
cause of the disappearance of these families. She was destroyed by burning,

which freed the people she had consumed. A sacred bundle was established by the young man. A buffalo robe represented the young girl, and twelve red sticks were carved to represent the twelve buffalo bulls.

Bundle transfer was traditionally from father to son, but the information on actual transfers is so limited that it was not possible to check this belief with actual transfers. The ceremony was not given after the buffalo herds disappeared.

The pledge to give the ceremony could be made either by an individual or by an age-grade society. In the case of the former, clan brothers of about the same age assisted by bringing their wives with food and goods. The owner of the sacred bundle would select twelve older men who had given the ceremony or who had sacred buffalo skulls, acquired through vision or purchase with bundles, to carry the red sticks. When an age-grade society gave the ceremony, the bundle-owner distributed the red sticks among the members of the next highest age-grade society who impersonated the buffalo bulls.

The ceremony was held in the giver's lodge. He paid those who carried the red sticks and the bundle-owner who set up the robe of First Pretty Woman on an ash stake to represent a young girl. These carriers of the red sticks met at the bundle-owner's lodge in the evening to receive their ceremonial paraphernalia, after which by four stages they approached the lodge where the ceremony was being held. At each stop the giver's wife would put down a robe and a corn ball.

Upon entering the lodge where the ceremonies were to be held, the carriers placed the red sticks in a row extending from the fireplace to the head of the lodge, and the image of First Pretty Woman was placed to the right of them.

During the afternoon the Black Mouths sent their criers through the village announcing the buffalo dances were to be held that evening. Any of the old men could go and sit on the right side nearer the door than the red-stick carriers. The young men came in with their wives, who wore only buffalo robes, and sat on the left side of the lodge. There was only one ceremonial song; it was sung four times. The young women brought by their husbands formed a single line, where each sat down on her heels and walked the length of the red boards. The woman in the lead must be one who had never had intercourse with anyone other than her present husband. The head of the line was a coveted position, and an attempt was sometimes made by an unqualified woman to lead the others over the red sticks. Then some man with whom she had had intercourse would laugh to make his presence known, whereupon she would drop out of line and take up the last place in the procession. The act of walking along the red sticks was known as "Walking with the Buffalo Bulls" or "Having Intercourse with the Buffalo Bulls." The women then returned to their places, put on their buffalo robes, and passed around the food to the old men representing the buffalo bulls and to the spectators.

The next performance was the "Giving the Wives" to the buffalo bulls. One of the young men, addressing his wife, would say, "Wife, I want you to help me to become a lucky man. I want you to walk with my father." The rule was for a young man always to select an old man of his father's clan. If the man selected did not choose to have intercourse with his "son's" wife, he would stop her before she reached the door.

One time when Red Coyote was selected, he said: "Stop right there, my 'granddaughter.' I want you to hold my medicine bundle now. Once I fasted four days in a ravine. While I slept, an owl came to me and said that I would be a lucky man and live to be old. I have killed an enemy, captured six horses, and struck three enemies. I pray that you will live a long time, be healthy, raise many children, and keep free of diseases." Both returned to their places and sat down.

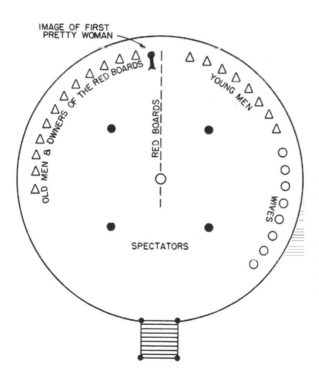

The arrangement of elders along with young men and their wives for the performance of the Mandan Buffalo Dance. Courtesy the Newberry Library, Chicago (Ayer E99 .M2 B68 1991, p. 317).

Each young man selected an old man to "walk with his wife." Some men stopped the women at the door and did not care to go outside with them; others went outside. In either case, the woman was given the old man's medicine bundle (vision bundle), which she clasped to her breast, believing that, by doing so, some of its powers would enter her body.

An unmarried man could participate by bringing his brother's or clan brother's wife. Men never brought women of other tribes who had recently married into the tribe, believing that the spirits of the red sticks would then help the other tribe. However, when such women had joined a Mandan clan, they could participate.

Sometimes, when a man refused to walk with his "granddaughter," her husband placed a filled pipe before him. This left the old man one of two choices: (1) he could walk with her, or (2) he could invoke the spirits of the north that sent storms driving the buffaloes to the Missouri River to help her and her husband. A woman was not offered to a man of her own clan or to immediate blood relatives.

Mrs. Good Bear recognized this as a separate ceremony at the lower village, Mitutanka, and did not believe that it was performed at Nuptadi in this form, as they had the buffalo-calling rites of the Snow Owl ceremony, which was similar in some respects to the Red Stick ceremony. Scattercorn verified this information by stating that Standing Bear, who owned the Red Stick Ceremony, came up early to Like-a-Fishhook Village (about 1845) together with the survivors of the lower village and that, after the Nuptadi survivors joined the other Mandans, both ceremonies were given but never at the same time.

The sacred myth belonging to the ceremony was related by Mrs. Good Bear.

Red Stick Ceremony Myth Related by Mrs. Good Bear

A long time ago there was a respectable young woman named Corn Silk who had then been single for several years. Many men wanted to marry her, but she always refused. One day her parents said, "Why don't you get married?" They scolded her, and she felt bad because they had quarreled. When night came, she went outside and lay on top of the doorway to the earth lodge to sleep and would not go into the lodge that night. She went to sleep.

When she awoke, someone was carrying her on his shoulders, and she knew that someone had her in his power. She couldn't get away. They went along until they came to his lodge. He put her in a bed, thinking that she was asleep, but she knew everything that happened. Then there was another woman, an owl, and a large grizzly bear in the lodge. The man asked Owl Woman to cook something for Corn Silk, and she began to prepare food. Then she said, "Corn Silk, you should get up and eat." Owl Woman brought water for her to wash with, and then she ate.

The man came in again and said to Owl Woman, "Send her into the woods to get fuel. Tell her to take the bear with her."

He walked out and then Owl Woman said, "You are a good and beautiful young woman, I am going to tell you what will happen to you. That man plans to eat you. That is why he brought you here. You must try hard to save your life. He will kill you when you get back from the woods, so be on your guard."

Corn Silk took the bear and the travois to bring the wood in with. The bear lay down while she gathered dry sticks, figuring all the time how she could get away. Owl Woman had said, "If you get to that sharp hill before he gets you, you will be safe." She picked up one of her lice while she was in the woods and thought that she would get away while the louse answered anyone who came along. She ran as fast as she could.

At that time the man came along and inquired where the girl was, and the louse replied, "In the woods." He waited. Corn Silk was nearly to the hill. The man went in to see where she was. He asked the bear where she had gone, and he replied that she asked him to lie down, so he did not know. He asked where she was, and the louse replied, "Here I am."

The man said, "I know where she is," and he ran toward the sharp hill to get her.

He came close and kept saying, "I will get you!" She had some waterbird feathers stripped down to work, like in quill work. She threw one of the feather sticks back, and thousands of these white birds [a bird on the lakes of the north, the land gull] flew up and beat him in the face, slowing him up.

When he got out of the flock, she threw back an elk-horn scraper which was used to flatten quills, asking help of the elk bulls, who appeared and hooked him. This slowed him up, but he passed them. He said, "I'll get you this time."

She had a pumice stone to smoothen the feathers with, and she threw that back. Sharp hills of pumice stone came up, and they caused him to fall often. About this time she reached the hill and found the door open. She ran in. A little boy named Breast was inside playing with a bow and arrow, but he did not pay any attention to the young woman who had come in. Soon Spirit Man was outside, and he called, "Send her out, or I will get you, too." The boy was shooting into the fireplace. Each time the man said, "I'll get you, too," the boy repeated it.

The man said, "This will be the last time that I will warn you."

The boy took up a pipe called "Tail Pipe" [a buffalo tail hide stuffed with sand until dry, when a hole was made in the end, leaving the tip hair on]. The boy picked up the pipe and filled it with tobacco, lighting it. The man was standing a short distance away. Breast took a deep suck on the pipe and blew the smoke toward the man, who fell down and died. He called to his sister to come outside and burn the body. They covered it with buffalo chips and burned the body until it was reduced to ashes.

When evening came, the little boy said, "Sister, I have quite a few brothers; some are foolish, and they are out hunting now, so you must go behind their beds and hide before they get here." She hid and they came in; they were all young men; they cooked a meal and talked of the hunt for a long while.

The little boy sat there and suddenly said, "I found something," but they paid no attention to him. He repeated it, but they paid no attention to him.

At last one said, "Our little brother said that he found something."

The others said, "Show us what you found."

After a long time he said, "I found a sister." They all agreed that they would have her for a sister, so the little boy said, "Sister, come out." She came out from hiding as a beautiful young woman.

All the young men called her sister, and one of them said, "It is a good thing that you reached here because that man kills people and eats them. It is a lucky thing that Breast was here. It won't do to keep you here all the time, so in a few days we will take you home again. You can stay two days and rest and then go home again."

The next day they told her that they were going hunting and that she was to stay with Breast through the day. They said to Breast, "Stay with our sister, and you must not go out anywhere at all." They said to the young woman, "Sister, we are saying this because there are many evil spirits who would take you away."

While they were gone, an old woman came along packing an old man like they carried babies. His face was ugly; his nose was dirty; he cried like a baby. All this was to try to get Corn Silk to look at him. She hung her head and would not look at him. The old woman was angry because Corn Silk would not look, but they went out.

Toward evening the brothers came home and inquired whether anyone had been there, and Corn Silk told of the old man and woman whom she would not look at. The brothers said, "We thought so; everyone will be after you. It is best for you to go home. We will let you take something along with you so that you will be safe. Then nobody will bother you." One of them pulled out a beautiful otter skin with the skull still in it. She wrapped it up to carry on her back. At the same time she pounded dry meat for her trip home. Her brothers said, "If anyone stops you or tries to give you anything to eat, you must refuse it. Do not eat with them."

She walked along until evening came, when she met a beautiful young girl who said, "My friend, I have a lodge. You should come and stay with me overnight." They went into a ravine. The woman had a wood-and-brush tepee. They went in, and she said, "My friend, I will give you something to eat." So she dished out a portion of a man's brain with a mountain-sheep spoon. Corn Silk took out the brain and gave it to the otter skull, which ate it all up. She slept there. While she slept, the other woman went away, for in the morning she was alone. She set the tepee afire and traveled along.

She walked all day until afternoon, when a small child came to her crying for its mother. She looked at it and knew that it was not a real human and passed it up. Soon she saw another and passed it up; still another cried, and she thought of taking it because it looked so pretty. She went on. It cried louder and louder. Toward evening she met another woman, who addressed her as "my friend" and asked her to her house in a ravine. It was another brush tepee. She said that she was cooking dried squash, but they were people's ears. Corn Silk said, "I have something here for you to eat," and she gave the dried meat to the woman. Corn Silk gave the ears to the otter skull. The skull ate all the ears. The other woman said she was glad Corn Silk ate all the squash. When Corn Silk awoke, she was alone. She set the tepee afire as before.

She traveled until nearly evening, when she met another baby; she passed a second one also. The third one was a very beautiful girl who was just learning to walk. The baby touched Corn Silk's dress, and she looked at it. She took it even though she had been told not to take anything. She packed the baby on her back. She came home with the baby girl the same evening. Everyone called that Corn Silk was back, and all admired the very pretty baby she had with her. Everyone heard about the baby and came to admire it. This went on for three days. One morning when the village awoke, an entire family was gone. The people wondered about it. The next morning another family had disappeared, and still a third family on the third morning. Some of the older people met and debated the cause of this and what could be done. It was something very mysterious, and they told the young men to stay up all night and keep watch. One young man said, "I will fast on the hills and see if I can find out what it is all about."

He cried all day, and a snowstorm and blizzard came up toward evening. In the night during the storm twelve buffalo bulls came along under the hill walking in the snow. They were walking toward the village. Each had a flat board about two feet long with hoofs, lungs, and a heart tied to the handle. They stopped at the foot of the hill near the young man, circled around, and sang their song.

First Pretty Woman was the name of the child which had been brought into the village, and the bulls gave the name. They said, "First Pretty Woman nearly ate up your village," and then they bellowed, pushing each other with their bodies. They were carrying the red sticks all this time. When they finished singing the song, the bulls went away and the young man returned to his village.

He said to the older men, "You wanted some young man to learn what has become of the people. I fasted on the hill to find out. While I was there, a storm came. I stood up against the wind and cried, and at the foot of the hill there appeared twelve buffalo bulls. They stood in a circle and sang a beautiful song. Each carried boards painted red. On the handles of each were hung heads, lungs, heart, and windpipe. They sang a song, and these words were in the song: 'First Pretty Woman ate up most of your people.'

"You must learn whether there is any child in the village named First Pretty Woman."

An old man said, "Corn Silk brought in a baby named First Pretty Woman, and that must be the one."

The older men called the Black Mouth Society, ordering them to go from lodge to lodge and find out who she was. They inquired the names of all the children in each family until they came to Corn Silk. They asked her if that was her own baby, and she said that it was. Then they asked the name and she replied, "First Pretty Woman."

Then the Black Mouths said, "That is the child we are looking for. We lost our families and something got them. We heard one of the young men say that First Pretty Woman was the name of the child who ate them. That must be the one, and we are going to take the baby from you."

Corn Silk replied, "She isn't mine because I picked her up on the prairie one morning at daybreak. Once the child flew down through the smokehole and came to me. I tickled her, and she laughed. I saw a piece of meat between her teeth and pulled it out. It was the fingernail of a human."

The Black Mouths took the baby along, called through the village that they had found the child, and directed the people to bring wood to burn her. They built a large fire and threw the child into the fire. She jumped out three times. The fourth time the baby burned, and its stomach swelled up and burst. All the people she had eaten came out and walked back to their lodges.

After that was done, this young man made up the ceremony. He made the sticks just like the ones he saw the buffaloes carrying. It was not in the dream but instead of the lungs he put on hoofs. It was the custom to put on this dance whenever the buffaloes were scarce, and then they came near the village. When the young man came back, he was the first to make these sticks. The old men met and came to his lodge to sing the song that went with the sticks. The young man's friends brought their wives, and the old men walked with them.

Alfred W. Bowers, "Red Stick Ceremony," in *Mandan Social and Ceremonial Organization* (Chicago: University of Chicago Press, 1950), 315–23; copyright © 1950 by the University of Chicago.

MONTHS OF YEAR AND PLANTS OR ANIMALS EXPECTED EACH MONTH

Herbert Spinden

Supported by Harvard's Peabody Museum, the anthropologist Herbert Spinden spent the summer of 1907 in Idaho, compiling information about the traditional culture of the Nez Perce Indians. In this report on his research, Spinden listed the tribal names for the months of the year. It is striking how changes in plant or animal behavior triggered new activities each month. Flowers (March) were succeeded by ripening roots (April), root-based bread (May), and the arrival of salmon (June) and eels (July). As they spoke the name of each month, Nez Perce people would be reminded of the creator's gifts.

According to the ancient calendar there were twelve months in the year. It is uncertain which of these months began the year, so they are here given from the starting point of our own calendar:

1st January.—*Wilū'pup*, meaning uncertain, said to be, "the middle of cold weather."

2nd February.—*Ălătămā'l*, "the month of swelling buds."

3rd March.—*Latī'tal*, "the month of flowers," *latis* meaning "flowers."

4th April.—*Kakītal'*, "the month of *kakit*"; *kakit* was a favorite food root much like kouse

5th May.—*Āpāāl'*, "the month of kouse bread"; kouse bread was made from the fresh roots gathered at this time.

6th June.—*Hil'lal*, "the month of the first run of the salmon."

7th July.—*Hasoal'*, "the month of eels," or *Qoiĭktsal*, "the month of blue-backed salmon."

8th August.—*Taiyaal*, meaning uncertain, possibly "the month of hot weather"; *taiyam* means "summer."

9th September.—*Wauwama aiakal*, "the month of salmon spawning at the heads of creeks."

10th October.—*Aiakal Pikūn'me*, "the month of spawning salmon on Snake river."

11th November.—*Hoplal*, "the month when tamarack (larch) trees lose their needles."

12th December.—*Saxliwāli*, "the beginning of cold weather," or "time of the fall deer hunt."

The four seasons of the year were named as follows:

Spring, *etaiyam.*
Summer, *taiyam.*
Fall, *saxnim'.*
Winter, *enim.*

Herbert Joseph Spinden, *The Nez Perce Indians* (Lancaster, Pa.: New Era Printing Co., 1908), 237–41.

FINDING SPIRIT HELPERS
Philip Minthorn

"Spirit helpers" were a gift from the supernatural world that played an important role in most Indian communities. The Umatilla people, who lived in what is now eastern Oregon, called these helpers "Weyekin." Weyekin offered humans a link to the invisible world of spiritual power; they brought a variety of gifts to their human partners. They provided vital information to troubled individuals and interceded with animals or other spirit beings to promote good crops, successful hunts, or happy relationships. These stories were compiled by a Umatilla elder in the first years of the twentieth century.

Beginning from the earliest times the children of the Indians were taught how they might best obtain their Weyekin, which would be their helper, adviser, guide, and comforter, both in daily life, in war, in hunting and fishing, in business, and in sickness. The instructions were on this wise. The child should rise early, bathe his body carefully by means of sweat bath and cold plunge, and cleanse his mouth far into his throat and stomach with willow twigs. Thus cleansed he should go alone into the woods or along the stream to commune with Nature until such time as some animal, bird, beast, or insect should in some manner communicate with him, in the natural way while walking, or while asleep in the visionary or ecstatic way. And what ever came to him and made a pact with him thus should become his Weyckin, his guiding star, his good angel in all after life. This was the normal way to find and get the Weyekin; but it might be obtained in other ways, for the Weyekin, like the wind, "bloweth where it will." So any experience might reveal to the seeker his Weyekin and permit his initiation into the Cult. One person might have a number of Weyekin at his service, especially was this true if he were educating himself to become a big medicine man or "Tuet." For if he was to overcome some special kind of sickness brought upon one of his patients by a different Weyekin, he must have a Weyekin of greater cunning, strength, or speed to outwit the other, and so work his cure. These Weyekin could communicate with their devotees by telepathy no matter how great the distance, or what obstacles were to be overcome or enemy blocking the way. So the Indian's world of imagination is peoples with these invisible Weyekin who work "malicious animal magnetism" on whom they will. Therefore, the personal Weyekin when found becomes a sacred thing, and even after embracing the Christian faith devotedly, no Indian, I believe, would willfully destroy his Weyekin. This spiritual alliance is kept secret. One man said to me, "If I told you about my Weyekin maybe it would storm and rain for many days."

The Indian medicine man has the adepts of occult science heavily handicapped, with his innumerable host of Weyekin to work for him. He has practiced the art of spirit communication for centuries, and explains the matter in more simple language, and with less vagaries, than these modern cults.

J. M. Cornelison, *Weyekin Stories* (San Francisco: E. L. Mackey, 1911), 7–8.

THE SEASONAL ROUND
Cecilia Bearchum

Here a member of the Umatilla community in eastern Oregon explains how the regular harvesting of plant resources renews her ties to her culture and ancestors.

They lived at the mouth of the Walla Walla River and up towards the Snake River, they were not nomads. They had a purpose in mind. When they moved it was because the food was seasonal. They moved towards the mountains in winter when it was time for either digging or for hunting. And when they moved they dug into the ground and lined it with tree mats and put all of their belongings into these storage areas. And then they covered them up and marked them so they knew where they were. They couldn't leave it in storage someplace in town or anything like that; there was no such place. So when they went to the mountains to gather roots they would bring them back to where they had things stored. That is where they would winter.

Different seasons you did different things. There was no calendar to tell you when you were supposed to do what, there was no one to tell you what season it was, because they knew the seasons themselves. And they did things according to the season. In springtime there was different things to take care of. Many folks went fishing; they called it the "spring run." They would then preserve their fish, they would dry it, you always hear about pemmican, they had the same thing with salmon. They took all the moisture out of it and they stored it for the winter. When I was growing up we still stored things in cellars, we still dried things, because there was no such thing as cold storage, or canning or salting, but everybody had a cellar.

Cecelia Bearchum, filmed interview by Sally Thompson, Tamástslikt Cultural Institute, Pendleton, Oregon, April 16, 2002.

"I AM SO THANKFUL . . ."
Lee Bourgeau

Here a Umatilla elder reflects on the continuing importance of her community's gathering traditions and the central role her tribe's treaty with the United States has played in protecting those traditions.

There's this place we've been going to for several years to gather berries, and we'd go up there and we'd be able to pick like six gallons in three hours. The berries are so thick, so big and so healthy we'd go back every year and gather in that same place. The kids would run around and play but we'd pick, and they'd help us a little bit. But a couple of years ago we went back with the intention of picking berries like we always have, and I jumped out of the car and I went running over this little hill down to where those bushes are and I was just shocked. I stood there and I looked around, and there were so few berries hanging on those bushes. It was painful. I just stood there and cried.

It is really painful to not be able to get the foods that we need. The elders teach us that during ceremonies we're supposed to set a full table, whatever the reason. Especially for the passing of one of our gatherers or our hunter-fishermen or somebody who's our drummer. We need to give them what we call the last supper, served at midnight during their wake. We recently laid a very important lady to rest; she was a gatherer all of her life, somebody who took care of the people. And she was a teacher; she taught me a lot of what I know. When she died we could barely get any of our traditional foods to put on the table for her and I always think very sadly of that. Which raises the question: if we don't have these traditional foods, how are we going to teach our children? How are they going to teach their children? The preservation of our ways is really a concern.

The attitude with treaties is that the federal government, in the treaty of 1855, didn't give the Nez Perce anything; they didn't give us anything. They took a lot from us. And what we did as a people is we reserved through those treaties, some rights: hunting and fishing and gathering. We reserved those rights, and I could never say it enough: I am so thankful for the wisdom of our elders in negotiating our treaties. I know there are other tribes that are not as fortunate as us, and I think about that whenever I go to our ancient fishing sites off the reservation. Or when we're picking huckleberries clear over on the Montana border I think about that, because that is way beyond the Nez Perce reservation boundaries. I'm just thankful for those people.

Lee Bourgeau, filmed interview by Sally Thompson, Spalding, Idaho, April 13, 2002.

CHAPTER FOUR

A Brilliant Plan for Living: Men and Women

Men and women contributed equally to the health and well-being of communities in Indian country. Their separate gifts were essential to the creation of human life. Their complementary contributions transformed animals into clothing, plants into food, and children into adults. Each gender made its own contribution to community life and each had specific responsibilities to fulfill. Working in groups—whether in hunting, farming, or the processing of raw materials into finished goods—drew men and women together, forging powerful bonds that provided Indian country communities with an essential source of unity and cohesion.

HIDATSA AGRICULTURE
Gilbert L. Wilson

Women owned the gardens filled with corn, beans, and squash that covered the river bottoms near the Arikara, Mandan, and Hidatsa villages on the Upper Missouri. Working in extended family groups or with fellow members of a ceremonial society, girls and women planted crops in the spring, weeded together in summer, and gathered the harvest in the fall. "Waheenee," or Buffalo Bird Woman, was born in 1839, and her memoir tells of many customs associated with traditional Hidatsa agriculture. Jeffery R. Hanson described the woman in the introduction to Wilson's book.

Buffalo Bird Woman, known in Hidatsa as Maxidiwiac, was born about 1839 in an earth lodge along the Knife River in present-day North Dakota. In 1845 her people moved upstream and built Like-a-fishhook village, which they shared with the Mandan and Arikara. There Buffalo Bird Woman grew up to become an expert gardener of the Hidatsa tribe. Using agricultural practices centuries old, she and the women of her family grew corn, beans, squash, and sunflowers in the fertile bottomlands of the Missouri River. In the mid-1880s, U.S. government policies forced the breakup of Like-a-fishhook village and the dispersal of Indian families onto individual allotments on the Fort Berthold Reservation, but Hidatsa women continued to grow the vegetables that have provided Midwestern farmers some of their most important crops.

In *Buffalo Bird Woman's Garden,* first published in 1917 as *Agriculture of the Hidatsa Indians: An Indian Interpretation,* the anthropologist Gilbert L. Wilson transcribed in meticulous detail the knowledge given by this consummate gardener. Following an annual round, Buffalo Bird Woman describes field care and preparation, planting, harvesting, processing, and storing of vegetables. In addition, she provides recipes for cooking traditional Hidatsa dishes and recounts songs and ceremonies that were essential to a good harvest. Her first-person narrative provides today's gardener with a guide to an agricultural method free from fertilizers, pesticides, and herbicides.

For many white Americans and Europeans, the very idea of farmer-Indians on the Great Plains is unfamiliar. Most people think of Plains Indians as the nomadic tribes who, mounted on horseback and free from agrarian ties to the soil, roamed the Plains in search of the buffalo. Hunters and warriors, provident with nature and fiercely resistant to subjugation, tribes like the Dakota, Comanche, Cheyenne, and Blackfeet have come to typify Plains Indian life. In "dime novels," fiction, movies, and history books, these Plains Indians have symbolized not only the drama and romanticism of the Old West, but a disappearing lifeway as well. The nomadic Plains tribes became, in the American mind, the quintessential Indians: standard-bearers of a bygone age, remembered for their noble qualities of courage, love of freedom, and a oneness with nature.

The other Plains Indian are those to whom popular sentiment and to a lesser extent historians have paid far too little attention. These are the Village Indians of the Great Plains, sedentary farming peoples whose ancient lifeways and contributions to history and civilization have gone largely unsung. In the Northern Plains, the Hidatsa, Mandan, and Arikara (known now as the Three Affiliated Tribes) were once numerous, powerful, and independent tribes controlling practically the entire Missouri River Valley in what is now North and South Dakota. Their cultural adaptations represent a much more ancient and indigenous Plains Indian tradition than the "typical" cultures of the nomadic Plains tribes, which depended on horses introduced by Euro-Americans.

The Hidatsa inherited a cultural legacy that had withstood the test of time. Archaeologists have named their lifeway the Plains Village Tradition and traced it back to A.D. 1100 in the Knife River–Heart River region of the Missouri Valley, the historic homeland of the Hidatsa and Mandan. The Plains Village lifeway reflects a stable cultural adaptation to specific ecological conditions in the Northern Plains. Agricultural peoples built permanent earthlodge villages where they would not be flooded, on the terraces of the Missouri and its tributaries. From these central communities the people took advantage of the opportunities that nature provided. The river channel provided abundant fish, mussel shells, and migratory waterfowl. The floodplains and bottomlands were used for garden plots and supplied extensive quantities of timber for building materials and fuel. The valley, with its characteristic gallery forests, offered habitat for a wide range of large and small mammals and birds, which were hunted by Plains Village peoples. Finally, the upland prairie teemed with bison, which were the major focus of Plains Village hunting parties. Thus the Plains villagers developed a successful and complementary dual economy based on agriculture and hunting which persisted well into historic times (that is, after the arrival of Europeans).

Agriculture provided the distinctive flavor of this lifeway. The commitment to permanent villages, the unique and complex architectural achievements shown in the earthlodges, the settlements and community plans of villages, and the ceramic traditions all testify to an agricultural legacy that lasted over seven centuries in the Northern Plains. This legacy is imbedded not only in the soil but also in the lives, minds, and hearts of those who inherited it, nourished it, and preserved it. It is to these people, the Hidatsa, Mandan, and Arikara, that historians and anthropologists have turned for this knowledge.

Before the 1830s, members of a large and powerful Hidatsa tribe farmed, hunted, and traded from their traditional villages near the mouth of the Knife River. The Hidatsa were divided into three closely related subgroups who, from about 1787 until 1834–45, maintained distinct and independent villages: the *Hidatsa-proper,* who inhabited Big Hidatsa village on the north bank of the Knife River; the *Awatixa,* who lived about a mile downstream from the Hidatsa-proper in Sakakawea village; and the *Awaxawi,* who lived in Amahami village about one mile south of Sakakawea at the mouth of the Knife River. *Wilson recorded the narrative of Buffalo Bird Woman:*

Beginning a Garden

My great-grandmother, as white men count their kin, was named Atąʿkic, or Soft-white Corn. She adopted a daughter, Mataʿtic, or Turtle. Some years after, a daughter was born to Atąʿkic, whom she named Otter.

Turtle and Otter both married. Turtle had a daughter named Icaʿwikec, or Corn Sucker; and Otter had three daughters, Want-to-be-a-woman, Red Blossom, and Strikes-many-women, all younger than Corn Sucker.

The smallpox year at Five Villages left Otter's family with no male members to support them. Turtle and her daughter were then living in Otter's lodge; and Otter's daughters, as Indian custom bade, called Corn Sucker their elder sister.

It was a custom of the Hidatsas, that if the eldest sister of a household married, her younger sisters were also given to her husband, as they came of marriageable age. Left without male kin by the smallpox, my grandmother's family was hard put to it to get meat; and Turtle gladly gave her daughter to my father, Small Ankle, whom she knew to be a good hunter. Otter's daughters, reckoned as Corn Sucker's sisters, were given to Small Ankle as they grew up; the eldest, Want-to-be-a-woman, was my mother.

When I was four years old, my tribe and the Mandans came to Like-a-fish-hook bend. They came in the spring and camped in tepees, or skin tents. By Butterfly's winter count, I know they began building earth lodges the next winter. I was too young to remember much of this.

Two years after we came to Like-a-fishhook bend, smallpox again visited my tribe; and my mother, Want-to-be-a-woman, and Corn Sucker, died of it. Red Blossom and Strikes-many-women survived, whom I now called my mothers. Otter and Turtle lived with us; I was taught to call them my grandmothers.

Clearing Fields

Soon after they came to Like-a-fishhook bend, the families of my tribe began to clear fields, for gardens, like those they had at Five Villages. Rich black soil was to be found in the timbered bottom lands of the Missouri. Most of the work of clearing was done by the women.

In old times we Hidatsas never made our gardens on the untimbered, prairie land, because the soil there is too hard and dry. In the bottom lands by the Missouri, the soil is soft and easy to work.

My mothers and my two grandmothers worked at clearing our family's garden. It lay east of the village at a place where many other families were clearing fields.

I was too small to note very much at first. But I remember that my father set boundary marks—whether wooden stakes or little mounds of earth or stones, I do not now remember—at the corners of the field we claimed. My mothers and my two grandmothers began at one end of this field and worked forward. All had heavy iron hoes, except Turtle, who used an old-fashioned wooden digging stick.

With their hoes, my mothers cut the long grass that covered much of the field, and bore it off the line, to be burned. With the same implements, they next dug and softened the soil in places for the corn hills, which were laid off in rows. These hills they planted. Then all summer they worked with their hoes, clearing and breaking the ground between the hills.

Trees and bushes I know must have been cut off with iron axes; but I remember little of this, because I was only four years old when the clearing was begun.

I have heard that in very old times, when clearing a new field, my people first dug the corn hills with digging sticks; and afterwards, like my mothers, worked between the hills, with bone hoes. My father told me this.

Whether stone axes were used in old times to cut the trees and under-growths, I do not know. I think fields were never then laid out on ground that had large trees on it.

Dispute and Its Settlement

About two years after the first ground was broken in our field, a dispute I re-member, arose between my mothers and two of their neighbors, Lone Woman and Goes-to-next-timber.

These two women were clearing fields adjoining that of my mothers; as will be seen by the accompanying map, the three fields met at a corner. I have said that my father, to set up claim to his field, had placed marks, one of them in the corner at which met the fields of Lone Woman and Goes-to-next-timber; but while my mothers were busy clearing and digging up the other end of their field, their two neighbors invaded this marked-off corner; Lone Woman had even dug up a small part before she was discovered.

However, when they were shown the mark my father had placed, the two women yielded and accepted payment for any rights they might have.

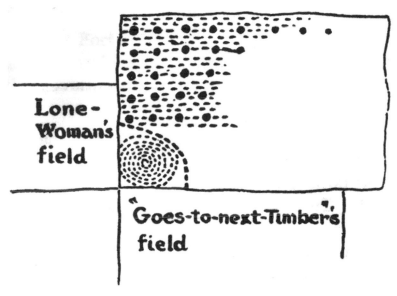

This diagram of a newly broken field was drawn under Buffalo Bird Woman's direction. The heavy dots represent corn hills; the dashes, the broken ground between, cultivated after the hills were planted. The circular area represents a portion of the garden whose ownership was in dispute. From Gilbert L. Wilson, *Buffalo Bird Woman's Garden* (St. Paul: Minnesota Historical Society Press, 1985). Courtesy the Newberry Library (Ayer oE99.H6 W337 1987, p. 10).

It was our Indian rule to keep our fields very sacred. We did not like to quarrel about our garden lands. One's title to a field once set up, no one ever thought of disputing it; for if one were selfish and quarrelsome, and tried to seize land belonging to another, we thought some evil would come upon him, as that some one of his family would die. There is a story of a black bear who got into a pit that was not his own, and had his mind taken away from him for doing so!

Turtle Breaking Soil

Lone Woman and Goes-to-next-timber having withdrawn, my grandmother, Turtle, volunteered to break the soil of the corner that had been in dispute. She was an industrious woman. Often, when my mothers were busy in the earth lodge, she would go out to work in the garden, taking me with her for company. I was six years old then, I think, quite too little to help her any, but I liked to watch my grandmother work.

With her digging stick, she dug up a little round place in the center of the corner; and circling around this from day to day, she gradually enlarged the dug-up space. The point of her digging stick she forced into the soft earth to a depth equal to the length of my hand, and pried up the soil. The clods she struck smartly with her digging stick, sometimes with one end, sometimes with the other. Roots of coarse grass, weeds, small brush and the like, she took in her hand and shook, or struck them against the ground, to knock off the loose earth clinging to them; she then cast them into a little pile to dry.

In this way she accumulated little piles, scattered rather irregularly over the dug-up ground, averaging, perhaps, four feet, one from the other. In a few days these little piles had dried; and Turtle gathered them up into a heap, about four feet high, and burned them, sometimes within the cleared ground, sometimes a little way outside.

In the corner that had been in dispute, and in other parts of the field, my grandmother worked all summer. I do not remember how big our garden was at the end of her summer's work, nor how many piles of roots she burned; but I remember distinctly how she put the roots of weeds and grass and brush into little piles to dry, which she then gathered into heaps and burned. She did not attempt to burn over the whole ground, only the heaps.

Afterwards, we increased our garden from year to year until it was as large as we needed. I remember seeing my grandmother digging along the edges of the garden with her digging stick, to enlarge the field and make the edges even and straight.

I remember also, that as Turtle dug up a little space, she would wait until the next season to plant it. Thus, additional ground dug up in the summer or fall would be planted by her the next spring.

There were two or three elm trees in the garden; these my grandmother left standing.

It must not be supposed that upon Turtle fell all the work of clearing land to enlarge our garden; but she liked to have me with her when she worked, and I remember best what I saw her do. As I was a little girl then, I have forgotten much that she did; but this that I have told, I remember distinctly.

Turtle's Primitive Tools

In breaking ground for our garden, Turtle always used an ash digging stick; and when hoeing time came, she hoed the corn with a bone hoe. Digging sticks are still used in my tribe for digging wild turnips; but even in my grandmother's lifetime, digging sticks and bone hoes, as garden tools, had all but given place to iron hoes and axes.

My grandmother was one of the last women of my tribe to cling to these old-fashioned implements. Two other women, I remember, owned bone hoes when I was a little girl; but Turtle, I think, was the very last one in the tribe who actually worked in her garden with one.

This hoe my grandmother kept in the lodge, under her bed; and when any of the children of the household tried to get it out to look at it, she would cry, "Let that hoe alone; you will break it!"

Gilbert L. Wilson, *Buffalo Bird Woman's Garden* (St. Paul: Minnesota Historical Society Press, 1987), xi–xiii, 9–13.

THE MEN AND THE WOMEN
C. C. Uhlenbeck

With this next story, Blackfeet elders taught a Dutch linguist about the separate gifts each gender brings to a community. Men and women were complementary halves of a social whole. The story recounts that in the beginning each gender had its own community. The women lived well—"their lodges were fine"—while the men "were very poor" because they didn't know how to make clothes or tipis or how to preserve meat.

The men traveled to the women's village carrying knives and bows—their only "useful things." As they approached, the chief of the women announced to her companions, "I shall go up there (to the men) first. I shall take my choice." The woman chief's first choice of men initially refused her, so she turned him into a lonely pine tree. The rest of the men were more cooperative. Ultimately the combination of the women's skills and the men's tools made for a prosperous society.

The men and the women of the ancient Peigans did not live about together in the beginning. The women lived about on the Porcupine hills [literally: Porcupine-tails] and made buffalo-corrals. Their lodges were fine. Their clothes were cow-skins. Their moccasins were of the same. They tanned the buffalo-hides, those were their robes. They would cut the meat in slices. In summer they picked berries. They used those [berries] in winter. Their lodges all were fine inside. And their things were just as fine. One was the chief of the women. That one led them about. And that one led them to make buffalo-corrals.

Now, the men were living about in the south. They were very poor. They made corrals. They had no lodges. They wore raw-hides [of buffalo] and antelope-hides for robes. They wore [the hide around] the gamble-joint of the buffalo for moccasins. They did not know, how they should make lodges. They did not know, how they should tan the buffalo-hides. They did not know too, how they should cut dried meat, [or] how they should sew their clothes. After a long while their chief told them: Let us look for the women. One useful thing of theirs were their [the men's] bows and arrows. They had [also] flint-knives. Those were the things, they had. And they went north over that way. They came to the Porcupine hills. There they stayed about. Then they found out, where the women were camping.

Their [the men's] chief Wolf-robe told them: Over there on that hill we shall sit in sight of those women. Then they came there. It was on the river, that the women were camped. Their [the women's] chief told them: Over there near the corral are the men sitting in sight. All these women were cutting meat. Their chief did not take off the clothes, she was cutting the meat with. They were told by her: I shall go up there first. I shall take my choice [from them]. When I come back, you will go up one by one. Now we will take husbands. Then she started up. Then she went up to all these men. She asked them: Which is your chief? [The men said:] This one here, Wolf-robe. She told him: Now we will take you for husbands. And then she walked to that Wolf-robe. She caught him. Then she started to pull him up. Then he pulled back. Then she let him loose. He did not like her clothes. Then she went back down. Then she entered her lodge. Then she began to dress up. When she came out gain, there was no such fine-looking woman [as she was]. Then she went up again. She got near the men. Wolf-robe jumped up already. She then walked away from him. And then he went in front of her. Then she went away from him again. It was another man, that that woman caught. Then she took him down to their [the women's] lodges. They came there. She said to him: Here is your lodge.

She told all these women: Now begin to go up. That one, that is very tall, [called] Wolf-robe, that is the Old Man. Don't take him for husband. And bring all those others down. That Wolf-robe would come in front of every one of these women, that came there. They would just walk away from him. [The women] would bring the others down. All these men were taken down. And there that Wolf-robe was standing up alone. He was told by that chief-woman: Turn into a pine-tree, right there were you stand. He got angry. He commenced to knock down that buffalo-corral. And then he turned into a pine-tree. And now till this day that buffalo-corral is still there, just as he knocked it down.

And he himself there turned into a pine-tree. In that way all these men and all these women came to be together. And that is what I know about them.

"The Men and the Women," in C. C. Uhlenbeck, *New Series of Blackfoot Texts* (Amsterdam: J. Müller, 1912), 167–71.

MY FAMILY
Marjorie Waheneka

A curator at the Umatilla Reservation's Tamástslikt Cultural Institute, Marjorie Waheneka has had a long career as a museum interpreter and administrator. In this excerpt from an interview in 2002, she describes how traditions of family loyalty and gender roles have continued to play a powerful role in tribal life.

My grandpa was a very strong believer in the sweathouse and he used to take care of it like a temple. We had it down by the river; we weren't allowed to play down there. We weren't allowed to swim in that part of the river because that is where when we got out we had to jump in. He kept that place very spotless and clean. It was a man's job to build a sweathouse, that was their duty and that's what he did. It didn't matter what time of year, when there was snow on the ground we were still out there sweating. We didn't have any indoor plumbing and that's how we used to take a bath in the morning.

I did a talk last week at our local charter school on our reservation and I asked the kids, "How many of you guys know what a sweat is?" and there were quite a few hands that went up. "So why do you go to sweat?" And it was good to hear the answers that I received: to pray, to cleanse yourself, to take away your aches and your pains. And that is really what it is all about; there was a very big spiritual significance for sweating.

The sweathouse was a process to just strengthen you from within because Indian people were always spiritual and they always gave thanks to the creator first thing in the morning. That is what we had to do, drink our water first thing in the morning and then we had to go jump in the river no matter what time of year, because like I said, we didn't have any indoor plumbing. We would have to go down to the river and jump in and get ready for school. My grandma always cooked a big breakfast for us and then we'd run out; you know the kids laugh because the older people say we had to walk for miles? Well, I used to have to walk at least half a mile to catch the bus and we were the last stop and then it would turn and go back. So that was the importance of it and I'm glad that my children were able to experience.

My grandma was a very traditional person; we had to go root digging, we had to go berry picking, we had to cut fish, we had to cut meat and dry it and watch the fire. We all had our duties, and there was separation.

There was a time we used to have to sit with them (grandmas and aunties) and just watch what they were doing and observe, whether it was beadwork or weaving or over preparation of food, we had to watch. Then there was the time they thought we had watched and listened enough, and we had to prepare it. It was our time to take over.

I remember I started my first beadwork project when I was eight years old. I got better, but my weaving I never could do. Weaving was a project that I just could not learn; I could not count the strings. My grandma used to take up my weaving so many times I just got so frustrated I never picked it up again. But beadwork and other things I still continue today.

My uncles were very traditional people and I used to get so disgusted with them because they had an alcohol problem, something that is very evident throughout Indian country. As I got older and we got closer together, especially after my grandmother passed away, my uncles became my elders and I never, ever questioned what they told me. There were things—because they were men you know it was a different perspective—when I started having children (I have three boys) the uncles didn't live long enough for my boys to experience, you know, manhood. First hunt, first fish and things like that; but they did teach them about the sweathouse, they did teach them about fishing and hunting. They took them out and my boys had to watch, and they also taught them about the river and the mountains, you know, boy things, something that I can't do. I was lucky they were able to experience that with their grandpas and that is something that they carry today. It's important and that's something that my son has kind of made me wake up to; my oldest son is twenty-two and he said to me one day, because my husband is in tribal government too, he told his dad when it was time for reelections, he says, "Dad, you know what, you better start being nice to my friends and my age group because we are old enough to kind of vote now." Armand kind of looked at him and he says, "It's true Dad; my friends don't think very much of you and they always ask me, 'Does your dad ever smile? Why is your dad always so mean looking?'" He said, "So dad, you better start changing; I'm old enough now to vote and so are my friends." It really is an awakening and my son is very open; he is very open about things like that, he is very truthful. When he is hurting he will let you know; when he is angry he'll let you know, so he is my eyes and ears.

Marjorie Waheneka, filmed interview by Sally Thompson, Tamástslikt Cultural Institute, Pendleton, Oregon, April 16, 2002.

FAMILIES AND CLANS AT FORT BERTHOLD
Malcolm Wolf and Tillie Walker

Two leaders from the reservation that is now the home to Mandans, Arikaras, and Hidatsas explained the continuing importance of family ties, clan loyalties, and gender roles in the life of their community.

Malcolm Wolf

The clanship system was a gift to my people by people from the heavens. We know there is a heaven some place; we call it the Happy Hunting Ground. Our clanship evolved from a spiritual being that came from the higher up. Our people also believe that there are people underground, and that this is where we came from. This would include the Hidatsa people and our Crow cousins. They were here too; we came from underground but that is another story. So on clanship, there were thirteen clans, thirteen young couples, thirteen lodges. Why do we have the clan here? Because we did not have any respect for anything or each other. That's how come our clanship came to be, by the way of a higher power. So that governs, that disciplines, that spiritually takes care of our people, so we had to take and we came along that way.

All of a sudden we had other people who came up the river and perished with a sickness; you won't believe what happened. We are told their sickness was so bad in their back it would go into their spine, their cartilages, and they would just die there. They were all standing and would go walking every which way, running from each other. That's what happened to us, the genocide, if you want to call it. How pitiful my people must have been at that time. That's why our clans were lost, because many people died. Then there was just seven left, so we joined together. Our clanship brought us together. You asked how do people get together after that and live together? Because of our clanship system; it is powerful because it was given to us by a higher power. That is why we bonded together, that's how we survived, and that's why we are still here today. There are very few people that have that; and we are very strong and we live by that today. That governs and gauges, socially, economically, you name it; we have two groups of clans and that governs what we do.

We have what we call the [native word], which is the three clans. Three clans came together and call themselves brothers and sisters. Because of what happened there's only a few left, but there will be more of us; we'll have families. You can be an orphan with no mother, no father, no brothers and sisters, but if you have a clan you still have family. That is the whole concept.

We don't have a word for aunt or uncle or cousin. We use "brother," "mother," or "grandpa"; that is how we are related. Cousins and nephews and nieces are our sons or our brothers or our sisters. An aunt we call [native word], that's my dad's clan's sisters. Those are the people that I would wait on. I would have a kill and I would take that meat to them first. I would let them take what they wanted and then I would go on back to my place, my lunch. That's how we took care of each other; we never owed each other, we didn't borrow. We gave to one another and never talked about it; that's how we bonded together, that's how we stayed together. It's a beautiful system. And you wonder how we did it, how did we survive? That's how we did it. It is sacred and if you can respect that then you are going to survive.

Tillie Walker

We grow up in a community in which you have many mothers, so if I call someone aunt, that is real different than calling someone mother. The whole idea is when you call somebody sister instead of cousin. Cousin means you are removed from that person and when you say sister that is part of you. All your clan is your sisters. All of your clan members are your brothers and your sisters in our society. This is still alive; this part is why I think we are survivors. We still call ourselves sisters. Not only that, but all of our father's brothers' children are our brothers and sisters and all of our mother's sisters' children are our brothers and sisters. We have a large number of people who are responsible to each other.

Malcolm Wolf and Tillie Walker, filmed interviews by Sally Thompson, Tribal Council Chambers, Fort Berthold Reservation, North Dakota, September 3, 2003.

CHAPTER FIVE

A Vast Network of Partners

In 1800, webs of trade, alliance, and competition linked all corners of the Indian country. Horses whose ancestors had first come to America with the Spanish were bred and traded from the Columbia plateau to the Missouri River. Steel tools and glass beads from Europe came up the Missouri and the Columbia Rivers and south from Lake Winnipeg, passing from communities there to trading partners in more remote areas. Other groups jostled one another for space: Sioux bands moved west, Arikaras moved north, Shoshones moved south, and farming and trading villages along the Missouri and Columbia Rivers struggled to maintain their independence and preserve their standing in the marketplace. All sought allies to help them hold off rivals. No single power dominated the region; it was governed instead by overlapping networks of trade, travel, and diplomacy.

Crossing the Rockies was one of the Lewis and Clark expedition's greatest feats, but for many Indian people living in the Pacific Northwest, traveling to and from "the Buffalo country" was an ancient custom. For example, the Nez Perces had long maintained trails that carried hunters and their families to the hunting grounds on the other side of the mountains. The following traditional story tells of the Nez Perce culture hero, Coyote, and his effort to bring buffalo back to the Northwest from the Plains. Earthy and irreverent, Coyote breaks the rules and frightens his buffalo friends, so they decide to remain with their kinsmen east of the mountains. The story underscores the tribe's familiarity with long-distance travel.

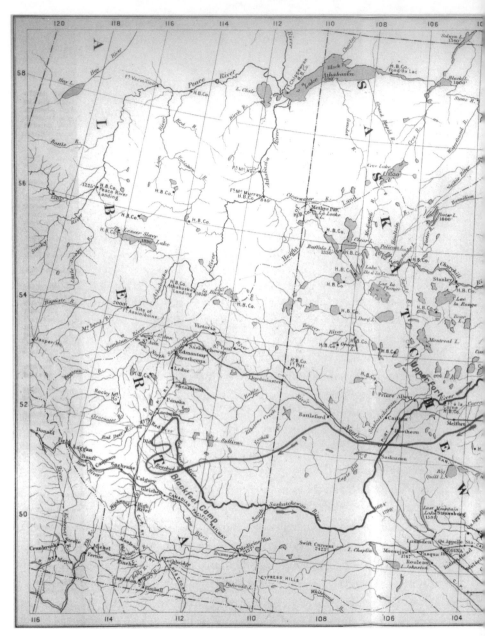

This map shows Anthony Hendry's route from York Factory, on the shores of Hudson Bay, to the Blackfeet hunting grounds. Hendry left York Factory in 1754, a half-century before the Corps of Discovery, returning the following summer. Courtesy the Newberry Library (Graff 1853).

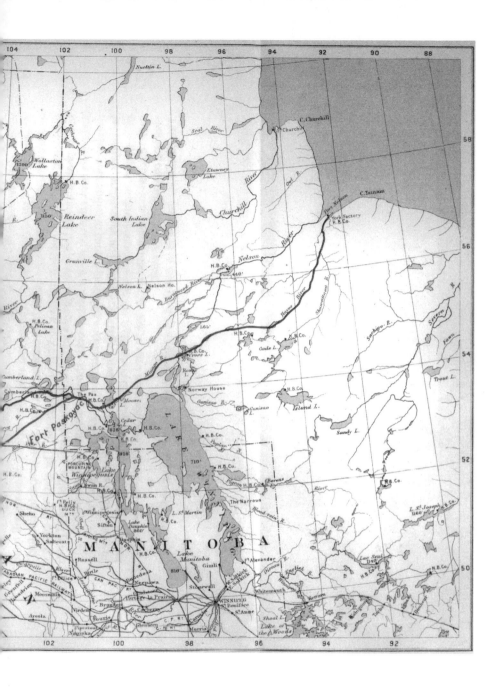

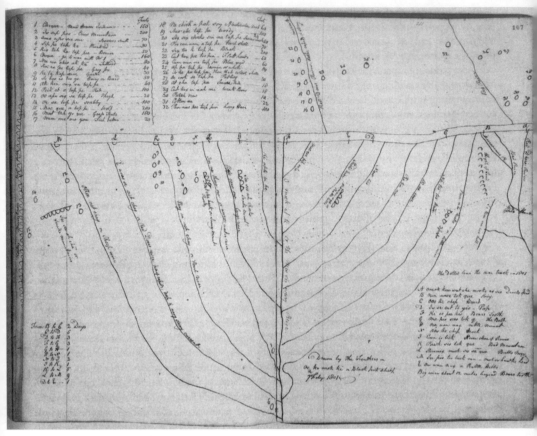

An Indian Map of the Different Tribes that inhabit on the East & West Side of the Rocky Mountains with all the rivers & other remarkbl. places, also the number of Tents etc. Drawn by the Feathers or Ac ko mok ki—a Black foot chief—7th Feby. 1801—reduced 1/4 from the Original Size—by Peter Fidler. Hudson's Bay Company Archives G.1/15. This remarkable document illustrates the extensive knowledge Native people possessed of their environment. Drawn in the snow by Ac ko mok ki, this map was copied onto paper by Peter Fidler, a Hudson's Bay Company trader. The map is oriented to the west; the double line represents the Continental Divide. Major peaks in the Rockies are noted with letters within that double line. Two rivers run west from the Rockies to the Pacific while seventeen rivers flow east, draining eventually into the Missouri River (represented by the line drawn down the center of the map). Courtesy the Newberry Library (Ayer 0E59.C25 W37 1997, p. 153).

COYOTE'S TRIP TO THE EAST
Haruo Aoki and Deward E. Walker

Coyote decided, "Now I'm going to the Buffalo Country; I'm going to where there are plains. I'm going after buffalo. I'll drive them over here, and we'll have buffalo for our own." He went fa-a-ar away, for many days. Finally he got to the Buffalo Country. He went over the mountains and came out of the timber. He kept walking, and finally he walked up to a buffalo bull.

There he sat—he was pitiful, skinny, and he had sores all over his body. His eyes were closed. "What happened?" Coyote asked, and he saw that the buffalo was very sick and ailing. Now Coyote played a trick on him and urinated on him; he urinated on his sores. Buffalo said, "Oh, Coyote, you're going too far." He got angry and stood up. Coyote ran and said, "No, my friend," and he turned around toward him. "No, I will make you horns, the very best. I will help you whenever you are in need." Buffalo replied, "Coyote, you're piling misery on misery for me. A young bull has taken all my cows. I fought with him, and as you see he defeated me. He almost killed me. Both my horns are broken, and look at my sores. Then you poked fun at me in this sad state." "No, my friend," Coyote said. "I'll make you good horns and I'll help you. We'll kill the bull who defeated you."

Then Buffalo said, "All right, Coyote," and Coyote made horns; he made very good and sharp ones out of a syringe tree. He made each one for him, and then he said, "You just rest, and then we'll go." Then the old bull got better, and he looked for the young bull. "They were there, somewhere; he took them over there." Then the old bull and Coyote followed. The sick one bellowed, and the young bull heard them, and the old bull saw the young one coming. Now they met, and they fought there. Coyote was there to help. They dashed at each other ferociously all day. And then, with his sharp horns, the old bull tore off the skin of his adversary.

Then Coyote made himself brave. He took bow and arrow and shot as the young bull went by, and soon he was stretched out dead. Oh, yes. Before this the old bull for whom Coyote made the horns said, "Now, (Coyote), you help me." Before Coyote would agree to help him, Buffalo had said, "If we defeat him, then I will give you thirty buffalo cows to take home." Then he said, "Now that we've finished this business, you take the thirty cows. Take good care of them. When you go into the mountains, go slowly and let them rest. Don't for any reason scare them. Take them gently and treat them well, and take them across to the other side of the mountains. These buffalo will grow bigger there." Coyote said, "All right, I'll do as you say."

Then Coyote followed them. The buffalo left and they rested; they ate grass, drank water, and sat down. And again when night came they would find a place. And there they slept, sitting on their haunches, while Coyote slept bunched up under a tree. Then they kept going, maybe for five nights, and then, there they were in the mountains. They stopped there for the night, and the buffalo were sleeping. Then Coyote started thinking, and he got up at night and looked them over—which one was the best? He touched them, and they got scared, these buffalo, and they stood up and dashed back home to the Buffalo Country. Then Coyote gave up, and he came back home alone. He had lost the buffalo. If only he'd followed the instructions of that bull who said, "Take them. Don't scare them for any reason." Then poor Coyote came home empty-handed.

"Coyote's Trip to the East," from Haruo Aoki and Deward E. Walker, *Nez Perce Oral Narratives* (Berkeley: University of California Press, 1989), 478–83.

INDIAN COUNTRY DIPLOMACY
Alexander Henry

Alexander Henry traveled the old Northwest as a trader for the North West Company and kept a journal of those travels from 1799 to 1814. His uncle of the same name founded the North West Company to compete with the Hudson's Bay Company in the lucrative northwest fur trade. Their records of native customs in the late eighteenth and early nineteenth centuries are among the most detailed available. Here, the younger Henry details his stay with the Cheyennes ("Schian") in 1806. He recounts their dealings in trade, diplomacy, and near war with the Mandans and Gros Ventres. In the process, glimpses of daily life are revealed, from the drying of meat and the layouts of tents, to horsemanship and examples of physical endurance. Le Borgne, a Hidatsa leader who plays a central role in this account, had met Lewis and Clark along the Upper Missouri earlier the same year. As a British trader, Henry was deeply suspicious of the Americans and their ambitions. The tensions revealed here—among Indians as well as between traders and tribal leaders—suggest the competitive environment the Americans entered as they traveled among people who sought to maintain their advantage in trade and diplomacy.

The Schian camp is situated in a delightful spot, on a level, elevated plain; in the rear, on the S. runs a rivulet, beyond which the river is bounded by high, barren hills, partly covered with large round stones. On the front or N. side runs the rivulet we crossed, and there the view extends no further than the hill we passed over. On the W., within about one-quarter of a mile, a range of high hills runs N. and S. On the E. the plain is more level for about five miles, when the view is terminated by high hills, mostly covered with large round stones; and indeed the level plains are nearly covered in the same manner. It is dangerous to chase buffalo, unless both horse and rider are accustomed to such rough, stony ground.

The camp consisted of about 120 leather tents (exclusive of small ones, or, as we call them, kitchens), nearly all new and as white as linen, and pitched with great regularity at certain distances apart, in the shape of a horseshoe—the opening or entrances facing N.; the large open space within the circle was unencumbered. Beside each large tent was a small one, which appeared to be the remains of an old one cut down—that is, the lower parts, having become rotten and damaged by the weather, had been cut off, reducing the former size about one-half. Such tents appear to be for the women's necessary occupations, such as cooking, preparing meat, dressing leather, etc. The spaces between the tents were occupied by stages for drying meat, all covered with buffalo flesh, the people having killed upwards of 200 of those animals two days ago. The extensive double-row circle of tents thus joined one another by a barricade of thinly sliced flesh drying in the sun. The frames for drying dressed skins and the horse and dog travailles were erected outside the camp. All the women appeared to be hard at work, stretching buffalo hides, dressing skins, slicing meat to dry, and working robes with straw and porcupine quills.

The language of these people, unlike that disagreeably harsh jargon of the Mandanes, has a pleasant sound. Some people pretend to say it has some affinity to the Kinistineaux tongue, particularly in the manner of counting from one to ten, which are nearly the same words; and it is supposed they originated from the same stock. But of this I am not a competent judge. My stay among them was too short and precious to make any inquiries; all I can pretend to say is, that the Schians formerly resided N. of the Missourie, on the river that still bears their name, and empties into Red river below Otter Tail lake. But from which direction they came to settle on Schian river I cannot say. They were formerly at peace with the Crees and Saulteurs, being considered their greatest friends. In general the men are tall, stout, and well-proportioned; their manners and customs appear to me to be nearly the same as those of the Sioux of the Plains.

We found them much more cautious than the Big Bellies, or even the Mandanes. They keep their tents, dishes, and spoons very clean; the latter are made out of the horns of the Rocky Mountain ram. They are much more decent and modest than their neighbors; all the men, and even boys, wear breech-clouts. They are very hard people to trade with. What few beaver skins they had were purchased without much trouble; but grizzly bear skins they value highly, and will take and return payment ten times before you can get one. It is a very hard task to deal with them; all must go by signs, unless one understands the Assiniboine language, and then he must get a Sioux to interpret. But some of them understand the Pawnee tongue, and as some of our party spoke that language, their conversation between one another was principally by means of an interpreter. The natives themselves can very well dispense with that, and communicate by signs; both parties being so accustomed to this manner of conversation that they comprehend each other with the greatest ease. I saw Le Borgne hold a conference with some of the Schians for more than an hour, during which not a word was spoken by either party, and all appeared to comprehend perfectly well every question and answer. The dress of these people, like that of all other natives of the plains, consists of leather. Many of the European dresses I saw were of Spanish manufacture. They generally pass the winter S. of the Black hills, about 20 encampments hence, which I suppose may be 80 or 100 leagues. Here, they say, is the source of two large rivers; one runs to the N.E. and the other to the S.; the former falls into the Missourie, below the Pawnee village, I believe, under the name of Rivière Platt; the other, of course, into the Gulf of Mexico. Near the sources of these two rivers they make their annual hunts of bear and beaver, in company with the Buffalo Indians, or, as some call them, the Caveninavish tribe, a very numerous nation inhabiting that part of the country. They consist of about 500 tents. I saw a few of them in this camp. The Schians, having made their winter's hunt, move northward. They sometimes dispose of their skins to the Pawnees and Sioux; or, if they find any traders from the Islenois [Illinois river], they deal with them. They are of a roving disposition, and seldom remain long in any one spot.

They informed us that last fall two Spaniards came up the river which runs to the S., in a wooden canoe or a boat loaded with goods, who passed the winter among them, disposed of all their property, and sold very cheap, giving a large double handful of gunpowder and 50 balls for one beaver. They told us that by spring the two men had collected such a quantity of skins that they were obliged to make another canoe; and even two could scarcely contain the packs, with just room for a man to sit behind to steer.

Affairs went on smoothly, and peace seemed to be settled; nothing was heard but singing throughout the camp; the young men were on horseback, as is a very common custom among the Missourie tribes. Almost every day, and particularly toward evening, the young men mount their horses and parade around the village singing; some times two or three will get upon the same horse to make their rounds. The women were also busy exchanging their corn for leather, robes, smocks, and dried provisions, as if at a country fair. Each one was anxious to dispose of her property to advantage, and to this end carried a load from tent to tent. But the numerous women of our party had overstocked the market, and many were obliged to keep half what they had brought, for want of buyers.

Just as the sun was going down, a number of Schians, Big Bellies, Mandanes, and others suddenly mounted on horseback, armed cap à pie, and rushed toward the rivulet N. of the encampment. There a large group soon collected, some on foot, others on horseback, and showed by their actions there was some misunderstanding which threatened hostilities. Everything was now in commotion and confusion—the men arming and saddling their horses; the women of our party collecting their horses and preparing for immediate departure, without any of the howling and bawling which is so common amongst them when danger threatens. Everyone exerted herself in sullen silence, though dismay was painted on every face; and in a few moments all were ready to start, should matters appear more alarming. Le Borgne's wives advised us to saddle also, and keep ourselves ready to move, in case of necessity. We accordingly did so, and stood awaiting the event of an affair which we suspected would end in a fight.

After remaining thus in suspense for some time, we were informed that the uproar proceeded from the presence of 12 Assiniboines, who, having arrived at the village just after we had left, and learned that the Big Bellies and Mandanes were more numerous than the Schians and Sioux, had followed our tracks to this camp. The Schians were fully determined to kill them, as these people are inveterate enemies. But as they came upon our road, and in a manner under the protection of our party, the latter were resolved to defend them, let the consequences be what they would. Le Borgne was one of the first to be informed of their approach; and, suspecting what might happen, he instantly ran out to meet them with his battle-ax in his hand. He took the chief, Old Crane, by the hand, telling him that he might advance into the camp without fear of danger. The Schians soon surrounded them, and wished to strike some of the Assiniboines; but Le Borgne, who was by this time joined by many of his own people, kept them at bay by flourishing his battle-ax. He desired them to desist; saying that if any of them were imprudent enough to hurt an Assiniboine whilst under his protection, he might advance and make the attempt, but the event would show who would be the most pitiful. Many of our party having assembled and surrounded the Assiniboines, the Schians were prevented from approaching within reach. Le Borgne then ordered his people to clear the way for them to enter the camp, which was accordingly done, notwithstanding the Schians were so anxious to oppose it that they offered Le Borgne five horses, not to interfere in the business. But he instantly presented these to the Assiniboines, as a convincing proof of his determination to defend them, conducted them to our tent, and placed a guard of young men over them. As our tent was not sufficiently large for us all, he separated some in other tents, and put a strong guard over each of them for the night. The Schians appeared enraged, and their chiefs made continual rounds on horse-back, haranguing in their own language, whilst the principal men of our party did the same. The uproar did not cease until dark, when matters appeared to be somewhat more settled; some of those who had before appeared most vexed came into our tent and smoked with our great men for some time; but the countenances of both parties betrayed the inward working of their minds, and it was evident that they were not pleased or even satisfied with each other. They often attempted to force a smile, but the expression was sinister.

Soon after the uproar had abated, Le Borgne sent orders for the women to unload and turn out their horses to feed. He had also desired us to unload and make ourselves easy, for as long as he could hold his battle-ax we had nothing to dread from the Schians; but he told us to tie our horses near the tent, and to be ready at a moment's warning in case of a surprise, as he was uncertain how matters might turn out. He then mounted and rode round camp at full speed, haranguing his people to the same purpose; he also forbade anyone to depart, as many of the women desired to take advantage of the darkness to escape from a place where they feared death.

About ten o'clock a young man came into our tent to inform Le Borgne that the Schians had stolen some of the Mandanes' horses, and that the latter had declared that, if the horses were not returned immediately, they would retaliate. This alleged insult added fuel to the flames; our great man got up in a rage and went out to inquire into the affair, declaring that if this report proved to be true, he would instantly spread death and destruction through the camp. He desired us to be in readiness to depart; but the night was so dark we could scarcely distinguish our own horses from others; and to adjust our saddles and baggages was almost impossible. While we were collecting our things, he returned and informed us that all was again quiet; that it was some of our own party who had taken the horses to go after others that had strayed, and that all had been found. Thus our minds were once more at ease, after a very disagreeable suspense. Still, we apprehended further disturbances, as we overheard Rattlesnake and some other resolute fellows declare vengeance on those dogs, as they termed the Schians, and they were only prevented from committing some rash action by Le Borgne. He is certainly a man of great prudence and circumspection; he never allows himself to be transported into such a passion as might commit him to any rash action; he does everything in a composed, deliberate, and cool manner. A fight on this occasion would not have been on fair terms, as the Schians, Sioux, and Buffalo Indians had only about 200 men, ill provided with fire-arms and ammunition, whereas our party mustered about 500 men, all well armed. Many of them had two guns and plenty of ammunition, as they had declined to part with those articles until we should be ready to depart, when they proposed to exchange them for horses. We passed an uncomfortable night; the Assiniboines were crowded in the same tent with us, and we were convinced that, should any disturbance take place, our tent would be the first attacked.

July 25th. At daybreak all were on the alert. I made several turns about camp, to observe what was going on, and entered some tents where I had been kindly received and well entertained, but found a great change in the physiognomy of these people; all were silent and sullen. None invited us into their tents as we passed; all turned their heads, and pretended not to see us.

At eight o'clock the preparations commenced for Le Borgne to adopt a son among the Schians. This ceremony is generally considered conclusive of peace among the different nations in these parts. The affair went on very slowly, and it was not without many speeches, smoking-matches, and persuasive arguments, that the medicine-tent was prepared. The Schians appeared very backward, indeed, and at first would neither bring tents enough to form the circle, nor lend a hand to erect them, while our party appeared very anxious to forward the business. After many obstacles had been surmounted the circle was formed with six leather tents, opening to the N. At nine o'clock the ceremony began by three of Le Borgne's principal mishinaways, or secretaries, taking their seats in the center of the tent which faced the open space. One of them, Two Crows, with great ceremony and many grimaces, untied the pipe-stem, adjusted the feathers, hairs, etc., and displayed it on a fathom of red strouds, whilst the other two secretaries were busy singing, one beating a drum, and the other keeping time with a rattle made of cabbrie hoofs. The stem being thus displayed, old General Chokecherry, who was sure to make himself busy upon every occasion, posted himself in front of the hut and uttered a long oration, inviting everybody to the ceremony. Many of our party accordingly took their seats on each side of the stem, but not a Schian or Sioux came near us. The singing recommenced, and continued for some time, after which the secretaries rose up from their seats; one of them, taking up the stem, marched off with it, dancing as he went to the drum and rattle, which the others sounded close behind him. One of them carried on his back a bull's head, whose nostrils and eyes were stuffed with hay. Next came a young man leading three horses, and after him a great crowd of our party, merely as spectators. They directed their course to the tent of the Schian whom Le Borgne intended to adopt, where the bearer of the stem danced for a few moments. Then one of the elder Big Bellies widened the door by pulling out the pegs from above and below; the three secretaries entered; and, after dancing before the intended son, who held down his head in a very sullen manner, presented him with the stem and rattle. At first he declined it, nor would he accept it for some time, but after a long conversation with his own people, he at last took it in a careless manner, and apparently much against his inclination. Le Borgne, who sat in the tent during all this part of the ceremony, wrapped up in an American flag, said not a word, but cast many a sardonic grin at his adopted son. At its conclusion he arose, and wrapped the flag around the adopted son, giving into his hand the three cords which tied the three horses at the door, which the Schian instantly handed to his wife. Le Borgne then took him by one arm, and Chief of the Wolves held him by the other; they thus raised him gently from the ground, and conducted him to the medicine tent, attended by the three secretaries with their music. On their arrival he was placed in the center, opposite the fathom of red strouds, holding the stem in his right hand; Le Borgne was seated on his right hand, and Chief of the Wolves on his left; near them were the three secretaries, who continued to sing and shake the rattle; the bull's head was placed opposite the cloth and son. The Big Bellies brought in some ammunition, and laid it upon the strouds; the son was directed to lay the stem over these articles, which he did accordingly. Our old general was again posted opposite the entrance of the shelter, where he was fully employed in his usual vocation of haranguing, inviting everyone to bring something to put under the stem. But all his eloquence was in vain; not a Schian came forward until some of their old men had gone the rounds making long speeches, when a few of the Schians appeared with some garnished robes and dressed leather, which were spread on the ground near the bull's head, which was then laid upon the heap. The Big Bellies next brought two guns, which they placed under the stem. The Schians put another robe or two under the bull's head. Our party were each time more ready to come forward with their property than the others were with theirs. The latter next brought some old, scabby, sore-backed horses for the bull's head. This compliment was returned by our party with corn, beans, ammunition, and a gun. General Chokecherry grew impatient, and reproached the Schians in a very severe and harsh manner for their mean and avaricious manner of dealing, in bringing forward their trash and rotten horses, saying that the Big Bellies were ready to give good guns and ammunition, but expected to receive good horses in return. In answer to this they were given to understand by the Schians that they must first put all their guns and ammunition under the stem, immediately after which the Schians, in their turn, would bring in good horses. As it was never customary in an affair of this kind for either party to particularize the articles to be brought to the stem or bull's head, but for everyone to contribute what he pleased of the best he had, this proposal induced our party to suspect the Schians had planned to get our firearms and ammunition into their own possession, that they might be a match for us, and commence hostilities. To prevent this, no more guns or ammunition were brought forward, and the Schians were told they must first produce some of their best horses; but to this they would not listen. After a few more trifles had been given in on both sides, the business came to a stand-still on the part of the Schians, who retired to their tents.

It was about 3 P.M. when affairs thus assumed a gloomy aspect; harangues were made through the camp by both parties, evidently not of a very amiable nature; frequent menaces were made by our party, and the other as often retorted. The ceremony was totally neglected and everybody left the spot. The adopted son went sullenly to his own tent; horses were collected on both sides; everyone was surly and gloomy; silence reigned throughout the camp, only broken by the neighing of horses and some few orations; the weather was hot and sultry. Water was only to be got at some distance, and was very filthy, both rivulets being dry except in stagnant puddles full of dung and urine, where hundreds of horses had been drinking and rolling. The impracticability of procuring any other had obliged us to use this water; but at this critical moment we could get none, as we did not think it prudent to separate from our main body to such a distance. I entered several tents, but in vain. I saw water in bladders and paunches, but it was refused me. At one time I caught hold of a bladder and a ram's horn to satisfy my thirst, but both were snatched away by one of the women, who were as sulky and sullen as the men. I was exasperated and choking with thirst, when I met a woman with a bladder full of this filthy beverage. Without any ceremony or asking her permission, as I was certain she would refuse me, I jerked the bladder out of her hands, cut a hole in it, and took a copious draught of the contents, which consisted of equal parts of horse dung, urine, and stagnant water. The woman made several unsuccessful attempts to recover the bladder, but I kept hold until my companions were fully satisfied also.

During this affray Le Borgne had been to the center of the camp and made a long speech, at the end of which he ordered all hands, men and women, to saddle and load instantly; but most of them were already prepared to depart, and only awaited his orders to march. The sun was about an hour high, when, in the greatest hurry, bustle, and confusion, the women saddled and loaded their horses as fast as possible, and began to file off by the route we came. By this time the men had become still more excited; everyone was armed and on horseback, with a ball in his mouth; haranguing went on throughout the camp; the horses were neighing and prancing impatiently, and instant battle threatened.

The women being all at some distance, Le Borgne ordered the men off and desired us to keep close by him. We all moved in a body, without any regular form of marching, and our horses at a slow walk. We were accompanied by the main body of the Schians, who mixed with our party and did not appear in the least afraid of our superior numbers, but with fierce countenances rode up to the most tumultuous of our party and vociferated to them with many significant signs and gestures. We really expected every moment to see some of them strike a fatal blow, and thus precipitate the conflict, as they certainly pushed our party to the last extremity. I could not help admiring the conduct of our commander-in-chief, Le Borgne; in all this tumult he said very little, and appeared quite unconcerned; but I observed he was always upon his guard, and that no Schian personally insulted him.

I was anxious to purchase one of their horses which had struck my fancy; he was a beautiful pied stallion four years old, the most spirited and swiftest beast I ever saw in the North West. The owner had promised him to me at the high price I offered, but as several Big Bellies also wanted him, and the owner wished to prevent jealousy, he desired me to keep up the payment until the moment I left, when he would deliver the horse. During the commotion in camp I went to him with my goods and demanded the horse, but he would not listen to me. One of the Big Belly war chiefs had offered him one of his wives, two horses, and the value of 50 skins in goods, but in vain. I met the fellow on this horse, and proposed once more to bargain, offering him the value of 100 skins in prime goods and my own horse; but he would not even return me an answer.

Having reached the eminence whence we had first seen the Schian camp we stopped, and formed into line abreast. Here both parties again disputed and argued with each other until many worked themselves up into such a frenzy as to foam at the mouth, especially the Schians, who appeared quite undaunted, and, I believe, would have fought like heroes. It was surprising to see what expert horsemen these people are; the agility of the beasts and the dexterity of the riders were astonishing. We proceeded, and soon overtook the women; when, observing the enemy still on the hill, in a menacing position, orders were given to halt. The women with the pack horses were placed in the center, and a large body of men were stationed around them as a guard. Le Borgne, accompanied by a large party, well armed, with their guns loaded and fresh primed, and balls in their mouths, returned to the Schians, who awaited their approach. We remained in suspense for some time, observing the motions of Le Borgne and his party, whom we every moment expected to see engaged in battle; but, after a short conference with the enemy, they returned, having, as they said, frightened the Schians back to camp.

Orders were given to push on with all speed possible, and instantly obeyed. Old men dispersed throughout the party, haranguing and encouraging the women to drive on fast, whilst young men were dispatched in every direction upon the hills to see that we were not surrounded. Thus we continued on our march until dark, when orders were given to halt and camp for the night. We found plenty of excellent water, which both men and beasts greatly needed, and I found it the pleasantest cordial I ever tasted.

Le Borgne told us the reason why he did not wish to push the affair to extremities was the great number of women and children who accompanied us, most of whom would have been destroyed; but he declared he would be revenged upon the Schians for the manner in which they had slighted his medicine stem. He directed his women to form a kind of intrenchment with his baggage and saddles, inside of which we slept with him and them. He desired us to fresh prime our guns, examine the flints, and be ready to fire at a moment's warning. He also ordered a number of young men to surround and watch the camp during the night. Everyone slept with his arms beside him. As our horses were tied at our feet, we were every moment in danger of being trampled; but as we were entirely free from mosquitoes, or any kind of troublesome flies, the horses were quiet. The poor beasts had eaten little for some days; they devoured the grass, which was of an excellent kind for them, upon this spot. Le Borgne had four mules, which were vicious brutes; when any other animal came near, they brayed and kicked enough to alarm the whole camp. The noise those animals kept up all night was hideous.

I could not but reflect upon the great fuss and uproar I had witnessed, and was surprised that it ceased without bloodshed. These people are certainly clamorous and noisy upon the most trifling occasion, and one unaccustomed to them would imagine every moment they were going to be at loggerheads. But many such affairs end in vociferation. Certainly some other nations, such, for instance, as the Saulteurs, would not have made half so much noise before beginning a battle. . . .

"Indian Country Diplomacy," in Alexander Henry, *New Light on the Early History of the Greater Northwestern Fur Trade* (New York: Francis P. Harper, 1897), 381–97.

NEZ PERCE TRADE
Otis Half Moon

Otis Half Moon, a National Park Service official, recounts the role of his Nez Perce ancestors in the trade networks of the Pacific Northwest just prior to the arrival of the American Corps of Discovery.

Trade is something that is very important to the tribe; the Nez Perce people were a trading people. If you look at where they were located, I mean as far as Idaho is concerned, what they call Idaho, there's one of two major passes into buffalo country, now what they call Lolo trail. Another one was the southern Nez Perce route. The buffalo hunting people also go west from there; you can go to the Columbia River country. And so the Nez Perce were very much middlemen, and trade was very, very important to the people.

The Nez Perce people used to go to the buffalo country a lot, and again sometimes to live with a tribe, and sometimes we fight with them. A good example was the Crows, the Crow Indians; you know they were a very numerous tribe over there, in the middle of the plains. And sometimes the Nez Perce fought them, sometimes they trade with them. If they were at peace, they would gather together, they would give thanks and tell stories and feast. Food was always very important, food is right in the middle of it; you get to share the foods and things. Years ago the tribes, the Crows and the Nez Perce, were allied.

Something which again shows up in the tribe's story is children. What they used to do was they would trade their wives with the Crows. It has been noted through fur trapper diaries. The fur trappers would say, "Boy, these Nez Perce and Crows are really close." The children conceived at this time period be a tangible proof of an alliance, tangible proof of a partnership.

You know today, in 2004, you go there to the northern plains and they grow camas. The Crows and the Cheyenne's they always want from the Nez Perce what we call [native word]. It's a root that grows in our mountains and we use it for smoking, and we use it in our sweat lodges, we use it just to chew on. The northern plains tribes like to grow [native word], and the rocky boys, they say, "Do you have any of the Nez Perce root?"

I mean this whole country that we call the Northern Plains, it was trade routes everywhere, going to and from every which way. I know from reviewing some of the maps of years ago that Lewis and Clark studied before their westward journey, there was nothing but a bare space: that's how many people perceive the country, as a bare space. It was not that at all. There were tribes everywhere going to and from trade centers. You had trader tribes and such; that's how we got along.

The horses was something that came up from Spain and from Mexico; that's how they get to all the tribes. All the tribes wanted the horse. I know some of the history books, they say the Nez Perce received the horse in 1720, 1730, and I dispute that. I know the Nez Perce date maybe 1680s, maybe even 1690s. At first the Spanish came up there with their horses among the Pueblos, the Navaho, and the Apaches, and the Comanches. This was like a brand-new weapon on the block, like even today, everyone wants nuclear weapons. Back in those days word must have spread so fast about this new creature that could make life so much easier: you can hunt better, you can travel further, you can carry your lodge faster, whatever. And I think those things were moved a lot more faster to the Northern Plains way before some of the experts say now. But again, it was a mode of wealth, horses, and Nez Perce were known for their horses, not only for the Appaloosa, which we created for all these years, but also other horses as well.

Otis Half Moon, filmed interviewed by Sally Thompson, Pendleton, Oregon, November 1, 2004.

PART 2

———◆◆◆———

CROSSING THE INDIAN COUNTRY

After his election to the presidency in 1800, Thomas Jefferson was eager to dispatch an expedition to explore the North American territory beyond the Mississippi River. Jefferson had long been interested in the West and he was well aware that both England and Spain were deeply engaged in the region. When Napoleon acquired Louisiana from Spain and planned for the reestablishment of a French empire in North America, Jefferson's interest only deepened. In 1803 the president appointed his personal secretary, Meriwether Lewis, to lead an expedition up the Missouri River. Within a few months, this project gained new momentum because the United States suddenly acquired the Louisiana Territory from the French.

Meriwether Lewis was born on a plantation near President Jefferson's Monticello and had a distinguished military career in the first years of American independence. He served in Ohio and Tennessee and at Detroit. He became Jefferson's secretary in 1800. In June 1803 Jefferson issued instructions to Captain Lewis. He ordered the American "Corps of Discovery" to explore the length of the Missouri River and to trace a route over the Rockies to the Pacific. The president wished to know the extent of the territory and the travel routes across it "for the purposes of commerce."

Soon after his appointment, Captain Lewis sought out a former comrade in arms, William Clark, and offered him joint command of the expedition. Clark's rural Virginia and Kentucky childhood included little formal schooling, but he was an accomplished horseman and frontier soldier. He had joined the U.S.

Army in 1792 and served in Ohio under General Anthony Wayne. It was there that he met Lewis. Clark had resigned his army commission and returned to Kentucky in 1796, but once Lewis offered him the chance to explore the West, he could not resist.

After a winter of preparation, Lewis, his co-commander Clark, and a core party of twenty-seven men set off from Wood River (Illinois) on May 14, 1804. The group included fourteen soldiers, nine civilian woodsmen, an interpreter, two boatmen, and Clark's slave York. Later that year they would add Toussaint Charbonneau, a French Canadian fur trader, and his Shoshone companion, Sakakawea. As they traveled west in 1804 and 1805, the corps devoted considerable time to diplomacy with Native peoples. Although they were cautious toward strangers, they were eager for directions and anxious to document the region's resources. They appreciated the traditional generosity and hospitality of tribal leaders, but they often underestimated the importance of reciprocating in kind. At times, Native Americans responded with suspicion to the heavily armed strangers. Those who had already established alliances with outsiders were usually less welcoming than those who saw the Americans as potential trading partners.

This section of the book begins with a chapter on what Americans knew (and didn't know) about the West in 1800, and then presents six telling moments during the Lewis and Clark expedition that illustrate the explorers' delicate interactions with Indians along the route. These chapters reveal how dependent the explorers often were on Native hospitality, and how differing perspectives and expectations often led to misunderstandings. During the expedition's return trip in 1806, the Americans' dwindling supplies and the burden of completing their mission caused the corps members to be impatient and even prone to violence.

The following timeline should help orient readers to the events described in the following seven chapters.

Major Events in the Lewis and Clark Expedition

1803
- Late in the year: Lewis and Clark and the Corps of Discovery assemble in St. Louis to begin preparations

1804
- May 14: The Corps of Discovery sets off from Camp Dubois (Wood River, Illinois).

- November 1: The corps establishes camp (Fort Mandan) near Mandan and Hidatsa villages along the Missouri River.

1805

- January 1: The Americans spend New Year's Day celebrating with the Mandans.
- April 7: The corps leaves the Mandan villages. A small party of men returns east, carrying a report and specimens back for Jefferson.
- June 2: The expedition comes to a fork in the river. The men think the northern fork is the correct one to follow and Lewis and Clark believe the southern fork is correct. After a few days of scouting, the entire party continues up the southern fork.
- June 13: The expedition reaches the Great Falls of the Missouri, proof that the captains had been correct in their decision to go with the southern fork.
- August 12: Now in the Rocky Mountains, the expedition ascends the Lemhi Pass, on the present-day border between Idaho and Montana.
- August 17: Lewis tries unsuccessfully to negotiate with a village of Shoshones for horses to cross the mountains.
- September 5: The expedition successfully acquires horses from a band of Salish Indians.
- September 20: After nearly starving in the Bitterroot Mountains, the corps emerges near modern-day Weippe, Idaho, where they are welcomed and fed by the Nez Perces.
- November 7: Storms on the lower Columbia River pin down the group for almost three weeks before it arrives at the Pacific.
- November 24: The corps establishes Fort Clatsop, near modern Astoria, Oregon.

1806

- March 23: The corps leaves Fort Clatsop and begins its journey east.
- May–June: The Americans rejoin the Nez Perces on the west side of the Bitterroot Mountains. They must wait for the snows before they are able to cross the range.
- July 3: After crossing the Bitterroots with Nez Perce guides, the corps splits into two parties and the Indians return home. Clark heads down the Yellowstone. Lewis takes a shortcut to Great Falls and explores the Marias River.
- July 27: The expedition has its deadly encounter with the Blackfeet.

- August 12: Downstream from the mouth of the Yellowstone, the two parties of the corps reunite.
- September 23: The Corps of Discovery arrives in St. Louis.

CHAPTER SIX

What Did the Americans Know?

In order to prepare his commander for the journey west, Thomas Jefferson sent Meriwether Lewis to Philadelphia to study with the nation's leading scientists and mapmakers. There the captain learned botany and cartography, but the information he gathered on the geography of Louisiana and the lifeways of the Missouri and Columbia River tribes was not much help in preparing him for his trip. The British had mapped the western coastline north of San Francisco, and French and Spanish traders had described the Indian communities on the Lower Missouri, but scholars knew very little about the North American interior, where the expedition would spend most of its time. When the Corps of Discovery embarked on its journey, the Indian country lay shrouded in mystery and fantasy.

The following selections provide a sample of the information available to the American explorers as they set off from St. Louis.

NOTES ON THE STATE OF VIRGINIA
Thomas Jefferson

While serving as the American ambassador in Paris in the year immediately follow-ing the Revolution, Thomas Jefferson became aware of the theory of Comte de Buffon, a French scientist who was then director of the Jardin du Roi in Paris. Buffon argued that American animals were generally smaller than those found in Europe and suggested that the American climate was hostile to healthy living. Jefferson prepared this report to give Europeans a better understanding of the New World and to counter Buffon's claims.

*In his report Jefferson made a number of careful observations regarding indig-
enous American plants and animals. Many sections reveal how little was known of
the territory west of the Mississippi. Jefferson even discusses the existence of giant
carnivorous mammoths in that little-known territory. The future president noted
Indian testimony that these animals existed and European travelers' reports of fossil-
ized skeletons of "unparalleled magnitude." If the animal existed, he believed it was
probably roaming the Far West. "He may well exist there now," Jefferson wrote. The
excerpt presented here contains his views on the West and his reflections on Native
Americans.*

Animals

Our quadrupeds have been mostly described by Linnaeus and Mons. de Buffon. Of these the Mammoth, or big buffalo, as called by the Indians, must
certainly have been the largest. Their tradition is, that he was carnivorous,
and still exists in the northern parts of America. A delegation of warriors from
the Delaware tribe having visited the governor of Virginia, during the present
revolution, on matters of business, after these had been discussed and settled
in council, the governor asked them some questions relative to their country,
and, among others, what they knew or had heard of the animal whose bones
were found at the Saltlicks, on the Ohio. Their chief speaker immediately put
himself into an attitude of oratory, and with a pomp suited to what he conceived the elevation of his subject, informed him that it was a tradition handed
down from their fathers, "That in antient times a herd of these tremendous
animals came to the Big-bone licks, and began an universal destruction of the
bear, deer, elks, buffaloes, and other animals, which had been created for the
use of the Indians: that the Great Man above, looking down and seeing this,
was so enraged that he seized his lightning, descended on the earth, seated
himself on a neighbouring mountain, on a rock, of which his seat and the print
of his feet are still to be seen, and hurled his bolts among them till the whole
were slaughtered, except the big bull, who presenting his forehead to the
shafts, shook them off as they fell; but missing one at length, it wounded him
in the side; whereon, springing round, he bounded over the Ohio, over the
Wabash, the Illinois, and finally over the great lakes, where he is living at this
day." It is well known that on the Ohio, and in many parts of America further
north, tusks, grinders, and skeletons of unparalleled magnitude, are found in
great numbers, some lying on the surface of the earth, and some a little below
it. A Mr. Stanley, taken prisoner by the Indians near the mouth of the Tanis-

see, relates, that, after being transferred through several tribes, from one to another, he was at length carried over the mountains west of the Missouri to a river which runs westwardly; that these bones abounded there; and that the natives described to him the animal to which they belonged as still existing in the northern parts of their country; from which description he judged it to be an elephant. Bones of the same kind have been lately found, some feet below the surface of the earth, in salines opened on the North Holston, a branch of the Tanissee, about the latitude of 36½ degrees North. From the accounts published in Europe, suppose it to be decided, that these are of the same kind with those found in Siberia.

. . . On the whole there seem to be no certain vestiges of the existence of this animal further south than the salines last mentioned. It is remarkable that the tusks and skeletons have been ascribed by the naturalists of Europe to the elephant, while the grinders have been given to the hippopotamus, or river-horse. Yet it is acknowledged, that the tusks and skeletons are much larger than those of the elephant, and the grinders many times greater than those of the hippopotamus, and essentially different in form. Wherever these grinders are found, there also we find the tusks and skeleton; but no skeleton of the hippopotamus nor grinders of the elephant. It will not be said that the hippopotamus and elephant came always to the same spot, the former to deposit his grinders, and the latter his tusks and skeleton. For what became of the parts not deposited there? We must agree then that these remains belong to each other, that they are of one and the same animal, that this was not a hippopotamus, because the hippopotamus had no tusks nor such a frame, and because the grinders differ in their size as well as in the number and form of their points. That it was not an elephant, I think ascertained by proofs equally decisive. . . .

For my own part, I find it easier to believe that an animal may have existed, resembling the elephant in his tusks, and general anatomy, while his nature was in other respects extremely different. From the 30th degree of South latitude to the 30th of North, are nearly the limits which nature has fixed for the existence and multiplication of the elephant known to us. Proceeding thence northwardly to 36½ degrees, we enter those assigned to the mammoth. The further we advance North, the more their vestiges multiply as far as the earth has been explored in that direction; and it is as probable as otherwise, that this progression continues to the pole itself, if land extends so far. The center of the Frozen zone then may be the Achmé of their vigour, as that of the Torrid is of the elephant. Thus nature seems to have drawn a belt of separation between these two tremendous animals, whose breadth indeed is not precisely known, though at present we may suppose it about 6½ degrees of latitude; to have assigned to the elephant the regions South of these confines, and those North to the mammoth, founding the constitution of the one in her extreme of heat, and that of the other in the extreme of cold. When the Creator has therefore separated their nature as far as the extent of the scale of animal life allowed to this planet would permit, it seems perverse to declare it the same, from a partial resemblance of their tusks and bones. But to whatever animal we ascribe these remains, it is certain such a one has existed in America, and that it has been the largest of all terrestrial beings. It should have sufficed to have rescued the earth it inhabited, and the atmosphere it breathed, from the imputation of impotence in the conception and nourishment of animal life on a large scale: to have stifled, in its birth, the opinion of a writer, the most learned too of all others in the science of animal history, that in the new world, "La nature vivante est beaucoup moins agissante, beaucoup moins forte": that nature is less active, less energetic on one side of the globe than she is on the other. As if both sides were not warmed by the same genial sun; as if a soil of the same chemical composition, was less capable of elaboration into animal nutriment; as if the fruits and grains from that soil and sun, yielded a less rich chyle, gave less extension to the solids and fluids of the body, or produced sooner in the cartilages, membranes, and fibres, that rigidity which restrains all further extension, and terminates animal growth. The truth is, that a Pigmy and a Patagonian, a Mouse and a Mammoth, derive their dimensions from the same nutritive juices. The difference of increment depends on circumstances unsearchable to beings with our capacities. Every race of animals seems to have received from their Maker certain laws of extension at the time of their formation. Their elaborative organs were formed to produce this, while proper obstacles were opposed to its further progress. Below these limits they cannot fall, nor rise above them. What intermediate station they shall take may depend on soil, on climate, on food, on a careful choice of breeders. But all the manna of heaven would never raise the Mouse to the bulk of the Mammoth.

To add to this, the traditionary testimony of the Indians, that this animal still exists in the northern and western parts of America, would be adding the light of a taper to that of the meridian sun. Those parts still remain in their aboriginal state, unexplored and undisturbed by us, or by others for us. He may as well exist there now, as he did formerly where we find his bones. If he be a carnivorous animal, as some Anatomists have conjectured, and the Indians affirm, his early retirement may be accounted for from the general destruction of the wild game by the Indians, which commences in the first instant of their connection with us, for the purpose of purchasing matchcoats, hatchets, and fire locks, with their skins. . . .

Indians

The Indian of North America being more within our reach, I can speak of him somewhat from my own knowledge, but more from the information of others better acquainted with him, and on whose truth and judgment I can rely. From these sources I am able to say, in contradiction to this representation, that he is neither more defective in ardor, nor more impotent with his female, than the white reduced to the same diet and exercise: that he is brave, when an enterprize depends on bravery; education with him making the point of honor consist in the destruction of an enemy by stratagem, and in the preservation of his own person free from injury; or perhaps this is nature; while it is education which teaches us to honor force more than finesse: that he will defend himself against an host of enemies, always chusing to be killed, rather than to surrender, though it be to the whites, who he knows will treat him well: that in other situations also he meets death with more deliberation, and endures tortures with a firmness unknown almost to religious enthusiasm with us: that he is affectionate to his children, careful of them, and indulgent in the extreme: that his affections comprehend his other connections, weakening, as with us, from circle to circle, as they recede from the center: that his friendships are strong and faithful to the uttermost extremity: that his sensibility is keen, even the warriors weeping most bitterly on the loss of their children, though in general they endeavour to appear superior to human events: that his vivacity and activity of mind is equal to ours in the same situation; hence his eagerness for hunting, and for games of chance. The women are submitted to unjust drudgery. This I believe is the case with every barbarous people. With such, force is law. The stronger sex therefore imposes on the weaker. It is civilization alone which replaces women in the enjoyment of their natural equality. That first teaches us to subdue the selfish passions, and to respect those rights in others which we value in ourselves. Were we in equal barbarism, our females would be equal drudges. The man with them is less strong than with us, but their woman stronger than ours; and both for the same obvious reason; because our man and their woman is habituated to labour, and formed by it. With both races the sex which is indulged with ease is least athletic. An Indian man is small in the hand and wrist for the same reason for which a sailor is large and strong in the arms and shoulders, and a porter in the legs and thighs.—They raise fewer children than we do. The causes of this are to be found, not in a difference of nature, but of circumstance. . . .

Before we condemn the Indians of this continent as wanting genius, we must consider that letters have not yet been introduced among them. Were we to compare them in their present state with the Europeans North of the Alps, when the Roman arms and arts first crossed those mountains, the comparison would be unequal, because, at that time, those parts of Europe were swarming with numbers; because numbers produce emulation, and multiply the chances of improvement, and one improvement begets another. Yet I may safely ask, How many good poets, how many able mathematicians, how many great inventors in arts or sciences, had Europe North of the Alps then produced? And it was sixteen centuries after this before a Newton could be formed. I do not mean to deny, that there are varieties in the race of man, distinguished by their powers both of body and mind. I believe there are, as I see to be the case in the races of other animals. I only mean to suggest a doubt, whether the bulk and faculties of animals depend on the side of the Atlantic on which their food happens to grow, or which furnishes the elements of which they are compounded? Whether nature has enlisted herself as a Cis or Trans-Atlantic partisan? I am induced to suspect, there has been more eloquence than sound reasoning displayed in support of this theory; that it is one of those cases where the judgment has been seduced by a glowing pen: and whilst I render every tribute of honor and esteem to the celebrated Zoologist, who has added, and is still adding, so many precious things to the treasures of science, I must doubt whether in this instance he has not cherished error also, by lending her for a moment his vivid imagination and bewitching language.

Thomas Jefferson, *Notes on the State of Virginia* (Philadelphia: R. C. Rawle, 1801), 43–79.

CHAPTER SEVEN

Celebrating the New Year and Surviving the Winter with the Mandans, January 1805

In November 1804, when the Americans established their winter camp near five Mandan and Hidatsa villages along the Upper Missouri River, they settled into life as the Indians' nearest neighbors. The explorers discovered that the tribes were firmly linked to the Canadian fur trade and that they worried about aggressive Sioux bands who were pressing them from the south. The Mandans and Hidatsas had many reasons to forge a partnership with the Americans and to put their community's traditional hospitality on display. The explorers were also eager for allies. They needed both food for the coming winter and information about the unknown territory ahead. As a result, the Americans muted their objections to the French Canadian fur traders who were living with the Indians and patiently traded with their neighbors.

WILLIAM CLARK DESCRIBES NEW YEAR'S DAY 1805

The Americans and the Mandans and Hidatsas displayed their common desire for friendship on New Year's Day 1805, when the American soldiers (and Clark's slave York) visited the two Mandan villages near their camp for extended rounds of dancing, feasting, and gift giving. William Clark described the day's activities in his journal.

The Day was ushered in by the Discharge of two Cannon, we Suffered 16 men[1] with their musick to visit the 1st Village for the purpose of Danceing, by as they Said the perticular request of the Chiefs of that village, about 11 oClock

I with an inturpeter & two men walked up to the Village (my views were to alay Some little miss understanding which had taken place thro jelloucy and mortification as to our treatment towards them.

I found them much pleased at the Danceing of our men, I ordered my black Servant to Dance which amused the Croud verry much, and Some what astonished them, that So large a man Should be active &c. &.

I went into the lodges of all the men of note except two, whome I heard had made Some expressions not favourable towards us, in Compareing us with the trabers from the north—Those Cheifs observed what they Sayed was in just [jest] & lafture.—just as I was about to return the 2d Chief and the Black man, also a Chief returned from a mission on which they had been Sent to meet a large party 150 of *Gross Ventres* who were on their way down from their Camps 10 Miles above to revenge on the *Shoe* tribe an injurey which they had received by a Shoe man Steeling a *Gross Venters Girl,* those Chiefs gave the pipe turned the party back, after Delivering up the girl, which the Shoe Chief had taken and given to them for that purpose. I returned in the evening, at night the party except 6 returned, with 3 robes, an 13 Strings of Corn which the indians had given them, The Day was worm, Themtr. 34° abov 0, Some fiew Drops of rain about Sunset, at Dark it began to Snow, and Snowed the greater part of the night, (the temptr for Snow is about 0) The Black Cat with his family visited us to day and brought a little meet.

Note

1. These included Ordway, and probably François Rivet, who earlier had "danced on his head" for the Indians.

"William Clark Describes New Year's Day, 1805," in *The Journals of the Lewis and Clark Expedition,* ed. Gary Moulton (Lincoln: University of Nebraska Press, 1987), vol. 3, 266–67.

JOHN ORDWAY DESCRIBES THE NEW YEAR'S CELEBRATION

Sergeant John Ordway also commented on the day, "January 1, 1805, was a day of rest." As this passage in his journal makes clear, the men were issued a ration of whiskey and the entire company crossed the river to Mitutanka, the nearest Mandan village. The Mandans welcomed the visit, responding with gifts of food and buffalo robes. Ordway noted that the "frolicking" continued into January 2. He did not appear to understand the obligations accompanying the hospitality being offered the Americans by the villagers.

Purchased by the government for three hundred dollars, the journal of "top sergeant" John Ordway was used by the Philadelphian Nicholas Biddle while he prepared the first official report of the expedition. Unfortunately, Biddle did not return it to the archives and it was "lost" until 1913.

Tuesday 1st Jany. 1805. cloudy but moderate. we fired a Swivel & drank a Glass. about 9 o.C. 15 of the party went up to the 1st village of Mandans to dance as it had been their request. carried with us a fiddle & a Tambereen & a Sounden horn. as we arived at the entrence of the vil. we fired one round then the music played. loaded again. then marched to the center of the vil, fircd again. then commenced dancing. a frenchman danced on his head[1] and all danced round him for a Short time then went in to a lodge & danced a while, which pleased them verry much they then brought victules from diffcrent lodges & of different kinds of diet, they brought us also a quantity of corn & Some buffalow Robcs which they made us a present off. So we danced in different lodges untill late in the afternoon. then a part of the men returned to the fort the remainder Stayed all night in the village—rained a little in the eve.

Note

1. This refers to François Rivet, a civilian engagé who accompanied the first phase of the expedition.

"John Ordway Describes the New Year's Celebration," in *The Journals of the Lewis and Clark Expedition,* ed. Gary Moulton (Lincoln: University of Nebraska Press, 1995), vol. 9, 107.

WILLIAM CLARK DESCRIBES THE MANDAN BUFFALO DANCE

This description of the Americans' attendance at a Red Stick or Buffalo Calling Ceremony during their winter with the Mandans appeared in the first history of the expedition. Unable to comprehend the ceremony's larger meaning, the explorers simply recorded what they saw at the time.

5th of January Satturday 1805

A cold day Some Snow, Several Indians visit us with their axes to get them mended, I imploy myself drawing a Connection of the Countrey from what information I have recved—a Buffalow Dance (or Medison) for 3 nights passed in the 1st Village, a curious Custom the old men arrange themselves in a circle

& after Smoke a pipe, which is handed them by a young man, Dress up for the purpose, the young men who have their wives back of the circle go to one of the old men with a whining tome and . . . the old man to take his wife (who presents necked except a robe) and—(or Sleep with him) the Girl then takes the Old man (who verry often can Scercely walk) and leades him to a Convenient place for the business, after which they return to the lodge, if the Old man (or a white man) returns to the lodge without gratifying the man & his wife, he offers her again and again; it is often the Case that after the 2d time without Kissing the Husband throws a nice robe over the old man & and begs him not to dispise him, & his wife.

(we Sent a man to this Medisan last night, they gave him 4 Girls)

all this is to cause the buffalow to Come newar So that They may kill thim.

"William Clark Describes the Mandan Buffalo Dance," in *The Journals of the Lewis and Clark Expedition,* ed. Gary Moulton (Lincoln: University of Nebraska Press, 1987), vol. 3, 268–69.

EXPLORING THE EXPLORERS: GREAT PLAINS PEOPLES AND THE LEWIS AND CLARK EXPEDITION
James P. Ronda

The Corps of Discovery was never alone in exploring the West. In fact, its members were far outnumbered by other explorers. The Natives they encountered throughout the Great Plains were doing some exploration of their own, discovering all they could about these newcomers. The Natives held just as many erroneous assumptions as the American captains, and relations between the two groups were often strained, comical, and even dangerous. James P. Ronda, author of the authoritative Lewis and Clark among the Indians, *examines the historical disconnect that exists due to scholars' failure to examine exploration from both sides.*

There are few stories that seem more commonplace than the narrative of the exploration of the American West. It is the stock-in-trade of countless textbooks, classroom lectures, and popular novels. In the traditional telling, European and American adventurers are the actors at center stage while Native Americans stand silently in the wings or have bit parts.

Much of exploration history labors under two burdens. First, we still see exploration events through the eyes of the European explorers themselves. Their stories become the only stories, their visions the only vision. For the most part exploration scholarship has not taken into account the ways Native and non-Native peoples worked together to probe a shared world. And scholars have not paid sufficient attention to Native voices as they give balance and meaning to the exploration encounter. Second, many recent accounts continue to envision exploration as simply a physical journey across a material landscape. Generations of artists and writers have sought to reveal exploration as a venture aimed at understanding self, place, and the other. Exploration was, and remains in the Space Age, an interior pilgrimage, a passage that Joseph Conrad dared call a journey into the heart of darkness.[1]

These observations carry special force when applied to the Lewis and Clark expedition. The Lewis and Clark story is an emblematic tale, one that transcends the particular events to represent larger cultural truths. Lewis and Clark's odyssey has become a touchstone event in the history of the American West, a part of something that might be called the tale of the tribe. But the telling of that tale has often been narrow in range and focus. Like the rest of exploration history, the Lewis and Clark narrative has been repeated as the exclusive adventures of white American males. We need to reimagine the Lewis and Clark voyage, not as a trip through empty space but as a mutual encounter between diverse peoples and cultures.[2]

The expedition was as much the object of exploration as it was the agent for exploring. Lewis and Clark were both explorers and the explored. Native people looked at the American expedition and saw a new world. Travelers on both sides of the cultural divide struggled to fit new faces, new words, new objects, and new ways of being into familiar patterns of meaning. What happened along the Missouri River was mutual discovery. When we say the word "explorer" we should see a native face as quickly as we see the face of a bearded stranger. So I propose that we turn the familiar Lewis and Clark story upside down, that we see it through native eyes. What we need to do is make Lewis and Clark the uncharted territory and native people the explorers. Then perhaps we can grasp the complexity of this American discovery.

Long before Lewis and Clark left St. Louis, they had a set of images and preconceptions about the land and peoples they would meet along the way. Those images, drawn from many sources, informed and directed the expedition throughout its journey. We might begin by asking what images, what previous experiences Great Plains native people had about Europeans before 1804.

For native people who called the northern plains home, white travelers were no novelty. By the time Lewis and Clark made their way up river, there was already half a century of contact between Plains peoples and the outsiders.

Beginning in the 1730s, first a trickle and then a steady stream of European visitors came to call. It was commerce, the traffic in furs, that brought men like David Thompson, James Slater, and René Jusseaume to the Mandan and Hidatsa villages. Those merchants simply became part of a vast and complex native trade system in place long before any French *coureurs de bois* or Hudson's Bay Company men came to the northern Plains.

From these contacts plains people fashioned a set of expectations about white outsiders. These men, always men, came in small numbers. The typical trading party counted perhaps five or seven men. In the fifty years before Lewis and Clark, the largest recorded European trading expedition had ten men.[3] By the 1780s those visits fell into an almost predictable seasonal cycle. The traders, especially those from Canada, arrived in late fall or early winter and stayed several weeks. Native people expected those weeks to be filled with business, the exchange of pelts and skins for ironware, textiles, guns, and luxury goods.

The business they neither expected nor welcomed was politics and diplomacy. European empire builders rightly understood that fur traders were agents of imperial expansion. Along with the usual goods to sell, the traders brought flags, medals, and other symbols of national sovereignty. While Indians often accepted such objects out of curiosity, respect, or hospitality, they did not think that those things in any way diminished native sovereignty or bound them to a distant great father. While most of the traders left once the exchanges were concluded, the villagers came to expect that a few might take wives and enter the native social world. These men, known as resident or tenant traders, became important intermediaries bridging the cultural divide. Two of them—René Jusseaume and Toussaint Charbonneau—played significant roles in the Lewis and Clark experience.

To these expectations about outsiders, we need to add one additional element. Early in the history of contact between native people and European traders, the goods that passed into native hands took on a special meaning. Meriwether Lewis grasped something of this when he wrote that Indians believed the first white traders "were the most powerful persons in the nation."[4] The apparent power of the whites—their technologies, seeming resistance to certain diseases, and exotic customs—could be shared with others by wearing or using things connected to the outsiders. A button, an awl, a gun, or an old tobacco box might have both utility in this world and a special force in the invisible but ever-present other world.

When the Lewis and Clark expedition came up the Missouri in 1804 the

Corps of Discovery presented native people with a spectacle at once familiar and yet strangely unexpected and unsettling. First there was the matter of size. What came up the river was by any standard a very large party, perhaps the largest yet seen on the Missouri. While the precise number remains elusive, there were at least forty men in the expedition company. And even a cursory look revealed a second unmistakable fact. These men were exceptionally well-armed. Trading parties always carried guns but no Indian could have confused this traveling infantry company for a traders' brigade. Weapons of all shapes and sizes—small cannons, pistols, rifles, muskets, and knives—were displayed for all to see. How this large, well-armed party sailed up river was also a source of wonder. St. Louis traders had used rafts, canoes, and perogues for river traffic. In the 1790s Spanish officials briefly experimented with small galleys but nothing could quite compare with the impressive keel-boat captained by Lewis and Clark. Here was a river craft unique in design and impressive in size.

Once the American expedition settled in to winter quarters at Fort Mandan, near present-day Bismarck, North Dakota, the sense of the new and the strange continued. The fort itself was an architectural curiosity. Mandan and Hidatsa villagers knew all about constructing very large earth lodges and they had seen an occasional trading party put up a crude post but the American fort was something altogether different. Walls, barracks, guards, and a locked gate—here was a new way to define space under Dakota skies. What happened in and around the fort was equally new and bewildering. Native people reasonably assumed that trade was the principal reason any party came to the Missouri. At first glance Lewis and Clark certainly looked like traders. Their bales of goods held a virtual country store—everything from knives and fish hooks to mirrors and calico shirts. And Lewis and Clark talked about trade, trade with St. Louis merchants who were part of an expanding American commercial empire. But commerce did not follow the words. While the soldiers at Fort Mandan were always ready to buy meat and corn, they showed no interest in pelts. These men were traders who did not trade.

The mystery of their intentions deepened as winter closed in. Earth lodge people always assumed that some of the resident traders would take village wives and become part of the family world. But the fort men were somehow different. They certainly sought the comforts of sex but made no moves to fulfill family obligations. For native women sex was bound up in family duties and, in the case of the buffalo-calling ritual, the quest for spirit power. Expedition men plainly saw intimate relations in a wholly different light. The bodies and some of the desires were the same; it was the meaning that did not translate across the divide.

What the captains said and did in their daily routine also did not square with previous plains experience. Squinting at the stars, recording temperatures, and collecting plant and animal specimens were strange things that demanded some explanation. Just as disturbing was all the American talk about the Great Father in Washington and the obedience owed to his wishes. During the Mandan winter, Lewis and Clark pursued an ambitious and ultimately unsuccessful diplomatic agenda. They sought to establish American sovereignty, to discredit Canadian rivals, and to forge an alliance with village peoples against the Sioux. A new political order had evidently come to the northern Plains, one that chiefs and elders now struggled to understand.

And there was one final part of the Lewis and Clark territory that demanded exploration. Most of the objects carried by the American explorers were now quite familiar to native people. European clothing, guns, all sorts of trade items—none of this was new. But there were some things, "curriossities" the captains called them, that were striking in form and function. When the Mandan Chief Black Cat visited the fort in late November 1804 he asked to see those objects. Out from their boxes came the latest wonders of western scientific technology. Surveying compasses, a precision chronometer, a sextant, and several telescopes—these things represented a reality as remote and mysterious as anything from NASA.[5]

To native eyes the space in and around the expedition was a new world. Here were people, objects, and ways of behaving that challenged previous assumptions. All exploration involves measuring images and preconceptions up against what is immediately seen. Along the Missouri, plains people began to explore the shadowy Lewis and Clark country just as other natives had done elsewhere since the 1490s. Even before the Mandan winter and its longer time for mutual discovery, river folk had tried to chart the expedition world. In early September 1804 Black Buffalo's band of Brule Sioux had an angry face-off with the Americans at the confluence of the Bad and Missouri rivers. That confrontation revealed Lewis and Clark as unwelcome intruders, commercial rivals bent on both political and economic dominion.[6]

Further up river the American party spent five days at the Grand River Arikara villages. Like other river people, the Arikaras had seen white traders and their goods. But the intentions and behavior of the captains, their fascinating technology, and the presence of the black slave York sparked intense interest. What came out of that encounter was a vivid set of stories, a kind of exploration folklore. Arikaras asked: who were these strangers, where did they come from, and what was the meaning of their journey? Pierre-Antoine Tabeau, a French trader well acquainted with the Arikaras, recorded many of those stories. Kakawita, Tabeau's leading informant, reported that Arikaras thought the Americans were on a special vision quest and had encountered terrible monsters along the way. A sextant, a magnet, and phosphorous were pointed to as evidence of spirit powers. And there was York. He was the clearest sign of the supernatural, "a large fine man, black as a bear who spoke and acted as one."[7]

Those plains and river folk—Sioux and Arikaras—had only a brief moment to explore the mysterious strangers. Genuine exploration takes time; it is the work of larger views and longer talks. The winter of 1804–05 at Fort Mandan was such a time. Here the American expedition was at rest, no longer defined by the traveling routines of up and out and on the way. For the Americans, exploration meant moving, measuring, observing, and recording. This was an abstract, almost detached process well-suited to the scientific spirit of the age. Landscape meant exploitable resources; people were objects to be studied and classified.

Native explorers pursued a different strategy. As hitherto unknown people, goods, and experiences entered the traditional circles of life, native people sought to maintain a harmonious balance between the old and the new. Exploration meant finding a suitable place for each new thing or person within the familiar framework. Indian explorers sought to domesticate the unknown, to name what seemed nameless. The native question was not so much "who are you" as "where do you fit?" To find the "fit" was to fix the meaning and keep all in balance. Indian explorers, and that means all native peoples of whatever age or gender, used simple but effective methods to probe the strangers. They looked at them, visited them, traded with them, shared all sorts of information, and on occasion made love with them. Lewis and Clark sought the new and gloried in it. Native explorers confronted the new, tried to soften its edges and make it like the old and the familiar.

Looking out from Fort Mandan, Lewis and Clark imagined a wilderness, a crowded wilderness but a wilderness nonetheless. From their earth lodges, Mandan and Hidatsa folk held a very different view of the landscape. When they surveyed the northern Plains they saw a great community of life. Fort Mandan, that odd one-house town, and its strange inhabitants were a challenge to the settled order of things. Here was something that needed to be folded into the everyday routines of life, made commonplace, and therefore comprehensible. Like European adventurers on their various travels, native discoverers undertook a journey to Fort Mandan, a journey of exploration and explanation. That voyage began by simply watching the strangers. For many plains people the American expedition was an almost irresistible tourist attraction. As the Lewis and Clark navy nosed its way up river into what is now North Dakota the banks were lined with curious onlookers. Sergeant John Ordway noticed that on many days the riverside galleries were packed with children.[8]

Once construction began on the fort there was even more to see. Native sidewalk superintendents observed everything from building the various quarters and rooms to setting the palisades and digging the latrines. As William Clark put it in one journal entry, Indian neighbors were "verry Curious in examining our works."[9] Little wonder, since the fort looked like no other piece of plains architecture. Its angular lines, vertical walls, heavy gate, and windows must have fascinated Indians more accustomed to the rounded lines of domed earth lodges.

For all the pleasures of seeing, looking was not enough for native explorers. Exploration demanded participation. It was not a spectator sport. Visiting was an essential part of any frontier culture, whether in tidewater Virginia or on the northern Plains. Fort Mandan was no isolated outpost, caught in the grip of a Dakota winter and cut off from the simple joys of human companionship. Long before Lewis and Clark came into the country, Mandan and Hidatsa villagers had brightened their winters with a steady round of visits to the lodges of friends and neighbors. Life in the winter camps could be harsh and hungry, but there also were times for storytelling and gossip. Once Fort Mandan was built, the Americans became part of the social web that bound the villagers together. Indians were drawn not only to the fort itself but to the many "curriossities" they found inside.

It had long been expedition policy to display all sorts of weapons and scientific instruments in an effort to impress Indians with American power. When Hidatsa chief Le Borgne came to visit in early March 1805, he was shown everything from Lewis's airgun to a spyglass. The Hidatsa promptly proclaimed these devices to be "Great Medicines." Whether impressed or not, many visitors found the objects both mysterious and compelling. Thermometers, quadrants, writing paper, and metal goods of all sorts were worth a special visit to the fort. It was as if Fort Mandan had become a living museum of white American life, familiar in some ways but novel in so many others.[10]

During most of the winter, Indians found an unfailing welcome at Fort

Mandan. And on most days, despite snow and falling temperatures, Indians came to explore the fort. Only once during the entire season were native people asked not to come calling. On Christmas day 1804 the expedition evidently wanted to do its own celebrating. Native neighbors were told that the festivities were part of a special "medicine day" for whites only.[11] On every other day the gates were open. Indian visitors brought a sense of friendship and good company. Visits usually meant sharing food and enjoying a dance or some fiddle music by Pierre Cruzatte. There must have been time to appreciate a fine bow, a good gun, or a skillfully decorated pair of moccasins. Visiting put names to faces and words to things. It humanized the unknown, softened its tough edges, and civilized the pale savages.

Plains people expected that strangers coming from afar made the journey to trade. Villagers used trade not only to enhance individual status but as a means to make and cement personal friendships. Indians who traded at the Mandan and Hidatsa villages were for the most part potential enemies or relatives of those killed in combat. Some means had to be found to stop possible violence and allow peaceful relations. Reflecting the fundamental native social reality that defined relatives as friends and outsiders as enemies, villagers and their trading partners created a ceremony in which strangers were made temporary, fictional relatives. Men who might later fight each other could for a brief time exchange goods, swap stories, and even share ritual practices as friends. Perhaps the bearded strangers could be made trading "relatives."

Lewis and Clark surely fit the image of traders. They came with all sorts of goods. And the Americans talked a trading game. A large part of the expedition's diplomacy was aimed at redirecting the Indian trade away from Canadian markets and toward a St. Louis–based commercial system. Not only did the Americans look like traders and talk like traders, they sometimes acted like traders. Fort Mandan became a busy marketplace where skilled native merchants brought corn and meat in exchange for metal and textile items. At one point during the winter the American expedition was so desperate for corn that Indians were offered war axes in exchange for food. Lewis and Clark diplomacy preached intertribal peace but the power of necessity put weapons in the hands of those same warriors.

It seemed to make sense that the American explorers were in fact a large group of traders. But somehow for Indians exploring Lewis and Clark, that answer didn't quite make sense. For all the goods and all the talk, the Americans did not behave like visitors from Canada. Fort Mandan had no fur warehouse. And these outsiders showed no inclination to become even temporary "relatives."

By January 1805 some Mandan villagers were beginning to doubt that the label "trader" fit their fort neighbors. Earth lodge gossip had it that the Americans were stingy bargainers, unable or unwilling to compete with their Canadian rivals. When William Clark bitterly complained about all this loose talk, two Mandan elders quickly reassured him that the words were only in "jest and lafture."[12]

But this explanation barely covered what an increasing number of Indians had come to believe. Lewis and Clark were not traders. And if they were not traders, who were they? Exploring the American explorers, village people had come up against an almost unanswerable question. The concept, the linguistic category employed to describe a large-scale expedition not for war, not for trade, not for hunting, simply did not exist. Warriors plotted war trails; merchants sought trade routes; hunters scouted game lands. Exploration apart from these activities was a pursuit utterly foreign to native peoples. Eventually Lewis and Clark hit upon an identity explanation that more completely fit the native universe of experience. Indians were told that the party was in search of distant, long-lost relatives.

Thomas Jefferson expected that his explorers would not so much march across the continent as question their way west. Deeply influenced by Enlightenment strategies, the president understood exploration as inquiry, not grand romantic adventure. Lewis and Clark went up the Missouri armed with a comprehensive set of questions on everything from botany and climatology to diplomacy and ethnography. Native explorers did not have such detailed question lists but they were inquirers nonetheless. One example here can stand for many. Few Indians were more regular visitors at Fort Mandan than Black Cat, chief of the Mandan village called Ruptáre. Lewis respected the quality of Black Cat's mind, calling him a man of "integrety, firmness, inteligence, and perspicuety."[13]

On a cold windy morning in November, Black Cat worked his way along the river bank to Fort Mandan. As Clark later recalled it, Black Cat "made Great inquiries respecting our fashions." We need to be sensitive to the many meanings of the word "fashion" as used by Clark. Black Cat was not especially interested in frontier *haute couteur,* the latest stylings from a nineteenth-century Bill Blass or Christian Dior. Fashion meant customs, habits, and ways of being. Black Cat had already seen the "curriossities." Now he wanted to understand something about the fabric of ordinary American life. What kind of a world produced and used such objects? Clark's journal is silent on the particulars. We don't know if Black Cat's questions headed toward the shape of American houses or the domestic relations between husbands and wives.

But whatever the questions, Black Cat must have found the process satisfying. Within a few days he was eagerly sharing what Clark called "little Indian aneck-dts."[14] The questions of exploration had sparked the dialogue of encounter.

Looking, visiting, questioning—this was exploring the new and the other on a personal level. But the American expedition posed a challenge on a much larger scale. That challenge was all about diplomacy—the complex web of relations between the native nations and their new neighbors. Lewis and Clark came to the Missouri with a diplomatic scheme that if implemented would have revolutionized the politics of the northern Plains. Were Lewis and Clark to have had their way, it would have indeed been a new world order. As agents of a young and ambitious imperial republic, the captains sought to proclaim American sovereignty and fashion an alliance of village peoples against the Sioux. Diplomacy was no new game for village chiefs and elders, but the American demands were so stiff that they called for another kind of exploring.

In hurried meetings and formal councils throughout the winter of 1804–05, native diplomats probed the territory that would come to be if Lewis and Clark prevailed. Typical of such gatherings were the exchanges at the end of October 1804. In a speech that was now a stock part of his repertory, Lewis sketched the outlines of a new political landscape on the Plains. There were the familiar themes—federal sovereignty, American trade, and intertribal peace. Such proposals did not seem extraordinary to the captains, but they did amount to substantial changes to the traditional ways the five Mandan and Hidatsa villages did business with both native and non-native outsiders.

At the end of the speech, Lewis introduced the most controversial feature in his plan. The assembled Indians must have known that the Arikara chief sitting in the council was more than a chance visitor. Now was the time to open the touchy issue of peace between the Arikaras and their Mandan and Hidatsa neighbors. That peace, so Lewis and Clark believed, was a necessary preliminary to a general village coalition against the Sioux. The captains did not record the words they used to propose the peace treaty but what does survive is evidence of a culturally significant gesture. Clark, by now familiar with the protocol of plains diplomacy, took a pipe, smoked it, and passed it to the Arikara chief. That pipe was in turn handed around to the Mandan and Hidatsa representative. Clark noted later, "They all smoked with eagerness."[15]

That eagerness did not mean assent. At most it meant that men like Black Cat were ready to begin a diplomatic exploration of what must have seemed suspect terrain. Black Cat, adept at probing other parts of that terrain, was equally skilled at feeling his way in the murk of diplomacy. Because the American explorers thought Black Cat was the most powerful Mandan chief, they were anxious to know his thoughts. At mid-day on 31 October Clark and interpreter René Jusseaume walked down to Black Cat's village. At Ruptáre Clark was welcomed "and with great ceremoney was Seeted on a roabe by the Side of the Chief." Black Cat placed a fine buffalo robe over Clark's shoulders "and after smoking the pipe with several old men around" began to speak.[16]

Black Cat's speech was a carefully worded reply to the American proposals. It was a response designed to reassure Lewis and Clark without tying the villages too closely to an uncertain policy and a chancy future. He went directly to the heart of the matter. Intertribal peace made sense, at least to elders and chiefs. Black Cat graphically illustrated what he saw as the benefits of such a peace, saying it would mean "they now could hunt without fear, and their womin could work in the fields without looking everry moment for the enemey." But this bright vision of a promising future did not mean that Black Cat was ready to become an American client. In his mind there were many unanswered questions. Earlier trader-diplomats, men like John Evans, had made extravagant promises about goods, markets, and protection against hostile outsiders. Those proved empty offers. Would the American ones be any better? The Great Father in Washington was only the most recent in a long line of distant sovereigns who handed out medals and flags. Each father asked much but in the end proved powerless and faithless. Would the chief of the American fires be any better? Later in November, Black Cat accepted a peace medal and an American flag. And there was his promise—made under considerable duress—to keep Union Jacks and King George medals out of his village.[17] Lewis and Clark imagined a plains diplomatic landscape filled with treaties, alliances, and the fixed bureaucracies of nation-states. Black Cat and his successors now had to explore that country. Such a journey would prove a perilous voyage, far more dangerous than any trek across the windswept plains.

T. S. Eliot once wrote that all exploring begins with an outward journey and ends with an interior passage back to one's inner self. Exploration is a kind of self-knowledge. When native people explored Lewis and Clark they may have come to know themselves with more clarity. Whether that happened or not, Indian explorers pursued the obvious strategies as they faced the new country. Looking, visiting, questioning, and counciling—all these were visible voyages made before the public gaze. But there was a final kind of discovery and exploration, one that was intensely personal and profoundly private. It was the exploration of the body, the intimate territory of another self.

Lewis and Clark knew that there would be liaisons between members of the expedition and Native American women. The captains accepted such relations as inevitable and thought about them in largely medical terms. For the practical captains, sex meant venereal disease. It was a clinical issue, something to be dealt with by doses of mercury from penis syringes. The American exploration strategy never considered sex as anything other than a physical problem or a momentary dalliance.

For Native American women on the northern Plains sexual relations with men other than their husbands took place within rigidly prescribed limits. In the buffalo-calling ceremony, wives of younger men courted and had intercourse with older men. Those intimate relations were like a conduit that transferred spiritual power and hunting skill from an older man to a younger one. When non-natives, both black and white, appeared on the scene, Indian women, and sometimes their spouses, sought them out. As Clark noted, "the Indians say all white flesh is medisan." In one especially revealing incident, an Arikara husband stood guard at the door of his lodge lest anyone interrupt the tryst between his wife and York.[18] Sex could appropriate power and place it in native hands. Here Indian women explored the intimate unknown, expecting to find great strength and a different kind of knowledge.

No nineteenth-century American exploring party made a fuller and more intimate record of its daily doings than the Lewis and Clark expedition. When expedition journal keepers encountered native women, the accounts they wrote revealed some things while concealing others. Journal entries made it plain that women were defined in terms of sexual identity, reproductive history, and domestic labor. Euro-American explorers were bound by those definitions, and blinded to the other ways that native women explorers might behave. What is either missing in or concealed by the journals are the ways native women explored the worlds beyond the sexual. Like native men, women must have studied the ways and means, the sights and sounds of the bearded strangers. That the strangers took no notice of that exploring activity diminishes both the written record and our appreciation of the larger exploration encounter.

It is not easy to judge how well native explorers came to know their strange neighbors. What did all the looking, visiting, questioning, talking, and lovemaking finally produce? Did native explorers succeed in "civilizing" the strangers? Did they give them new names or influence their behavior? There are no certain answers to these questions. There is no scholarly edition of documents and maps called *The Journals of Black Cat*. What survives are evocative fragments hinting at a major effort of mind and spirit, the struggle to know the other. Two unrelated events at the end of the winter of 1804–05 can tell us something about the Indian enterprise to understand what had quite suddenly become a new world.

In early March 1805 the Hidatsa chief Le Borgne came to Fort Mandan for a meeting with Lewis. As the two men talked through an interpreter, there was a buzz of commotion in the Hidatsa delegation. Finally the chief explained what was going on. "Some foolish young men had informed him that there was a black man in the party." Le Borgne doubted that any man was wholly black. Perhaps the man in question was simply wearing black paint in mourning for a lost relative. With that, Lewis produced Clark's slave York. In that moment Le Borgne the explorer had to confront what seemed the unthinkable, the unimaginable. Was York a man, was he really black? Clark heard later that Le Borgne was "astonished" by the sight of York. The chief examined York closely and then "spit on his hand and rubbed in order to rub off the paint." York quickly grasped what was going on, pulled off the bandana from his head, and showed Le Borgne his hair. Amazed by black skin and curly hair, the Indian was convinced that York was "of a different species from the whites."[19]

If Le Borgne was bewildered by his foray into the unknown, Black Cat's more extensive exploration of the Lewis and Clark world produced a larger measure of understanding. On a warm day in early April 1805, just before the American explorers left for the Pacific, Black Cat had a final visit with the captains. They smoked together and then the Indian gave Clark "a par of excellent Mockersons."[20] Smoking and a gift—perhaps gestures that acknowledged an exploration enterprise at least partially fulfilled. Clark now had a place in Black Cat's world. The pipe and the moccasins said as much. What happened along the Missouri was a continuation of a process that began in 1492. Two very different worlds collided and out of that collision came something new and unsettling. Black Cat, Le Borgne, Lewis, and Clark—all were new world explorers bound together in the common cause of discovery.

Notes

1. Exploration historiography is discussed at length in James P. Ronda, *The Exploration of North America* (Washington, D.C.: American Historical Association, 1992).

2. The full range of Lewis and Clark scholarship is discussed in James P. Ronda, "The Writingest Explorers: The Lewis and Clark Expedition in American Historical Literature," *Pennsylvania Magazine of History and Biography* 112 (October 1988): 607–30.

3. W. Raymond Wood and Thomas D. Thiessen, eds., *Early Fur Trade on the Northern Plains: Canadian Traders among the Mandan and Hidatsa Indians, 1738–1808* (Norman: University of Oklahoma Press, 1985), table 1.

4. Lewis, "Observations and Reflections, August, 1807," in Donald Jackson, ed., *Letters of the Lewis and Clark Expedition with Related Documents, 1783–1854,* 2 vols., 2nd ed. (Urbana: University of Illinois Press, 1978), 2:698.

5. Gary E. Moulton, ed., *The Journals of the Lewis and Clark Expedition,* 8 vols. to date (Lincoln: University of Nebraska Press, 1983–), 3:242. Hereafter cited as JLCE.

6. James P. Ronda, *Lewis and Clark among the Indians* (Lincoln: University of Nebraska Press, 1984), 27–41.

7. Annie H. Abel, ed., *Tabeau's Narrative of Loisel's Expedition to the Upper Missouri* (Norman: University of Oklahoma Press, 1939), 200–201.

8. Milo M. Quaife, ed., *The Journals of Captain Meriwether Lewis and Sergeant John Ordway* (Madison: State Historical Society of Wisconsin, 1916), 159.

9. JLCE, 3:238.

10. JLCE, 3:310–11; Quaife, ed., *Journals of Lewis and Ordway* (note 8 above), 186.

11. Quaife, ed., *Journals of Lewis and Ordway* (note 8 above), 174.

12. JLCE, 3:267.

13. JLCE, 3:289.

14. JLCE, 3:237, 238, 240, 311, quotations 237 and 311.

15. JLCE, 3:208–11, quotation 209.

16. JLCE, 3:218.

17. JLCE, 3:218–19, 242.

18. "Biddle Notes," in Jackson, ed., *Letters* (note 4 above), 2: 503, 538; JLCE, 3:209, 268.

19. "Biddle Notes," in Jackson, ed., *Letters* (note 4 above), 2: 539.

20. JLCE, 4:13–14.

James P. Ronda, "Exploring the Explorers: Great Plains Peoples and the Lewis and Clark Expedition," *Great Plains Quarterly* 13, no. 2 (Spring 1993): 81–90.

LEWIS AND CLARK AMONG THE MANDANS AND HIDATSAS
Calvin Grinnell and Tillie Walker

The modern community at the Fort Berthold Indian reservation, the current home of the Mandans, Hidatsas, and Arikaras, contains many men and women who hold the oral history of the Americans' winter with their ancestors two centuries ago. Among these elders are two educators who shared some of that history in an interview.

Calvin Grinnell

Well, the visit to our villages I don't think was very much of a significant event. I've heard some things from the tribal members I've talked to that Lewis and Clark, the whole party, was pretty aromatic, I guess you might say. Here was a party of thirty to forty men working day and night trying to move these boats upriver and obviously wouldn't have time to bath. They stank; they didn't smell very good. It rings true to me, you know, men being what they are, they don't really concern themselves with it and a dip in the Missouri River isn't going to wash that smell away; it might even add to it a little.

The Hidatsa saw them coming upriver; they had just come from the Sioux camps where they had had some skirmishes. Apparently some rivals were shot, so obviously the Lewis and Clark expedition was adopting the best-offense-is-a-good-defense policy. They showed all their military might, shooting off their air gun, and that didn't sit well with the Hidatsa leadership, who made the comment that they are shooting off their ammunition and wasting it when they should share.

Tillie Walker

I think anything you read about us has been written by a white man. If you looked at the Lewis and Clark journals you would not realize there were villages with woman and children, grandpas and grandmas, aunts, and mothers and fathers. That is really missing and that is the part that of our story we need to tell. These were communities that had been built and had been developed by the Mandan people and the Hidatsa people. There was no one that came and said you have to have this Constitution; they built a society that really cared about each other. They cared about the children; they cared about the elderly. They had a process that took care of those needs and that is the part that I feel is missing.

The family was never part of the journals at all. Somehow they have all of these stories of these women walking and carrying large loads of corn. It looked like they were slaves with the men walking in front. Well, the men were standing in front to protect; if they were carrying the corn and somebody ambushed them they would all be dead. Those men were the protectors of the village and the family. The corn belonged to the woman of the household. They were going to trade; the men weren't going to trade, *they* were going trade. It was the woman who owned everything. They owned the homes and they owned the gardens. When you read the journals you don't get that story.

Calvin Grinnell, filmed interview by Sally Thompson, Fort Berthold Reservation, North Dakota, September 4, 2003; Tillie Walker, filmed interview by Sally Thompson, Fort Berthold Reservation, North Dakota, September 3, 2003.

CHAPTER EIGHT

Trading for Horses and Finding Their Way, August–September 1805

By the end of the summer of 1805, the Corps of Discovery had struggled past the Great Falls of the Missouri and entered the labyrinth of peaks and valleys that marked their entry into the eastern slopes of the Rocky Mountains. The Americans were beginning the most dangerous segment of their journey. With mounting dread they realized the Rockies were like no other mountain range they had ever seen. Instead of neat ridges separating eastern and western slopes, the explorers discovered immense snow-capped peaks separating valleys that ran in every direction. The weather was turning cold and there was no clear path to the west.

Thanks to a fantastic stroke of luck—and Sekakawea's assistance—the Americans befriended a band of Shoshones who happened to be led by the woman's brother, Cameahwait. Beseiged by hostile—and well-armed—Indian neighbors, the Shoshones eagerly traded horses and directions for the Americans' goods. But Cameahwait and his kinsmen were impatient, eager to leave for their fall hunt in the buffalo country. They agreed to help the Americans through Lemhi Pass in modern Idaho and to leave them an elderly guide named Toby, but they quickly turned back toward the Plains. They left the Americans heading north into the Bitterroot Valley, near modern Missoula, Montana. The expedition's success was far from assured. The explorers needed horses and directions. And time was running short. On September 5 they met a part of Salish hunters and their families. The group was riding a magnificent collection of horses.

William Clark's journal entry for September 5, 1805, describes the Americans' formal meeting with the Salish hunting party. (Clark referred to the Salish erroneously as "Flatheads.") Clark reports that English communication was translated successively into French, Hidatsa, Shoshone, and Salish. Responses followed a similar five-step process and required "so many different languages" that "we therefore proceeded to the more intelligible language of presents." Clark reported "buying" eleven "elegant" horses from the Salish in exchange for seven of the group's worn out ponies and "a few articles of merchandise." Sergeant Ordway noted that they now had "40 good pack horses." But clear directions remained a concern.

September 3

A Cloudy morning, horses verry Stiff Sent 2 men back with the horse on which Capt Lewis rode for the load left back last night which detained us untill 8 oClock at which time we Set out. The Country is timbered with Pine Generally the bottoms have a variety of Srubs & the fur trees in Great abundance. hills high & rockey on each Side, in the after part of the day the high mountains closed the Creek on each Side and obliged us to take on the Steep Sides of those Mountains, So Steep that the horses Could Screcly keep from Slipping down, Several Sliped & Injured themselves verry much, with great dificuelty we made miles & Encamped on a branh of the Creek we assended after Crossing Several Steep points & one mountain, but little to eate I killed 5 Pheasents & The huntes 4 with a little Corn afforded us a kind of Supper, at dusk it began to Snow (& rain) at 3 oClock Some rain. The (last) mountains (we had) to the East Covered with Snow. we met with a great misfortune, in haveing our last Thmometer broken by accident, This day we passed over emence hils and Some of the worst roade that ever horses passed our horses frequently fell (Country a) Snow about 2 inches deep when it began to rain which termonated in a Sleet (killed Seven) our genl. Courses nearly North from the R.

September 4

A verry cold morning every thing wet and frosed, we detained untill 8 oClock to thaw the covering for the baggage &c. &c. groun covered with Snow, we assended a mountain & took a Divideing ridge which we kept for Several

Miles & fell on the head of a Creek which appeared to run the Course we wished to go, I was in front, & Saw Several of the Argalia or Ibex decended the mountain by verry Steep decent takeing the advantage of the points and best places to the Creek, where our hunter killed a Deer which we made use of and prosued our Course down the Creek to the forks about 5 miles where we met a part of the (*Flat head*) nation of 33 Lodges about 80 men 400 Total and at least 500 horses, those people recved us friendly, threw white robes over our Sholders & Smoked in the pipes of peace, we Encamped with them & found them friendly but nothing but berries to eate a part of which they gave us, those Indians are well dressed with Skin Shirts & robes, they Stout & light complected more So than Common for Indians, The Chiefs harangued untill late at night, Smoked our pipe and appeared Satisfied. I was the first white man who ever wer on the waters of this river.

September 5

A Cloudy morning we assembled the Chiefs & warriers and Spoke to them (with much dificuely as what we Said had to pass through Several languajes before it got in to theirs, which is a gugling kind of languaje Spoken much thro the Throught) we informed them who we were, where we Came from, where bound and for what purpose &c. &c. and requsted to purchase & exchange a fiew horses with them, in the Course of the day I purchased 11 horses & exchanged 7 for which we gave a fiew articles of merchendize. those people possess ellegant horses.—we made 4 Chiefs whome we gave meadels & a few Small articles with Tobacco; the women brought us a few berries & roots to eate and the Principal Chief a Dressed Brarow, otter & two Goat & antilope Skins.

Those people wore their hair (as follows) the men Cewed with otter Skin on each Side falling over the Sholrs forward, the women loose promisquisly over ther Sholdrs & face long Shirts which Coms to the anckles & tied with a belt about their waste with a roabe over, the have but fiew ornaments and what they do were are Similar to the Snake Indians, They Call themselves Eoote-lash-Schute and consist of 450 Lodges in all and divided into Several bands on the heads of Columbia river & Missouri, Some low down the Columbia River.

September 6

Some little rain, purchased two fine horses & took a Vocabiliary of the language litened our loads & packed up, rained contd. untill (2) 12 oClock we

Set out at 2 oClock at the Same time all the Indians Set out on Ther way to meet the Snake Indians at the 3 forks of the Missouri. Crossed a Small river from the right we call Soon after Setting out, also a Small Creek from the North all three forks Comeing together below our Camp at which place the Mountains Close on each Side of the river, We proceeded on N 30 W. Crossed a Mountain and Struck the river Several miles down, at which place the Indians had Encamped two days before, we Proceeded on Down the River which is 30 yds. wide Shallow & Stoney. Crossing it Several times & Encamped in a Small bottom on the right side. rained this evening nothing to eate but berries, our flour out, and but little Corn, the hunters killed 2 pheasents only—all our horses purchased of the (flat heads) oote lash Shutes we Secured well for fear of their leaveing of us, and watched them all night for fear of their leaving us or the Indians prosuing & Steeling them.

"Down the Lolo Trail," in *The Journals of the Lewis and Clark Expedition,* ed. Gary Moulton (Lincoln: University of Nebraska Press, 1987), vol. 5, 185–90.

SERGEANT JOHN ORDWAY ON THE SALISH

Perhaps because he was aware of how much the men were suffering from the mountain cold and how worried they were about the path forward, Sergeant Ordway was more descriptive than Clark (and more grateful to the Indians) in his journal entry.

September 3

We Set out as usal, and proceeded on up the branch a Short distance further up the branch then took the mountain and went up and down rough rockey mountains all day. Some places So Steep and rockey that Some of the horses fell backwards and roled to the bottom. [one] horse was near being killed. crossed a nomber of fine Spring branches. Some places obludged to cut a road for to git along thro thickets &C. Some of the balsom fir trees on the branches are about 100 and fifty feet high, and Strait. . . . we dined at a branch eat the last of our pork &.C. Some of the men threaten to kill a colt to eat they being hungry, but puts it off untill tomorrow noon hopeing the hunters will kill Some game. towards evening we assended a mountain went Some distance on the top of it then went down in to a cave near the head of a branch running nearly an opposite course from the branch we dined on at noon. We Camped in this cove. Several Small Showers of rain. So we lay down wet hungry and cold came with much fatiguc 11 miles this day.

September 4

The morning clear, but very cold, the ground covred with frost. our mockasons froze. the mountains covred with Snow. a mountain Sheep Seen by one of the men who was a hunting the horses. we delayed untill about 8 oClock A. M. then thoughed our Sailes by the fire to cover the loads and Set out. ascended the mountain on to the dividing ridge and followed it Some time. the Snow over our mockasons in places. we had nothing but a little pearched corn to eat the air on the mountains verry chilley and cold. our fingers aked with the cold proceeded on descended the mountain down a rough way passed through a large thicket of pine and balsom fer timber in which we killed a dozen partridges or fesents. went down in to a valley on a branch running on about a north course and halted. our hunter killed a deer on which we dined. our guide and the young Indian who accompanied him eat the verry guts of the deer. Saw fresh Sign of Indians. proceeded on down this valley towards evening we arived at a large encampment of the flat head nation of Indians about 40 lodges and I Suppose about 30 persons, and they have between 4 or 5 hundred horses now feeding in the plains at our view and they look like tollarable good horses the most of them, they received us in a friendly manner. when our officers went to their lodges they gave them each a white robe of dressed skins, and spread them over their Shoulders and put their arms around our necks instead of Shakeing hands as that is their way they appeared glad to See us. they Smoaked with us, then gave us a pleanty Such as they had to eat, which was only Servis berrys and cheeries pounded and dryed in Small cakes. Some roots of different kinds. our officers told them that we would Speak to them tomorrow and tell th[em] who we were and what our business is and where we are going &C. these natives are well dressed, descent looking Indians. light complectioned. they are dressed in mo Sheep leather Deer & buffalow robes &C. they have the most curious language of any we have Seen before. they talk as though they lisped or have a bur on their tongue. we Suppose that they are the welch Indians if their is any Such from the language. they have leather lodges to live in Some other Skins among them. they tell us that they or Some of them have Seen bearded men towards the ocean, but they cannot give us any accurate of the ocean but we have 4 mountains to cross to go where they saw white men which was on a river as we suppose the Columbian River. came miles to day and pitched our Camp near the creek on the right of the Indian Lodges. considerable of large pitch pine timber in this valley our hunter killed another Deer this evening.—

September 5

A clear cool morning. the Standing water froze a little. the Indian dogs are so ravinous that they eat Several pair of the mens Moccasons. a hard white frost this morning. Several men went out to hunt our officers purchased Several horses of the natives after Counsiling with them. they are a band of the Flat head Nation our officers made four chiefs gave them meddles 2 flags Some other Small presents and told them our business and that we were friends to all the red people &C. which they appeared verry friendly to us. they have a great stock of horses but have no provision only roots and berrys, at this time but are on their way to the Meddison River or Missourie whire they can kill pleanty of buffalow. our officers bought 12 horses from them and gave a Small quantity of Marchandize for each horse. our officers took down Some of their language found it verry troublesome Speaking to them as all they Say to them has to go through Six languages, and hard to make them understand. these natives have the Stranges language of any we have ever yet Seen. they appear to us as though they had an Impedement in their Speech or brogue on their tongue. we think perhaps that they are the welch Indians, &C. they are the likelyest and honestest we have seen and are verry friendly to us. they Swaped to us Some of their good horses and took our worn out horses, and appeared to wish to help us as much as lay in their power. accommodated us with pack Saddles and chords by our giving them any Small article in return [towa]rds evening our hunters came in had kild 1 deer.

September 6

A clear cold morning, we packed up our baggage the natives got up their horses also and Struck their Lodges in order to Set out for the Missourie. we have now got 40 good pack horses and three Colts. four hunters were furnished horses without loads in order to hunt constant. about 1 oClock we Set out again on our journey. the natives Set out at the Same time for the Missourie we proceeded on soon crossed a large creek in this valley then Soon took the mountains. one of the hunters left us. we went over a Mountain about 7 miles and descended down the Mountain on a creek and Camped. eat a little parched corn. light Sprinkling of rain, through the course of this day—

"Ordway: Across the Rockies," in *The Journals of the Lewis and Clark Expedition,* ed. Gary Moulton (Lincoln: University of Nebraska Press, 1987), vol. 9, 217–20.

CHAPTER NINE

Rescued by the Nez Perces

Despite their fresh mounts and new directions, the explorers encountered bad weather and mounting danger in the weeks following their meeting with the Salish. Captain Lewis stopped writing in his journal (he was silent from September 10 to September 18) and Clark scouted ahead for a clear trail. "From this mountain," Clark wrote on September 15, "I could observe high rugged mountains in every direction as far as I could see." The next day it began to snow. On September 18 Clark and a few men broke off from the main party to search for food. But two days later his small group suddenly found itself in "level pine country." The men had arrived at Weippe Prairie, in modern Idaho, a camas-digging site visited each fall by Nez Perces and other Indians. Clark saw three young boys and gave them presents. Soon a man came to greet them; he took them to a "large spacious lodge," where "great numbers of women gathered around me with much apparent signs of fear." They were served "buffalo meat, dried salmon, berries and roots in different states." Luckily, the expedition had encountered another group interested in forging alliances with well-armed strangers.

WILLIAM CLARK ON HIS ENCOUNTER WITH THE NEZ PERCES

Clark's description of the days prior to his meeting with the Nez Perces carried a sense of desperation. The Americans pressed on as the weather worsened and their trail grew harded and harder to follow. Finally on September 20, Clark discovered the Nez Perce root gatherers. Clark began distributing presents almost as soon as he stumbled

*onto Weippe Prairie. His hosts responded by feeding their guests. Soon a male "chief"
invited them to his lodge, later taking Clark to the camp of Twisted Hair. Clark's
host drew him a map of the river system leading to the Pacific. The Nez Perces showed
the Americans a stand of pine that could be used for making dugout canoes. Within
a few days, expedition members were hard at work on these vessels. When they set off
down river on October 7, Twisted Hair was with them. Within a month, the Americans reached the Pacific.*

September 20

I Set out early and proceeded on through a Countrey as ruged as uial passcd
over a low mountain into the forks of a large Creek which I kept down 2 miles
and assended a Steep mountain leaveing the Creek to our left hand passed
the head of Several dreans on a divideing ridge, and at 12 miles decended the
mountain to a leavel pine Countrey proceeded on through a butifull Countrey
for three miles to a Small Plain in which I found maney Indian lodges, at the
distance of 1 mile from the lodges I met 3 boys, when they Saw me ran and
hid themselves searched . . . found gave them Small pieces of ribin & Sent
them forward to the village a man Came out to meet me with great Caution
& Conducted (me) us to a large Spacious Lodge which he told me (by Signs)
was the Lodge of his great Chief who had Set out 3 days previous with all the
Warricrs of the nation to war on a South West derection & would return in 15 or
18 days. the fiew men that were left in the Village aged, grcat numbers of women
geathered around me with much apparent Signs of fear, and apr. pleased they
(those people) gave us a Small piece of Buffalow meat, Some dried Salmon
beries & roots in different States, Some round and much like an onion which
they call (*Pas she co*) quamash the Bread or Cake is called Pas-she-co Sweet,
of this they make bread & Supe. they also gave us the bread made of this root
all of which we eate hartily, I gave them a fiew Small articles as preasents, and
proceeded on with a Chief to his Village 2 miles in the Same Plain, where we
were treated kindly in their way and continued with them all night Those two
Villages consist of about 30 double lodges, but fiew men a number of women
& children; They call themselves *Cho pun-nish* or *Pierced Noses;* their dialect
appears verry different from the (flat heads) Tushapaws altho origneally the
Same people. They are darker than the (Flat heads) Tushapaws (I have seen)
Their dress Similar, with more beads white & blue principally, brass & Copper
in different forms, Shells and ware their haire in the Same way. thcy are large
Portley men Small women & handsom fetued (featured) Emence quantity of

the quawmash or *Pas-shi-co* root gathered & in piles about the plains, those roots grow much an onion in marshey places the seed are in triangular Shell on the Stalk. they Sweat them in the following manner i.e. dig a large hole 3 feet deep Cover the bottom with Split wood on the top of which they lay Small Stones of about 3 or 4 Inches thick, a Second layer of Splited wood & Set the whole on fire which heats the Stones, after the fire is extinguished they lay grass & mud mixed on the Stones, on that dry grass which Supports the Pâsh-Shi-co root a thin Coat of the Same grass is laid on the top, a Small fire is kept when necessary in the Center of the kile &c.

I find myself verry unwell all the evening from eateing the fish & roots too freely. Sent out the hunters they killed nothing Saw Some Signs of deer.

"William Clark on His Encounter with the Nez Perces," in *The Journals of the Lewis and Clark Expedition,* ed. Gary Moulton (Lincoln: University of Nebraska Press, 1987), vol. 5, 219–25.

WOTOLLEN TELLS OF RED BEAR
Lucullus McWhorter

A Nez Perce story recorded a century after the explorers' first visit places Clark's description of hospitality and diplomacy in a different light. In the early twentieth century, Wotollen, a grandson of one of the chiefs who played host to Clark, explained that when the Americans suddenly arrived, an elder woman named Watkuweis had urged her leaders not to hurt them. The story of her effort appears here.

Among the tribal notables who canoed down the Clearwater to meet Lewis and Clark where Lewiston, Idaho, now stands, was Hohots Ilppilp [Red Grizzly Bear], in time abbreviated to Red Bear. Wotollen [Hair Combed Over Eyes], a grandson of this renowned warrior, chief, and prophet, contributed the following, his son, Many Wounds, interpreting.

Red Grizzly Bear was a chief famous among the tribes. His bravery as a warrior was attested by the eighty wounds he carried, received in battles. From these scars, in later years, he was known as Many Wounds. He knew and took part in all the wars of his day. Always a leader, when foraying he went ahead of his band; no one ever traveled in front of him.

Whether night or day, on foot or on horseback (I cannot explain the mystery) some kind of foresight was with him. Even if an enemy were at a distance and invisible, Many Wounds would drop into a trance of prophecy, and while thus sleeping he beheld all enemies passing before him. Everything pertaining to the enemies: the kind to be met, whether the meeting would be that same sun or the next, the number of scalps that would be taken and the kind of horses they would secure. This happened a number of times. Of most wonderful strength, he used principally his right hand and arm in battle. He was known everywhere west of the great mountains [Rockies] even to the big waters [Pacific].

Chief Red Bear first learned of white people through a girl of his band living on Tamonmo.[1] When small she was stolen by the Blacklegs in the buffalo country, who sold her to some tribe farther toward the sunrise. In time she was bought by white people, probably in Canada, where she was well treated. It is a long story; how in time, carrying her little baby, she ran away and after several moons reached the friendly Selish, who cared for her and brought her in a dying condition to her own people at White Bird. Her baby had died on the way. She was called Watkuweis [Returned from a Faraway Country].

She told of the white people, how good they had been to her, and how well she liked them. When the first two white men, Lewis and Clark with their followers, came, Watkuweis said to her people, "These are the people who helped me! Do them no hurt!"

This was why the strange people had been received in friendship.[2] There had been a prophecy about Red Bear and a new people, which was thus fulfilled in 1805. He met the strangers. They first have a smoke. If no smoke, then they must fight. Red Bear made presents of dressed buckskins, and they gave him beads and a few other articles. They afterwards found the white man's gifts to be cheap.

The canoes made by Lewis and Clark to descend the Snake and Columbia rivers were made from five yellow pine trees given them for the purpose by Chief Walammottinin [Hair or Forelock Bunched and Tied]. The explorers first met him when fishing in the Kooskooskie Smaller River, now the Clearwater. It was in this chieftain's care that they left their horses and cached goods, all of which they found in the best of condition upon their return the following year.

After visiting the explorers, Red Bear returned to his home near the mouth of White Bird Creek, Salmon River. When he died, he left good council, good instructions for his people. The whites owe honor to his memory.

My father, Chief Black Eagle, was the son of Chief Red Bear, Sr., who met Lewis and Clark. I am his grandson. I have seen one hundred and four snows [1926].

Chief Red Bear, most famed of his generation and the youngest of six brothers, grew up under the rigorous, Spartanlike schooling universal among the tribes. From the time he was about ten years of age, he swam across the Salmon River and back (at a point a short distance above the mouth of the White Bird), every morning—for five consecutive winters.[3] Wotollen continued:

It was during the days of youthful training and development that Red Bear went on foot to Slate Creek[4] to look for flint arrowheads where there had been fighting. It was morning and he stayed until late evening. Starting for home he had gone a good distance when it grew dark. He lay down by the trail and slept. In a dream he beheld a great, bloodstained grizzly bear approaching. Awakening, he sprang to his feet, but no bear was to be seen. Silently he resumed his buffalo robe and dozed off, only to be aroused a second time by the same fearful vision, which vanished as he leaped erect. He again lay down and as he drowsed the monster bear appeared for the third time. This time the boy did not awaken entirely, and a voice spoke to him:

"Do not be afraid. You see my body. Blood is all over it. When you become a man, when you go to war and do fighting, you shall receive many wounds. Wounds shall cover your body. Blood like this from my body will course down your limbs. But you will not die. After these wars, and fights, because of your wounds and bloodstains people will call you *Hohots Ilppilp* [Red Grizzly Bear]."

When this boy had grown to young manhood, and had received arrow and spear wounds in battle, he told his father and the people about seeing the blood-reddened grizzly bear, and what it had said to him. From that time he was known as Red Bear, and was made a chief. He was a strong brave warrior.

After taking his name the new chief never used a gun in battle. There were only a few fire-rock [flintlock] guns, and ammunition was scarce. He had a club made from the hard heavy syringa found growing along the canyon streams. It was nearly arm's length, and entirely unlike the stub-handled, stone-headed war club of the foot warriors. With this tied to his wrist by a thong loop, he would rush into battle. The Bannocks all learned to know and fear him.

At one time when going up Little Salmon, at a place now called Biggins, he discovered a war band of Snake or Bannock Indians coming toward him on the trail. There was a small creek with large rocks intervening. He hid his gun and secreting himself, he waited the advance of the hated enemy. They were out for fighting or stealing horses. When they drew near, Red Bear sprang from hiding and downed the foremost warrior before his presence was fully known. In the confusion he killed others of the startled foe, who recognizing their unconquerable enemy, swam the Little Salmon to safety.

Other similar exploits are also ascribed to Red Bear. He bore eighty distinct scars received in conflict, from which, in later years, he was known as Many Wounds. In comparison, the great Chief Red Cloud of the Sioux had to his credit eighty coups for as many distinctive deeds of personal valor in battle.[5]

Such was the "Bloody Chief," who spoke in council with Dr. Elijah White, first United States Indian agent to enter the Pacific Northwest, taking office in 1842. Of this Nez Perce chieftain Dr. White says:

Soon the Bloody Chief arose—not less than ninety years old—and said: "I speak today, perhaps tomorrow I die. I am the oldest chief of the tribe; was the chief chief when your great brothers, Lewis and Clark, visited this country. They visited me, and honored me with their friendship and counsel. I showed them my numerous wounds received in bloody battle with the Snakes; they told me it was not good, it was better to be at peace; gave me a flag of truce; I held it up high; we met and talked. We never fought again. Clark pointed to this day, to you and this occasion; we have long waited in expectation; I can say no more; I am quickly tired; my voice and limbs tremble. I am glad to live to see you and this day, but I shall soon be still and quiet in death."[6]

Red Grizzly Bear, whose name appears twelfth in the list of the signers of the Treaty of Walla-Walla, June 11, 1855, there spelled "Ha-ha Still-pilp," was a son of the senior Chief Red Bear, or Many Wounds, the "Bloody Chief" of Dr. White's council. The eldest son of Red Bear was Koolkooltom, Sr., Selish for "Red Arrow Point." He was a mighty warrior and a great prophet. He led in fights against the Cheyennes in particular. Another son, Koolkooltom, Jr., lived at White Bird and was wealthy in cattle. Not a warrior, but a prophet, he inherited his father's mantle. He died on the Salmon River before the 1855 Treaty. His son, who took his illustrious grandfather's name, was a scout for General Howard against his own tribe in the conquest of 1877, but he did not enlist under his ancestral name. Blacktail Eagle, who will figure in these pages, was the youngest son of Red Bear, Sr.

Notes

1. *Tamonmo:* ancient name of the Salmon River, meaning "unknown."

2. The seriousness with which the Watkuweis story is accepted by responsible members of the Nez Perce tribe is amply attested in the following contribution by Many Wounds, May 7, 1930:

"In the buffalo days a girl was missing from a Nez Perce hunting camp in Montana. In after snows, when she came back to her own people, she told her story to Chief Red Bear, to whose band she belonged. Told how she was sold by an enemy people to a different tribe, where she was a slave. Then she was sold to white people, who kept her as one of their own kind. This story soon spread through all the Nez Perce nation.

"Our oral history says that she received a baby, then escaped to return to her own country. When about halfway on the trail, the baby died and she buried it. She was by blood a Bannock but was reared as a Nez Perce from before her memory. She was given the name *watkuweis* which means "returned" (from being lost).

"She told history about the whites and every Nez Perce listened on that day. Told how the white people were good to her, treated her with kindness. Her story opened much friendship for the future. It was worth good to both whites and Indians.

"That is why the Nez Perces never made harm to the Lewis and Clark people in 1805. We ought to have a monument to her in this far West. She saved much for the white race.

"I feel proud about her. I should call her peacemaker between Indian race and white race! We must remember her fine qualities and wonderful long trip only to die at home."

The following comment was made by interpreter War Singer. "*Watkuweis* means any person or domestic animal that returns from a different district or country. Thus *watkuweis* or *watkuese* means 'returned from a far country.' She called the whites, *Allimah* [From Near Water]. This was because they had first come in boats from the sea, as she had learned in Canada. Thus Watkuweis saved the lives of those early white explorers at the Weippe. She told her people that the whites had given her good treatment after she was sold to them."

For similar versions of the foregoing see Kate C. McBeth, *The Nez Perce since Lewis and Clark* (New York: F. H. Revell, 1908), 24–25. Also, Eliza Spalding Warren, *Memoirs of the West* (Portland, 1917), 7.

3. Five is a mystic number in the Dreamer religious cult.

4. *Eausninma* is the Nez Perce name of Slate Creek, Idaho. *Eaus* is an old term almost forgotten by the tribe. Ninety-four-year-old (1986) Phillip Evans says it means the oar or pole used in poling boats, not the flat oar.

5. F. W. Hodge, ed., *Handbook of American Indians North of Mexico,* Bulletin 30, Bureau of American Ethnology, Smithsonian Institution (Washington, D.C.: Government Printing Office, 1907), II, 359.

6. A. J. Allen, *Ten Years in Oregon: Travels of Doctor E. White and Lady* (Ithaca, N.Y., 1850), 185.

"Wotollen Tells of Red Bear," in Lucullus McWhorter, *Hear Me, My Chiefs!* (Caldwell, Idaho: Caxton Printers, 1952), 16–24.

ASPECTS OF NEZ PERCE CULTURE: LANGUAGE, TERRITORY, AND THE ANNUAL CYCLE

Deward E. Walker

The century between the arrival of the American strangers and Wotollen's retelling of that arrival was a time of immense change for the Nez Perces. American goods often eased the burdens of daily life for many of the explorers' trade partners, yet they eroded cultural signposts such as language, territories, and seasonal living. The Nez Perce language is rooted in the ancient Sahaptian language, indigenous to the Columbia Basin. The Nez Perces have been anthropologically divided by dialect into upper and lower divisions. The immense diversity of vegetation and game in their homelands provided them with an abundance of goods for centuries. This diversity increased with the introduction of the horse after 1700.

Language

Nez Perce (nez'pərs) is closely related to Sahaptin (Rigsby 1965; Aoki 1963) in the Sahaptian language grouping that dominates the southern Plateau. Neither historical linguistics nor archeological research (Leonhardy and Rice 1970) has produced evidence that the Sahaptians have ever resided outside the Columbia Basin. Existing research shows only that they are ancient dwellers of the Columbia Basin with possible external connections to the Penutian superfamily (Swadesh 1956).

Territory

Nez Perce territory centered on the middle Snake and Clearwater rivers and the northern portion of the Salmon River basin in central Idaho and adjacent Oregon and Washington. In 1800 there were over 70 permanent villages ranging from 30 to 200 individuals, depending on the season and type of social grouping (Walker 1958–64). About 300 total sites have been identified, including both camps and villages (Schwede 1970).

The Nez Perce have been divided into Upper and Lower divisions, primarily on dialect grounds. The Upper Nez Perce were oriented more toward a Plains lifeway. The Nez Perce are also very closely related linguistically, culturally, and socially to the Sahaptin speakers of Oregon and Washington, including the Palouse, Walla Walla, Yakama, Umatilla, and Wayampam, and with them form an intertribal ceremonial congregation (Anastasio 1972).

Their territory was marked by a diverse flora and fauna, as well as by temperature and precipitation patterns reflecting sharp variations in elevation. The deep canyons cut by the Clearwater, Salmon, and Snake rivers encouraged seasonal subsistence migrations, a pattern typical of other Plateau tribes (Marshall 1977; Walker 1987).

Annual Cycle

Large game animals taken by the Nez Perce included elk, deer, moose, mountain sheep, and goat, as well as black and grizzly bear. After obtaining the horse (after 1700), the Nez Perce made annual trips to Montana to secure bison and to engage in trade and various other forms of exchange. Smaller game animals were taken as needed, including rabbit, squirrel, badger, and marmot. Birds taken included ducks, geese, grouse, sage hens, and birds of prey for ceremonial reasons. The Nez Perce were fortunate in having numerous anadromous fish and many streams well suited for fishing. With their complex fishing technology, they took the chinook, coho, chum, and sockeye varieties of salmon; dolly varden, cutthroat, lake, and steel-head varieties of trout; several kinds of suckers; whitefish; sturgeon; lampreys; and squawfish. Their average per capita consumption of fish is estimated at over 500 pounds per annum (Walker 1967).

In the early spring when the cache pits had been emptied of stored food, the Nez Perce began their communal drives in the river valleys, with snowshoe hunting in deep snow and trips by canoe down the Snake and Columbia rivers to intercept the early salmon runs. Although hunting was fundamental and continuous, it was of lesser importance during the seasons of salmon runs when all able-bodied adults turned to fishing where many thousands of pounds were customarily caught and processed (Walker 1967). As the spring progressed, salmon began arriving in Nez Perce territory, and the early root crops were taken at lower elevations.

Men were the principal fishermen, but women assisted in splitting, drying, and storing the fish. Hook and line, spears, harpoons, dip nets, traps, and weirs were all used in various ways (Walker 1967). Large traps and weirs were usually constructed communally by villages and regulated by a fishing specialist who regulated the fishing and divided the catch. Weirs and traps, constructed close to winter villages, often were located on smaller lateral streams. Salmon were also speared and netted from canoes and dipping platforms on the major tributaries. Fish were mostly sun-dried and smoked for winter storage, while the more succulent parts were consumed immediately.

Roots in higher areas such as Weippe did not often ripen until mid-August (Harbinger 1964). The basic root staple was camas, but bitterroot, couse, wild carrot, and wild onion were also important. Fruits gathered included serviceberries, gooseberries, hawthorn berries, thornberries, huckleberries, currants, and chokecherries. Pine nuts, sunflower seeds, and black moss added to the abundant vegetable and fruit inventory of gathered foods.

By midsummer the Nez Perce would typically leave their villages in the lower river valleys and move into the highlands where later-growing crops were harvested, highland streams fished, and hunting intensified. The fall salmon runs, fall hunting, and gathering of late root and berry crops provided winter food stores, and brief bison hunting trips into Montana over the Lolo and other passes augmented winter supplies of meat. Hunting forays into Montana usually included members of neighboring tribes such as the Umatilla, Cayuse, and Yakama and were led by warriors (Anastasio 1972). Some Nez Perce groups would stay in the Plains for several years at a time, and few winters passed that did not see some Nez Perce wintering with the neighboring Flathead. By November most travel ceased, and the Nez Perce settled into their winter villages until the cycle began again in the early spring (Walker 1973:56).

Deer and elk were taken communally by encirclement methods similar to those used by many other tribes. Decoys and scarecrows were used to entice them into areas where they could be easily dispatched. Fire and horses were employed in driving deer and elk into traps. A variant of the lake entrapment used by other tribes consisted of driving deer and elk into larger rivers where they could be easily dispatched from canoes and from horseback. The ambush was a popular hunting method, especially in prehorse days when it was used for bison by pedestrian Nez Perce hunters in Montana. Deadfalls were popular for larger game as were snares for birds and smaller game. There is some evidence for use of rattlesnake poison on arrow tips in certain types of hunting (Walker 1973:56).

Women dug roots with crutch-handled digging sticks. Some wooden containers were made, but coiled basketry was the major form of container. Food was stored in baskets in bark and grass-lined cache pits located on well-drained hillsides and in parfleche bags. Some horn spoons and drinking cups were made, but most spoons and bowls were of wood. Distinctive stone pestles were used with both basketry (with a stone base) and wooden mortars, primarily to grind meat and roots. Splitting wedges were made of antler. Club and ax heads were of stone hafted with a combination of antler, wood, and rawhide. Bows were made of syringa and yew, frequently backed with sinew.

Roots and meats were boiled in baskets by stone-boiling and baked in large earthen ovens. Generally, meat was broiled by attaching it to a wooden frame or to sticks inserted in the ground around an open fire. Roots were crushed and formed into loaves and biscuits for storage and later eaten in soups and stews.

References

Anastasio, Angelo. 1972. "The Southern Plateau: An Ecological Analysis of Inter-group Relations." *Northwest Anthropological Research Notes* 6 (2): 109–229.

Aoki, Haruo. 1963. "On Sahaptian-Klamath Linguistic Affiliations." *International Journal of American Linguistics* 29 (2): 107–12.

Harbinger, Lucy. 1964. "The Importance of the Food Plants in the Maintenance of Nez Perce Cultural Identity." M.A. thesis, Washington State University, Pullman.

Leonhardy, Frank C., and David G. Rice. 1970. "A Proposed Culture Typology for the Snake River Region, Southeastern Washington." *Northwest Anthropological Research Notes* 4 (1): 1–29.

Marshall, Alan G. 1977. "Nez Perce Social Groups: An Ecological Interpretation." Ph.D. diss., Washington State University.

Rigsby, Bruce. 1965. "Linguistic Relations in the Southern Plateau," Ph.D. diss., University of Oregon, Eugene.

Schwede, Madge. 1970. "The Relationship of Aboriginal Nez Perce Settlement Patterns to Physical Environment and to General Distribution of Food Resources." *Northwest Anthropological Research Notes* 4 (2): 129–36.

Swadesh, Morris. 1956. "Problems of Long-Range Comparison in Penutian." *Language* 32 (1): 17–41.

Walker, Deward E. Jr. 1958–64. Nez Perce Field Notes. Manuscripts in D. Walker's possession.

——. 1967. "Mutual Cross-Utilization of Economic Resources in the Plateau: An Example from Aboriginal Nez Perce Fishing Practices." In *Washington State University, Laboratory of Anthropology, Report of Investigations* 1.

——. 1973. *American Indians of Idaho.* Volume 1: *Aboriginal Cultures.* Anthropological Monographs of the University of Idaho 2. Moscow, Idaho.

——. 1987. "Native Americans and Cultural Impact Analysis: The Proposed Nuclear Waste Repository at Hanford." *Proceedings of the Symposium on Waste Management,* vol. 1 (Tucson: University of Arizona, College of Engineering and Mines).

"Nez Perce," in *Handbook of North American Indians,* ed. Deward E. Walker (Washington, D.C.: Smithsonian Institution Press, 1998), vol. 12, 420–21.

CHAPTER 10

New Year's Day 1806 and the Oregon Winter

During the winter following their arrival on the Oregon coast, the expedition's commanders grew increasingly worried about completing their mission. Although President Jefferson had told them that they might meet American or British ships once they arrived on the Pacific Coast, none appeared. The company was nearly out of supplies and, worse, the captains were unsuccessful in bargaining with the local Chinook-speaking Clatsops, who were savvy traders (British and Canadian merchants were already regular visitors to the area, so the Americans' merchandise had little appeal). The enlisted men spent too much time socializing with the Indians. Supplies, particularly of the trade goods the captains needed for trading with local Indians, were getting low. And the damp weather was unfamiliar and difficult.

While the rising tensions at the American headquarters had many sources, the most important was the Corps of Discovery's lack of knowledge about the Chinook-speaking communities clustered along the Columbia and its tributaries. Connected both to coastal communities and to inland peoples in modern Oregon and Washington, the Chinooks were accomplished traders and diplomats. They had established regular ties to Europeans beginning about a generation before the Americans' arrival on the coast. By 1805, these people were regularly exchanging guns, iron pots, and other metal goods for sea otter pelts destined for sale in China. They were not particularly impressed by the company of hungry and impoverished U.S. soldiers.

MERIWETHER LEWIS ISSUES NEW ORDERS

On New Year's Day 1806, Captain Lewis issued a new set of general orders: the gates to the Americans' compound—"Fort Clatsop"—would close at sunset and all Indians would be "put out of the fort." Indians who became "troublesome" at any time would be removed. Everyone would take a turn at guard duty. And anyone who traded or gave away government property would be "tried and punished." The "frolicking" at Fort Mandan was now long forgotten.

Fort Clatsop, January 1st 1806

The fort being now completed, the Commanding officers think proper to direct: that the guard shall as usual consist of one Sergeant and three privates, and that the same be regularly relieved each morning at sunrise. The post of the new guard shall be in the room of the Sergeants rispectivly commanding the same. the centinel shall be posted, both day and night, on the parade in front of the commanding offercers quarters; tho' should he at any time think proper to remove himself to any other part of the fort, in order the better to inform himself of the desighns or approach of any party of savages, he is not only at liberty, but is hereby required to do so. It shall be the duty of the centinel also to announce the arrival of all parties of Indians to the Sergeant of the Guard, who shall immediately report the same to the Commanding officers.

The Commanding Officers require and charge the Garrison to treat the natives in a friendly manner; nor will they be permitted at any time, to abuse, assault or strike them; unless such abuse assault or stroke be first given by the natives. nevertheless it shall be right for any individual, in a peaceable manner, to refuse admittance to, or put out of his room, any native who may become troublesome to him; and should such native refuse to go when requested, or attempt to enter their rooms after being forbidden to do so; it shall be the duty of the Sergeant of the guard on information of the same, to put such native out of the fort and see that he is not again admitted during that day unless specially permitted; and the Sergeant of the guard may for this purpose imploy such coercive measures (not extending to the taking of life) as shall at his discretion be deemed necessary to effect the same.

When any native shall be detected in theft, the Sergt. of the guard shall immediately inform the Commanding offercers of the same, to the end that such measures may be pursued with rispect to the culprit as they shall think most expedient.

At sunset on each day, the Sergt. attended by the interpreter Charbono and two of his guard, will collect and put out of the fort, all Indians except such as may specially be permitted to remain by the Commanding offercers, nor shall they be again admitted untill the main gate be opened the ensuing morning.

At Sunset, or immediately after the Indians have been dismissed, both Kales shall be shut, and secured, and the main gate locked and continue so untill sunrise the next morning: the water-gate may be used freely by the Garrison for the purpose of passing and repassing at all times, tho' from sunset, untill sunrise, it shall be the duty of the centinel, to open the gate for, and shut it after all persons passing and repassing, suffering the same never to remain unfixed long than is absolutely necessary.

It shall be the duty of the Sergt. of the guard to keep the kee of the Meat house, and to cause the guard to keep regular fires therein when the same may be necessary; and also once at least in 24 hours to visit the canoes and see that they are safely secured; and shall further on each morning after he is relieved, make his report verbally to the Commandg officers.—

Each of the old guard will every morning after being relieved furnish two loads of wood (each) for the commanding offercers fire.

No man is to be particularly exempt from the duty of bringing meat from the woods, nor none except the Cooks and Interpreters from that of mounting guard.

Each mess being furnished with an ax, they are directed to deposit in the room of the commanding offercers all other public tools of which they are possessed; nor (are) shall the same at any time hereafter be taken from the said deposit without the knoledge and permission of the commanding officers; and any individual so borrowing the tools are strictly required to bring the same back the moment he has ceased to use them, and no case shall they be permited to keep them out all night.

Any individual selling or disposing of any tool or iron or steel instrument, arms, accoutrements or ammunicion, shall be deemed guilty of a breach of this order, and shall be tryed and punished accordingly.—the tools loaned to John Shields are excepted from the restrictions of this order.

"At Fort Clatsop," in *The Journals of the Lewis and Clark Expedition,* ed. Gary Moulton (Lincoln: University of Nebraska Press, 1987), vol. 6, 156–58.

These passages reveal some of Captain Lewis's darkest assessments of Native Americans. They were written amidst the gloom and boredom of the Oregon winter and mark a striking counterpoint to the image of stalwart heroism through which we often recall the expedition's commander.

Thursday February 20th 1806

Permited Collins to hunt this morning he returned in the evening unsuccessfull as to the chase but brought with him some cranberries for the sick. Gibson is on the recovery fast; Bratton has an obstinate cough and pain in his back and still appears to be geting weaker. McNeal from his inattention to his disorder has become worse.

This forenoon we were visited by *Tah-cuma* principal Chief of the Chinnooks and 25 men of his nation. we had never seen this chief before his a good looking man of about 50 years of age reather larger in statue than most of his nation; as he came on a friendly visit we gave himself and party some thing to eat and plyed them plentifully with smoke. we gave this cheif a small medal with which he seemed much gratified. in the evening at sunset we desired them to depart as is our custom and closed our gates. we never suffer parties of such number to remain within the fort all night; for notwithstanding their apparent friendly disposition, their great averice and hope of plunder might induce them to be treacherous. at all events we determined allways to be on our guard as much as the nature of our situation will permit us, and never place our selves at the mercy of any savages. we well know, that the treachery of the aborigines of America and the too great confidence of our countrymen in their sincerity and friendship, has caused the disctruction of many hundreds of us. so long have our men been accustomed to a friendly intercourse with the natives, that we find it difficult to impress on their minds the necessity of always being on the guard with rispect to them. this confidence on our part, we know to be the effect of a series of uninterrupted friendly intercourse, but the well known treachery of the natives by no means entitle them to such confidence, and we must check it's growth in our own minds, as well as those of our men, by recollecting ourselves, and repeating to our men, that our preservation depends on never loosing sight of this trait in their character, and being always prepared to meet it in whatever shape it may present itself.–

The Mule deer are the same with those of the plains of the Missouri so frequently mentioned. we met with them under the Rocky mountains in the Neighbourhood of the Chopunnish nation on the Kooskooske river, but have not seen them since nor do we know whether they exist in the interior of the great plains of Columbia or on their lower border near the mountains which pass the river about the great falls. The Elk is the same with that found in much the greatest portion of North America, they are common to every part of this country, as well the timbered lands as the plains, but are much more abundant in the former than the latter The large brown woolf is like that of the Atlantic States and are found only in the woody country on the Pacific Ocean imbracing the mountains which pass the Columbia between the great falls and rapids of the same. the large and small woolves of the plains are the inhabitants principally of the open country and the woodlands on their bor-ders and resemble in their habits and appearance those of the plains of the Missouri precisely. they are not abundant in the plains of Columbia because there is but little game on which for them to subsist.—

Friday March 14th 1806

This morning we sent a party after the two Elk which Collins killed last eve-ning, they returned with them about noon. Collins, Jos. Fields and Shannon went in quest of the flock of Elk of which Collins had killed those two. this evening we heared upwards of twenty shot, and expect they have fallen in with and killed a number of them. Reubin Fields and Thompson returned this evening unsuccessfull having killed one brant only. late in the evening Drewyer arrived with a party of the Clatsops who brought an indifferent canoe some hats and roots for sale. the hats and roots we purchased, but could not obtain the canoe without giving more than our stock of merchandize would lisence us. I offered him my laced uniform coat but he would not exchange. The Salmon Trout are seldom more than two feet in length they are narrow in proportion to their length, at least much more so than the Salmon or red charr. the jaws are nearly of the same length, and are furnished with a single series of small subulate streight teeth, not so long or as large as those of the Salmon. the mouth is wide, and the tongue is also furnished with some teeth. the fins are placed much like those of the salmon. At the great falls we met with this fish of a silvery white colour on the belley and sides, and a bluish light brown on the back and head. in this neighbourhood we have met with another speceis which dose not differ from the other in any particular except in point of colour. this last is of a dark colour on the back, and it's sides and belley are tallow with transverse stripes of dark brown. sometimes a little red is intermixed with these colours on the belley and sides towards the head. the eye, flesh, and roes are like those described of the Salmon. the white speceis which we found below the falls was in excellent order when the salmon were entirely out of season and not fit for uce. the speceis which we found here on our arrival early in November had declined considerably, reather more so indeed than the red Charr with which we found them ascociated in the little rivulets and creeks. I think it may be safely asserted that the red Charr and both speceis of the salmon trout remain in season longer in the fall of the year than the common Salmon; but I have my doubts whether either of them ever pass the great falls of the Columbia. The Indians tell us that the Salmon begin to run early in the next month; it will be unfortunate for us if they do not, for they must form our principal dependence for food in ascending the Columbia, above the falls and it's S. E. branch to the mountains. the mountain or speckled trout are found in the waters of the Columbia within the mountains. They are the same of those found in the upper part of the Missouri, but are not so abundant in the Columbia as on that river. we never saw this fish below the mountains but from the transparency and coldness of the Kooskooske I should not doubt it's existing in that stream as low as it's junction with the S E. branch of the Columbia.—The *bottle nose* is the same with that before mentioned on the Missouri and is found exclusively within the mountains.—

"Meriwether Lewis on the Clatsops," in *The Journals of the Lewis and Clark Expedition,* ed. Gary Moulton (Lincoln: University of Nebraska Press, 1987), vol. 6, 330–31, 414–15.

JOHN ORDWAY ON RELATIONS WITH THE CLATSOPS

By March 1806, the American commanders were eager to begin the journey home. Confident that friendly relations with the Nez Perces and other tribes would assure them speedy passage over the Rockies, they could be certain, despite the grueling journey ahead of them, that they could be back in St. Louis by fall. On the eve of their departure, the Americans tried to acquire an additional canoe from the Chinook leader of a nearby village. When more was demanded than they felt they should pay, Lewis proposed stealing the vessel. He suggested that the Indians had taken an abandoned elk carcass during the winter and the canoe was proper payment for the "theft." Sergeant Ordway's view of the situation was more candid.

Tuesday 18th March 1806—a Showery morning of rain and hail. Some Thunder. we repair the Small canoea. 4 men went over to the prarie near the coast to take a canoe which belonged to the Clotsop Indians, as we are in want of it. In the evening they returned 2 of them by land and killd. an Elk. The others took the canoe near the fort an concealed it, as the chief of the Clotsops is now here.

"John Ordway on Relations with the Clatsops," in *The Journals of the Lewis and Clark Expedition,* cd. Gary Moulton (Lincoln: University of Nebraska Press, 1987), vol. 9, 277–78.

CHAPTER ELEVEN

Friends and Trading Partners on the Upper Columbia

In late March 1806, the Corps of Discovery abandoned their Oregon "fort" and began the journey home. With their stolen canoe and meager supplies, they presented a pitiful image as they traveled through the wealthy trading villages along the Columbia River. The Americans traded for whatever supplies they could obtain (regularly preferring dog meat to salmon), but they also pressed the bounds of hospitality by occasionally begging for food.

WILLIAM CLARK DESCRIBES MEETING THE WALLA WALLAS AND UMATILLAS

By April 27, Lewis and Clark and their men had passed Celilo Falls and reached the far side of the coastal and Columbia River trading networks. Here they met Walula, Yakama, Cayuse, and Umatilla communities, groups that the Chinook had prevented from reaching the American and Hudson's Bay traders on the coast and who were eager to participate in trade with outsiders. The members of these communities sought the Americans' friendship as well as the power of their weapons. That April day the Walulas traded ten dogs to the soldiers for "provision," and one of their leaders, Yellepit, presented Clark with a magnificent white horse.

April 27

This morning we were detained untill 9 AM in consequence of the absence of one of Shabono's horses. the horse being at length recovered we Set out and to the distance of 15 miles passed through a Country Similar to that of yesterday. (passed Muscle Shell rapid) and at the experation of this distance again approached the river, and are rocky abrupt and 300 feet high. we assended the hill and marched through a high plain 10 miles where we again returned to the river. we halted altho we had not reached the *Wal-lah-lal-lah* village as we had been led to believe by our guide who informed us that the village was at the place we Should next return to the river, and the considiration of our haveing but little provisions had been our inducement to make the march we had made this morning. we collected Some of the dry stalks of weeds and the Stems of Shrubs or weeds which resemble the Southern wood; made a Small fire and boiled a Small quantity of our [boiled] jurked meal on which we dined; while here we were met by the principal Chief of the *Wal lah wal lah* Nation and Several of his nation. this chief by name *Yel lep-pet* had visited us on the morning of the 19th of Octr. at our encampment imedeately opposit to us; we gave him at that time a Small Medal, and promised him a large one on our return. he appeared much gratified at Seeing us return. he envited us to remain at his village 3 or 4 days and assured us that we Should be furnished with a plenty of Such food as they had themselves, and Some horses to assist us on our journey. after our Scanty repast we Continued our March accompanied by Yelleppit and his party to the Village which we found at the distance of Six miles, Situated on the North Side of the river. about 16 miles below the enterance of Lewis's river. This Chief is a man of much influence not only in his own nation but also among the neighbouring tribes and nations.—the village Consists of 15 large mat Lodges. at present they Seam to Subsist principally on a Species of Mullet which weighs from one to 3 pds. and roots of various discriptions which those plains furnish them in great abundance. They also [furnish] take a fiew Salmon trout of the white kind. *Yelleppet* haranged his village in our favor intreated them to furnish us with fuel & provisions and Set the example himself by bringing us an armfull of wood, and a platter with 3 rosted mullets. the others Soon followed his example with respect to fuel and we Soon found ourselves in possession of an ample Stock, they burn the Stems of the Shrubs in the plains, there being no timber in this neighbourhood of any discription. we purchased 4 dogs of those people on which the party Suped hartily haveing been on Short allowance for near 2 days. the Indians retired when we requested them this evening and behaved themselves in every respect very well. the Indians informed us that there was a good road Which passed from the Columbia opposit to this Village to the enterance of Kooskooske on the S. Side of Lewis's river, they also informed us, there were a plenty of Deer and Antilopes on the road with good water and grass. we knew that a road in that direction if the Country would permit it would Shorten the rout at least 80 miles. the Indians also inform us that the County was leavel and the road good, under those circumstances we did not hesitate in pursueing the rout recommended by our guide and Corroberated by *Yelleppit* and others. we Concluded to pass our horses over early in the morning.—made 31 miles to day—

April 28

This morning early the Great Chief *Ye I lip pet* brought a very eligant white horse to our Camp and presented him to me Signifying his wish to get a kittle but being informed that we had already disposed of every kittle we could possibly Spare he Said he was Content with what ever I thought proper to give him. I gave him my *Swoard,* 100 balls & powder and Some Small articles of which he appeared perfectly Satisfied. it was necessary before we entered on our rout through the plains where we were to meet with no lodges or resident Indians that we Should lay in a Stock of provisions and not depend altogether on the gun. we derected R. Frazer to whome we have intrusted the duty of makeing the purchases, to lay in as maney fat dogs as he could procure; he Soon obtained 10. being anxious to depart we requested the Chief to furnish us with Canoes to pass the river, but he insisted on our remaining with him this day at least, that he would be much pleased if we would consent to remain two or three days, but he would not let [him] us have Canoes to leave him this day. that he had Sent for the *Chim-na-pums* his neighbours to come down and join his people this evening and dance for us. We urged the necessity of our proceeding on imediately in order that we might the Sooner return to them, with the articles which they wishd ... brought to them but this had no effect, he Said that the time he asked Could not make any considerable difference. I at length urged that there was no wind blowing and that the river was consequently in good order to pass our horses and if he would furnish us with Canoes for that purpose we would remain all night at our present encampment, to this proposition he assented and Soon produced a Canoe. I Saw a man who had his knee Contracted who had previously applyed to me for Some Medisene, that if he would fournish another Canoe I would give him Some Medisene. he readily Consented and went himself with his Canoe by means of which we passed our horses over the river Safely and hobbled them as usial—. We found a *Sho Sho ne* woman, prisoner among those people

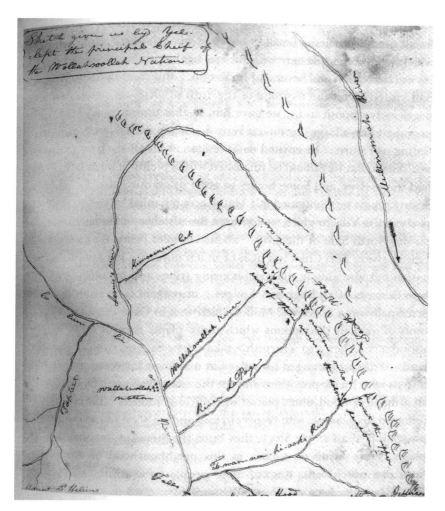

The Corps of Discovery's visit to the upper Columbia River in spring 1806 produced more than celebrations and pledges of friendship. Lewis and his host Yellepit drew this map of the confluence of the Columbia and Snake rivers. Courtesy the Newberry Library (Ayer G1380.A84. 1982 v. 7, p. 175).

by means of whome and *Sah-cah gah-weah,* Shabono's wife we found means of Converceing with the *Wallahwallârs.* we Conversed with them for Several hours and fully Satisfy all their enquiries with respect to our Selves and the Object of our pursute. they were much pleased. they brought Several disordered persons to us for whome they requested Some Medical aid. one had his knee contracted by the Rhumitism (whome is just mentioned above) another with a broken arm &c. to all of whome we administered much to the gratification of those pore wretches, we gave them Some eye water which I believe will render them more esential Sirvece than any other article in the Medical way which we had it in our power to bestow on them Sore eyes Seam to be a universial Complaint among those people; I have no doubt but the fine Sands of those plains and the river Contribute much to the disorder. The man who had his arm broken had it loosely bound in a peice of leather without any thing to Surport it. I dressed the arm which was broken Short above the wrist & Supported it with broad Sticks to keep it in place, put in a Sling and furnished him with Some lint bandages &c. to Dress it in future. a little before Sun Set the Chim nah poms arrived; they were about 100 men and a new women; they joined the Wallah wallahs who were about 150 men and formed a half Circle arround our camp where they waited verry patiently to See our party dance. the fiddle was played and the men amused themselves with danceing about an hour. we then requested the Indians to dance which they very Chearfully Complyed with; they Continued their dance untill 10 at night. the whole assemblage of Indians about 350 men women and Children Sung and danced at the Same time. most of them danced in the Same place they Stood and mearly jumped up to the time of their musick. Some of the men who were esteemed most brave entered the Space around which the main body were formed in Solid Column and danced in a Circular manner Side wise. at 10 PM. the dance ended and the nativs retired; they were much gratified in Seeing Some of our Party join them in their dance. one of their party who made himself the most Conspicious Charecter in the dance and Songs, we were told was a Medesene man & Could foretell things, that he had told of our Comeing into their Country and was now about to Consult his God the moon if what we Said was the truth &c. &c.

April 29

This Morning Yelleppit furnished us with 2 Canoes, and We began to nansport our baggage over the river; we also Sent a party of the men over to collect our horses. we purchased Some deer and chappellell this morning. we had now a Store of 12 dogs for our voyage through the plains. by 11 A. M. we had passed the river with our party and baggage but were detained Several hours in consequence of not being able to Collect our horses. our guide now informed us that it was too late in the evening to reach [to] an eligible place to encamp; that we Could not reach any water before night. we therefore thought it best to remain on the Wallah wallah river about a mile from the Columbia untill the morning, accordingly encampd on the river near a fish Wear. this weare Consists of two Curtains of Small willows wattled together with four lines of withes of the Same Materials extending quite across the river, parralal with each other and about 6 feet asunder. those are Supported by Several parrelals of poles placed in this manner those Curtains of willows is either roled at one end for a fiew feet to permit the fish to pass or are let down at pleasure. they take their fish which at present are a Mullet only of from one to 5 pounds Wt. with Small Seines of 15 or 18 feet long drawn by two persons; these they drag down to the Wear and rase the bottom of the seine against the willow Curtain. they have also a Small Seine managed by one person, it bags in the manner of the Scooping Nets; the one Side of the Net is Confined to a Simicircular bow of half the Size of a mans arm and about 5 feet long, the other Side is confined to a Strong String which being attatched to the extremities of the bow forms the Cord line to the Simicurcle. The Wallah wallah River discharges it's Self into the Columbia on it's South Side 15 miles below the enterance of Lewis's River, or the S. E. branch. a range of hills pass the Columbia just below the enterance of this river. this is a handsom Stream about 4½ feet deep and 50 yards wide; it's bead is composed of gravel principally with Some Sand and Mud; the banks are abrupt but not high, tho' it does not appear to overflow; the water is Clear. the Indians inform us that it has it's Source in the range of Mountains in view of us to the E. and S. E. these Mountains commence a little to the South of Mt. Hood and extend themselves in a S Eastwardly direction terminateing near the Southern banks of Lewis's river Short of the rockey Mountains. *Ta wan na hiooks* river, river Lapage and River all take their rise on those [N. Side of] Mountains. the two principal branches of the first of those take their rise in the Mountain's, Jefferson and Hood. those Mountains are Covered at present with Snow. those S W. Mountains are Covered with Snow at present tho' do not appear high. they Seperate the Waters of the Multnomah from those of the Columbia river. they appear to be 65 or 70 miles distant from hence. The Snake indian prisoner informed us that at Some distance in the large plains to the South of those Mountains there was a large river running to the N. W. which was as wide as the Columbia at this place, which is nearly 1 mile. this account is no doubt Somewhat exagurated but it Serves to evince the Certainty of the Multnomah being a very large River and that it's waters are Seperated from the Columbia by those Mountains, and that with the aid of a Southwardly branch of Lewis's river which pass around the Eastern extremity of those mountains, it must water that vast tract of Country extending from those Mountains to the Waters of the Gulf of Callifornia. and no doubt it heads with the Rochejhone and Del Nord.

We gave Small Medals to two inferior Chiefs of this nation, and they each furnished us with a fine horse, in return we gave them Sundery articles among which was one of Capt Lewis's Pistols & Several hundred rounds of Amunition. there are 12 other Lodges of the Wallahwallah Nation on this river a Short distance below our Camp. those as well as those beyond the Columbia appear to depend on their fishing weres for their Subsistance. those people as well as the Chym na poms are very well disposed, much more So particular their women than they were when we decended the river last fall. Most of them have long Shirts and leggins, good robes and Mockersons. their women were the truss when they Cannot precure the Shirt, but very fiew are Seen with the former at the present. I prosume the Succcess of their Winters hunt has produced this change in their attere. they all Cut their hair in the fore head, and most of the men ware the two Cews over each Sholder in front of the body; Some have the addition of a fiew Small plats formed of the eare locks, and others tigh a Small bundle of the docked foretop in front of the fore head. their [amusements] orniments are Such as discribed of the natives below, and are worn in a Similar manner. they insisted on our danceing this evening but it rained a little the wind blew hard and the weather was Cold, we therefore did not indulge them.—Several applyed to me to day for medical aides, one a broken arm another inward fever and Several with pains across their loins, and Sore eyes. I administered as well as I could to all. in the evining a man brought his wife and a horse both up to me. the horse he gave me as a present. and his wife who was verry unwell the effects of violent Coalds was placed before me. I did not think her Case a bad one and gave Such medesine as would keep her body open and raped her in flannel. left Some Simple Medesene to be taken. we also gave Some Eye water 1 G. of Ela v V. & 2 grs. of Sacchm Stry. to an ounce of water and in that perpotion. Great No. of the nativs about us all night.

"William Clark Describes Meeting the Walla Wallas and Umatillas," in *The Journals of the Lewis and Clark Expedition,* ed. Gary Moulton (Lincoln: University of Nebraska Press, 1987), vol. 7, 174–77, 179–81, 183–86.

After their difficult winter on the coast the meeting with the Umatillas was encourag-
ing to the Americans. But the men were ready to move upriver to the Nez Perces. The
Indians urged them to stay. "They were much pleased," Sergeant Ordway reported,
"[they] said they would dance day and night until we return."

April 26

We got up our horses. took a light breakfast of a little dry Elk meat and Set out
proced on over a low level Sandy plain about 12 miles & halted & dined on a
little dry Elk meat as we have nothing else. the day warm. we delayed about 1
hour and preceed on a number of the natives followed us who are mooveing
up the . . . & Some of them are going over the rockey mountn. to kill buffaloe
. . . considerable of Snow on the mountains to the South & S East. Came . . .
odd miles this day & Camped on the bank of the river, only small willows to
burn &C—

April 27

A little rain fell the latter part of last night we Set out as usal and proceed. on
Soon passd. a Small village of 3 lodges then assended a high plain where we
Saw an extensive country around us & not a tree to be Seen came about 20
miles before we halted & delayed a Short time eat a little dry meat & let our
horses feed a Short time and proceed on about 5 miles further and arived at
a large village of the wal-a-wal tribe, at the commencement of a low barron
Smooth country where we Camped bought a fat dog to each mess. these natives are numerous their is another village on the opposite Side of the river
& a great number of horses. we get different kinds of roots and fresh Salmon
trout & Suckers &C. all these Savages are glad to See us and appear verry
friendly.—

April 28

A clear pleasant morning. our Indian guides who are going over the mountains with us inform us that their is a nearer way across the plains to the forks
of Lewises river at the entrence of Kooskooske which is a Smooth way and
only 3 days march to that place which is allmost as near again as to follow the

river round. So our officers conclude to cross the river at this place & take the near way. So we purchased 6 dogs from the natives to take with us. our Intrepters wife found a woman of hir own nation who was a prisoner among these Indians, and as they could Speak together our officers Spoke to the head chief & told him our business and that the white people would Supply them with marchandize at the head of the Missourie &C. asked for canoes to cross the river they Said they wished us to Stay with them to day as we lived a great way off, and they wished to See us dance this evening& begged on us to Stay this day. So our officers concluded to Stay this day. the head chief brought up a good horse & Said he wished to give it to us but as he was poor he wished us to give him Some kind of a kittle, but as we could not Spare a kittle Capt. Clark gave his Sword a flag and half pound of powder & ball for the horse. we took our horses across the river. our officers made another chief gave him a meddle &C. in the afternoon an number of Indians came to our officers who were diseased the lame and many with Sore eyes and lame legs & arms &C. our officers dressd. their wounds, washed their eyes & gave them meddicine and told them how to apply it &C. the chief called all his people and told them of the meddicine &C. which was a great wonder among them & they were much pleased &C. the Indians Sent their women to gether wood or Sticks to See us dance this evening. about 300 of the natives assembled to our Camp we played the fiddle and danced a while the head chief told our officers that they Should be lonesome when we left them and they wished to hear once of our meddicine Songs and try to learn it and wished us to learn one of theirs and it would make them glad. So our men Sang 2 Songs which appeared to take great affect on them. they tryed to learn Singing with us with a low voice. the head chief then made a Speech & it was repeated by a warrier that all might hear. then all the Savages men women and children of any Size danced forming a circle round a fire & jumping up nearly as other Indians, & keep time verry well they wished our men to dance with them So we danced among them and they were much pleased, and Said that they would dance day and night untill we return. everry fiew minutes one of their warries made a Speech pointing towards the enimy and towards the moon &C. &C which was all repeated by another meddison man with a louder voice as all might hear. the dance continued untill about midnight [when] the most of them went away peaceable & have behaved verry clever and honest with us as yet, and appear to have a Sincere wish to be at peace and to git acquaintance with us &C &C—

April 29

We bought 2 more dogs to take us across the plains and a little Shappalell & other roots &C. we borrowed a canoe from the Indians and crossed over the Columbia to the South Side above the mouth of the river which we took to a byo where we passd. down last fall, and got all our baggage across the river and got up our horses. our guide telling us that it was a long distance to water, & further than we could go this day. So we mooved over 1 mile on the bank of the river which is named the wal-a-wal-a River near a large village of the wal-a-wal-a nation where we Camped again. these Savages have wers made of willows across this little river where they catch large quantityes of Salmon trout, Suckers, &C. we bought a little Commass roots, Shappalell and a fiew more dogs &C. the most of the Savages moved across the river also, & they have a vast Site of horses. Capt. Lewis made a chief gave him a meddle. he gave a fine horse in return as a present. another chief who Capt. Clark made yesterday brought up another fine horse and made him a present of. we purchased another by giving a Small quantity of powder and ball. these natives are the kindest and the most friendly to us than any we have yet Seen.—they have lately been at war with the Snake nation and many of them were kild. one of our men lift a Steel trap on the other Side—

"Sergeant Ordway Describes the Umatillas," in *The Journals of the Lewis and Clark Expedition,* ed. Gary Moulton (Lincoln: University of Nebraska Press, 1995), vol. 9, 298–300.

THE COLUMBIA RIVER TRADE NETWORK
Theodore Stern

As shown on Raymond Wood's map of trade networks reproduced in chapter 1, the Columbia River, and particularly the Dalles, was a major crossroads in North American trade networks prior to the arrival of Europeans. With patience and the right trade items at their disposal, Lewis and Clark could have obtained everything they needed for the return journey from the people living along this river.

The drainage of the Columbia River, that great avenue of communication, from aboriginal times has been the locus of an exchange system that formed one of the expressions of Plateau culture. It drew in turn upon regions beyond that drainage; within the Plateau, it drew from proximate segments of the Thompson-Fraser river system to the north: on the west, it ranged both north and south along the Pacific coast within the cultural province of the Northwest Coast; in the south, it drew upon the fringe regions belonging to the provinces of California and the Great Basin: while on the east, particularly after the advent of the horse, it reached across the Rockies into the Missouri drainage of the Plains. Eventually it had continental extensions (Wood 1972).

Meriwether Lewis and William Clark described the system in 1805–1806. Five regionally distinct entities participated in the exchange, of which four were Indian. There were those dwelling in villages where the river cuts through the Cascades, who dominated portages around falls, and thus controlled passage: those on the lower river and coast, who traded with them; and those who came seasonally to trade—one from the western Plateau and one from the mountainous country east of them in the foothills of the Rockies (Lewis and Clark 1902, 2:148–54). The fifth group was coastal traders, by that time largely American, whose seasonal calls, in the words of the explorers, formed "the soul of this trade." They cannot have been responsible for initiating the exchange network: they had only breached into a traffic already in existence.

At the center lay those villages situated along the Columbia between Celilo Falls, just upriver from The Dalles, and the Cascades, a distance of roughly 50 miles. These were first the villages of the Western Columbia River Sahaptin bands and the Chinookan-speaking Wasco, Wishram, and White Salmon. Not only did these villages dominate passage along the river, strewn as it was with obstacles, but they were favored with local conditions within which they had developed the production of salmon pemmican, both for their own use and for trade. Yearly, they dried and pulverized salmon, packing it in baskets lined with salmon skin, holding some 100 pounds apiece. Stored in stacks of 12, the pemmican baskets provided the captains, and subsequent scholars, the basis for calculating the total amount consigned each year to trade, which Griswold (1970:21) estimated to have been a million pounds. This delicacy, still recalled with pleasure by elderly Indians, was traded in several directions. It was highly sought on the lower river, for the fresh-run salmon caught there in abundance were too fat, and the climate too humid, to produce a satisfactory pemmican. Above The Dalles to the mouth of the Snake, where other conditions were favorable, the dearth of firewood, said the captains, made it often necessary to burn dried salmon for fuel; and not enough was left for pemmican (cf. Hunn 1990:184f). Klamath, trading northward from their well-stocked lakes and marshes, found the pemmican so admirable an article that they seem to have copied it in their local whitefish (Gatschet 1890, 2:116). Finally, even Plains tribes seem to have traded for it.

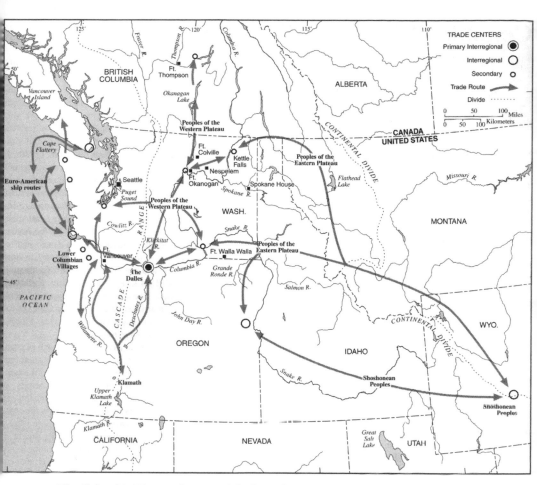

The Columbia River trade network in the early nineteenth century. A comparison of this map with the map of precontact trade routes reveals how European traders fit themselves into the American Indian economy. Courtesy the Newberry Library (Ref. E77 H25 1998, p. 642).

This was but a single item in a complex exchange of products. In local environments there flourished plants and animals that entered into the stream of trade. Such, for example, was wapato root in the lower valley, berries in numerous localities, or on the coast sea fish, eulachon oil, and whale oil and blubber. There were shells from the coast and other raw materials elsewhere. Moreover, there were a myriad of local manufactures that were eagerly sought in trade. Thus, the trading network had the consequence not only of enlarging local diets and enriching local cultures but also of encouraging local specialization in production while, through the dissemination of foods, material, and products, it diminished the cultural distinctiveness of participant peoples (Wood 1972:164).

The Dalles, which lay at the juncture of the Northwest Coast and the Plateau, was the great center for inter- and intra-regional exchange. There, diverse peoples congregated from late springtime into late summer, bringing with them their trading goods (Lewis and Clark 1902, 2:150; cf. Murdock 1980:132). Lewis and Clark observed that those from the western Plateau brought skins, mats, silk grass, and bread made from couse root (Cutright 1989:410), which they exchanged for wapato, horses, beads, and items from the coastal traders, now retraded. Those from the foothills of the Rockies, such as the Nez Perces, brought beargrass, horses, camas root, as well as buffalo robes and other skins that they had secured, either through their own hunting or in trade with the Flathead. These they exchanged for wapato, salmon pemmican, and trade beads.

From the south, in the nineteenth century, came Klamath who, together with the related Modoc, raided Shasta, as well as the Achumawi and Atsugewi of the Pit River drainage, carrying off women and children as slaves, together with loot such as bows and watertight baskets. Together with wokas (pond lily seeds) and other local products, Klamath traders brought these articles northward along the Klamath Trail to trade, either with the Chinookan tribes at the falls of the Willamette or, making their way to the Tygh Valley villages on the Deschutes, traded with the Wasco for horses, parfleches, and salmon pemmican. Slaves were a commodity much sought on the lower Columbia, as well as along the northern reaches of the Northwest Coast. To secure them, Lower Chinook, at the mouth of the Columbia, raided southward along the Oregon coast (Ray 1938:52).

The Lower Chinook sought to dominate all trade with the coastal traders. Their own trading parties made their way north to the Makah, at Cape Flattery, through whom they acquired both Makah products and items traded south from the related Nootka, of southern Vancouver Island. Among products from this quarter were dentalium shells, slaves, and Nootka canoes.

Within the network, many of the participant peoples exchanged not only their own products but also surplus stocks of items received in trade from others. When a whale washed up on the Tillamook coast, south of the mouth of the Columbia, Clark met parties of Lower Chinook and Clatsop from the lower river trading with the Tillamook for whale oil and blubber. In turn, the Clatsop received a party of Cathlamet, from above them on the Columbia, who bartered wapato for at least part of their stock of the whale. "In this manner," wrote Lewis, "there is a trade continually carried on by the natives of the river each trading some article or other with their neighbors above and below them; and thus articles which are vended by the whites at the entrance of this river, find their way to the most distant nations inhabiting it's [*sic*] waters" (Thwaites 1904–5, 3:329, 338). At The Dalles, the Klikitat, inveterate traders, sold their imbricated baskets to the Nez Perce for buffalo robes, in turn bartering the robes with the Wishram for salmon pemmican (Spier and Sapir 1930:227). The villagers at The Dalles readily bought goods for resale (Teit 1928:122).

References

Cutright, Paul Russell. 1989. *Lewis and Clark: Pioneering Naturalists.* Lincoln: University of Nebraska Press.

Gatschet, Albert S. 1890. *The Klamath Indians of Southwestern Oregon.* 2 vols. Contributions to North American Ethnology 2. Washington: U.S. Geological and Geological Survey of the Rocky Mountain Region. Pt. 1, Ethnographic Sketch. Reprinted by Shorey Book Store, Seattle, Wash., 1966.

Griswold, Gillett. 1970. "Aboriginal Patterns of Trade between the Columbia Basin and the Northern Plains." *Archeology in Montana* 11 (nos. 2–3): 1–96. Originally issued as M.A. thesis in anthropology, Montana State University, Missoula, 1954.

Hunn, Eugene. 1990. "The Plateau Area." In *Native North Americans: An Ethnographical Approach,* edited by D. L. Boxberger. Dubuque, Iowa: Kendall/Hunt.

Lewis, Meriwether, and William Clark. In *History of the Expedition under the Command of Captain Lewis and Clark, 1804-5-6,* edited by Elliot Course. 2 vols. Chicago: McClurg.

Murdock, George Peter. 1980. "The Tenino Indians." *Ethnology* 19 (no. 2): 129–49.

Ray, Verne F. 1938. "Lower Chinook Ethnographic Notes." *University of Washington Publications in Anthropology* 7 (no. 2): 29–165.

Spier, Leslie, and Edward Sapir. 1930. "Wishram Ethnography." *University of Washington Publications in Anthropology* 3 (no. 3): 151–300.

Teit, James A. 1928. "The Middle Columbia Salish." Edited by Franz Boas. *University of Washington Publications in Anthropology* 2 (no. 4): 83–128.

Thwaites, Reuben G., ed. 1904–5. *Original Journals of the Lewis and Clark Expedition, 1804–1806.* 8 vols. New York: Dodd, Mead, 1904–5. Reprint, New York: Antiquarian Press, 1959; New York: Arno Press, 1969.

Wood, Raymond W. 1972. "Contrastive Features of Native North American Trade Systems." In *For the Chief: Essays in Honor of Luther S. Cressman; by Some of His Students,* edited by Fred W. Voget and Robert L. Stephenson, 153–69. Foreword by Theodore Stern. University of Oregon Anthropological Papers 4.

Theodore Stern, "The Columbia River Trade Network," in *The Handbook of North American Indians,* ed. Deward E. Walker, vol. 12 (Plateau) (Washington, D.C.: Smithsonian Institution Press, 1998), 641–43.

CHAPTER TWELVE

A Confrontation in Montana

In early June 1806, a group of Nez Perce guides led the Corps of Discovery back over the Bitterroot Mountains into modern Montana. The Americans had spent most of the previous month with the Nez Perces, waiting for the snows to clear from the mountain passes. The Indian guides remained with the Americans for a month. On July 3, with the party safely on the eastern slope of the Rockies, Captain Lewis and nine other men set off to explore the north bank of the Missouri. The remainder of the group descended the Yellowstone River, passing through the country of the Crow Indians. The two groups would rendezvous on August 12.

MERIWETHER LEWIS DESCRIBES A VIOLENT ENCOUNTER
WITH THE BLACKFEET

On July 26, Lewis's small party encountered fifteen young Blackfeet men in the hills near the Two Medicine River in modern Glacier County, Montana. A cordial meeting produced a decision to camp together. Lewis presented the leader of the group with a small flag and a peace medal. Using sign language, Lewis interviewed the Blackfeet late into the night. He told them the Americans were now allied with the young men's traditional enemies: the Nez Perces, Salish, and Shoshones.

On the morning of July 27, the young Indians—perhaps alarmed by Lewis's speech of the night before—suddenly grabbed some of the Americans' precious guns and tried to escape. Private Reuben Fields seized one of the thieves and stabbed him in the heart; Meriwether Lewis pursued and shot dead another man who confronted him with a rifle. Lewis then set the Indians' "baggage" ablaze and retrieved the flag

168

he had given out the night before. He left the peace medal around the neck of one of the dead warriors.

July 26, 1806

The moring was cloudy and continued to rain as usual, tho' the cloud seemed somewhat thiner. I therefore posponed seting out untill 9 A. M. in the hope that it would clear off but finding the contrary result I had the horses caught and we set out biding a lasting adieu to this place which I now call camp disappointment. I took my rout through the open plains S.E. 5 ms. passing a small creek at 2 ms. from the mountains wher I changed my direction to S. 75 E. for 7 ms. further and struck a principal branch of Maria's river 65 yds. wide, not very deep, I passed this stream to it's south side and continued down it 2 ms. on the last mentioned course when another branch of nearly the same dignity formed a junction with it, coming from the S. W. this last is shallow and rappid; has the appearance of overflowing it's banks frequently and discharging vast torrents of water at certain seasons of the year. the beds of both these streams are pebbly particularly the S. branch. the water of the N. branch is very terbid while that of the S. branch is nearly clear not withstanding the late rains. I passed the S. branch just above it's junction and continued down the river which runs a little to the N of E 1 ms. and halted to dine and graize our horses. here I found some indian lodges which appeared to have been inhabited last winter in a large and fertile bottom well stocked with cottonwood timber. the rose honeysuckle and redberry bushes constitute the undergrowth there being but little willow in this quarter both these rivers abov their junction appeared to be well stocked with timber or comparitively so with other parts of this country. here it is that we find the three species of cottonwood which I haw remarked in my voyage assembled together that speceis common to the Columbia I have never before seen on the waters of the Missouri, also the narrow and broad leafed speceis. during our stay at this place R. Fields killed a buck a part of the flesh of which we took with us. we saw a few Antelopes some wolves and 2 of the smallest speceis of fox of a redisli brown colour with the extremity of the tail black. it is about the size of the common domestic cat and burrows in the plains. after dinner I continued my rout down the river to the North of Eat about 3 ms. when the hills putting in close on the S side I determined to ascend them to the high plain which I did accordingly, keeping the Fields with me; Drewyer passed the river and kept down the vally of the river. I had intended to decend this river with it's course to it's junction with the fork which I had ascended and from thence have taken across the country obliquely to rose river and decend that stream to it's confluence with Maria's river. the country through which this portion of Maria's river passes to the fork which I ascended appears much more broken than that above and between this and the mountains. I had scarcely ascended the hills before I discovered to my left at the distance of a mile an assembleage of about 30 horses, I halted and used my spye glass by the help of which I discovered several indians on the top of an eminence just above them who appeared to be looking down towards the river I presumed at Drewyer. about half the horses were saddled. this was a very unpleasant sight, however I resolved to make the best of our situation and to approach them in a friendly manner. I directed J. Fields to display the flag which I had brought for that purpose and advanced slowly toward them, about this time they discovered us and appeared to run about in a very confused manner as if much allarmed, their attention had been previously so fixed on Drewyer that they did not discover us untill we had began to advance upon them, some of them decended the hill on which they were and drove their horses within shot of it's summit and again returned to the hight as if to wate our arrival or to defend themselves. I calculated on their number being nearly or quite equal to that of their horses, that our runing would invite pursuit as it would convince them that we were their enimies and our horses were so indifferent that we could not hope to make our escape by flight; added to this Drewyer was seperated from us and I feared that his not being apprized of the indians in the event of our attempting to escape he would most probably fall a sacrefice. under these considerations I still advanced towards them; when we had arrived (at the distance of) within a quarter of a mile of them, one of them mounted his horse and rode full speed towards us, which when I discovered I halted and alighted from my horse; he came within a hundred paces halted looked at us and turned his horse about and returned as briskly to his party as he had advanced; while he halted near us I held out my hand and becconed to him to approach but he paid no attention to my overtures. on his return to his party they all decended the hill and mounted their horses and advanced towards us leaving their horses behind them, we also advanced to meet them. I counted eight of them but still supposed that there were others concealed as there were several other horses saddled. I told the two men with me that I apprehended that these were the Minnetares of Fort de Prarie and from their known character I expected that we were to have some difficulty with them; that if they thought themselves sufficiently strong I was convinced they would attempt to rob us in which case be their numbers what they would I should resist to the last extremity prefering death to that of being deprived of my papers instruments and gun and desired that they would form the same resolution and be allert and on their guard. when we arrived within a hundred yards of each other the indians except one halted I directed the two men with me to do the same and advanced singly to meet the indian with whom I shook hands and passed on to those in his rear, as he did also to the two men in my rear; we now all assembled and alighted from our horses; the Indians soon asked to smoke with us, but I told them that the man whom they had seen pass down the river had my pipe and we could not smoke untill he joined us. I requested as they had seen which way he went that they would one of them go with one of my men in surch of him, this they readily concented to and a young man set out with R. Fields in surch of Drewyer. I now asked them by sighns if they were the Minnetares of the North which they answered in the affermative; I asked if there was any cheif among them and they pointed out 3 I did not believe them however I thought it best to please them and gave to one a medal to a second a flag and to the third a handkerchief, with which they appeared well satisfyed. they appeared much agitated with our first interview from which they had scarcely yet recovered, in fact I beleive they were more allarmed at this accedental interview than we were. from no more of them appearing I now concluded they were only eight in number and became much better satisfyed with our situation as I was convinced that we could mannage that number should they attempt any hostile measures. as it was growing late in the evening I proposed that we should remove to the nearest part of the river and encamp together, I told them that I was glad to see them and had a great deel to say to them. we mounted our horses and rode towards the river which was at but a short distance, on our way we were joined by Drewyer Fields and the indian. we decended a very steep bluff about 250 feet high to the river where there was a small bottom of nearly ½ a mile in length and about 250 yards wide in the widest part, the river washed the bluffs both above and below us and through it's course in this part is very deep; the bluffs are so steep that there are but few places where they could be ascended, and are broken in several places by deep nitches which extend back from the river several hundred yards, their bluffs being so steep that it is impossible to ascend them; in this bottom there stand tree solitary trees near one of which the indians formed a large simicircular camp of dressed buffaloe skins and invited us to partake of their shelter which Drewyer and myself accepted and the Fieldses lay near the fire in front of the sheter. with the assistance of Drewyer I had much conversation with these people in the course of the evening. I learned from them that they were a part of a large band which lay encamped at present near the foot of the rocky mountains on the main branch of Maria's river one ½ days march from our present encampment; that there was a whiteman with their band; that there was another large band of their nation hunting buffaloe near the broken mountains and were on there way to the mouth of Maria's river where they would probably be in the course of a few days. they also informed us that from hence to the establishment where they trade on the Suskasawan river is only 6 days easy march or such as they usually travel with their women and childred which may be estimated at about 150 ms. that from these traders they obtain arm amunition speriutuous liquor blankets &c in exchange for wolves and some beaver skins. I told these people that I had come a great way from the East up the large river which runs towards the rising sun, that I had been to the great waters where the sun sets and had seen a great many nations all of whom I had invited to come and trade with me on the rivers on this side of the mountains, that I had found most of them at war with their neighbours and had succeeded in restoring peace among them, that I was now on my way home and had left my party at the falls of the missouri with orders to decend that river to the entrance of Maria's river and there wait my arrival and that I had come in surch of them in order to prevail on them to be at peace with their neighbours particularly those on the West side of the mountains and to engage them to come and trade with me when the establishment is made at the entrance of this river to all which they readily gave their assent and declared it to be their wish to be at peace with the Tushepahs whom they said had killed a number of their relations lately and pointed to several of those present who had cut their hair as an evidince of the truth of what they had asserted. I found them extreemly fond of smoking and plyed them with the pipe untill late at night. I told them that if they intended to do as I wished them they would send some of their young men to their band with an invitation to their chiefs and warriors to bring the whiteman with them and come down and council with me at the entrance of Maria's river and that the ballance of them would accompany me to that place, where I was anxious now to meet my men as I had been absent from them some time and knew that they would be uneasy untill they saw me. that if they would go with me I would give them 10 horses and some tobacco. to this proposition they made no reply, I took the first watch tonight and set up untill half after eleven; the indians by this time were all asleep, I roused up R. Fields and laid down myself; I directed Fields to watch the movements of the indians and if any of them left the camp to awake us all as I apprehended they would attampt to seal [steal] our horses. this being done I fell into a profound sleep and did not wake untill the noise of the men and indians awoke me a little after light in the morning.—

July 27, 1806

This morning at day light the indians got up and crouded around the fire, J. Fields who was on post had carelessly laid his gun down behid him near where his brother was sleeping, one of the indians the fellow to whom I had given the medal last evening sliped behind him and took his gun and that of his brothers unperceived by him, at the same instant two others advanced and seized the guns of Drewyer and myself, J. Fields seing this turned about to look for his gun and saw the fellow just runing off with her and his brothers he called to his brother who instantly jumped up and pursued the indian with him whom they overtook at the distance of 50 or 60 paces from the camp sized their guns and rested them from him and R Fields as he seized his gun stabed the indian to the heart with his knife the fellow ran about 15 steps and fell dead; of this I did not know untill afterwards, having recovered their guns they ran back instantly to the camp; Drewyer who was awake saw the indian take hold of his gun and instantly jumped up and sized her and rested her from him but the indian still retained his pouch, his jumping up and crying damn you let go my gun awakened me I jumped up and asked what was the matter which I quickly learned when I saw drewyer in a scuffle with the indian for his gun. I reached to seize my gun but found her gone, I then drew a pistol from my holster and terning myself about saw the indian making off with my gun I ran at him with my pistol and bid him lay down my gun (at the instant) which he was in the act of doing when the Fieldses returned and drew up their guns to shoot him which I forbid as he did not appear to be about to make any resistance or commit any offensive act, he droped the gun and walked slowly off, I picked her up instantly, Drewyer having about this time recovered his gun and pouch asked me if he might not kill the fellow which I also forbid as the indian did not appear to wish to kill us, as soon as they found us all in possession of our arms they ran and indeavored to drive off all the horses I now hollowed to the men and told them to fire on them if they attempted to drive off our horses, they accordingly pursued the main party who were drving the horses up the river and I pursued the man who had taken my gun who with another was driving off a part of the horses which were to the left of the camp, I pursued them so closely that they could not take twelve of their own horses but continued to drive one of mine with some others; at the distance of three hundred paces they entered one of those steep nitches in the bluff with the horses before them being nearly out of breath I could pursue no further, I called to them as I had done several times before that I would shoot them if they did not give me my horse and raised my gun, one of them jumped behind a rock and spoke to the other who turned arround and stoped at the distance of 30 steps from me and I shot him through the belly, he fell to his knees and on his wright elbow from which position he partly raised himself up and fired at me, and turning himself about crawled in behind a rock which was a few feet from him. he overshot me, being bearheaded I felt the wind of his bullet very distinctly. not having my shotpouch I could not reload my peice and as there were two of them behind good shelters from me I did not think it prudent to rush on them with my pistol which had I discharged I had not the means of reloading untill I reached camp; I therefore returned leasurely towards camp, on my way I met with Drewyer who having heared the report of the guns had returned in surch of me and left the Fieldes to pursue the indians, I desired him to haisten to the camp with me and assist in catching as many of the indian horses as were necessary and to call to the Fieldes if he could make them hear to come back that we still had a sufficient number of horses, this he did but they were too far to hear him. we reached the camp and began to catch the horses and saddle them and put on the packs. the reason I had not my pouch with me was that I had not time to return about 50 yards to camp after geting my gun before I was obliged to pursue the indians or suffer them to collect and drive off all the horses. we had caught and saddled the horses and began to arrange the packs when the Fieldses returned with four of our horses; we left one of our horses and took four of the best of those of the indian's; while the men were preparing the horses I put four sheilds and two bows and quivers of arrows which had been left on the fire, with sundry other articles; they left all their baggage at our mercy. they had but 2 guns and one of them they left the others were armed with bows and arrows and eyedaggs. the gun we took with us. I also retook the flagg but left the medal about the neck of the dead man that they might be informed who we were. we took some of their buffaloe meat and set out ascending the bluffs by the same rout we had decended last evening leaving the ballance of nine of their horses which we did not want. the Feildses told me that three of the indians whom they pursued swam the river one of them on my horse. and that two others ascended the hill and escaped from them with a part of their horses, two I had pursued into the nitch one lay dead near the camp and the eighth we could not account for but suppose

Captain Lewis shooting an Indian.

This illustration by an anonymous artist was published with the 1812 edition of Sergeant Patrick Gass's journal of the expedition. It presents a fairly accurate picture of Captain Lewis's confrontation with two young Blackfeet men. After one young Blackfeet leveled his gun at the commander, Lewis (who was hatless in 1806) fired, mortally wounding his adversary. Courtesy the Newberry Library (Graff 1521).

that he ran off early in the contest. having ascended the hill we took our course through a beatiful level plain a little to the S of East. my design was to hasten to the entrance of Maria's river as quick as possible in the hope of meeting with the canoes and party at that place having no doubt but that they would pursue us with a large party and as there was a band near the broken mountains or probably between them and the mouth of that river we might expect them to receive inteligence from us and arrive at that place nearly as soon as we could, no time was therefore to be lost and we pushed our horses as hard as they would bear. at 8 miles we passed a large branch 40 yds. wide which I called battle river. at 3 P. M. we arrived at rose river about 5 miles above where we had passed it as we went out, having traveled by my estimate compared with our former distances and couses about 63 ms. here we halted an hour and a half took some refreshment and suffered our horses to graize; the day proved warm but the late rains had supplyed the little reservoirs in the plains with water and had put them in fine order for traveling, our whole rout so far was as level as a bowling green with but little stone and few prickly pears. after dinner we pursued the bottoms of rose river but finding inconvenient to pass the river so often we again ascended the hills on the S. W. side and took the open plains; by dark we had traveled about 17 miles further, we now halted to rest ourselves and horses about 2 hours, we killed a buffaloe cow and took a small quantity of the meat. after refreshing ourselves we again set out by moon light and traveled leasurely, heavy thunderclouds lowered arround us on every quarter but that from which the moon gave us light. we continued to pass immence herds of buffaloe all night as we had done in the latter part of the day. we traveled untill 2 OCk in the morning having come by my estimate after dark about 20 ms. we now turned out our horses and laid ourselves down to rest in the plain very much fatiegued as may be readily conceived. my indian horse carried me very well in short much better than my own would have done and leaves me with but little reason to complain of the robery.

"Meriwether Lewis Describes a Violent Encounter with the Blackfeet," in *The Journals of the Lewis and Clark Expedition,* ed. Gary Moulton (Lincoln: University of Nebraska Press, 1987), vol. 8, 127–37.

A BLACKFEET ENCOUNTER
Patrick Gass

Captain Lewis had left a portion of his detachment on the Missouri when he and his party rode north to explore the prairies surrounding the Missouri River. One of those left behind was Patrick Gass. On June 28 Gass reported that his squad's "pleasant" morning of hunting at the mouth of the Maria's River was interrupted by the arrival of Lewis and his companions. The captain had ridden more than a hundred miles to put as much distance as possible between himself and the Blackfeet, and he quickly related his version of events, especially that the Americans had ridden south "as fast as possible." Because Gass published his journal in 1812, his was the first printed version of the encounter.

Saturday 26th. The morning was cloudy. Eight of us went back to Willow creek for the other canoe, and the rest of the party[1] were employed in taking down the canoes and baggage to the lower end of the portage, where the periogue had been left.[2] It rained very hard all night, which has made the plains so muddy, that it is with the greatest difficulty we can get along with the canoe; though in the evening, after a hard day's labour, we got her safe to Portage river, and the men run her down to the lower landing place, where we encamped. A few drops of rain fell in the course of the day.

1. Ordway says Colter and Potts ran the canoes down the rapids to the lower portage camp.
2. Where the white pirogue was hidden near the lower portage camp below Belt Creek, Chouteau County, Montana, on June 18, 1805.

Sunday 27th. In a fine clear pleasant morning, myself and one of the men crossed the river with the horses, in order to go by land to the mouth of Maria's river: the rest of the party here are to go by water. We proceeded on through the plains about twenty miles, and in our way saw a great many buffaloe. We then struck Tansy or Rose river,[1] which we kept down about ten miles, and encamped. The land along this river is handsomely covered with Cotton wood timber and there is an abundance of game of different kinds. In our way we killed a buffaloe and a goat [probably a pronghorn]. The wolves in packs occasinally hunt these goats, which are too swift to be run down and taken by a single wolf. The wolves having fixed upon their intended prey and taken their stations, a part of the pack commence the chase, and running it in a circle, are at certain intervals relieved by others. In this manner they are able to run a goat down. At the falls where the wolves are plenty, I had an opportunity of seeing one of these hunts.

1. Teton River, Chouteau County, Montana.

Monday 28th. The morning was fine and pleasant, and at an early hour we proceeded down the river. In our way we killed six goats or antelopes and seven buffaloe; and about one o'clock came to the point at the mouth of Maria's river, where we met with the party who had come down from the falls by water, and who had just arrived; and also unexpectedly with Captain Lewis and the three men who had gone with him. They had joined the party descending the river this forenoon, after riding one hundred and twenty miles since yesterday morning, when they had a skirmish with a party of the Prairie Grossventres, or Bigbellied Indians who inhabit the plains up Maria's river; of which they gave the following account. On the evening of the 26th Captain Lewis and his party met with eight of those Indians, who seemed very friendly and gave them two robes. In return Captain Lewis gave one of them, who was a chief, a medal; and they all continued together during the night; but after break of day the next morning, the Indians snatched up three of our men's guns and ran off with them. One Indian had the guns of two men, who pursued and caught him; and one of them killed him with his knife; and they got back the guns. Another had Captain Lewis's gun, but immediately gave it up. The party then went to catch their horses, and found the Indians driving them off; when Captain Lewis shot one of them, and gave him a mortal wound; who notwithstanding returned the fire, but without hurting the Captain. So our men got all their own horses but one, and a number of those belonging to the Indians, as they ran off in confusion and left every thing they had. Our men then saddled their horses, and made towards the Missouri as fast as possible; after Captain Lewis had satisfied himself with respect to the geography of the country up Maria's river.

We this day took the articles out of the place of deposit, and examined the large red periogue we left here,[1] and found it too rotten to take down the river. We therefore took what nails out of it we could, left our horses on the plains and proceeded down the river. About the time we started a heavy gust of rain and hail, accompanied with thunder and lightning came on and lasted about an hour, after which we had a cloudy wet afternoon, and in the evening we encamped about twenty-five miles below the forks.

1. They cached the red pirogue on an island in the then mouth of Marias River, on June 10, 1805.

"Patrick Gass on Blackfeet Encounter," in *The Journals of the Lewis and Clark Expedition,* ed. Gary Moulton (Lincoln: University of Nebraska Press, 1996), vol. 10, 258–59.

A BLACKFEET VERSION OF THEIR ENCOUNTER WITH THE AMERICANS
Olin Wheeler

In the 1890s, the Northern Pacific Railroad hired Olin Wheeler, a journalist, to compile an annual magazine called Wonderland, *which featured articles on the region's scenic and historic sites. In preparation for the centennial of the Lewis and Clark expedition, Wheeler was asked to provide a modern portrait of the explorers' route.*

Wheeler visited the Blackfeet homeland and interviewed George Bird Grinnell, an anthropologist who had spent many years studying the tribe. Grinnell told Wheeler the story of Wolf Calf (1793?-1895), one of the young men involved in the skirmish with Lewis and the Americans in 1806. According to Grinnell, Wolf Calf and his friends had not known who the Americans were; they had tried to capture the

Americans' guns and horses out of youthful bravado. Such "captures" were a central element of Plains warriors' competitive culture.

Through the courtesy of George Bird Grinnell, I am enabled to present a brief account of Captain Lewis's fight with the Blackfeet, which came from one of the Indians engaged in it, and to give also a picture of the Indian himself.

Mr. Grinnell, in his years of affiliation with and study among the Blackfeet, made a friend of old Wolf Calf, for many years the most aged of the Piegan Blackfeet. He was a mine of ancient lore [Mr. Grinnell states], and was quite willing to talk freely on all historical subjects. When he died he was supposed to be considerably over one hundred years old, and, as nearly as I could figure it, he was one hundred and two, in 1895. He used often to speak of men in the tribe, whom I regarded as very aged, as mere boys, and to say that when he was growing up and old enough to go to war, they had not yet been born.

Regarding the meeting with Captain Lewis, Mr. Grinnell continues:

He told me that he was with a war party to the south when they met the first white men that had ever come into the lower country. They met these people in a friendly fashion, but the chief directed his young men to try to steal some of their things. They did so, and the white men killed the first man with their "big knives." This was the man killed, I suppose, by Fields. Afterwards the Indians ran off some of the horses of the white men. The name of the first man killed was Side Hill Calf, or Calf Standing on a Side Hill.

Regarding the point where the fight occurred:

Wolf Calf located this place as on the hills immediately south of Birch Creek, where the town of Robare, Teton County, now stands.

The old man did not know who Lewis and Clark were, but his story agrees so exactly with that given in the Journal that I cannot doubt that this was the Indian side of the occurrence. He must have been a young boy at the time, but in the old war days boys of nine and ten years not infrequently went on the war path.

In reply to my inquiry as to any attempt of the Indians to pursue Lewis, Mr. Grinnell said that Wolf Calf distinctly gave me the idea that the Indians were badly frightened, felt that they had been punished, and I think he ended his story with, "then we all ran away." I have no doubt in my own mind that they flew north about as fast as Lewis flew south and east.

"A Blackfeet Version of Their Encounter with the Americans," in Olin Wheeler, *The Trail of Lewis and Clark* (New York: Putnam, 1976), 308–16.

PART 3

———————◆◆◆———————

A NEW NATION COMES
TO THE INDIAN COUNTRY

The Lewis and Clark expedition had little immediate impact on the Indian country. The Corps of Discovery had failed to find an easy route to the Pacific and few people wanted to follow its difficult path. Nevertheless, the expedition had established a U.S. presence in the Trans-Mississippi West. In addition, the information the explorers compiled helped Americans understand that a vast new territory lay along the western border. As citizens began thinking about national expansion, their attention would shift westward.

For forty years, American expansion into the Missouri River basin and beyond was gradual. A profitable fur trade encouraged outposts and new settlements, but there was little wholesale movement of eastern populations to either the Plains or the Pacific Coast. That situation changed in the 1840s. A dispute between Mexico and Americans in Texas grew into a confrontation that culminated in war. The spoils of that conflict included modern Arizona, New Mexico, California, Utah, and Nevada. At the same time, the settlement of a long-standing border dispute with Great Britain secured the American title to Oregon and Washington. And in 1849, the discovery of gold in California sparked a rush of prospectors and adventurers to that new American territory. In the 1850s, these migrations began to change the character of the territory first visited by the Corps of Discovery. Gold rushes drew Americans to Oregon, Idaho, and Montana and the promise of new agricultural land attracted additional settlers to follow in the prospectors' wake. The coming of the railroads in the second half of the century completed the transformation of the region: the first railroad to link Chicago to the Mississippi was opened in 1854, and the first transcontinental route began operation in 1869. In the following three decades three additional rail lines forged links between eastern cities and the Pacific. By 1900, Americans had a new name for the Indian country. They now called it simply "the West." This process was not peaceful; rather it was punctuated by displacement, violence, and military conflict.

This section of the book focuses on the experiences of Native American groups that the Corps of Discovery encountered on its journey to the Pacific. It illustrates the ways in which different aspects of American expansion—the fur trade, mining, homesteading, ranching, and the "Americanization" efforts of missionaries and schoolteachers—altered and undermined the traditions and institutions of the Indian country.

CHAPTER THIRTEEN

Two Views of Western North America

This chapter presents two maps of the Indian country. The first map appeared just prior to large-scale American migration to the West. The second appeared as that migration was reaching its peak.

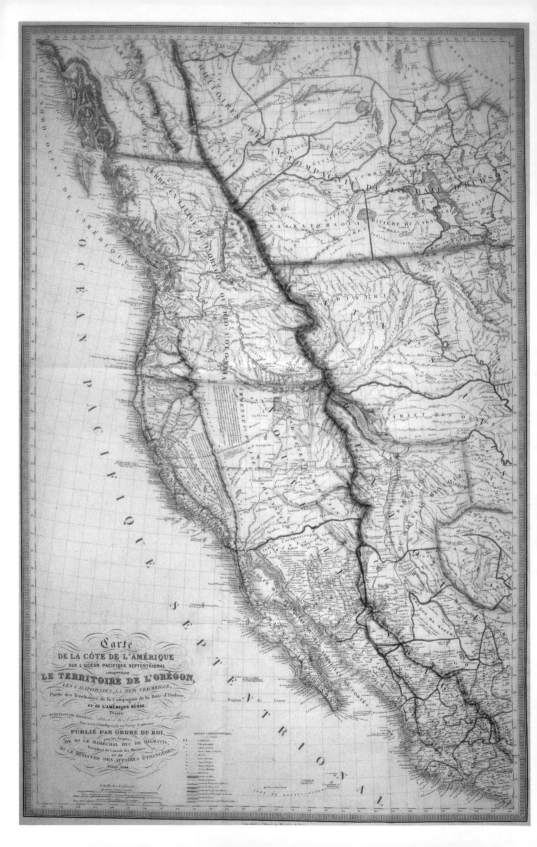

Opposite page: This map illustrates the complex loyalties and jurisdictions that characterized the Indian country four decades after the Lewis and Clark expedition. Produced in 1844 by Eugene Duflot de Mofras, a French diplomat stationed in Mexico City, the map shows Texas as an independent country, Mexico broken into several autonomous provinces, the Canadian prairies as the private property of the Hudson's Bay Company, Alaska as part of the Russian empire, and Oregon as a territory "in litigation" between the United States and Great Britain. Fine print on the map indicates that vast territories were ruled by Indian nations—"Osages," "Mandans," and others. Eugene Duflot de Mofras, "Carte de la Côte de l'Amérique," detail, from *Exploration du Territoire de l'Oregon, des Californies et de la mer Vermeille, executée pendant les années 1840, 1841 et 1842* (Paris: A. Bertrand, 1844). Courtesy the Newberry Library (Graff 1169).

Following pages: Barely forty years after de Mofras produced his complex map of western North America, the Chicago publisher Rand McNally produced an atlas for schoolchildren. The United States now claimed complete authority over the former Indian Country lands. "The United States, 1884," in *Dollar Atlas of the United States and Canada* (Chicago: Rand McNally, 1884). Courtesy the Newberry Library (RnMcNally Atlas folio D6 1884, pp. 18–19).

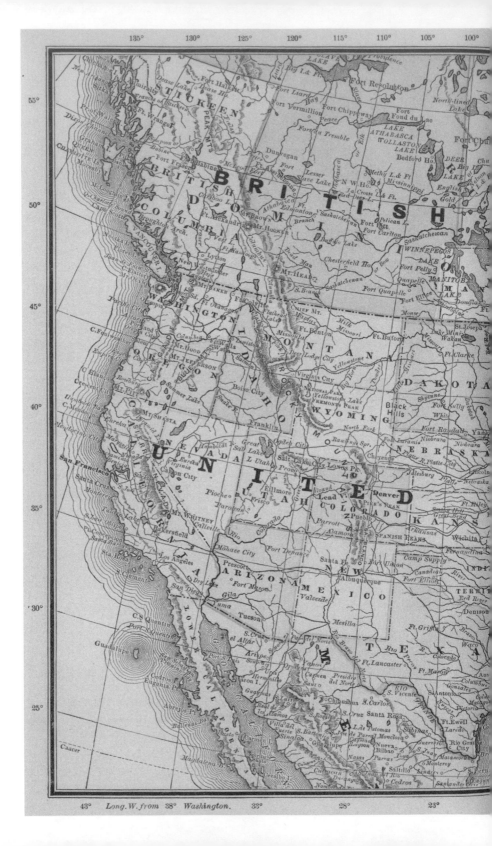

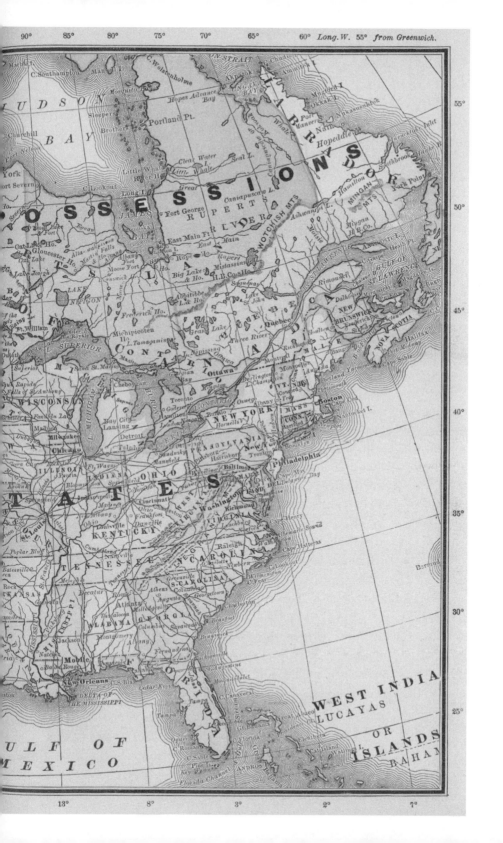

CHAPTER FOURTEEN

The Fur Trade

For the first third of the nineteenth century, the fur trade formed the basis for most of the interaction between representatives of the United States and the people of the Indian country. With the entry of the Americans into the fur trade in the wake of the Lewis and Clark expedition, that enterprise grew dramatically in scale. St. Louis became the epicenter of the trade and American corporations based in that city dominated commerce along the Missouri.

The early nineteenth-century American fur trade relied on the abundant supply of fur-bearing animals in the Indian country, as well as the availability of Native American labor and the diplomatic skill of the fur traders. Among the pioneers of the western fur trade were John Colter and George Drouillard, Corps of Discovery veterans. These "mountain men" carried tools, cloth, and other trade goods west to Indian trading centers and exchanged them for valuable furs and buffalo hides.

The expanded fur trade brought profound changes to the Indian country. Commercial trading posts created new, mixed-heritage communities and encouraged Native people to devote the bulk of their time to gathering and processing furs. Sustained contact with outsiders also brought new diseases to Indian communities and encouraged overhunting of fur-bearing animals. By 1840 the fur trade had brought prosperity to many and had made John Jacob Astor America's first millionaire. At the same time it disrupted local Native American economies by displacing a system of combined subsistence and trade with a more purely cash economy.

THE STATE OF THE FUR TRADE, 1831
Joshua Pilcher

This report illustrates how high the geopolitical stakes could be in the early nine-teenth-century American fur industry. A veteran trader who had done business in St. Louis for decades, Joshua Pilcher (1790–1843) traveled to the Rockies and Oregon in the 1820s in search of new opportunities. Frustrated by the Canadian Hudson's Bay Company agents who dominated the territory, Pilcher urged the national govern-ment to expel the British from the Northwest. He predicted that whoever controlled the Columbia River trade "will also command the navigation and commerce of the Pacific." By stating the issue in global terms, Pilcher underscored the national inter-ests at stake in a continental fur trade.

The Present State of the Fur Trade

As early as the year 1805, the Northwest Company had extended its opera-tions to the waters of the Columbia; and an agent or partner of that concern passed the winter on Clark's fork, about 350 miles above its junction with the main Columbia, at the time Captains Lewis and Clark were at the Pacific. A short time after *their* return to the United States, a company was organised and fitted out by Mr. Astor, of New York, under the superintendence of W. P. Hunt, Esquire, of St. Louis, for the purpose of prosecuting the fur trade on the Columbia. The chief establishment of this company was made at the mouth of the Columbia, and called Astoria; and, notwithstanding the opposition it had to encounter from the Northwest Company, the country being then rich in furs, the proprietors of the American Company had good grounds to hope for the most favorable results. A circumstance, however, soon occurred, which blasted their expectations, and made it necessary for them to close their busi-ness, and abandon the country. The commencement of the war with England in 1812 presented difficulties in the prosecution of their business which they had not expected; and they were, in consequence, induced to dispose of their interest in that country to the Northwest Company, and abandon it. From that time until about the year 1821, the Northwest Company remained in the quiet possession of the country, unopposed in a trade from which they must have derived immense profits. It is true, that, in the year 1818, the establishment at the mouth of the Columbia, which had been sold by the American Company to the Northwest, was delivered to an agent of the American Government, conformably to the stipulations of the treaty of Ghent, respecting all parts which have fallen into the hands of the British during the war. This may have been considered as a formal delivery of the whole country; but it appears to have been, understood by all parties at the time as a mere nominal transaction, as that company remained in possession, and continued to prosecute their business; and the right to occupy that country for the term of ten years was secured to them by a treaty entered into by our minister at London, and subsequently ratified by the proper authorities.

They accordingly continued their operations until the year 1821, free from all competition—their great rival in the fur trade, the Hudson's Bay Company, never having extended its operations to the west of the mountains in that quarter. About this time, these two rivals found it necessary to put an end to an unprofitable strife, from which they had no longer any thing to expect but a waste of means, and an increase of that hostile spirit which had frequently produced the most inveterate rencounters, and resulted in the loss of many lives. With this view they formed a union; the Northwest Company sold out its stock and establishments to that of the Hudson's Bay, and ceased to exist as a company; and, in this sale, their establishments on the Columbia were of course included.

From that until the present time, the Hudson's Bay Company have remained the sole occupants of the Columbia river. It is true that they have sometimes met with a transient opposition from some hunters from this country, who are probably licensed to trade on the Columbia, but whose real pursuits are that of trapping; but the Hudson's Bay Company may, nevertheless, be considered the sole occupants, as they are the only persons who have any pretensions to a regularly settled system of business, or who have any establishments in that country. Both the Hudson's Bay Company and citizens of the United States engage in trapping, and each suffer occasionally from the attacks of the Indians. And here I take occasion, as an act of justice to the gentlemen of the Hudson's Bay Company, to say that I saw nothing to justify the opinion that they excited the Indians to kill and rob our citizens. Our laws prohibit the practice of trapping and hunting; but it would seem to be the very height of injustice to prohibit our own citizens from doing upon our own territories what the British are allowed to do, and equally absurd to suppose that the same treaty which covers their operations will not cover ours also. About three hundred men who may be considered citizens of the United States are now engaged in the business, some, with much profit to themselves, others with great loss; but all with advantage to the United States, as, from their exertions, the supply of furs are obtained, which are indispensable to the hatting manufactories. As for the fur trade itself, it is laboring under the most serious difficulties, and calls loudly upon the aid and sympathy of the Federal Government. In the first place, the woollen goods used in the trade are loaded with duties to the amount of about sixty per cent., which gives an advantage to that amount to the British traders along the northern wilderness frontier, without being of any advantage, that I can see, to domestic manufacturers, as they make no goods of the same kind. These duties ought, therefore, in my opinion, to be abolished; and it is difficult to conceive of any advantage derived from the revenue obtained from this source, equal to the injury done to the fur trade by their continuance. In the next place, American furs have to pay duties in every foreign country to which they are exported, while furs from every country in the world are imported duty free. Under such circumstances, it is no wonder that the trade has been a perilous one in the United States.

Having abandoned the trade myself, I can now express my sentiments upon this subject without fear of incurring the imputation of having acted from interested motives.

Face of the Country

The country must be viewed under three distinct regions—

1st. The mountain region, drained by the upper waters of the Multnomah, Lewis's river, Clark's river, and McGilvray's river; all of which fall into the Columbia on its south side.

2d. The plains which lay between the foot of the mountains and the head of tide water.

3d. The tide water region, which extends from the foot of the plains to the sea.

My personal observation was chiefly confined to the first of these regions, over which I travelled from south to north, and spent about a year in making six or seven degrees of latitude, which I traversed in many directions. Lewis's river, where I crossed it, affords some very extensive fertile low grounds, which appeared suitable for any kind of culture. The valleys were well covered with such grass as is common in all parts of the Columbia; and besides these, I found the white clover in great abundance. This was so unexpected that I was, induced to make some inquiries, and was informed that blue grass, timothy, and clover, were common in the country, and among its spontaneous productions. The northern branches of Lewis's river issue from rugged mountains, covered with almost impenetrable forests of pine and cedar. The upper parts of Clark's river present the same general appearance; but there are several situations on this river which would admit of settlements to a considerable extent; and though not comparable in fertility of soil to the rich lands of Missouri and Illinois, yet superior to many of the inhabited and cultivated parts of the Atlantic States, where powerful communities have grown up. The Flathead lake, and its rich and beautiful valley, are on this fork, and vie in appearance with the beautiful lakes and valleys of Switzerland. At the foot of the mountains, according to information there is a belt or strip of fertile land, similar to what is seen at the foot of the Alleghany and Blue Ridge.

The second region, consisting of the plains, is sandy, destitute of timber, quite unfit, in general, for cultivation, and famous only for the fine horses that are found among the Indians.

The third region is heavily timbered, and intermixed with considerable tracts of fertile soil, and, towards the sea, is bound in by mountains, which line the coast, and through which all the waters of the valley of the Cumberland issue, by one channel, into the ocean. To the question, how far a nation of people could subsist west of the Rocky mountains, it might be answered, comparatively, by referring to the east side of the Alleghanies. The resources of agriculture might be something inferior; for grazing and raising stock; superior, and for the salmon fishery, perhaps the very finest in the world. These fish enter the mouth of the Columbia, ascend all its tributaries, and run, when not impeded by great falls, to the heads of the creeks in the mountains. They will pass falls of sixteen feet. I have myself seen myriads, in the course of a few hours, pass the Kettle falls of the Columbia, just below the mouth of Clark's fork, which are about that height. They are the main resource of the Indians; and to a civilized people, acquainted with taking, and curing them with salt, of which the Indians have none, they would be a great article of subsistence and exportation. . . .

Passes through the Mountains

The most erroneous ideas prevail upon this head. The Rocky mountains are deemed by many to be impassable, and to present the barrier which will arrest the westward march of the American population. The man must know but little of the American people who supposes they can be stopped by any thing in the shape of mountains, deserts, seas, or rivers; and he can know nothing at all of the mountains in question, to suppose that they are impassable. I have been familiar with these mountains for three years, and have crossed them often, and at various points between the latitude 42 and 54; that is to say, between the head waters of the Rio Colorado of the gulf of California, and the Athabasca of the Polar sea. I have, therefore, the means to know something about them, and a right to oppose my knowledge to the suppositions of strangers. I say, then, that nothing is more easily passed than these mountains. Wagons and carriages may cross them in a state of nature without difficulty, and with little delay in the day's journey. Some parts are very high; but the gradual rise of the country, in the vast slope from the Mississippi to the foot of the mountains, makes a considerable elevation without perceptible increase, and then the gaps or depressions let you through almost upon a level. This is particularly the case opposite the head of the Platte, where I crossed in 1827, and which has already been described. I have crossed here often, and always without delay or difficulty. It is, in fact, one of the best passes, and presents the best over-land route from the valley of the Mississippi to the mouth of the Columbia, and would follow the line of the Platte and Lewis's river. Another pass, following the line of the Missouri and the Columbia, by water, would be up the Missouri to the Great falls, two thousand five hundred and seventy-five miles from St. Louis, and a clear navigation all the way; thence due north one hundred and fifty miles, through a low gap, to Clark's river; thence down the river, making some portages, to near the principal falls, and then overland sixty miles to the main Columbia. The Hudson's Bay Company use this route now in trading up Clark's river. From thence down the Columbia to the sea.

Extent and Configuration of the Country

From the dividing ridge of the Rocky mountains is about nine or ten degrees of longitude, say about five hundred miles, in a straight direction from the sea; from the head of the Multnumah in the south to the source of the Columbia in the north, is about fourteen degrees of latitude, or about nine hundred miles, in a strait line. These distances would give a superficial content of three hundred and sixty thousand square miles, which is much larger than the principal kingdoms of Europe. The form or configuration of the country is the most perfect and admirable which the imagination can conceive. All its outlines are distinctly marked; all its interior is connected together. Frozen regions to the north, the ocean and its mountainous coast to the west, the Rocky mountains to the east, sandy and desert plains to the south; such are its boundaries.

Within, the whole country is watered by the streams of a single river, issuing from the north, east, and south, uniting in the region of tide water, and communicating with, the sea by a single outlet.

Such a country is formed for defence; and whatever power gets possession of it will probably be able to keep it. Several years ago the maxim was proclaimed by President Monroe, and re-echoed by the whole American people, that no part of this continent was open to European colonization. Since that time, the settlements of the Hudson's Bay Company have been formed in the valley of the Columbia; and this company acts under the charter, the treaties, and the acts of Parliament of the British crown. It is rich in wealth, strong in power, and efficient in its organization. It is second only to the East India Company, and, like it, has immense territories and innumerable tribes of natives, besides its own proper strength, under its command. This company, thus backed by the power of the British Government, may bring the maxim of President Monroe to a practical decision.

After making these remarks upon the soil, climate, extent, and configuration of this country, it is hardly necessary to intimate that the power which possesses it will also command the navigation and commerce of the Pacific ocean.

Number and State of the Indians

These may be stated at thirty thousand souls, exclusive of the Snake Indians. This estimate is not a random guess, but founded on accurate information, derived from the Hudson's Bay Company. The Snakes are exceedingly numerous, and range through the mountains. None of these Indians cultivate anything; they depend upon hunting and fishing, and of course are exposed to the extremes of feasts and famine. The salmon fishery is their great resource; and to avail, themselves of it, they assemble from great distances, and collect along the banks of the river, and principally at the different falls, from the head of tide water to the main source of the river in the Rocky mountains. They cure these fish without salt, by drying in the sun. In the absence of game and fish, they are driven to every extremity to sustain life—devouring every bird, beast, insect, and creeping thing they can get hold of, and tearing up the ground for roots. Those in the plains and gorges of the mountains are excellent horsemen. In point of temper and disposition, they are milder than the Indians east of the mountains, and in morals more honest; but this may be an effect of the discipline of the Hudson's Bay Company, for I never saw Indians in a state of nature who would not steal to which may be added three other bad qualities, to wit: begging, drinking, and lying. On the other hand, they have the virtue of hospitality, and offer without request a part of their food to every traveller.

They use their arms with great dexterity on horseback, while pursuing the game at full speed; and are capable of becoming a very formidable enemy, as irregular cavalry, when properly trained.

These observations I address to you, sir, as an organ of communication with the President. As an American citizen, anxious for the prosperity of my country, I deem it my duty to communicate to the Government the observations which I have made upon the state of things to the west of the Rocky mountains. Aiming at truth, brevity, and precision, and to the presentation of prominent points, I have omitted personal details and minute descriptions, and endeavored to exhibit in one view the facts which it may be necessary for the Government to possess.

Joshua Pilcher, "Letter to Secretary of War Regarding the Present State of the Fur Trade," in *Message to the President Regarding the State of Fur Trade* (Washington, D.C.: Committee of Military Affairs, 1831), 17–21.

AN OVERVIEW OF THE WESTERN FUR TRADE
David J. Wishart

Unlike Joshua Pilcher, an observer with a vested interest, the modern geographer David Wishart tried to offer a balanced view of the fur trade. Among the dimensions Wishart addresses here—and which Pilcher did not consider—are the environmental impact of this new industry and its role in preparing for the eventual American occupation of the Indian country.

The sweep across the North American continent has traditionally been described in heroic terms, and the blemishes which stained each period of frontier settlement have tended to fade with time. Perhaps, as Bellow's protagonist Moses Herzog wrote (to himself), "we have fashioned a new Utopian history, an idyll, comparing the present to an imaginary past, because we hate the world as it is."[1] Certainly the fur trade has generally been represented as a glorious episode in the opening of the West,[2] and the trapper, in Goetzmann's words, is "a figure of American mythology rather than history."[3]

There is, as Sauer has argued, "a dark obverse" to this romanticised view of American history.[4] The fur trade was an early stage in the progressive dissipation of the American environment. In any assessment of the fur trade as a frontier stage of occupance both the practical accomplishments and the destructive environmental impact should be weighed.

The assessment begins with the actors, who were a small, diverse group of men. The trappers and traders were complex characters, and their motivations for entering the fur trade were varied and probably ambiguous. They were generally young men in their twenties and thirties. The majority of the trappers were married, although the American Fur Company preferred single men. They were mostly drawn from rural areas of Canada, the Midwest, and the Upper South.[5] There is reason to believe that the Rocky Mountain Trapping System attracted a rougher type of individual than the Upper Missouri Fur Trade which, by comparison, was a steady, mundane occupation. To Edwin Denig the trappers were a "desperate set of men," more outlandish and brutal than the traders, and more than half-Indian in appearance and habits.[6]

At least three stereotypes have been used to categorise the Rocky Mountain trappers.[7] Each one, like most reasonable stereotypes, is partly valid. The trapper has been portrayed as an epic hero who confronted and partially tamed the wilderness. Conversely, he has been cast as an outsider, a daring but degraded character who was escaping the strictures of a civilised society. To these standard stereotypes Goetzmann has added a third which seems to be most tenable: the trapper was a Jacksonian man, an "expectant capitalist" like most other Americans of that time. Goetzmann substantiates his thesis with statistical evidence which indicates that a primary motivation for participating in the fur trade was to accumulate capital quickly. This capital could subsequently be invested in more permanent and less demanding occupations.[8]

Each of these stereotypes draws support from the contemporary literature of the fur trade. Zenas Leonard ... was an expectant capitalist who entered the Rocky Mountain Trapping System with the hope of making a fortune from what he termed a "toilsome occupation."[9] In this endeavour, unlike most of his peers,[10] Leonard was partially successful. Following the disintegration of Bonneville's schemes in 1835, Leonard returned to Clearfield County, Pennsylvania, with $1,100 accumulated capital from five years' labour. Some of his colleagues, however, were unwilling or unable to leave the Rocky Mountains:

> Many were anxious to return to the States, but feared to do so, lest the offended law might hold them responsible for misdemeanors committed previous to their embarking in the trapping business, and others could not be persuaded to do so for any price—declaring that civilized life had no charms for them.[11]

Some trappers, therefore, were escapists who, in Russell's words, had been "banished to the wilderness" by "some mishap in life."[12] Others, like Russell, were romantics who developed an attachment to the remote, solitary life in the

Rocky Mountains.[13] Most, perhaps, were simply men trying to earn a living. The categories overlap and in any one trapper motivations surely varied with time, experience, even with mood.

Like most frontiersmen, the trappers and traders predominantly viewed the environment with antipathy. Romanticism was not allowed to interfere with the pragmatic aspects of making the wilderness productive.[14] The trappers and traders were determined to draw from the environment any resource that was easily exploitable and valuable. When the resources of one area were depleted they moved on to exploit other areas of frontier opportunity. This was characteristic of the settlement process in North America which, in Zelinsky's words, "can be viewed as a series of environmental traumas or conflicts, in each of which the modern American has won the immediate decision through a technical knockout."[15]

The fur trade was never an important part of the American economy; only in one year (1833) during the 1820s and 1830s did fur exports from the United States exceed $800,000.[16] However, contrary to Clayton, the fur trade was extremely important in the regional economy of the Trans-Missouri West, particularly with reference to the growth of St. Louis.

St. Louis was the major collecting and dispersing depot for furs and trade goods. It is estimated that from 1807 to 1840 an average of $200,000–$300,000 worth of furs were channelled annually through St. Louis to the east coast and Western Europe. The value of the return flow of trade goods was about the same.[17] This represents an early stage in Vance's mercantile model of settlement, and it supports Harold Innis's thesis that the trade in staples was of basic importance to the economic development of North America.[18] The fur trade stimulated the early growth of St. Louis, established a spirit of enterprise, and resulted in an accumulation of knowledge and capital that was a prerequisite to the diversification of the wholesaling base of the city.

Thomas Jefferson, it may be recalled, envisaged the fur trade as the overture to the American settlement of the west. In this geopolitical context the fur trade accomplished a great deal. The leading trappers were well aware of the catalytic role they were playing in the settlement process. In their 1830 letter to John Eaton, the Secretary of War, Smith, Jackson, and Sublette warned of the danger of British activities in Oregon, and they emphasised that the American government should counteract this presence by utilising the transcontinental routeway which the trappers had established. Having thus stated "the facts," Smith, Jackson, and Sublette felt that they had "complied with their duty, and rendered an acceptable service to the administration."[19]

The trappers completed the initial work of American exploration in the West. It was an unsophisticated process compared to the scientific, government-sponsored surveys which followed after 1840. Generally the trappers' explorations were a by-product of the search for furs. Nevertheless, this conversion of second-degree and third-degree geographical knowledge into first-degree knowledge expressed on maps was a major achievement of the fur trade.[20] By 1840 the transcontinental trails were established, the main tenets of western geography were known, and the West had become, in Goetzmann's words, "a place to move into—to occupy and settle and develop."[21] Jefferson's vision of the fur trade as a preliminary stage in the settlement of the West had been realised.

The fur trade was instrumental in the establishment of two of the most important routeways in the early development of the West—the Missouri River and the Oregon Trail. The Missouri River never fulfilled its promise as a transcontinental channel of commerce and migration: The Passage to India proved to be no more than a "macrogeographical dream."[22] The Missouri River did, however, afford access to the northern Great Plains and Rocky Mountains. In the three decades following 1840 the river was used as a transportation line by fur traders, miners, the military, and, eventually, by settlers. Dependable steamboat service, first introduced on the upper Missouri by the American Fur Company in 1831, continued to expand and reached a peak in the decade 1860 to 1870. Thereafter the railroads cut across the plains from Iowa, Minnesota, and the eastern Dakotas, and the river route was truncated.

William Ashley and Jedediah Smith established the concept of a central route to the Pacific in the 1820s. In the following decade Nathaniel Wyeth, Captain Bonneville, and Joe Walker added substance to this concept and proved the practicality of the Oregon and California trails. Walker, Tom Fitzpatrick, and Caleb Greenwood, amongst other trappers, continued to apply their accumulated geographical knowledge in the 1840s by guiding emigrant trains to the Pacific. Justifiably this forging of the emigrant trails has been described as "the climax of the 'mountain man' era of western exploration."[23]

After the collapse of the Rocky Mountain Trapping System the trappers formed the vanguard of American settlement in Oregon, California, and New Mexico. Fehrman in his statistical analysis of the biographical sketches that were included in Hafen's "Mountain Man" series concluded that 90.5 percent of the trappers (218 men) eventually died to the west of the Mississippi. The four areas of Missouri (41), California (39), New Mexico (31), and Oregon (28) accounted for 64 percent of these men.[24]

This migration of what Merk derisively called "broken-down trappers" is epitomised by Robert Newell's exhortation to his colleague and brother-in-law Joe Meek in 1840:

"Come," said Newell to Meek, "We are done with this life in the mountains— done with wading in beaver-dams and freezing or starving alternatively—done with Indian trading and Indian fighting. . . . Let us go down to the Wallamet and take farms."[25]

There the trappers formed "a nucleus of a steadily growing pioneer force."[26] With typical frontier versatility they engaged in a wide variety of occupations, both in farming and in trade. They were often successful because men were in short supply on the frontier, particularly men with accumulated capital (no matter how small) and experience. Many trappers became prominent members of these embryonic communities. Joe Meek, for example, was Oregon's first sheriff, elected in 1843, and first U.S. Marshall, appointed in 1848. Robert Newell was elected to membership in Oregon's first territorial legislature in 1849 and in the same year he was named one of the three United States sub-Indian agents for Oregon Territory. As Zelinsky has pointed out in his Doctrine of First Effective Settlement, "the activities of a few hundred, or even a few score, initial colonizers can mean much more for the cultural geography of a place than the contributions of tens of thousands of new immigrants a few generations later."[27]

This trickle of American settlers to Oregon swelled into a flood after 1843. To the British Oregon remained primarily a "company frontier"; to the Americans it was part of their "natural frontier" and their national destiny. In 1841 Governor Simpson responded with a "counter-immigration" policy, but his efforts were in vain. Four years later the Hudson's Bay Company moved the headquarters of the Columbia District north to Fort Victoria on Vancouver Island, and the "Oregon Question" was virtually settled.[28]

In a spatial sense, however, the influence of the fur trade on the northern Great Plains and Rocky Mountains was generally rather transitory. Derwent Whittlesey, writing in 1929, argued that the human occupance in an area could be divided into discrete stages, each stage being linked genetically "to its forbear and to its offspring."[29] Perhaps the structure of an oil painting is analogous to this process of sequent occupance. Each successive layer of paint builds on the foundation of previous layers and largely obliterates them. Eventually only remnants of the earlier layers show through on the landscape. The fur trade influenced the stages of occupance which followed close after, but its imprint was soon erased from the land by new forms of use.

The geography of the missionary frontier on the northern Great Plains and in Oregon was greatly influenced by the existent network of the fur trade. This is hardly surprising, because the missionaries, like the traders, arranged their system primarily to afford access to the Indians.

The missionaries who worked among the Indians on the Upper Missouri in the 1840s and 1850s used the trading posts as bases and the company steamboats for transportation. The American Fur Company welcomed the missionaries, believing that peaceful, christianised Indians would make more dependable producers. The trading posts became the nucleii of later Catholic parishes in the Dakotas and Montana.[30]

In Oregon the mission frontier on the Columbia Plain and to the west of the Cascades was closely fitted to the patterns of the fur trade. In the second half of the 1830s missionaries (such as Marcus Whitman and Henry Spaulding) travelled with the fur parties to Oregon, and in subsequent years the Platte Overland Route served as the main line of communication between the missions and their headquarters in New England. The missions were located near the Hudson's Bay Company posts for the purposes of protection, companionship, and access to the Indians and the main routes of travel. The influence of the fur trade was fundamental. Indeed, in Meinig's opinion, "without that established framework, the Oregon missions could have been neither inaugurated nor maintained."[31]

Until 1870 the military frontier closely traced the general pattern of transportation and locations established during the fur trade. The forts, like the trading posts, were generally built on the terraces of the Missouri, within easy reach of the river for the bulk transportation of men and goods, but above the level of the flood waters. Ideally the sites provided fresh water, grass for forage, and flat land for the same type of small-scale agriculture that had been practised around the trading posts.

There was, however, very little continuance of site, as opposed to situation, even before 1870. Of 68 military forts established on the northern Great Plains from 1846 to 1891 only six were built around the nucleus of a former trading post.[32] In 1855, for example, the army purchased Fort Pierre from the American Fur Company to serve as a base for operations against the Dakota. They soon found that Fort Pierre was quite unsuitable for its new role. The buildings were in poor repair, there was insufficient pasture for the animals, and there was no fuel within twenty miles. A quarter of a century of continued occupance by traders had exhausted the resources of the surrounding country. Consequently in 1857 Fort Pierre was abandoned. By 1859 the post lay in ruins.[33]

After 1870 military forts were dispersed throughout the northern Great Plains to protect the emigrant routes, the Bozeman Trail, and the workers on the Union Pacific and Northern Pacific Railroads, and to support the relentless campaign that was waged against the Indians after the Battle of the Little Big Horn. By the 1880s the military had virtually crushed the resistance on the northern Great Plains and the surviving Indians were incarcerated on reservations. The fur trade, mission, and military frontiers—geographic systems which were predicated in one form or another on the Indians—gave way to new patterns on the land. Thereafter towns developed as central places on an agricultural frontier not as entrepots in a mercantilist system.

Symbolically the northern loop of the Oregon Trail, which traced the North Platte and Sweetwater to the Big Sandy and Green, was abandoned after 1870 when the Union Pacific was built *on* a direct route across the Great Divide Basin. The Oregon Trail, Vance explains, "was located where nature came closest to maintaining the traveler rather than where the effort was least." The Union Pacific on the other hand (and subsequently Interstate 80) were established along lines of "least wasted effort" in an attempt to reduce overall costs.[34] South Pass, the most important gateway in the early settlement of the West, is now crossed by Highway 28, a rather remote state road. Contrary to Turner, a neat continuity of routes did not exist on this frontier.[35] Instead routes were altered as the purposes of transportation changed.

In comparison with later stages of frontier settlement the fur trade barely scratched the surface of the West. The trappers and traders were too few in number, too limited in technology, and too focused in their objectives of exploitation for it to be otherwise. The fur trade did, however, set the pace for subsequent Euro-American activity in the West. The attitude of rapacious, short-term exploitation which was imprinted during the fur trade persisted after 1840 as the focus shifted from furs to minerals, timber, land, and water.

The fur trade did, of course, result in a serious depletion of beaver reserves throughout the northern Great Plains and Rocky Mountains. Yet, as Denig noted in 1854, beaver populations quickly rebounded after 1840 once the pressure of continuous overtrapping was removed:

> This animal has been trapped and killed to such an extent as to threaten his entire extinction, though for the last 10 or 12 years, since beaver trapping by large bodies of men has been abandoned, they have greatly increased.[36]

Even in the Rocky Mountains total depletion was averted by the decline in the demand for beaver pelts in the late 1830s (aided, perhaps, by favourable trends in the natural cycle). The beaver was given a "breathing-time," wrote Ruxton in 1849, "and this valuable fur-bearing animal, which otherwise would, in the course of a few years, have become extinct, has now a chance of multiplying, and will in a short time again become abundant."[37] By the late 1840s beaver were again numerous on the Arkansas and Platte rivers and in the parks of Colorado.

Nevertheless, unregulated trapping continued throughout the second half of the nineteenth century, often as a secondary activity by miners and farmers. By 1900 in Colorado, for example, beaver populations were again dangerously low.[38] Thereafter, largely as a result of the pioneering work of Aldo Leopold who sparked the wilderness movement, beaver were protected by state legislation. Public trapping was restricted to designated periods of the year and in the twentieth century the streams of the western United States once again teem with beaver.

Protection, of course, came almost too late for the bison herds. By 1890, when many Americans first became aware of the dimensions of the slaughter, less than 1,000 bison remained as remnants of the once massive herds. As early as 1840, as a result of hunting by the trappers and the Indians, bison were no longer found to the west of the Rocky Mountains. On the northern Great Plains, however, the great destruction came not before 1840 but in the 1870s when the railroads afforded easy access for hide hunters and so-called sportsmen who systematically destroyed the herds. Even as late as 1854, Denig opined that "Buffalo are very numerous and we do not, after 20 years experience, find that they decrease in this quarter, although upward of 150,000 are killed annually throughout the extent of our trade."[39]

Nevertheless, the attitude of unconstrained exploitation was inculcated during the initial stages of the Upper Missouri Fur Trade. The traders began the process of depletion by furnishing the producing Indians with guns and a commercial incentive to produce hides and tongues above the needs of their own subsistence and inter-tribal trade. The herds were saved from greater destruction before 1840 only because the market and the scale of production were limited.[40]

The fur trade was also directly responsible for extensive deforestation of the riparian woodlands along the upper Missouri. Large supplies of wood were needed to stoke the steamboats, to construct the batteaux, and to build, maintain, and heat the trading posts. By 1854, for example, Fort Pierre consumed 1,000 cords of wood each year. Wood for construction was carried on rafts from 80 miles above the post and wood for fuel was hauled more than ten miles.[41]

The repercussions of this deforestation were also felt by the village Indians on the upper Missouri. In the second half of the 1840s the Mandan-Hidatsa were forced to move their villages 40 miles upstream from the traditional Knife River sites because of a serious shortage of wood. The traders, being dependent on the Indians for production, followed suit and built a trading post, Fort Berthold, at the new site.

According to Chittenden, "The relation of the trader to the Indian was the most natural and congenial of any which the two races have ever sustained toward each other."[42] The traders and the Indians interlocked in what Spicer has called a non-directed form of culture contact.[43] Neither culture was locally dominant but each accepted innovations from the other according to its needs. The traders adopted Indian foods and clothes, assimilated Indian geographic knowledge, were subject to Indian laws, and were encouraged by the companies to unite with Indian women. The Indians in turn welcomed the trade goods that the traders brought and willingly expanded their production of robes to meet the new demands.

Yet in the process of this contact the relationship between the Indian and the trader soured. The Indians became increasingly reliant on European trade goods, and the deleterious effects of alcohol and disease strained the existing social systems. The introduction of new commercial motivations weakened the traditional religious aspects of hunting which had given meaning and cohesion to Indian societies. The Indian was co-opted as a partner in the destruction of his most fundamental resource, the bison herds. Unintentionally, unthinkingly, the fur trader undermined the Indian societies and paved the way for a settlement process that would eventually result in the dispossession of the Indians' lands and in the shattering of Indian culture.

Viewed in the broadest sense the fur trade was the vanguard of a massive wave of Euro-American colonisation which brought into contact two sets of cultures with disparate and irreconcilable ways of life. The native Americans were, to use Dasmann's terminology, ecosystem people.[44] They were dependent on a single ecosystem, or at the most a few adjacent ecosystems, for their survival. If they violated the ecosystem—by persistent bison overkill, for example—then their very existence was jeopardised. Intimately connected with the land by livelihood and religion, ecosystem people were basically conservationist.

The fur trappers and traders were biosphere people. They were not dependent on a single ecosystem, but drew support (equipment, trade goods, supplies, markets) from many areas. As biosphere people the trappers and traders possessed a licence for unconstrained exploitation that was untenable for a people who were totally dependent on the ecosystem. They were able to exert great pressure on the environments of the northern Great Plains and Rocky Mountains with relative impunity. When these environments had been stripped of their furs the trappers and traders simply turned to other resources and to other areas. The impact of this exploitation was destructive to the physical environment and to the native inhabitants alike. Perhaps it is through this dark lens, rather than through the rosy lens of frontier romanticism, that the fur trade of the West should be viewed.

Notes

1. S. Bellow, *Herzog* (Greenwich, Conn: Fawcett Publications, 1965), 202–3.

2. See, for example, the treatment in J. A. Hawgood, *America's Western Frontiers* (New York: Knopf, 1967), 93–128. On the other hand, R. A. Bartlett in *The New Country* (New York: Oxford University Press, 1974) devotes considerable attention to the fur trade as a destructive form of occupance.

3. W. H. Goetzmann, "The Mountain Man as Jacksonian Man," *American Quarterly* 15 (1963): 402.

4. C. O. Sauer, "Theme of Plant and Animal Destruction in Economic History," *Journal of Farm Economics* 20 (1938): 49.

5. R. J. Fehrman, "The Mountain Men—A Statistical View," in L. R. Hafen, *The Mountain Men and the Fur Trade of the Far West* (Glendale, Calif.: Arthur H. Clark, 1965), 9–15.

6. J. C. Ewers, *Five Indian Tribes of the Upper Missouri* (Norman: University of Oklahoma Press, 1961), 149.

7. H. L. Carter and M. C. Spencer, "Stereotypes of the Mountain Man," *Western Historical Quarterly* 6 (1975): 17–32. See also, H. N. Smith, *Virgin Land: The American West as Symbol and Myth* (New York: Vintage, 1950), 88–98.

8. Goetzmann, "The Mountain Man as Jacksonian Man," 402–15.

9. W. F. Wagner, *Leonard's Narrative* (Cleveland: Burrows Brothers, 1904), 280–82.

10. H. L. Carter, *Dear Old Kit* (Norman: University of Oklahoma Press, 1968); see also M. C. Spencer, "Stereotypes of the Mountain Man," *Western Historical Quarterly* 6 (1975): 26.

11. Wagner, *Leonard's Narrative*, 281.

12. Osborne Russell, *Journal of a Trapper,* edited by Aubrey L. Haines (Lincoln: University of Nebraska Press, 1965), 84.

13. Russell strove to express his feelings for the Rocky Mountains. See, for example, his description of the Lamax Valley of northwestern Wyoming and the poem which he wrote as a eulogy to his life as a trapper. Ibid., 46, 153–54.

14. R. Nash, *Wilderness and the American Mind* (New Haven: Yale University Press, 1973), 65.

15. W. Zelinsky, *The Cultural Geography of the United States* (Englewood Cliffs, N.J.: Prentice Hall, 1973), 61.

16. J. L. Clayton, "The Growth and Economic Significance of the American Fur Trade, 1790–1890," in *Aspects of the Fur Trade* (St. Paul: Minnesota Historical Society, 1967), 71–72.

17. H. M. Chittenden, *The American Fur Trade of the Far West*, vol. 1 (New York: F. P. Harper, 1902), 8.

18. J. E. Vance Jr., *The Merchant's World* (Englewood Cliffs, N.J.: Prentice Hall, 1970), 148–59; H. A. Innis, *The Fur Trade in Canada* (New Haven: Yale University Press, 1962), 383–402.

19. Quoted in D. L. Morgan, *Jedediah Smith and the Opening of the West* (Lincoln: University of Nebraska Press, 1967), 343–48.

20. The concept of graduations of geographic knowledge is presented in J. L. Allen, "An Analysis of the Exploratory Process: The Lewis and Clark Expedition of 1804–1806," *Geographical Review* 62 (1972): 13–39.

21. W. H. Goetzmann, *Exploration and Empire* (New York: Knopf, 1906), 179.

22. Allen, "An Analysis of the Exploratory Process," 39.

23. Goetzmann, *Exploration and Empire*, 169.

24. Fehrman, "The Mountain Men—A Statistical View," in Hafen, *The Mountain Men and the Fur Trade of the Far West*, vol. 10, 14.

25. F. F. Victor, *The River of the West* (Newark: Bliss, 1870), 204.

26. F. Merk, ed., *Fur Trade and Empire: George Simpson's Journal, 1824–1825* (Cambridge, Mass.: Belknap Press, 1968), xxvii.

27. Zelinsky, *Cultural Geography of the United States*, 14.

28. D. W. Meinig, *The Great Columbia Plain: A Historical Geography, 1805–1910* (Seattle: University of Washington Press, 1968), 115, 146–47.

29. D. Whittlesey, "Sequent Occupance," *Annals*, Association of American Geographers, vol. 19 (1929), 162–65.

30. J. E. Sunder, *The Fur Trade on the Upper Missouri, 1840–65* (Norman: University of Oklahoma press, 1965), 100.

31. Meinig, *The Great Columbia Plain*, 130.

32. R. H. Mattison, "The Military Frontier on the Upper Missouri," *Nebraska History* 37 (1956): 159–82; and "The Army Post on the Northern Plains, 1865–1885," *Nebraska History* 35 (1954): 17–44.

33. F. T. Wilson, "Old Fort Pierre and Its Neighbours," *South Dakota Historical Collections* 1 (1902): 259–440.

34. J. E. Vance Jr., "The Oregon Trail and the Union Pacific Railroad: A Contrast in Purpose," *Annals*, Association of American Geographers, vol. 60 (1961), 357–79.

35. F. J. Turner, *The Significance of the Frontier in American History* (Madison: State Historical Society of Wisconsin, 1894). Turner wrote (p. 13) that "the buffalo trail became the Indian trail, and this became the trader's 'trace'; the trails widened into roads, and the roads into turnpikes, and these in turn were transformed into railroads."

36. J. N. B. Hewitt, ed., *Indian Tribes of the Upper Missouri*, Forty-sixth Annual Report of the Bureau of American Ethnology, 1928–29 (Washington, D.C.: Government Printing Office, 1930), 411. The artist Rudolph Kurz made the same point in 1851 when he wrote: "The low price placed on their skins is to the advantage of the beavers. There are said to be a great many of them not far from here [Fort Union]." J. N. B. Hewitt, *The Journal of Rudolph Friederich Kurz* (Fairfield, Wash.: Viking Press, n.d.), 81.

37. G. F. Ruxton, *Adventures in Mexico and the Rocky Mountains* (London: John Murray, 1849), 239–40.

38. R. R. Lechleitner, *Wild Mammals of Colorado* (Boulder, Colo.: Pruett, 1969), 125–26.

39. Hewitt, *Indian Tribes,* 410.

40. The traders did occasionally try to limit robe production, but the motives were economic, not conservationist. In 1838, for example, Ramsey Crooks advised Chouteau to "restrain the Indians from over-exploiting." There was a poor demand for robes that year and Crooks feared that the market would be swamped and the price would fall. R. Crooks to Pratte, Chouteau and Co., 28 July 1838, *American Fur Company Letterbooks.*

41. "Fort Pierre in 1854," *New York Daily Tribune,* 6 April 1854, reprinted in *Museum of the Fur Trade Quarterly* 2 (1975): 8–9.

42. Chittenden, *American Fur Trade of the Far West,* vol. 1, 8.

43. E. H. Spicer, "Types of Contact and Processes of Change," in E. H. Spicer, ed., *Perspectives in American Indian Culture Change* (Chicago: University of Chicago Press, 1961), 517–44.

44. R. Dasmann, "Future Primitive," *CoEvolution Quarterly* 11 (1976): 26–31.

CHAPTER FIFTEEN

New Settlers

Three events near midcentury unleashed a flood of American settlement across the Indian country. In 1846 a treaty with Great Britain fixed the northern boundary of the United States at the forty-ninth parallel, securing the Americans' title to the Columbia River country. Two years later, the discovery of gold in California began a rush that attracted 250,000 people to what had been a distant province of the young Republic of Mexico. And at almost the same moment the Treaty of Guadalupe Hidalgo, ending the Mexican-American war, transferred a massive arc of new territory to the United States. Suddenly, the United States became a continental power.

Settlers, merchants, and entrepreneurs headed west, their transit sped by such popular routes as the Oregon Trail, and later by the railroad. Eager to set up American institutions across the Indian country, they assumed that the land was theirs, and that their needs superseded those of the existing Indian communities. By the centennial of the Lewis and Clark expedition in 1904, more than six million new people had moved to the territory visited by the Corps of Discovery.

THE TREATY OF 1855

With the settlement of the Oregon boundary dispute with Great Britain and California's admission to the Union in 1850, American settlers suddenly had a target for their western fantasies. In addition to gold, easterners could dream of vacant land and new beginnings. Neither the United States government nor the boosters who trafficked in wagons, supplies, or land tried to stop this process. But government officials in both Washington, D.C., and the West were aware that the California gold rush had unleashed a riot of violence against the state's Indians and that new waves of settlers could do the same in Oregon. In 1853, President Franklin Pierce appointed a thirty-five-year-old West Point graduate, Isaac Stevens, to be the Oregon Territory's first governor. Pierce charged Stevens with arranging for the sale of Indian lands in the new territory and creating a method for separating Natives from the oncoming American pioneers. In the summer of 1855 Stevens traveled to the inland portion of his new domain to meet with leaders of the upper Columbia tribes, many of whom had hosted the Corps of Discovery a half-century earlier. Stevens persuaded the leaders to sell some of their land in exchange for federal subsidies and a guarantee that they could retain smaller homelands and continue to harvest fish from the rivers. Similar agreements were reached at the same time with the Nez Perces, the Middle Columbia groups (including many Chinook-speakers), and the Yakamas.

Popular histories properly condemn the United States for having "broken" many of its treaties, but it is important to recall that when they were negotiated, agreements like this one reflected compromises on both sides and promises that the signatories believed would be kept. In this case, the tribes understood that they were ceding huge tracts of land. At the same time, they believed the United States would exert its power to protect them and to live up to its promise to allow them to continue to hunt and fish in their traditional places within their homeland even if those places were outside the boundaries of their new reservation homes. Eventually it would take the United States Supreme Court and the steel backbone of federal officials to enforce those promises, but no one could deny that they were written into the original agreement.

Articles of agreement and convention made and concluded at the treaty-ground, Camp Stevens, in the Wall-Walla Valley, this ninth day of June, in the year one thousand eight hundred and fifty-five, by and between Isaac I. Stevens, governor and superintendent of Indian affairs for the Territory of Washington, and Joel Palmer, superintendent of Indian affairs for Oregon Territory, on the part of the United States, and the undersigned chiefs, head-men, and delegates of the Walla-Wallas, Cayuses, and Umatilla tribes, and bands of Indians, occupying lands partly in Washington and partly in Oregon Territories, and who, for the purposes of this treaty, are to be regarded as one nation acting for and in behalf of their respective bands and tribes, they being duly authorized thereto; it being understood that Superintendent I. I. Stevens assumes to treat with that portion of the above-named bands and tribes residing within the Territory of Washington, and Superintendent Palmer with those residing within Oregon.

ARTICLE 1. The above-named confederated bands of Indians cede to the United States all their right, title, and claim to all and every part of the country claimed by them included in the following boundaries, to wit: [Describes territory in present eastern Oregon and Washington] : Provided, however, That so much of the country described above as is contained in the following boundaries shall be set apart as a residence for said Indians, which tract for the purposes contemplated shall be held and regarded as an Indian reservation; to wit: Commencing in the middle of the channel of Umatilla River opposite the mouth of Wild Horse Creek, thence up the middle of the channel of said creek to its source, thence southerly to a point in the Blue Mountains, known as Lees Encampment, thence in a line to the head-waters of Howtome Creek, thence west to the divide between Howtome and Birch Creeks, thence northerly along said divide to a point due west of the southwest corner of William C. McKays land-claim, thence east along his line to his southeast corner, thence in a line to the place of beginning; all of which tract shall be set apart and, so far as necessary, surveyed and marked out for their exclusive use; nor shall any white person be permitted to reside upon the same without permission of the agent and superintendent. The said tribes and bands agree to remove to and settle upon the same within one year after the ratification of this treaty, without any additional expense to the Government other than is provided by this treaty, and until the expiration of the time specified, the said bands shall be permitted to occupy and reside upon the tracts now possessed by them, guaranteeing to all citizen[s] of the United States, the right to enter upon and occupy as settlers any lands not actually enclosed by said Indians: Provided, also, That the exclusive right of taking fish in the streams running through and bordering said reservation is hereby secured to said Indians, and at all other usual and accustomed stations in common with citizens of the United States, and of erecting suitable buildings for curing the same; the privilege of hunting, gathering roots and berries and pasturing their stock on unclaimed lands in common with citizens, is also secured to them. And provided, also, That if any band or bands of Indians, residing in and claiming any portion or portions of the country described in this article, shall not accede to the terms of this treaty, then the bands becoming parties hereunto agree to reserve such part of the several and other payments herein named, as a consideration for the entire country described as aforesaid, as shall be in the proportion that their aggregate number may have to the whole number of Indians residing in and claiming the entire country aforesaid, as consideration and payment in full for the tracts in said country claimed by them. And provided, also, That when substantial improvements have been made by any member of the bands being parties to this treaty, who are compelled to abandon them in consequence of said treaty, [they] shall be valued under the direction of the President of the United States, and payment made therefore.

ARTICLE 2. In consideration of and payment for the country hereby ceded, the United States agree to pay the bands and tribes of Indians claiming territory and residing in said country, and who remove to and reside upon said reservation, the several sums of money following, to wit: eight thousand dollars per annum for the term of five years, commencing on the first day of September, 1856; six thousand dollars per annum for the term of five years next succeeding the first five; four thousand dollars per annum for the term of five years next succeeding the second five, and two thousand dollars per annum for the term of five years next succeeding the third five; all of which several sums of money shall be expended for the use and benefit of the confederated bands herein named, under the direction of the President of the United States, who may from time to time at his discretion, determine what proportion thereof shall be expended for such objects as in his judgment will promote their well-being, and advance them in civilization, for their moral improvement and education, for buildings, opening and fencing farms, breaking land, purchasing teams, wagons, agricultural implements and seeds, for clothing, provision and tools, for medical purposes, providing mechanics and farmers, and for arms and ammunition.

ARTICLE 3. In addition to the articles advanced the Indians at the time of signing this treaty, the United States agree to expend the sum of fifty thousand dollars during the first and second years after its ratification, for the erection of buildings on the reservation, fencing and opening farms, for the purchase of teams, farming implements, clothing, and provisions, for medicines and tools, for the payment of employees, and for subsisting the Indians the first year after their removal.

ARTICLE 4. In addition to the consideration above specified, the United States agree to erect, at suitable points on the reservation, one saw-mill, and one flouring-mill, a building suitable for a hospital, two school-houses, one blacksmith shop, one building for wagon and plough maker and one carpenter and joiner shop, one dwelling for each, two millers, one farmer, one superintendent of farming operations, two school-teachers, one blacksmith, one wagon and plough maker, one carpenter and joiner, to each of which the necessary out-buildings. To purchase and keep in repair for the term of twenty years all necessary mill fixtures and mechanical tools, medicines and hospital stores, books and stationery for schools, and furniture for employees.

The United States further engage to secure and pay for the services and subsistence, for the term of twenty years, [of] one superintendent of farming operations, one farmer, one blacksmith, one wagon and plough maker, one carpenter and joiner, one physician, and two school-teachers.

ARTICLE 5. The United States further engage to build for the head chiefs of the Walla-Walla, Cayuse, and Umatilla bands each one dwelling-house, and to plough and fence ten acres of land for each, and to pay to each five hundred dollars per annum in cash for the term of twenty years. The first payment to the Walla-Walla chief to commence upon the signing of this treaty. To give to the Walla-Walla chief three yoke of oxen, three yokes and four chains, one wagon, two ploughs, twelve hoes, twelve axes, two shovels, and one saddle and bridle, one set of wagon-harness, and one set of plough-harness, within three months after the signing of this treaty.

To build for the son of Pio-pio-mox-mox one dwelling-house, and plough and fence five acres of land, and to give him a salary for twenty years, one hundred dollars in cash per annum, commencing September first, eighteen hundred and fifty-six.

The improvement named in this section to be completed as soon after the ratification of this treaty as possible.

It is further stipulated that Pio-pio-mox-mox is secured for the term of five years, the right to build and occupy a house at or near the mouth of Yakama River, to be used as a trading-post in the sale of his bands of wild cattle ranging in that district: And provided, also, That in consequence of the immigrant wagon-road from Grand Round to Umatilla, passing through the reservation herein specified, thus leading to turmoils and disputes between Indians and immigrants, and as it is known that a more desirable and practicable route may be had to the south of the present road, that a sum not exceeding ten thousand dollars shall be expended in locating and opening a wagon-road from Powder River or Grand Round, so as to reach the plain at the western base of the Blue Mountain, south of the southern limits of said reservation.

ARTICLE 6. The President may, from time to time at his discretion cause the whole or such portion as he may think proper, of the tract that may now or hereafter be set apart as a permanent home for those Indians, to be surveyed into lots and assigned to such Indians of the confederated bands as may wish to enjoy the privilege, and locate thereon permanently, to a single person over twenty-one years of age, forty acres, to a family of two persons, sixty acres, to a family of three and not exceeding five, eighty acres; to a family of six persons and not exceeding ten, one hundred and twenty acres; and to each family over ten in number, twenty acres to each additional three members; and the President may provide for such rules and regulations as will secure to the family in case of the death of the head thereof, the possession and enjoyment of such permanent home and improvement thereon; and he may at any time, at his discretion, after such person or family has made location on the land assigned as a permanent home, issue a patent to such person or family for such assigned land, conditioned that the tract shall not be aliened or leased for a longer term than two years, and shall be exempt from levy, sale, or forfeiture, which condition shall continue in force until a State constitution, embracing such land within its limits, shall have been formed and the legislature of the State shall remove the restriction: Provided, however, That no State legislature shall remove the restriction herein provided for without the consent of Congress: And provided, also, That if any person or family, shall at any time, neglect or refuse to occupy or till a portion of the land assigned and on which they have located, or shall roam from place to place, indicating a desire to abandon his home, the President may if the patent shall have been issued, cancel the assignment, and may also withhold from such person or family their portion of the annuities or other money due them, until they shall have returned to such permanent home, and resumed the pursuits of industry, and in default of their return the tract may be declared abandoned, and thereafter assigned to some other person or family of Indians residing on said reservation: And provided, also, That the head chiefs of the three principal bands, to wit, Pio-pio-mox-mox, Weyatenatemany, and Wenap-snoot, shall be secured in a tract of at least one hundred and sixty acres of land.

ARTICLE 7. The annuities of the Indians shall not be taken to pay the debts of individuals.

ARTICLE 8. The confederated bands acknowledge their dependence on the Government of the United States and promise to be friendly with all the citizens thereof, and pledge themselves to commit no depredation on the property of such citizens, and should any one or more of the Indians violate this pledge, and the fact be satisfactorily proven before the agent, the property taken shall be returned, or in default thereof, or if injured or destroyed, compensation may be made by the Government out of their annuities; nor will they make war on any other tribe of Indians except in self-defense, but submit all matter of difference between them and other Indians, to the Government of the United States or its agents for decision, and abide thereby; and if any of the said Indians commit any depredations on other Indians, the same rule shall prevail as that prescribed in the article in case of depredations against citizens. Said Indians further engage to submit to and observe all laws, rules, and regulations which may be prescribed by the United States for the government of said Indians.

ARTICLE 9. In order to prevent the evils of intemperance among said Indians, it is hereby provided that if any one of them shall drink liquor, or procure it for others to drink, [such one] may have his or her proportion of the annuities withheld from him or her for such time as the President may determine.

ARTICLE 10. The said confederated bands agree that, whenever in the opinion of the President of the United States the public interest may require it, that all roads highways and railroads shall have the right of way through the reservation herein designated or which may at any time hereafter be set apart as a reservation for said Indians.

ARTICLE 11. This treaty shall be obligatory on the contracting parties as soon as the same shall be ratified by the President and Senate of the United States.

In testimony whereof, the said I. I. Stevens and Joel Palmer, on the part of the United States, and the undersigned chiefs, headmen, and delegates of the said confederated bands, have hereunto set their hands and seals, this ninth day of June, eighteen hundred and fifty-five.

ISAAC I. STEVENS, [L. S.]
Governor and Superintendent Washington Territory.

JOEL PALMER, [L. S.]
Superintendent Indian Affairs, O. T.

PIO-PIO-MOX-MOX, HIS X MARK,
   HEAD CHIEF OF WALLA-WALLAS. [L. S.]

MEANI-TEAT OR PIERRE, HIS X MARK. [L. S.]

WEYATENATEMANY, HIS X MARK, HEAD CHIEF OF CAYUSES. [L. S.]

WENAP-SNOOT, HIS X MARK, HEAD CHIEF OF UMATILLA. [L. S.]

[Thirty-two band leaders added their marks to the agreement at this point.]

Treaty with the Wallawalla, Cayuse, etc., 1855, June 9, 1855, 12 Stats., 945, Ratified Mar. 8, 1859.

AMERICAN ATTITUDES TOWARD TREATIES
Isaac Ingalls Stevens

When negotiating the Treaty of Walla-Walla and other similar agreements, Governor Isaac Stevens had assured the Oregon and Washington tribes that their new homelands would be reserved for their exclusive use. However, three years after the treaty was signed, Stevens published this Circular Letter *promoting non-Indian settlement in the Washington Territory. In his letter, Stevens described the Columbia River country's mild climate and fertile land and praised the region's abundant fisheries and densely forested mountains. Notably, he did not mention the local tribes; nor did he point out that thousands of square miles of the Northwest were guaranteed to Indians by federal treaty and were therefore not available for settlement.*

Just as many of the emigrants to Oregon were unaware of the local tribes' treaty rights, tribal leaders in the 1850s did not know that east of the Rockies politicians and entrepreneurs were encouraging Americans to travel west and invade the Indian homelands. At the treaty grounds where the negotiating sessions for the Treaty of Walla-Walla took place, one of the government representatives had warned the Indians that they needed a secure title to their lands because whites would soon arrive in unimaginable numbers. He told the chiefs that new settlers would appear "like grasshoppers on the plains." The insect analogy was not entirely accurate. The migrations west were not the same as animal migrations that were seasonal and temporary. The Americans wanted to settle the Indian country and to replace the Indian communities there with farms and cities.

Circular Letter

Having received many letters of inquiry in regard to Washington Territory, and the best route of emigration thither, I have concluded to publish this circular letter for the information of persons who are desirous of locating in that section of our country. As regards the resources of the Territory, its climate, soil, and present condition, the circular letter of his Excellency Fayette McMullin, the present Governor of Washington, is so just, comprehensive, and complete, that but little is left for me to do except to republish his letter, with the statement that I am able to endorse his views from a personal knowledge of that Territory, acquired during a residence of more than four years, and after a careful personal observation of nearly all parts of it, and to furnish some notes in regard to routes for the use of emigrants. I will also, in connection with this paper, republish a memorial of the citizens of the Territory, setting for the advantages and character of the country on, and adjacent to, Gray's Harbor and the Chehalis river.

I will also refer the public to a recent work by James G. Swan, esq., entitled "The Northwest Coast, or Three Years in Washington Territory," which gives an accurate and graphic account of the country and its resources, and is a work to be entirely relied upon.

Finally, I will refer the public to my report of the exploration of the northern route for a Pacific railroad, wherein my views, and those of the several gentlemen in charge of the exploring parties, are given at much length of the country from the Upper Mississippi to the Pacific coast. A general description of the Territory of Washington will be found in that report. Of some portions the description is very minute.

The proper route of emigration westward becomes of great importance in consequence of the troubles in Utah. There is a good wagon road from the western frontier, via the South Pass, to Fort Hall, and thence down the Columbia valley. At old Fort Walla Walla emigrants will cross the Columbia river and take the road on the Nachess Pass of the Cascades to Puget sound.

The route from the vicinity of the South Pass, westward and northward to Snake river, has been much improved, in consequence of the explorations of F. W. Lander, esq., the past season, and guides can, without doubt, be found who are familiar with the country.

Should the Utah troubles break up this route, then emigrants leaving the usual trail near Fort Laramie, and skirting the eastern base of the Wind River mountains in the direction of the Upper Yellow Stone, will find a well watered and well grassed country all the way to the tributaries of the Missouri; and crossing the Rocky mountains by a pass leading from the Wisdom tributary of the Missouri to the Hell Gate river, follow this river down to its connection with a route north of the Missouri from Lake Superior and the Upper Mississippi.

The country from some 175 miles north of Laramie, and to the eastward, has been explored the past season by Lieut. Warren, and the character of the whole country, from the line of his explorations to those of the parties of the exploration of the Northern Pacific Railroad route, especially of Lieut. Mullan on the Wisdom and other tributaries of the Missouri, and in the Flathead country, is well known from the many trappers and mountain men who have frequented that region, as also from the Indians.

Emigrants from the Upper Mississippi or from the great lakes will find an excellent natural wagon road, with grass and water all the way to Fort Benton, near the great falls of the Missouri. The country is well known, to the Bois de Sioux, in Minnesota; thence to Fort Union, at the mouth of the Yellow Stone, no trouble will be found in getting guides. The distance from St. Paul's to Fort Union is 715 miles. There will be some four or five camps where the bois de vache will be the fuel. From Fort Union to Fort Benton is 377 miles; the route is traveled with wagons many times each year by the fur companies. There is water, wood, and grass all the way from Fort Benton to Hell gate; the route is by the northern Little Blackfoot or "Mullan's" trail, over which wagons were taken in March, 1854, and in 1856 the distance is about 240 miles. The Little Blackfoot empties into the Hell Gate, 55 miles, before reaching the debouche of the Hell Gate river, in the Bitter Root valley, and at that point connects with the route already referred to, leading from the Wisdom, over the Rocky Mountain divide, to the Hell Gate river. Thence, the route will be down the Bitter Root river to the mouth of the St. Regis de Borgia creek; thence, up that creek, to the crossing of the Coeur d'Alene mountains; thence, down the Coeur d'Alene river, to the Coeur d'Alene mission; thence, either by the crossing of the Spokane at Antoine Plante's, or the guts of the Coeur d'Alene lake, the emigrant can reach the Walla Walla valley.

Heavily laden wagons were taken by me from the Dalles, via the Walla Walla valley, in 1855, to the Spokane, at Antoine Plante's.

On this route the emigrant would have to do some work, from a point about 30 miles below Hell Gate to a point about 30 miles above Antoine Plante's, a distance of 150 miles; or, if he took the route of the guts of the Coeur d'Alene lake, there would be work from the point on the Bitter Root, 30 miles below Hell Gate, to 10 miles beyond the guts of the Coeur d'Alene in either case about 150 miles. Ten wagons, with a few extra hands and a few tools, could open the trail in thirty days. The whole distance from Fort Benton to old Fort Walla Walla would be, in round numbers, about five hundred miles.

From Antoine Plante's there are good routes both for wagons and packs to Colville, the headquarters of the gold region; the distance being in round numbers about ninety miles.

The distance from St. Paul's, or the western end of Lake Superior, to old Fort Walla Walla would be about 1,600 miles, and thence to the Sound about 1,840 miles. By crossing the Columbia river, a little above the mouth of the Snake, where there is a good crossing, the distance would be about 1,800 miles; there is wood, water, and grass in abundance the whole distance. The only precaution is, that emigrants moving in large bodies, in passing up the Regis de Borgia, and thence down the Coeur d'Alene, should not camp altogether, but form some days move in several camps.

The distance from Fort Leavenworth to Puget Sound via the South Pass and Snake river would be about 2,100 miles. From Fort Leavenworth via the route north of Laramie, and thence to the Wisdom and Hell Gate rivers to Puget Sound, about 1,950 miles.

Emigrants moving in bodies, using the necessary precautions, and treating the Indians with justice and kindness, would not be molested by them till after crossing the Coeur d'Alene mountains and arriving upon the great Columbia plains, where the military force now in the Walla Walla valley would afford protection to them.

The best time to start from the Upper Mississippi would be about the middle of May. The crossing of the Cascades should not be made later than October.

Emigrants moving north of the Missouri could have provisions and effects sent up the Missouri by steamers to Fort Union, and thence by keel-boats to Fort Benton. This is the plan adopted by the fur companies, who, however, generally run their steamers above Fort Union, sometimes as high as the mouth of Milk river, and then transfer the goods to the keel-boats.

As the Missouri is navigable for light-draught steamers to Fort Benton for seven months of the year (at all seasons except when obstructed by ice,) and as the Columbia is navigable to Priest's Rapids, above the mouth of Snake river, and probably the Snake is navigable to the mouth of the Palouse, a point of the route from the Coeur d'Alene to Fort Walla Walla, the importance of the northern route as a line of emigration is obvious; for the distance between the navigable waters of the two rivers does not exceed five hundred miles, and probably not four hundred and fifty miles.

In addition to the statements made by Gov. McMullin, I will say that east of the Cascade mountains good land is found in large bodies, as in the re-entering of Snake river, including the valleys of the Walla Walla river and its tributaries, a farming and grazing region, sufficient for a population of one hundred thousand souls; west of the Coeur d'Alene and Bitter Root mountains, where, for a breadth of one hundred miles, the soil is not only good but equal to the western prairies; and in the southern part of the Yackama country. On the Spokane, and in the region towards Colville, there is much good land and excellent locations for farms. The Flathead country is one-third arable, and at least equal to the Alleghany region in Pennsylvania and Virginia. In these valleys are delightful resting places for emigrants and stock. The grasses are good all through the winter, with but a small number of days of cold weather.

Persons wishing to emigrate to Washington Territory from the Eastern States for the purposes of lumbering, fishing, or trading, will find the easiest mode of conveyance to be by water, either by the present lines of steamers semi-monthly from New York to San Francisco, and from thence by sailing vessels or steamers to Puget sound, or the Columbia river; or they can take the cheaper method of a sailing vessel via Cape Horn. A company of emigrants could either charter or buy a suitable vessel, and after arriving at their destination readily sell or load her on their own account with coal or timber.

The whale, cod, and salmon fisheries of Washington Territory offer great inducement to that class of our citizens engaged in those pursuits; and the proximity of the coal mines and forests of timber to navigable waters offer peculiar advantages to those persons engaged in commercial business.

The mouth of the Columbia river, Shoalwater bay, Gray's harbor, as well as Neah bay, near the entrance of the Straits de Fuca, as well as the other ports of the Straits and Sound, afford good locations for the above class of emigrants. The land of the coast is very good, though heavily timbered; and in the vicinity of Gray's harbor and Shoalwater bay there is an extensive country having most abundant and nutritious grasses summer and winter.

Lumbering operations are also carried on on the Columbia river, as at Cathlamet, Oak Point, Wahuyal, Cascades, and other places; and the Columbia bottom, from its mouth to the Cascades, had an exceedingly fertile soil, though a portion, from the annual overflow in June, is better adapted to grazing than to crops. There are several valleys and bottoms of rivers flowing into this portion of the Columbia, offering great inducements to settlers as the Cowlitz river.

Emigrants desirous of locating in the Columbia valley can, at the Dalles, take steamers and land at any point on the river; and it is expected that steamers will run the present season on the Upper Columbia from the mouth of the Des Chutes, some eleven miles above the Dalles, to Fort Walla Walla. Sailing vessels have been running on this portion of the river the last year. As vessels have little or no freight returning, emigrants could send their effects down the river if they should find it difficult to haul them in consequence of a loss of cattle, or the cattle becoming thin and weak from the long journey.

Emigrants should, however, in this connexion, bear in mind the two portages at the Dalles, (eleven miles,) and the Cascades, (two and one half mile to five miles, according to the stage of water).

ISAAC I. STEVENS
Delegate in Congress from Washington Territory.
Washington City, February 1, 1858.

Isaac Stevens, *Circular Letter to Emigrants* (Washington: George S. Gideon, Printer, 1858).

A MODERN INDIAN LEADER REFLECTS ON THE TREATY OF 1855
Marjorie Waheneka

Marjorie Waheneka, the curator at the Tamástslikt Cultural Institute near Pendleton, Oregon, was a consultant to the Lewis and Clark and the Indian Country exhibit at the Newberry Library. Here she recalls an attempt to explain the significance of her tribe's agreement with the United States for contemporary schoolchildren on the Umatilla reservation. For her, the treaty is far more than a legal document; it plays a role in many aspects of family and community life.

I went to the charter school last week to do a presentation on tribal culture and history and I asked the group if they knew what the Treaty of 1855 was. They all looked at one another with kind of, well, you know, who's going to answer; nobody really wanted to be the first one to say anything. Finally one young man got brave and he raised his hand and he said, "Well, it was made so we could go hunting and fishing," and I said, "Do you know what else we are allowed to do with that treaty?" And then another boy says, "Well, it gives us the right, well, not me, not boys," but he said, "that is when the women can go pick berries and dig roots." And then I said, "Does anybody know how big our reservation is? Who can tell me how big our reservation used to be?" And, you know, that is when they went blank and they all just looked at each other.

Before the 1855 treaty we had 6.4 million acres of land; once the treaty was made with the government our land base shrunk down to 172,000 acres and we were also relocated to the southern part of our tribal boundaries into

Oregon, into our ceded area. And it's a scary fact because I am a traditional person and I belong to the Indian religion.

I'm a root gatherer, I'm a berry picker, and I picked this up because that is what our family did. And when I moved back to the reservation in 1974 my aunt came down because she was the head digger; she came down and said, "Your mom and I, we used to be the youngest in line. I'm asking if you will come out and go digging with us because we aren't getting any younger and we need young people. It's time you are home now; you need to continue." I remember I looked at my grandma and my grandma got me ready; she made all my wind dresses; she showed me how to cut out moccasins and made me new moccasins. She actually brought out some bags, some root bags that she had put away for a number of years, so they were brand new. Even some flat bags that you bring the roots home it, called storage bags, and then she actually got me a digger, so she got me ready. And I had to go sweat; my grandpa made sweat for me, and for seven days I had to go before sunrise; before the sun came up I had to go the sweathouse. So I went seven days in a row to get ready, and my grandma had everything ready for me to go out. She made everything in a little bundle and tied everything up and said, "This is what you take." I remember saying, "Do I have to fill all them bags?" And she said, "Well, you have to feed a lot of people. That's why you are going out, it's not just for us. You are going out for the community; you have a lot of roots to dig."

I remember they both stressed over and over: clear thoughts, clear your mind, good thoughts, good words, and a good heart, that's what you have to have. Don't go out mad, don't get angry at anybody, don't have any bad words or bad feelings about somebody isn't carrying their load or doing their share. Don't have any kind of thoughts; just go and do your own work because you don't want to get anybody sick, you don't want to make them ill, because if you have those bad feelings and bad thoughts you are gathering that up and that's what you are feeding the people and that's not good, that's not why you are out there. It was hard. It was something that I never really had practiced before and I tried very hard to follow their advice and it is scary because each year now, I have been doing this since 1974 and our line goes from oldest to youngest; I have gradually now made my way up the line and I am fifth from the very beginning now.

Its scary because every year . . . they (others in the community) are not committed, they don't really understand what it is all about, and we were getting frustrated because there was maybe just five of us—myself, my mother-in-law, and about four of my aunts—and there was a few of my in-laws, but we didn't know if everyone was going to show up. Because we have more than that, more women and children, but it is always a question of, are they going to come or are they going to find an excuse not to come? And finally my uncle, my uncle-in-law, I think he could see the frustration that we have, and he stood up and said,

I admire you ladies for the work that you are doing. I don't know if you realize this or not but you are doing a very big job that I don't think anybody pats you on the back for. But what I am going to tell you, I commend you for what you are doing. Whether you realize it you are still practicing our treaty rights of 1855. I've seen it go from my mother, I've seen my grandmother go and then I've seen my mother, but I don't have any girls, just you nieces that continue this and I have grand nieces now that are at the end of this line. Our family has always been a traditional family and we still continue to live and practice those rights that were given to us. And it scares me because I wonder when you folks quit, when you folks get old enough to retire, who is going to take that over? It's a scary thought because I wonder if anybody else, if the other ladies that have come and gone that do it whenever they feel like it, they're not truly committed or they do it to be a part of the group for show, they aren't thinking in the right way, they're not having that knowledge. They are losing out.

And it is a scary thought that I know my boys and my nieces and nephews, whether they want to or not, I take them out digging.

My nieces, they think it is hard work and it is dirty because they have to dig in the dirt and stuff—well, you know, why do we have to do it, we don't need the roots—but it upsets me because, well, you know, maybe if you consumed it, really did eat some of this stuff, you would have different feeling about it. It is a scary thought because there are not too many who dig for camas and there are many others who abuse the treaty rights.

We have had trouble on our reservation with poachers. Some of our own tribal people hunting out of season, fishing out of season. And sometimes we have had people that have reported poachers on the reservation. My son recently found a full deer; the only thing that was gone was the horns and the legs and they left everything else there. He came home and was just mad; he said, "Mom, I couldn't believe that, I don't understand that." He said, "I never thought I'd see that," and he was mad; he said, "You know, its gonna make me more mad if I find out it was Indian people that did that, that would make me more mad. You know it still would make me mad if it was a white person that did it, but to waste all of that . . ." He was real upset; it is a scary thing; I really don't know.

Now one of the biggest efforts that our charter school is attempting to do is to get more culture and tradition and heritage to our students there. But there are only, like, forty-two students there right now; that is why you have to keep pounding it in, to keep repeating the words, to keep repeating the thoughts to these young people, because it is up to them, it is up to them. I'm glad that I'm the way I am. My sons, my nieces and nephews, they all say I'm sounding like a grandma now. That is just a compliment to me because I am just repeating words that were taught to me and my grandma used to tell me. Grandma Deloris from Priest Rapids used to say, you guys will be throwing dirt on me, I'll be six feet under and I'll still be talking, and it's true. She said I'm just borrowing these words from you. Hopefully, she said, when I'm gone, the words I am telling you, you are going to be telling your kids or your grandchildren. My kids, my sons, get tired of me but now it's a compliment to hear my sons telling me things now of what they see, what's going on, what their friends do. They don't like what even some of their cousins are doing that is disrupting our cycle. They are few, but even a few, like my grandma used to say, you are planting seeds; just keep watering it and it'll grow. Your words are your water but you have to do it in a good way, she says, don't be mean about it, talk to them in a good way and you'll water that seed.

Marjorie Waheneka, filmed interview by Sally Thompson, Tamástslikt Cultural Institute, Pendleton, Oregon, November 1, 2004.

CHAPTER SIXTEEN

Miners

From the days of Columbus, European expansion was driven by stories of gold and silver waiting to be gathered up by energetic explorers. In the nineteenth century, Americans often rushed to Native lands to claim what they saw as their share of these rumored riches. Such episodes usually terrified local Indian communities because they attracted groups of young men who were traveling without families and often prone to violence.

The Nez Perce Gold Rush

Among the most traumatic gold rushes in the nineteenth century was one triggered by the discovery of gold on lands the Nez Perces had reserved for themselves in their 1855 agreement with Governor Stevens. In February 1860, Elias Pierce, a veteran of the California gold rush, discovered gold on a sand bar in the Clearwater River near where the Corps of Discovery had built its canoes in the fall of 1805. Within a year, thousands of miners were streaming onto Nez Perce lands, many attracted by rumors of gold strikes also on the Salmon River. The invasion of their reservation set off disputes between the Nez Perces and young miners who were often unaware that they were trespassing on tribal property. These conflicts were exacerbated by arguments within the tribe over how best to respond to the crisis.

At the same time, publishers contributed to the new gold rush by selling hastily assembled guides to the area. The map reproduced here, published by Daniel W. Lowell and Company at the height of the excitement, failed to mention the Nez Perces or to indicate that the new mines were located on tribal land. Unwilling to force miners

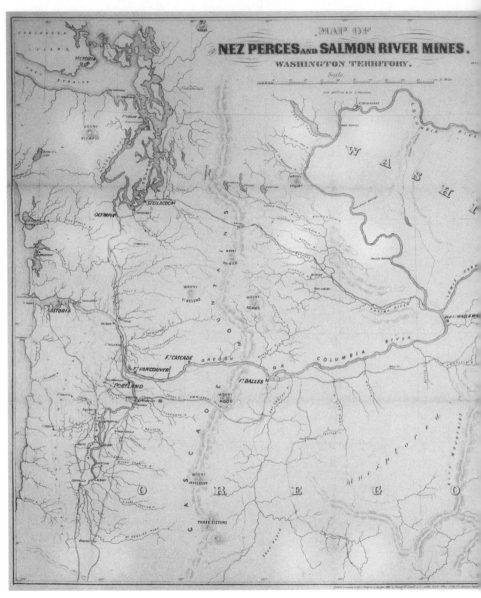

In 1861 prospectors who had heard rumors of gold strikes on the Salmon River began to trespass land reserved for the exclusive use of the Nez Perces in their 1855 treaty with the United States. This map doesn't mention the Nez Perce presence in the area or the fact that prospectors would be traveling across tribal property. The original

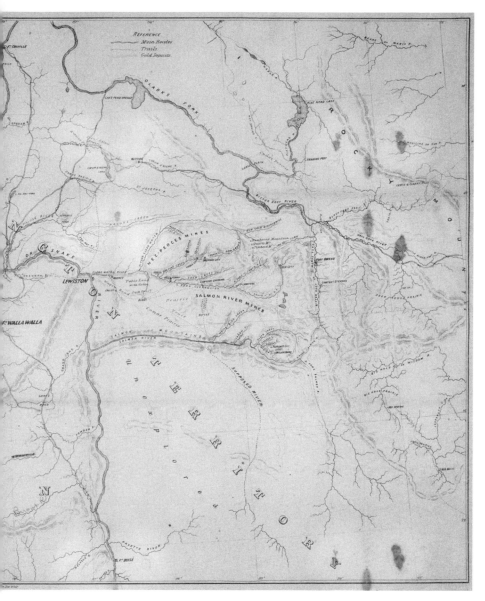

edition of the map indicated the Salmon River with a hand-colored gold marking.
Daniel W. Lowell and Company, *Map of the Nez Perces and Salmon River Gold Mines
in Washington Territory. Compiled from the Most Recent Surveys* (San Francisco: Whit-
ton, Waters, and Company, 1862). Courtesy the Newberry Library (Graff 2551).

from tribal property, federal officials convened a treaty council in May 1863 and pressured a group of Nez Perce chiefs to accept a 90 percent reduction of their homeland.

Many other tribes suffered in similar ways from the onrush of prospectors and would-be miners. Perhaps the most famous displacement of Indians in the West took place in modern South Dakota. In 1868 the United States signed a treaty with the Teton Sioux recognizing their ownership of the lands in Dakota Territory west of the Missouri River. Six years later, Colonel George Armstrong Custer led an expedition through the Black Hills in the western portion of these reserved lands to investigate rumors that the area contained gold. Custer's positive report set off a rush to the hills similar to the one witnessed by the Nez Perces a decade earlier. Many believe that the fury unleashed against Custer and his men a few years later at the Little Big Horn was fueled by resentment over his role in sparking the American invasion of the Black Hills.

NEZ PERCE VIEWS OF THE LAND

Sue Whalen

When Lewis and Clark first came into contact with the Nez Perces, the lands on which the Indians lived were not individually owned but were collectively used for the benefit of families. The land defined who the Nez Perces were, and it was managed through reciprocity and balance. The Native people believed then and now in the unity of the physical and spiritual universe. The earth's annual rebirth is cause for celebration, and thanks must always be offered for the food and provisions that come out of it. As Sue Whalen points out in this brief essay, collective ownership and a tribe's sense of spiritual relationship to the land could not be accommodated by the Americans' laws.

Central to understanding any aspect of the way of life of the Nez Perce Indian Nation is an understanding of their integral relationship to their country. The Nez Perce culture is not a body of abstract ideas; it is a way of life, and at the center of that way of life is the earth.

The lands of the Nez Perces lay in what is presently Northeastern Oregon, and in Southeastern Washington and West Central Idaho as well, near the lands of their neighbors, the Cayuse, Walla-Walla, Yakama, Umatilla, and Palouse nations. This was the country of the Ne-me-pu, the name by which the Nez Perces call themselves.[1] They were part of their land in a way that European and Euroamericans did not, and still generally do not, comprehend.

This lack of comprehension (where it is not a deliberate excuse for dealing arbitrarily with Indian lands) results from the basic difference in the way the European and the American Indian peoples look at the land.

First, briefly consider the European way of regarding lands, transferred to this continent through immigration and conquest. When one of European background speaks of the earth, he calls it "land," and to him land is a resource to be used as he chooses. Land equals "property," and property is assigned a value, according to the equivalent amount of goods or money it can be traded or sold for. Man is the owner of the land, and as owner he decides how the land is used, what it grows, and assumes the right to sell or trade his parcel of land to others whenever he chooses, provided he can secure the price he thinks it is worth. Although all people may become sentimentally attached to a given locale, permanent tenancy has never been consistent with the European idea of property. Whenever another place will serve a man's uses better than his present location, he is usually willing to put sentiment aside and move.

The Nez Perce way of regarding lands (like the way of most Indian peoples) differs entirely from the European way. When a Nez Perce speaks of the land, according to the traditional concepts of his people, he speaks of the earth. The earth itself has meaning. It is the earth that gives special meaning to the lives of the people. Rather than being a resource for man's use, the earth is the source of all life and provides all man's needs. Man does not use the land to create products that fulfill his wants; he gathers what the earth freely provides.

A Nez Perce valued the earth not for what it represented in goods or money, but for its being the source of his life and providing all he needed. He did not own the land; rather he belonged to a particular part of the earth, and owed a responsibility to it. Belonging to the place of his birth, he did not feel free to exchange it for another place. He did not desire to abandon his responsibility to his country.

The earth was the mother of all life, and the mother of the people. It was as the Cayuse leader Stachas told Governor Isaac Stevens at the 1855 Treaty Council: "This is our mother this country, as if we drew our living from her."[2] Owhi, a Yakama, said at this council, "It is the earth that is our parent. . . ." He also said, "God made our bodies from the earth. . . . Shall I give the lands that are a part of my body?"[3] This close relationship between man and the earth was explained quite clearly by Richard Half Moon, of Lapwai, Idaho, during an interview in August, 1970. Speaking of the way in which the Nez Perces had traditionally been associated with the earth, Mr. Half Moon said, "Man comes from the earth, and at his death he returns to it," likening this to a literal acceptance of the expression in the Christian Bible: "Dust thou art, to dust returneth."[4]

The earth, like a mother, cares for the people. The Cayuse Tauitau attempted to explain this relationship to the Stevens commission (clearly, an unreceptive audience). Tauitau said,

> The Earth says, that God tells me to take care of the Indians on this earth: the Earth says . . . feed them right. God named the roots that he should feed the Indians on: the water speaks the same way: God says feed the Indians upon the earth: the grass says the same thing: feed the horses and cattle . . . the Earth and water and grass says God has placed me here to produce all that grows upon me, the trees, fruit, etc.[5]

Notes

1. Richard A. Half Moon, interview, August 27–29, 1970, Lapwai, Idaho.
2. From "A True copy of the Record of the official proceedings at the Council in the Walla Walla Valley, held jointly by Isaac I. Stevens Gov. & Supt. W. T. and Joel Palmer Supt. Indian Affairs O. T. on the part of the United States with the Tribes of Indians named in the Treaties made at that Council, June 9th and 11th, 1855" (hereafter called 1855 Treaty Journal).
3. 1855 Treaty Journal.
4. Richard Half Moon interview.
5. 1855 Treaty Journal.

Sue Whalen, "The Nez Perces' Relationship to Their Land," *Indian Historian* 4, no. 3 (1971): 30–33.

A NEZ PERCE HISTORIAN ON THE IMPACT OF MINERS ON HIS TRIBE
Otis Half Moon

The son of former tribal chair Richard Half Moon (a consultant to Sue Whalen in the preparation of the article reproduced above), Otis Half Moon has had a long career as an interpreter, historian, and administrator with the National Park Service. In an interview, he discussed the history of tribal lands on his reservation and explained the tribe's outlook on the Rocky Mountain landscape.

In 1855 the land that was set aside to our people, a lot of things happened to that piece of ground. It's really a sad story as far as looking at the land base today. They told us that no white man would be allowed to come on our reservation without our endorsement or authorization or our blessing. In

1860 they discovered gold on our reservation and people go crazy over gold. Next thing you know you got gold miners coming in every which way to our reservation, every which way. They went up there and they wanted to find more gold. Some of our people, the leaders at that time, thought they would go up there and dig this rock, some tribal members made a little money off of it. They had a tow, like a boat that ran across back and forth like a ferry to carry the miners across for a certain amount of dollars. So some of them were making money off it, the tribal people.

But they (the whites) didn't leave. They started homesteading in that area and squatting on the land. The government found itself in an awkward position. What are we going to do? We have got all these Anglo people all over the Nez Perce reservation which we told them we weren't going to allow and all of sudden what are we going to do? We'll make another treaty! In 1863 another treaty was made and it made the land even smaller. It also divided many of the Nez Perce people. It divided us completely because some of them did not sign it and some of the leaders did sign it. The ones that signed this treaty were ones that were within the boundaries of the new reservation and they are pretty much the present-day boundary of what we have today. They were the Christian leaders. The ones outside the reservation did not sign it. People like Joseph, Looking Glass, White Bird, many others who were outside the boundary area. As far as they were concerned, as far as what the tribal government did, they didn't agree with it. They didn't have to abide by it. The soldiers, or the treaty commissioners, said the majority of the Nez Perce signed so therefore you all have to abide by it, they had formal law. This led to the war of 1877.

And then later on in 1890s, 1885 I think it was, pushing 1890, was what they called the Dawes Act. With that they allotted out so many acres of Nez Perce land and they only had a certain amount that was set aside for general tribal ownership; the rest was opened up to homesteading. So again you have a mad rush of white people moving on to reservation areas. Alice Fletcher, who was one of the women at the time to help allot this land to the people, she tried to give the best land to the Nez Perce people. She was threatened many times in Lewiston, "You are giving the good stuff to the Indians, they don't know what to do with it!" But she did it anyway. I really respect that lady for what she tried to do.

It destroyed the reservation, the Dawes Act. It also did something else; some of the tribal people could start selling their land as well. Nez Perce were not farmers; some of them tried to go on farming but it was tough times, and they couldn't do it. Sometimes a man would turn around and sell portions of his land just to get some money to feed his family. Today, if you look on the present-day Nez Perce reservation, we own probably about 13–14 percent of it. The Dawes Act did us wrong. Even nowadays in 2004, in these last few years, I am not quite sure if the policy still stands. We are buying it back from them, this land; we are getting back these pieces of ground. I know there is a law right now, they are giving some of BLM [Bureau of Land Management] land back to the tribe, but again, you know that causes a lot of bad feelings with the state. The state of Idaho views it as being taken out of tax rolls and therefore they'll be losing money. But as we see it, we are getting back our land.

Otis Half Moon, filmed interview by Sally Thompson, Pendleton, Oregon, November 1, 2004.

CHAPTER SEVENTEEN

Ranchers

After the American Civil War, while homesteaders built farms in California and the Pacific Northwest and miners filed claims across the Rockies, cattle and sheep ranchers moved into the arid northern Plains to raise food for the nation's growing cities. Native people were unhappy about the displacement of buffalo by stock animals, but many tribal communities found ranching offered them an attractive way to make a living. Particularly in the wake of the destruction of the buffalo herds, the stock industry allowed for a seasonal round of herding activities and did not require a drastic shift in community social traditions or gender roles.

But ranching attracted thousands of outsiders to the Indian country. Newcomers quickly exhausted the available public lands and pressed western tribes to open new areas for cattle and sheep. White ranchers also urged the Office of Indian Affairs (later renamed the Bureau of Indian Affairs) to permit them to graze their herds on what they viewed as unused Indian lands. And once the arid West was organized into states and began sending representatives to Washington, D.C., the region's political leaders began campaigning for the construction of federally funded dam and irrigation projects. By the end of the nineteenth century, the Indian communities along the Lewis and Clark route were feeling the impact of these economic and environmental changes. Many groups lost control over their land and water resources to cattle and sheep men, while still others watched helplessly as public works projects inundated and destroyed their homes.

CATTLE FOR INDIANS
John M. Thayer

This request for special inspectors to certify the quality of the cattle being sent to Indian communities along the Upper Missouri reflects a moment of self-interested benevolence. Senator John M. Thayer of Nebraska wanted to see Missouri River Indians become ranchers because he knew they needed a new food source and because he wanted to incorporate them and their lands into the growing American cattle industry.

Thayer's letter is addressed to Secretary of the Interior Jacob D. Cox. The son-in-law of the evangelical leader Charles Grandison Finney, Secretary Cox had argued that if reservations were staffed by missionaries and supplied with tools and livestock, the Indians would soon be "elevated in the scale of humanity."

Sir,

I would advise that *special inspectors* be sent out to examine and receive the cattle now being delivered under the contract of J. A. Morrow for furnishing cattle to the upper Missouri Indians. I have good evidence that the cattle [furnished] to be delivered will fall far below one thousand pounds to the head.

The men to inspect these cattle should be *incorruptible,* for effort will be made to buy them up. Men who are strangers to the contractors, *and who are unapproachable,* should be sent out to receive the cattle. The herds which have started up, I am informed, will fall generally far below the weight required.

Very Respectfully

JOHN M. THAYER

John M. Thayer, manuscript letter to J. D. Cox, Secretary of the Interior, October 17, 1870, Newberry Library.

INDIAN RANCHERS
Carolyn Gilman

The Indian Office first issued cattle to Indians for food, but in the 1890s federal officials began encouraging the tribes to develop commercial herds as a way to generate jobs and cash. The Mandan, Hidatsa, and Arikara families whose lands were now combined to form the Fort Berthold reservation began building such a herd in 1891. In winter Indian ranchers kept the cattle close to their Missouri River homesteads, while in summer they set the animals loose on the surrounding prairies. Within a decade many families were engaged in this new enterprise, sending hundreds of head of cattle to eastern stockyards each year.

The Hidatsa had a story about how cattle came to be. Only Man and First Creator, the first two beings on earth, split up the job of creation. They made the river and the plains and the badlands. To populate them, First Creator made the buffalo. But Only Man picked up a dead wolf and created a white man and the spotted cows the white man raised. When First Creator saw what Only Man had done he said, "You are foolish to make these things." The white men were "a queer kind of men,—they will always be greedy!" And the spotted cows all had short hair, too short to protect them from the winter. "That is so," said Only Man; and so he opened a hole in the earth and sent all the spotted cattle down underground. "But," he said, "when [the] buffalo are all gone they will come again and cover this earth as buffaloes [did]" (Beckwith 1938:16–17; Wilson 1906:29–30).

And that is what happened.

Although the spotted cattle were a second-best solution, the Hidatsa came to be grateful for Only Man's gift. The dry, rugged range land where the buffalo had flourished was perfect for raising cattle. Where the white man's agriculture had failed the tribe, ranching succeeded.

The government first issued cattle to the Hidatsa in 1891. "At first they issued one cow to each family," said Goodbird. "At the time I began farming there were about thirty-five head of cattle in the herd which we kept at Independence. These cattle we had to feed through the winter. We saw that every farmer had a barn for their cattle. . . .

"All the cattle of the Indians at Independence were let run out on the prairie. There was at that time no fence around the reservation, which was quite large, over eight hundred thousand acres. . . . Every cow and steer was branded. My brand was the letters SU on the right shoulder. All the [Hidatsa] cattle were branded on the right thigh and the Ankara cattle on the left thigh" (Murphy 1893:3; Wilson 1913:72–73).

There were problems to overcome before the raising of livestock took hold. For one thing, Hidatsa customs were not geared to the profit motive. "We Indians have a custom," said Goodbird, "that when we kill an animal we send a present to our friends. When I slaughter a steer, I send ten pounds to Wolf Chief and ten pounds to each of the other families of my friends in

Independence. In this way half the steer is gone to my friends, but when my friends kill a steer they do likewise, and always remember me.

"But this custom of ours makes it so that it does not pay to keep pigs or do a great deal that white men want us to do. It is hard for us to break our Indian customs. . . . I kept a pig last year and fed it a good deal of corn and worked hard so as to keep it, but when I killed it in the fall, the pig's meat lasted me and my family only four days. . . . I would keep pigs but what is the use of raising pigs when our custom makes us give away the meat?" (Wilson 1913:154).

Even more crucial was the problem of land. Ranching required much more land than farming, and the 160-acre allotments were woefully inadequate. The unallotted range away from the river became crucial to the Indians' self-sufficiency. Yet the government intended to sell off that land to white settlers. In 1909 a special agent strongly recommended that this step not be taken. "The ability of these Indians to develop the stock raising industry depends upon their keeping a considerable range," he said. But a communally owned cattle range undermined the government's zeal for private property. Anything that "would involve the continuance of that communal system" was looked on as "a backward step" by the Office of Indian Affairs (Allen 1909:3; Leupp 1907:2).

Despite these hurdles, the residents of Independence generally took to ranching. The work had a seasonal rhythm based on the natural cycles of weather and breeding. In the spring the men rounded up the herd to brand and castrate the new calves. Then they left the cattle alone on the range until about July 10, when the bulls were put in with the herd. During summer the Indians cut and stored hay to feed the cattle in winter. In August or early September, a second roundup was held. More branding and castrating was done, and grown cattle were chosen to be shipped away to market (Goodall 1912:1–2).

A roundup, like a buffalo hunt, involved the whole community. Families camped in tents near the roundup grounds. The younger men then left to find the cattle. "We rode on horseback," Goodbird said, "and surrounded the herd in a long line with our ponies. . . . We Indians drove our cattle to the edge of a high, steep bank over the Missouri River." The older men waited on the hills, smoking their pipes, to spy the herders coming back. When they were seen, their horses glistening with sweat, the cry would go up, "Here they come!"

The cattle were penned in a corral against the cliff. Then, said Goodbird, "the agent appointed a man to brand the calves. The branding iron was heated in a fire and the calves were roped by the neck by a man who went in with a lariat, on foot. We did not rope from horseback at that time. . . . The brand was the same as the mother's, in order to establish the right owner" (Wilson 1913:74; Baker 1984).

After fall roundup the cattle were sent to market. At first the people of Independence sold to local ranchers, but later they realized they could get a better price by taking the cattle east to St. Paul or Chicago. Accordingly, yearly cattle-selling trips became the custom. In 1900 Wolf Chief was selected by his neighbors to make the journey. It was his first taste of the big city.

"Myself & Water Chief, Henry Bad Gun, Louis Baker, & Frank Packineau . . . gathered up steers & fat cows between here & [the] Little Missouri," Wolf Chief said. "This was my district—everybody wanted me to go, & wanted me to bring money back. . . . I drew no pay for taking [the] cattle. . . . Our custom is not to charge one another" (Wilson 1916:88, 90).

They drove the cattle to the railroad stockyard at Hebron, N.Dak., where the stock commissioner counted the cattle and charged them five cents a head for shipping. Then they loaded the cattle onto the train. The men rode in the caboose, sleeping on bare board shelves that served for bunks. A German livestock dealer from Hebron named Charlie Weigel went along to translate for them (Van Dersal 1902:45–46).

"We expected to find [the] price when we came to St. Paul," Wolf Chief said. "We reached St. Paul & crossed [the] Mississippi on [a] high bridge & came to [the] stockyards in So. St. Paul. Got in about noon." But when they arrived, Charlie Weigel found out that the price for cattle was higher in Chicago. So the men decided to go on.

The Hidatsa called the train má'ti aku tidía, or "boat that runs." After leaving St. Paul, "There was a bad hill there and our train got stuck. . . . We stopped [a] little while till another engine came & pushed us up. Then he went awful fast. Weigel said, '[The] road is good here [and the] engineer will go fast.' It was awful fast, kind of dangerous & pretty near we went off our seats."

They got into Chicago at about 9:00 A.M. The "day was kind of smoky— whether air is that way in town I [do] not know. . . . They turned our cattle in [at the] stockyard again & [we] went to [a] hotel. . . .

"We had fine visiting that day. [We] went to [the stockyard of Swift & Co. They showed us . . . [the] room where they killed pigs. [A] man had chains in his arms, snapped [them] on [the] leg of [the] pig and fastened [it] to a wheel, and a man cut [the pig's] throat, [the] next take off [the] hair. So each one did something [to the] pig sliding along till all done & ready for packing" (Wilson 1916:88–91).

Another big attraction was Lake Michigan. "I asked and I heard [the] lake was 60 miles [in width]. I couldn't see any hills on [the] other side but saw steamboats.

"We . . . watched [the] water come up & go down & come up again. We never saw the Missouri do that. We thought also in this city they haul water from this lake. Afterward we learned a big ditch took all the bad water and ran it in the lake so we didn't try to drink the lake water" (Wilson 1916:94).

There were less pleasant sights, as well. "Back of a hotel in Chicago they threw old foods that they did not want any more on their tables. I saw some poor women, dirty and in rags, take off the covers of the cans, and they took out the food to eat. I said to myself, 'These poor white women must be hungry,' and I did not understand how this could be in Chicago where there was so much food. If an Indian man is hungry—, no matter what he has done or how foolish he has acted, we will always give him food. That is our custom. There are many white customs which I do not understand and which puzzle me very much" (Wilson 1915:28–29).

The men could not sell their cattle on the same day they arrived, but they decided to see where the cattle were being kept. "We went in & walked around a kind of fence. Lots of corrals there. We saw lots of cattle all mixed. We found few of our own. We were scared, thinking now we would lose some of our cattle.

"We got back to [the] hotel in eve[ning]. Had supper & Weigel told us, 'All go [out] in [a] bunch. That's best, for you fellows might get lost.' That scared us too, for we don't know city customs.

"He said, 'You must not go to any bad house—they will take your money & might kill you!'" (Wilson 1916:91–92).

They slept that night in the hotel. "In the morning I heard a bell ring and I thought it must be time for breakfast. I arose and, as was my custom, prepared to bathe, I had on my breech clout as we Indians wear and took a sheet from the bed and went down and washed my face. Other men were there and they looked at me and seemed curious. I had no moccasins on but I had the sheet and breech clout on. While I was washing, the owner of the hotel came and asked me:

"'Why don't you put your clothes on?'

"'Because it is too hot,' I answered.

"He went away not looking pleased but said no more. Then I went into the dining room and men and women were eating their breakfast. I sat with the sheet draped about my waist but with my shoulders bare and I noticed that all the people stared at me and seemed curious, but I did not care; that was my custom for I was an Indian and I followed Indian custom. They could think what they chose. After I ate, I went upstairs and put on my white men's clothes.

"Now I should like to ask you, Mr. Wilson, why those people looked at me. If you are on our reservation and you follow your custom we think that is all right and if you choose to follow our custom we think that is all right also. When I was in Chicago I followed my Indian custom and I do not see why any white man could find fault with me" (Wilson 1915:27–28).

After breakfast, they went back to the stockyards. They "Found lots of cowboys there & they . . . told us to cut out our cattle. We worked all day at this, hard to do too, [for] the cowboys didn't help us much [and] we were afoot."

They slept at the hotel again that night. The next morning they went to the livestock commission merchant's office and he paid them for their cattle. Wolf Chief insisted that the checks be made out to the individual cattle owners, not to the agent. He got $2,000 for his own cattle. The "Commissioner gave [me the] checks in [a] big envelope & sealed it. 'Don't lose this, for there is lots of money here.'"

"I won't lose it unless I lose my life," Wolf Chief replied (Wilson 1916:92–93, 89).

On the way back, they stopped for three days in St. Paul to talk to a government commissioner about some late treaty payments. Later, as he sat in the hotel restaurant, Wolf Chief thought to himself how he was surrounded by "Lots of people [in] fine clothes. . . . They had big rooms, big houses, and lots of foods & I thought of home and our cabins & how we lived & dressed & I wondered if we would ever live in big houses & have fine clothes. There were so many white people—and [they] lived so well. These white people I thought must have more power or are different people from mine. All [the] time I was eating I thought this.

"Girl waiters waited on us and I thought they had sweet faces & nice clothes. I wished they were [at] home, & I would get after one as my wife or sweetheart. But I knew customs were different [here]. But at home if I were young, I would.

"We had beef steak every meal & eggs, & I thought to myself: Well, I learned these white people's ways. I will put on fine shoes and underclothes & [a] good watch & hat & hair cut and I am just like one of those rich men in [the] city.

"When I got back I distributed [the] money, & gave [out the] checks. I gave a feast when I did so and distributed the money. The people were all glad" (Wilson 1916:95–96).

Trips like Wolf Chief's grew more common as ranching became the mainstay of the reservation's economy. "Cattle raising by the Indians has proved pretty successful," Goodbird said in 1913. "Members of my own family now own about thirty head of cattle and I own, in addition to these, fifteen horses. Our Indians here at Independence own about three hundred head of cattle." By 1915, the Indian-owned livestock on the reservation numbered 2,596 cattle and 3,274 horses. The Hidatsa were finding their way to a new prosperity (Wilson 1913:90; Michael 1915:2).

References

Allen, Edgar A. 1909. Report of August 11. Central Classified Files, U.S. Office of Indian Affairs, Records Group 75, National Archives, File 659813109 FB916.

Baker, Cora. 1984. Interview with Carolyn Gilman and Mary Jane Schneider, Mandaree, N.D., July 11.

Beckwith, Martha Warren. 1938. *Mandan-Hidatsa Myths and Ceremonies.* Memoirs of American Folk-Lore Society, vol. 32.

Goodall, Anow. 1912. Letter to Commissioner of Indian Affairs. Oct. 10. Central Classified Files, U.S. Office of Indian Affairs, Records Group 75, National Archives, File 659813109 FB916.

Leupp, F. E. 1907. Letter to H. C. Hansbrough, Dec. 19. Central Classified Files, U.S. Office of Indian Affairs, Records Group 75, National Archives, File 96497/07 FB 916.

Michael, L. F. 1915. "Inspection Report. Fort Berthold Reservation and Schools," Oct. 17. Central Classified Files, U.S. Office of Indian Affairs, Records Group 75, National Archives, File 113333/15 FB 910.

Murphy, John S. 1893. Letter to Commissioner of Indian Affairs. Feb. 24. Field Letters to the Commissioner, May 31, 1892–May 4, 1893, pp. 387–88, U.S. Office of Indian Affairs, Records Group 75, National Archives Branch, Kansas City, Mo.

Van Dersal, Samuel. 1902. *Van Dersal's Stock Growers Directory of Marks and Brands for the State of North Dakota, 1902.* Bismarck, N.D.: Samuel Van Dersal.

Wilson, Gilbert L. 1906. Diary, vol. 3. Gilbert Wilson Papers, Minnesota Historical Society.

———. 1913. Field Report, vol. 13. Gilbert Wilson Papers, Minnesota Historical Society.

———. 1915. Field Report, vol. 17. Gilbert Wilson Papers, Minnesota Historical Society.

———. 1916. Notebook, vol. 35. Gilbert Wilson Papers, Minnesota Historical Society.

Carolyn Gilman and Mary Jane Schneider, *The Way to Independence: Memoirs of a Hidatsa Indian Family, 1840–1920* (St. Paul: Minnesota Historical Society), 242–51.

CHAPTER EIGHTEEN

Missionaries and Teachers

By 1900 Native Americans could no longer maintain their traditional life-ways without interference from outsiders. Surrounded by new states, new businesses, and new settlers, tribal communities faced constant disruption. Believing there was no alternative but to force tribes to adapt to these new conditions, government agents, teachers, and state-subsidized missionaries set out to transform tribal communities. Instruction in the benefits of private property, Christianity, and fluency in the English language was a basic element of this assimilation campaign.

While eager to maintain their community traditions, Native Americans were also aware that changing conditions required new skills. Government-sponsored schools and missions provided much-needed food and clothing as well as instruction in English. Unfortunately, the Americans viewed this Indian cooperation as a sign that Native Americans had accepted the superiority of Western ways over their own. The experiences of the Blackfeet are just one example of this painful process.

SCHOOLS AS PLACES OF DISCIPLINE AND INSTRUCTION
United States Office of Indian Affairs

United States authorities operated four types of schools for young people in the Indian country: off-reservation boarding schools, such as the Carlisle Indian Industrial School in Pennsylvania; on-reservation boarding schools; day schools; and mission schools. All federally supported schools operated under a single set of rules issued by the Indian School Service, a division of the Office of Indian Affairs. These rules reveal the coercive nature of the government's education program. To foster the development of "good habits" Indian school administrators were told to withhold rations from parents who did not send their children to school (Rule 19) and to arrest and imprison anyone who interfered with official work (Rule 21). Administrators were also told that visits home by children "should be as brief and infrequent as possible" (Rule 54).

NOTE: These rules for the Indian school service, having received the approval of the honorable Secretary of the Interior, are hereby promulgated for the government of Indian schools. All rules, regulations, and circulars inconsistent with or contrary to their provisions are repealed. It should be the duty of all employees to familiarize themselves thoroughly with these rules.

W. A. JONES,
Commissioner of Indian Affairs.
June 8, 1898.

Rules for the Indian School Service

1. The preparation of Indian youth for the duties, privileges, and responsibilities of American citizenship is the purpose of the governmental plan of education. This implies training in the industrial arts, the development of the moral and intellectual faculties, the establishment of good habits, the formation of character, and preparation for citizenship. The development of this plan should be through the medium of permanent and well directed efforts.

2. Indian schools are divided into nonreservation boarding schools, reservation boarding schools, and day schools.

3. These schools should be conducted upon lines best adapted to the development of character, and the formation of habits of industrial thrift and moral responsibility, which will prepare the pupil for the active responsibilities of citizenship.

4. The administration of the Indian-school service is vested in the Commissioner of Indian Affairs, subject to the direction of the Secretary of the Interior.

Superintendent of Indian Schools

5. It shall be the duty of the superintendent of Indian schools, under the direction of the Commissioner of Indian Affairs, to assist in the administration of the educational work of Indian schools; to organize Government schools for

Indian youth; to prepare courses of study and circulars of instruction concerning the educational management of the schools and methods of instruction; to examine and recommend textbooks and other school appliances; to visit and inspect Indian schools, and from time to time to report to the Commissioner of Indian Affairs concerning their condition, defects, and requirements, and to perform such other duties as he may direct.

Supervisors of Indian Schools

6. There shall be five supervisors of Indian schools, each being assigned to a supervisor's district.

7. The supervisors' districts as at present constituted are as follows:

No. 1. Schools located in the States of Utah, Colorado, Kansas, Oklahoma, and Indian Territory, and the Territory of New Mexico, with the exception of the Navajo Reservation.

No. 2. Schools located in the States of Nevada, California, the Territory of Arizona, the Navajo Reservation in New Mexico, and schools in Oregon south of the forty-third parallel of latitude.

No. 3. Schools of Nebraska, South Dakota with the exception of the Standing Rock Reservation, and the Pipestone School in Minnesota.

No. 4. Schools in Oregon north of the forty-third parallel of latitude, Washington, Idaho, Montana, and Wyoming.

No. 5. Schools in the remainder of the States.

These districts may be changed from time to time by special order of the Commissioner of Indian Affairs whenever he deems it for the best interest of the service.

8. It shall be the duty of supervisors of Indian schools to organize and inspect the various Indian schools in the districts to which they may be assigned, and to perform such other duties connected with the Indian school service as may be imposed upon them by the Commissioner of Indian Affairs.

9. The supervisor has general oversight of all schools in his district, both Government and contract, including public schools in which Indian children are educated at Government expense. He must acquaint himself with the educational status and needs of each reservation and of all the Indians in his district, and report from time to time to the Indian Office the facts and his recommendations. After each inspection of a school he will make a special report upon the same with definite recommendations. He must visit each school as often as practicable and note its organization, grading, promotion

of pupils, discipline, and methods of instruction (personally examining the classes), character and condition of school buildings and premises, culinary and other domestic arrangements, industries taught and how they are carried on, amount of land cultivated and stock cared for, what improvements or extent of industrial training and plant will be advantageous and practicable; the character, efficiency, and adaptability for the position occupied of each school employee; sufficiency in quality and quantity of subsistence supplies, clothing, furniture, books, and apparatus; and particularly the tone of the school and the methods employed for developing moral character in the pupils. Buildings in course of erection should be especially examined to ascertain if materials and workmanship are good and thorough and in accordance with contract, and the necessity for enlargement, repair, or remodeling of buildings should have careful attention. He shall examine critically all school records and see that they are properly kept. The supervisor must do all in his power to increase the attendance of pupils at school, and he must impress upon parents and children the necessity of education and industrial training.

10. During the closing and vacation months each supervisor is expected to visit schools in his district and determine by suitable tests what children are ready for transfer from reservation and nonreservation boarding schools to other schools. He will ascertain, as far as possible, the name of the school to which it is desirable to transfer each child, and whether or not the consent of the parents will be obtainable, and transmit to the Commissioner of Indian Affairs lists of names of such pupils, together with any data or information necessary, as rapidly as the same may be collected. He will also report lists of pupils ready for transfer whose continuance at their respective schools may be specially desirable, together with reasons for their continuance. . . .

Agents

12. The agent, under the rules and regulations of the Indian Office, has charge of, and is held responsible for, all school work among the Indians on his reservation. He shall enforce these rules and regulations with firmness and tact, and promote by all legitimate means in his power educational work intrusted to his care. He shall visit and inspect all schools on his reservation as often as necessary, keep informed of their condition and requirements, the advancement or retrogression of the pupils, the manner, and methods of employees in the discharge of their duties, and make quarterly reports of all

matters of general interest to the Indian Office. He shall see that the pupils have proper training in all respects; that abundant and wholesome food, suitable clothing, sufficient fuel, and an ample supply of good water is provided; that sanitary laws and regulations are complied with; that the buildings are kept in repair and are properly heated, lighted, ventilated, and cared for; that the dormitories are not overcrowded, and that proper medical attendance and supervision are afforded.

13. The agent shall, as far as practicable, place in school all Indian youth over 5 and under 18 years of age for whom he has accommodations.

14. No Indian youth over 18 years of age shall be admitted to any Indian school without the consent of the Commissioner of Indian Affairs; but when kindergarten facilities are provided, with the consent of the Commissioner of Indian Affairs, children may be enrolled at 4 years of age.

15. The placing of Indian youth in nonreservation schools should be accomplished with the consent of the parents and agent. The consent of the agent is not a mere perfunctory act upon his part, but in every instance he must look carefully into all the surroundings and conditions of the children proposed for transfer, and be fully satisfied that their best interest will be subserved.

16. When the children have arrived at an age when they can properly appreciate the benefits of further educational advantages, every effort must be made, to induce both parents, guardians, and children to avail themselves of the opportunity presented.

17. Before attempting to collect pupils on a reservation, representatives of nonreservation schools must first report to the agent, who will accord to all properly accredited representatives every facility for securing eligible pupils for transfer. After completing his work, the representative shall submit to the agent a full list of children secured, giving names and ages, and the agent shall carefully canvass this list and strike therefrom the names of all children whose parents refuse to consent, or who, in his opinion, should not be sent away from home. He shall then cause the school or agency physician to make a thorough examination of each child and submit to him in writing the result. Only those reported sound and healthy must be transferred.

18. A complete record of all children transferred from the reservation must be kept by the agent, which record should show names, parents or guardians, tribe, age, date of transfer, and by whom, and for what school collected. Should a child return to the reservation, date of return and physical condition at the time must be noted on this record.

19. The law provides that "the Secretary of the Interior may, in his discretion, withhold rations, clothing, and other annuities from Indian parents or guardians who refuse or neglect to send or keep their children of proper school age in some school during a reasonable portion of each year," and in all cases where it is deemed advisable by the agent to so withhold rations, clothing, or annuities from parents or guardians he will report fully all the facts and reasons for his recommendations to the Commissioner of Indian Affairs for his action. This does not apply to pupils leaving school without proper authority, who are to be returned to the school without delay.

20. When notified by the superintendent of a reservation boarding school or by the teacher of a day school on his reservation of the fact that a pupil enrolled on the agency on which the school is located has left the school without permission, the agent shall promptly return such pupil to the school.

21. Should any parent, guardian, or other person harboring the pupil fail or refuse to deliver him the agency police and school employees, or either of them, shall arrest and return such pupil under the order of the agent. Agency police and school employees are authorized and empowered to arrest and bring before the agent for suitable punishment any person or persons who may hinder them in their lawful performance of this duty.

22. Parents, guardians, or other persons who may obstruct or prevent the agent from placing Indian children of the reservation in the schools thereof, shall be subject to like penalties; provided, that these regulations shall not be construed as authorizing the removal of Indian children from their reservation to be placed in a school outside of such reservation without the consent of the parents or guardians of the children by law required to be first obtained.

23. When the agent is notified of the return to his reservation of a pupil of a nonreservation school, he shall take the necessary steps to inform himself as to the legitimacy of his return. Should he find that the pupil can not produce satisfactory evidence of proper authority for his return, a full report of all the facts must be made promptly to the Indian Office, and the superintendent of the school notified thereof.

24. The agent shall keep to date a census of children of school age on his reservation. Opposite each child's name he shall place the name of the school, if any, which the child attends, and at the close of each fiscal year a copy of this census shall be forwarded to the Indian Office.

25. The agent shall not require of the superintendent of a school under his charge anything inconsistent with his position. He shall give directions in regard to the duties of school employees and other school matters through

the superintendent, and all his orders and directions must be obeyed, subject, however, on appeal, to the approval of the Commissioner of Indian Affairs.

26. Over a bonded school within the limits of his agency or adjacent thereto the agent shall exercise advisory supervision and cooperate with the superintendent in every effort for the general welfare of the school, assisting, if necessary, with his police force, in maintaining order, preventing desertions, returning runaways, and enforcing attendance.

27. The agent shall report quarterly the cost of all articles issued to each Government school under his charge during the quarter.

28. He shall, immediately after the close of each quarter, report to the Indian Office the name, tribe, age, and sex of each pupil, and number of days the pupil has attended school during the quarter.

29. He shall, at the close of each month, cause the superintendents and day-school teachers of the schools under his charge promptly to prepare a monthly report of the attendance upon each school and forward it immediately to the Indian Office.

30. At the close of each fiscal year he shall submit in his annual report a full report of all educational work under his supervision during the year, accompanying the same with special reports of the superintendents and day-school teachers.

31. About April 1 of each year he shall submit a list of such positions and salaries as he shall deem necessary for the ensuing fiscal year, accompanying the same with a list of the positions and salaries for the current fiscal year.

32. Not later than September 1 in each year he shall submit, in order that the Indian Office may prepare its annual estimate for support of schools for the succeeding fiscal year, a separate estimate for each school under his charge, showing the amount which in his opinion will be required for its successful conduct. This report should be a clear and definite statement of the requirements of the school.

33. On April 1 and December 1 in each year he will submit an "Efficiency report" of all employees at his schools, prepared by the superintendents thereof, together with such remarks and recommendations as he may desire.

34. It shall be the duty of the agent to visit all public schools within the limits of his reservation and adjacent thereto in which Indian pupils are taught, and from time to time report upon their condition and efficiency.

35. Applications for contracts with public schools will be referred to the nearest Indian agent, and it shall be his duty to investigate the application and indorse his recommendations thereon before transmitting it to the Indian Office.

36. When special reports are called for, the agent will promptly prepare and forward them. . . .

Reservation School Superintendents

42. Superintendents and principal teachers in charge of boarding schools under agents are the executive officers of the agent, through whom the affairs of the school are administered.

43. The superintendent shall have general charge, under the direction of the agent, of the school premises, including buildings and grounds allotted for school purposes, and be responsible for the care and proper protection of the same.

44. He will also keep an account of all Government property that may be in his possession directly or indirectly, in order that proper and accurate returns of the same may be made as the agent may direct. Superintendents will be expected to keep themselves fully advised as to the condition of all Government property, stores, etc., in their charge, and to advise the agent from time to time when, in their judgment, such property, etc., becomes unserviceable, that prompt measures may be taken for the disposition of the same by condemnation or otherwise.

45. He shall keep on file a map of the school grounds, plans of buildings, and data with reference to the same.

46. He shall have the immediate control of the school, be responsible for its discipline, for the character, conduct, and efficiency of the employees, for the gradation, classification, and promotion, of pupils, their moral and industrial welfare and progress, and the distribution of labor among the employees. He shall act as principal teacher, unless a principal teacher is provided for the school.

47. He shall arrange a program of schoolroom exercises and industrial work, and assign employees to their duties and responsibilities in accordance therewith, defining the work of each. He shall decide upon the hours of recitation and industrial work for each pupil and approve the daily details.

48. As the occasion demands, he shall hold meetings with the school employees for consultation as to the general welfare of the school.

49. In his intercourse with employees he shall be courteous and kind, and support them within the lawful limits of their authority.

50. He shall issue his orders to the heads of the various departments, and hold each one to a strict account for their proper performance. His criticism

of the conduct and work of employees must be in private, and the strict rules of official courtesy must at all times be maintained.

51. In cases of controversy or want of harmony, which the superintendent is unable to settle amicably, the entire matter must be referred to the agent. If the agent is not able to restore cordial relations, all the facts must be reported to the Commissioner of Indian Affairs.

52. The superintendent, when it is practicable, should reside in the school building. He shall personally inspect daily the various departments of the school, and at least twice a week inspect the dormitories and hospital.

53. All cases of infectious or contagious diseases must be promptly reported by the physician, nurse, or matron to the superintendent, who shall take immediate steps for the isolation of the patients. He shall take special care to isolate cases of pulmonary tuberculosis, providing antiseptic cuspidors and using every precaution to prevent the disease from communicating itself to others through sputa or breathing of infected air.

54. The superintendent shall use all proper means within his power to retain pupils in continuous attendance at the school during the entire year, except when the school is closed for vacation. Visits of pupils to their homes should be as brief and infrequent as possible.

55. The superintendent shall keep on file a full and complete record of all pupils enrolled at the school, preserving carefully both their Indian and English names. At the end of each school year after enrollment there should be added an entry as to the physical, moral, and intellectual standing and progress of the pupils, and, finally, the date and reason of separation from the school.

56. He shall keep the agent fully advised, by written reports, as to the new pupils entering the school, showing names, sex, age, tribe, residence, date of entering school, together with such other data as may be required.

57. The superintendent shall keep the agent advised of all prospective changes in the employee force of his school.

58. At the close of each fiscal year he shall submit an annual report, giving a full history, for the year, of the school and of each of its departments. For the preparation of this report he may require written reports from the employees under him.

59. He shall, at the date on which the general efficiency reports of employees are required, prepare the same for submission to the agent, and transmission by him, with his approval or disapproval.

60. It shall be the duty of superintendents and acting superintendents

of Indian schools to receive and control all mail matter addressed to pupils of their respective schools who are minors, and to withhold the same from delivery where, in their opinion, it contains unmailable or otherwise improper communications or articles. All mail matter so retained shall be promptly turned over to the postal authorities. Other improper communications shall be returned to the writer or forwarded to the Indian office for further disposal.

61. During the absence of the superintendent of the school his duties shall, for the time being, devolve upon the principal teacher, if there be one for the school; but if there is no principal teacher, then the superintendent, with the approval of the agent, shall designate one of the employees to act for him during his absence.

62. The superintendent, where there is no industrial teacher, shall designate some one of his industrial force to have the special care of the school grounds; and it shall be the duty of this employee, by himself and through details, to keep the same in a neat and artistic manner. . . .

Physician

66. The school physician, while responsible to the superintendent and under his orders, shall have charge of all sanitary matters connected with the school.

67. The school hospital shall be under his immediate supervision; he shall prescribe its general regimen, give instructions in particular cases, and decide upon the admission and dismissal of patients. The employees of the school hospital shall be under his immediate direction, though, their duties shall be assigned them by the superintendent.

68. He shall thoroughly examine pupils proposed for transfer to other schools, and, when requested, he shall examine Indian children previous to their admission to reservation schools with reference to incurable, infectious, or contagious diseases that might affect other pupils or be seriously aggravated by the confinement incident to school work.

69. He shall make to the Indian Office, through the superintendent, a monthly and an annual report of the sanitary condition of the school, and shall keep a permanent record of all cases treated.

70. In addition to his professional duties, he shall, at the request of the superintendent, give the pupils simple instruction in the elements of physiology and hygiene, explaining particularly the necessity for proper habits in eating and drinking, cleanliness, ventilation, and other hygienic conditions; the

manner of treating emergency cases, such as hemorrhage, fainting, drowning, sunstroke, etc. Classes of the most advanced and intelligent pupils should be instructed in regard to the nursing and care of the sick.

71. Where there is no school physician these duties will devolve upon the agency physician, so far as practicable. He shall be subject to the orders of the agent, but in all cases shall be ready to comply, so far as practicable, with the wishes and suggestions of the superintendent. If an agency physician fails to give proper attention to the school hospital, or the medical or sanitary needs of the school, a statement of the case should be presented by the superintendent to the agent, and, if the circumstances seem to demand it, the agent may refer the case to the Indian Office. . . .

Manual Training Teacher

76. The manual training teacher shall have charge of the classes in manual training. He shall teach the application of the arts and sciences to the mechanical trades, including the proper care and use of tools. The importance of this branch of school work can not be overestimated, as this teacher has the supervision of all mechanical industries of the school, partly to render the work of these industries more systematically effective and partly in order to bring about in a mutually methodical and effective way the needed organic connection between the class-room work and the mechanical industries. Without such supervision and direction the mechanical industries will scarcely rise above the dignity of shops. Their chief aim will be to satisfy the economic needs of the school. To these the educational features of the respective industries will be even more or less subordinated. The Indian boys detailed to the shops will remain mere apprentices and will rarely, if ever, be students of their trades; but while it is proper that the school shops may be made self-sustaining by turning out serviceable work in sufficient quantity, it must not be overlooked that their chief purpose lies in the direction of the educational features of their work. When there is no regular carpenter for the school, he shall also perform the duties appertaining to that position.

Matron

77. The matron, subject to the directions of the superintendent, shall be responsible for the domestic management of the school. She shall have the care and oversight of the dormitories and, either personally or through her

assistants, shall see that the beds are properly cared for; that the toilet of the girls is carefully made each morning; that the clothing of the pupils is kept in proper condition, and that care and attention are given the sick pupils.

78. The matron shall see that the work in the kitchen, laundry, sewing room, dining room, dairy, and other departments of domestic economy is properly performed. She shall make the necessary details of girls for such work and for instruction in these departments.

79. The matron is expected ordinarily to reside in the girls' building, where she can at all times have supervision over the girls.

80. The matron shall have charge of assistant matrons, and shall assign to them their various duties.

81. One of the assistant matrons shall, in connection with the industrial teacher, have the care of the boys' buildings, and the small boys shall be specially under her supervision and oversight. . . .

Laundress

85. The laundress, with the assistance of the pupils, shall do the washing and ironing required for the school. Laundering for employees may be done in the school by the laundress, if such work will not interfere with the proper discharge of her duties or necessitate the employment of an assistant laundress; but if such laundering is done, the employees must pay for the same—the pay to be given to the pupils and laundress who perform the work, upon basis approved by the superintendent.

Cook

86. The cook, with the assistance of the pupils, who shall be regularly detailed for that work, shall prepare all food required for the school, attend to setting the tables, washing the dishes, and cleaning the lamps each day; see that everything in the kitchen and dining room is kept in proper order, and that the kitchen and dining room are locked at night. . . .

United States Office of Indian Affairs, *Rules for the Indian School Service* (Washington, D.C.: Government Printing Office, 1898), 25–28.

THE INDIAN OFFICE AND BLACKFEET "PROGRESS"
Charles H. Burke

When Commissioner of Indian Affairs Charles H. Burke issued this optimistic report on the Blackfeet Indians in 1922, he affirmed that a new five-year program to develop Blackfeet agriculture was producing positive results. Oddly, he chose to support this assessment with testimony from a "prominent club woman of Terre Haute, Indiana" rather than with the statements of tribal leaders.

There is no reason to doubt the sincerity of Commissioner Burke. However, like all of its predecessors, Burke's five-year program would fail. Traditional family farming was not suited to the arid climate of the Blackfeet reservation. In 1934 a survey of economic conditions revealed that only 15 percent of reservation families were self-supporting and that the community's average annual family income was $150, far below the minimum needed for survival.

The Blackfeet Indian Reservation, Montana, is located immediately south of the Canadian border, and the winters are long and severe, the growing season being correspondingly short and the agricultural possibilities of the reservation limited. Nevertheless, the Indians of this reservation have made remarkable progress within the past two years as the result of a comprehensive five-year program adopted in the spring of 1921. This year practically every Indian family in the Heart Butte District, where most of the full-bloods reside, had a vegetable garden and small patch of grain, and many of them not only raised sufficient potatoes for their own use, but had a surplus to sell.

A flour mill was installed for the purpose of making flour from the wheat grown by the Indians. This year for the first time, not a pound of flour will be shipped in by the Government. The agency flour contract has been canceled, and the Indians will be supplied with flour made on the reservation from wheat which they themselves produced.

In 1921, the first year of the campaign, 115 Indians cultivated 3,750 acres, producing, among other things, 5,000 bushels of wheat and 1,000 bushels of potatoes. This year 476 Indians cultivated 5,975 acres, producing 7,000 bushels of wheat and 5,500 bushels of potatoes.

A sawmill was erected for the purpose of providing lumber to improve the Indian homes. An old, blind, full-blood Indian was highly elated when he heard the sawmill whistle for the first time, and said: "I was never happier in my life than when I heard the sawmill whistle blow." He also had a friend take him out into the wheat field so that he could feel the growing grain with his own hands, as he could not see it.

The total population of the reservation is slightly over 3,000 which represents an increase of [8]50 in the past 10 years. During the winter of 1920–21 free rations were issued to over 2,000 Indians, while last winter the number on the ration roll was less than 1,000.

A prominent club woman of Terre Haute, Indiana, visited the reservation several months ago, and after her return wrote me, in part, as follows:

> As for the fields, it is amazing what has been accomplished in the short year and one-half, which Mr. Campbell has had charge. Think of walking in wheat fields extending to my chest, and I am no weakling, oats and barley ditto. Of course, I realize that this was the product of virgin soil, but also developed under unschooled hands, except as to instruction, which must be more or less perfunctory, coming from the capacity of one man, the farmer in each district. Never in Indiana and Illinois, where we believe we can farm, have I seen such crops.
>
> I walked over the gardens where hidden in the soil were great tubers, potatoes, turnips, rutebagoes, beets, onions, and cabbages all ready for the root cellar this winter.

After a visit to the reservation last July, Mr. R. H. Russell, a prominent citizen of Spokane, Washington, wrote me as follows:

> I spent eight days, driving in cars, going from one Indian home to another. I visited dozens of them. I found the inside of their homes clean, showing every evidence of being well-kept at all times. At each home nice pieces of grain (wheat and oats, wheat predominating in acreage) were to be seen which had been harvested or harvesting was under way. These grain crops are good notwithstanding nearly all of them were sown in raw sod late last spring.
>
> I found the Indians and their families enjoying the best of health. Their appearance and actions were sufficient evidence that they have plenty to eat and are contented. I was [out] with the superintendent, Mr. F. C. Campbell, one day and we covered a large territory visiting many homes and inspecting their grain and gardens. They manifested great pride in showing Mr. Campbell the results of their combined efforts. They treated the superintendent with the greatest respect, respect almost bordering on adoration. They listened closely to all his instructions, beginning at once executing his orders with much pride. I noticed quite a rivalry among them to excel in doing the things, thus bringing out the results that would be most pleasing to Mr. Campbell.

I have been in close touch with different Indian tribes about all my life, and I am quite [confident] the Blackfeet are the most intelligent and respond more readily to uplifting influences than any tribe I have ever before observed.

General Hugh L. Scott, U.S. Army, retired, a member of the Board of Indian Commissioners, also visited the reservation last fall and wrote me as follows:

I have been going about all over the Blackfeet country at the request of the superintendent, Mr. F. C. Campbell, and in his company, and I think it will please you to know the results he is accomplishing.

He is a man of great sympathy for the Indian, of untiring energy, firm and wise in his management. I see a vast difference everywhere since my last visit. The town pump from which water had heretofore been drawn by women in a Montana blizzard, a disgrace . . . to every administration, still stands but has been replaced by an adequate water system, and two new cottages have relieved the crowded condition of the employees.

But more than all, Mr. Campbell has regenerated the spirit of the Indians. Everywhere we see crops; from 5 to 12 acres of wheat and oats; 3 or 4 of potatoes with garden produce. The flour and sawmills are in operation. The Indians show their crops with the greatest pride and joy. Mr. Campbell goes about among them for days at a time, into every field instructing and encouraging the owners. His system of organizing them into chapters in each section is bringing great results. They love and respect him highly, and he is gaining over the malcontents common to every agency who must join with him or be left behind by their own people.

He has waked up the hope and pride of the Blackfeet people, and if given sheep and supported by your Office will in the time set for the working out of his plan (five years) effect the regeneration of his people.

Without making any invidious comparisons, I may say that no tribe of Indians in the United States has made better progress during the past two years than the Blackfeet. This progress was well exemplified by their exhibition at the Montana State Fair this fall, which attracted the attention of thousands of the industrial program outlined for the Indians of this reservation, under the leadership of Superintendent F. C. Campbell, who is a man of long and varied experience in the Indian Service, thoroughly interested in the Indians, and who is doing everything in his power to promote their welfare.

It may be of interest to mention briefly the salient features of the program. The Indians of the reservation have been organized into what is known as the "Piegan Farming and Livestock Association," the purpose of which is to promote agriculture and stock raising, to advocate a higher standard of living with better homes and farm equipment, and to promote a spirit of cooperation among the Indians.

This association is divided into 28 local chapters, each with an Indian president, vice-president, and secretary.

Each chapter is provided with farming equipment consisting of plows, harrows, seeders, mowing machines, hay rakes, and grain binders, placed in charge of the president, who becomes responsible for its disposition and care, for loan to the Indian farmers of his chapter.

The meetings of the separate chapters are held every two weeks, at which the members exchange ideas regarding farm work. There have been two general meetings of the association, as a whole, during the present year (1922), attended also by the wives of the Indian farmers, who show much interest in the program as it affects them, their children and their homes.

One of the principal workers in the association is Bird Rattler, president of one of the local chapters. When recently interviewed through an interpreter he said:

> I am very much interested in what our people are doing, and greatly pleased with the way they are doing it; and that they will be able to get through the coming winter with plenty of food in their houses. I am now using in my house flour ground up from my last year's crop of wheat. Last year I had 3 acres of wheat and this year I doubled it, and besides had in two big patches of potatoes. . . . Mr. Campbell gave us a big encouragement when he put in the flour mill, and when he furnished us with machinery it made us anxious to put in much more crops.

Besides the development along agricultural lines, the program includes getting the Indians started in the live stock industry on an individual basis. To accomplish this, each Indian is being given sufficient wire to fence a 49-acre tract, and cows, sheep, pigs, and poultry will be sold to them to be paid for in easy payments extending over a period of five years.

Last winter many of the Indians not otherwise employed earned [*illegible*] thousand dollars by cutting wood in the forest and hauling it to the agency, the superintendent paying them so much a cord for it. When able-bodied Indians applied to him for rations saying that they had no money and could not get work, they were afforded the opportunity of cutting the wood into stove-lengths, being paid therefore in cash.

There are, of course, many Indians on the reservation too old to work and who have no resources. In order that they may be adequately provided for, a sort of "Old Folks Colony" is being established, which consists of separate cottages for each such family, so as to simulate as far as possible the individual home life to which the occupants have been accustomed, and thus avoiding institutionalism which the Indians do not like.

Charles H. Burke, *Progress of the Blackfeet Indians,* Bulletin 18 (Washington, D.C.: Office of Indian Affairs, 1922), 1–4.

A BLACKFEET EDUCATOR DISCUSSES THE IMPORTANCE OF LEARNING THE BLACKFEET LANGUAGE
Darrell Robes Kipp

Darrell Robes Kipp attended schools in Montana before enrolling in the Harvard Graduate School of Education. When he completed his training at Harvard, Kipp returned to his home reservation in northwestern Montana and began to explore ways of improving the educational lives of children there. Before long he became convinced that the key to that improvement was recognizing the value of Blackfeet history and culture. Kipp represents a new generation of Native American educators who define "progress" not only as the acquisition of the majority culture's skills, but also as the absorption and assimilation of Native traditions and values. His position is diametrically opposed to the teachings of nineteenth-century missionaries and government agents.

In 1896 the Blackfeet were reduced to living in a refugee camp thirty miles south of here. And the U.S. government came in and said, well, we want to take away the mountains now, and they said, no, you've taking all the rest, we want to be allowed to lease, you are not going to seize of our land. And so after three days of negotiations the government commissioners took their leaders aside and said, well, we'll just stop feeding you. And so you realize that, if you tell this to a group of people already in a refugee camp barely surviving, and you take away their last hope of survival, then the whole negotiation process switches, and these the leaders of this tribe then no longer are negotiating; they're now negotiating for their lives. And then we respect them because they negotiated for survival, and they said go ahead, take it, take whatever you want as long as we survive. And when we exited this refugee camp, there was only 1,400 Blackfeet left in Montana. So between then and now, everything on the part of this tribe had been a renegotiating the reality of those years. That's what we're doing. . . .

The images of Native Americans that you typically see are images we respect. We appreciate them. We hold them in high esteem: pictures of our elders, pictures of the early-day lifestyle of our people. They're important, but America in general, and educators, and communicators, and university people, and others have to realize that these are images of the past. Today, Native Americans are very much a part of the modern world, and we're part of the trek that all Americans are making. And it's important that we begin to instill new images of us as Native people. And some of the most beautiful people in the world are Native American children; all children are beautiful, no doubt. But to really see the new image of Native America is to go and film young Indian children on the move, et cetera, after school. And you see a group of them walking down the street or you see them riding their bikes or you'll see them heading for the playground or football field or the soccer field, or off with their musical instrument to go somewhere, you begin to see the vitality, you begin to see the attractiveness, the beauty of, the essence of that tribe.

And I guess the irony is these people never went away; they thought we were going to vanish—they thought we were going to disappear—and ironically, our birth rate right now in our community is four times that of the rest of the state. You can traverse much of the landscape that was settled by the early homesteaders, the early-day people who came out and thought they could farm in the dry-land farms of eastern Montana, all those places are deserted. And you could traverse the small towns of Wyoming and North Dakota and Montana and there's nothing left there anymore. There's a gas station and a post office and a bar; everything's combined. And so there's even a lot of books written today that refer to the waning of the West. These people that came in and attempted to make the land adapt to them found out that in the final analysis the land and nature was not going to adapt to their needs, to their wants, to their desires. And if they wanted to be farmers when they came, during the good years they made it; when nature and the land decided it was time for a drought or dry land, there was nothing they could do.

And because they preached—followed—the American dream, their children left those places in droves, never to return. Native Americans have lived here thousands of years, thousands of years. The Blackfeet, the Pikuni lived here thousands of years. And consequently they don't try to make the land adapt to them; they adapted to the land. And I believe even today the reasons that Indian reservations are the only places flourishing population-wise. People say, well, gosh, they have the highest unemployment rate, there's no jobs there, there da da-da da-da, why are people going there?

It's because they're a homogeneous people and they have biological bonds, geographical bonds, heritage bonds, language bonds that are part of a continuum thousands of years old. And that's why Indian people are always homesick and always can't wait to get back home; sooner or later they end up back here. And I think that is a part of the legacy of the Lewis and Clark commemorative, that two hundred years ago maybe they thought they would be gone; and I guess if there's anything such as a prophecy, that if there's anybody around here two hundred years from now, they're certainly going to be Native Americans, will be here too, so they're not going to disappear.

Darrell Robes Kipp, filmed interview by Sally Thompson, Piegan Institute, Browning, Montana, September 9, 2004.

PART 4

<hr/>

THE INDIAN COUNTRY TODAY

Today, Native Americans living in the lands visited by Lewis and Clark two centuries ago belong to two nations. They are American citizens, working in their communities, paying taxes, sending their young people to serve in the military, and speaking out on public issues. But these people also belong to tribes that continue to view their homelands as part of Indian country, a country that demands a different kind of loyalty and service.

Indian people are proud to live in the United States, but they are also determined to sustain the values and practices of the ancient Indian country. The documents in this part of the volume will introduce communities and individuals who are working successfully to rebuild and maintain Native traditions in the twenty-first century. People participating in this effort do not feel divided loyalties. They believe that by building a better Indian country, they are building a better America.

CHAPTER NINETEEN

Salmon Restoration

In the summer of 1855 most of the Indians living along the Columbia River signed treaties that ceded millions of acres to the United States in exchange for secure titles to fixed "reservations," the right to fish on their new homelands without restriction, and an assurance that tribal members could continue fishing at all of their "usual and accustomed stations" in the future, regardless of where those "stations" might be. "This agreement," the Umatilla Indians have noted, "was our 'contract' with America."

In the twentieth century, the Columbia River tribes, together with other tribes along the Pacific Coast, fought to preserve their right to fish at their "usual and accustomed stations." Their struggle was long and difficult, but in the end the tribes' position prevailed. In the wake of their success, the Columbia River tribes now work collectively to protect and restore salmon habitats and to preserve community traditions that honor and celebrate their ties to this vital food source.

THE BOLDT DECISION RECOGNIZES A TREATY RIGHT TO FISH

Over the past 150 years, U.S. courts have frequently upheld the terms of the 1855 treaties negotiated by Isaac Stevens, but the Indians' fishing grounds have changed dramatically. Massive hydroelectric dams have transformed the swift-running Columbia into a series of giant reservoirs that supply power and irrigation water to the public, while interrupting salmon migration patterns from the Pacific to the Rocky Mountains. Migrating fish are now blocked by impregnable barriers and harmed by rising water temperatures. Fish hatcheries, "ladders" that help salmon bypass some dams, and special protective laws have saved some species from extinction, but the tribes' "right" to fish today often seems an empty promise. In this modern atmosphere, the State of Washington took the position that it was no longer practical to enforce tribal fishing rights. The state's attorneys argued that Indians did not deserve any special privilege when it came to taking fish from the Columbia and other rivers in the region. In 1974 Federal District Court Judge George Boldt ruled on this matter. When the Supreme Court of the United States affirmed his decision in 1979, it became the basis for most future legal rulings on the question of rights guaranteed by treaty.

Since tribal on-reservation treaty-right fishing is exclusive, fish taken from stations on a reservation shall not be included in any allocation of fish between treaty and non-treaty fishermen. Therefore, the *amount* or *quantity* of any species of fish that may be taken off reservation by treaty right fishing during a particular fishing period can only be limited by either:

(a) The number of fish required for spawning escapement and any other requirements established to be reasonable and necessary for conservation, and

(b) The number of harvestable fish non-treaty fishermen may take at the tribes' "usual and accustomed grounds and stations" while fishing "in common with" treaty right fishermen.

As used above, "harvestable" means the number of fish remaining to be taken by any and all fishermen, at usual and accustomed grounds and stations, after deducting the number of fish required for spawning escapement and tribal needs. . . .

By dictionary definition and as intended and used in the Indian treaties and in this decision "in common with" means *sharing equally* the opportunity to take fish at "usual and accustomed grounds and stations"; therefore, non-treaty fishermen shall have the opportunity to take up to 50% of the harvestable number of fish that may be taken by all fishermen at usual and accustomed grounds and stations and treaty right fishermen shall have the opportunity to take up to the same percentage of harvestable fish, as stated above. . . .

The right of a Treaty Tribe to harvest anadromous fish outside reservation boundaries arises from a provision which appears in each of the Stevens' treaties and which, with immaterial variations, states:

The right of taking fish, at all usual and accustomed grounds and stations, is further secured to said Indians, in common with all citizens of the Territory. . . .

It is the responsibility of all citizens to see that the terms of the Stevens' treaties are carried out, so far as possible, in accordance with the meaning they were understood to have by the tribal representatives at the councils, and in a spirit which generously recognizes the full obligation of this nation to protect the interests of a dependent people.

From the earliest known times, up to and beyond the time of the Stevens' treaties, the Indians comprising each of the treating tribes and bands were primarily a fishing, hunting and gathering people dependent almost entirely upon the natural animal and vegetative resources of the region for their subsistence and culture. They were heavily dependent upon anadromous fish for their subsistence and for trade with other tribes and later with the settlers. Anadromous fish was the great staple of their diet and livelihood. They cured and dried large quantities for year around use, both for themselves and for others through sale, trade, barter and employment. With the advent of canning technology in the latter half of the 19th Century the commercial exploitation of the anadromous fish resources by non-Indians increased tremendously. Indians, fishing under their treaty-secured rights, also participated in this expanded commercial fishery and sold many fish to non-Indian packers and dealers.

The taking of anadromous fish from usual and accustomed places, the right to which was secured to the Treaty Tribes in the Stevens' treaties, constituted both the means of economic livelihood and the foundation of native culture. Reservation of the right to gather food in this fashion protected the Indians' right to maintain essential elements of their way of life, as a complement to the life defined by the permanent homes, allotted farm lands, compulsory education, technical assistance and pecuniary rewards offered in the treaties. Settlement of the West and the rise of industrial America have significantly circumscribed the opportunities of members of the Treaty Tribes to fish for subsistence and commerce and to maintain tribal traditions. But the mere passage of time has not eroded, and cannot erode, the rights guaranteed by solemn treaties that both sides pledged on their honor to uphold.

The treaty-secured rights to resort to the usual and accustomed places to fish were a part of larger rights possessed by the treating Indians, upon the exercise of which there was not a shadow of impediment, and which were not much less necessary to their existence than the atmosphere they breathed. The treaty was not a grant of rights to the treating Indians, but a grant of rights from them, and a reservation of those not granted. In the Stevens' treaties, such reservations were not of particular parcels of land, and could not be expressed in deeds, as dealings between private individuals. The reservations were in large areas of territory, and the negotiations were with the tribes. The treaties reserved rights, however, to every individual Indian, as though described therein. There was an exclusive right of fishing reserved within certain boundaries. There was a right outside of those boundaries reserved for exercise "in common with citizens of the Territory."

United States v. State of Washington, March 22, 1974, 384 Federal Supplement 343, 406–7. (The U.S. Supreme Court's 1979 decision upholding Judge Boldt's decision is: Washington v. Washington State Commercial Passenger Fishing Vessel Association, 443 U.S. 658–708.)

CONFEDERATED TRIBES OF THE UMATILLA INDIAN RESERVATION STATEMENT ON SALMON RESTORATION

After their victory in the fishing rights cases of the 1970s, the Columbia River tribes formed a fish commission to regulate tribal harvesting of salmon and oversee community efforts to restore and protect salmon habitats. Since then they have worked in unison and individually to restore the fragile ecosystem of the Columbia River Basin, often with mixed results. Each tribe approaches the task from its own perspective, but all share a commitment to sustaining the presence of salmon in their cultures and personal lives. Tribal people in the Columbia Basin are not only proud of the treaty provisions their ancestors negotiated in 1855, but they are acutely aware of the responsibility that treaty "right" places on them to protect the health of the salmon population into the future. The Confederated Tribes of the Umatilla Indian Reservation (CTUIR) are a part of this process and in 1995 created the Columbia Basin Salmon Policy, declaring the fish to be in a state of crisis. This policy is seen as a call not only to tribal people of the Columbia Basin to restore and preserve their relationship with the salmon, but also to the people of the United States, to remember the guarantee of this stewardship.

For thousands of years, salmon thrived in the Columbia Basin. Salmon always have been central to our religion and our culture, and we honored them accordingly. We had plenty of salmon to sustain us and plenty more to trade with others from far away. In less than 150 years, the newcomers to our homeland have driven the once-plentiful salmon to the brink of extinction. Many salmon species already are gone forever.

It is not just the salmon which are endangered. Salmon are only a small symptom of a dying ecosystem. It is the Columbia Basin and the Pacific Ocean which are endangered. The salmon are telling us that the mountains, valleys, plains, rivers, and ocean are all sick. Many other species now face extinction.

For thousands of years, we managed our resources with respect. This land was rich in natural resources when the first non-Indians arrived. The wasteful and disrespectful practices of the last 150 years have used up nearly all of these resources, creating ugly conflicts between those people now dependent on them.

These resources would be healthy if the Treaty of 1855 had been honored, and if the United States Government had honored its own laws. Salmon, sturgeon, eels, and many other fish face certain extinction unless immediate and drastic changes are made in the human management of the Columbia Basin and the Ocean. Salmon have been a source of sustenance, a gift of religion, and a foundation of culture for our people since time immemorial. Their existence is vital and linked to ours. We will not allow them to go extinct.

We have the answers to this problem. We can save the salmon and make the economy of the Pacific Northwest even stronger at the same time. We must implement plans which meet not only our needs, but the needs of our grandchildren and their grandchildren. . . .

The Treaty of 1855 is our "contract" with America. It is much more than a contract, however. Under the United States Constitution, the Treaty of 1855 is considered "the Supreme Law of the Land." The United States Government has a solemn obligation under both its own laws and under international laws to uphold our Treaty. This obligation extends to the individual States which make up the United States, and to the individual citizens of the United States.

The Federal Government, in addition, has a special Trust Responsibility to protect Tribal resources. This doctrine has been recognized by the United States Supreme Court and was first articulated by the first Chief Justice, John Marshall. This doctrine recognizes that States and citizens often are hostile to Tribes and greedy for our resources. It places a special obligation upon the United States Government to protect our people, our rights and our resources from those who do not honor our Treaty.

The Federal Government, however, is responsible for much of the hostility that we and our Treaty rights face. The conflict between salmon and other economic interests in many cases was the direct result of Federal actions. For instance, Federally constructed dams encouraged non-Indians to become dependent on the water we reserved for the fish. Now, non-Indian hydropower and irrigation interests view themselves as pitted against the restoration of the Treaty-reserved water needed by the fish.

It is the Policy of the CTUIR that:

1. Our Treaty, in which we gave the people of the United States over 6.4 million acres of land rich with resources, has been violated. Our Treaty rights must be honored, and our Treaty resources restored.

2. The Federal Government has breached its Trust Responsibility to this and other Tribal Nations by managing the Columbia Basin and the Pacific Ocean in a way which has destroyed our Treaty resources.

3. In many cases, the conflict between our Treaty rights and other economic interests was caused by Federal actions. These situations are a particularly outrageous violation of the Federal Trust Responsibility. The Federal Government has an obligation to fix the conflicts it has created. Specifically, the Federal Government must restore our Treaty resources, and take responsibility for the resulting impacts on other users of those resources.

4. The Federal Government's Trust Responsibility requires that it protect and restore the salmon, sturgeon, and eels, and the Columbia Basin–Pacific Ocean habitat they require.

5. We will use our Sovereign powers to protect ourselves by using whatever means necessary to protect and restore the Columbia Basin and its Treaty-protected fish, wildlife, plant, water and cultural resources. . . .

6. We call upon the Federal and State Governments to enforce the laws and policies you have adopted. If compliance were met with the National Forest Management Act, the Clean Water Act, the Northwest Electric Power Planning and Conservation Act, and the Endangered Species Act, among others, the Columbia River salmon would not be on the brink of extinction. We support these laws and call for Congressional and administrative efforts to implement and strengthen them where necessary.

7. The policy of using hatcheries in lieu of protecting habitat in the mainstem and tributaries has failed. Restoration plans must be comprehensive, using both habitat restoration (mainstem and tributary) and supplementation.

. . .

11. We call upon all other Tribal Nations in the Pacific Northwest to join with us to protect Tribal resources and Tribal people. The time for burying age-old conflicts is at hand. Let us join together as Indian People to protect what is rightfully ours and to show the non-Indian world that salmon, shellfish and wildlife can survive along with people and industry.

12. We call upon the non-Indian citizens of the United States to learn and understand from Indian people, and to remember what promises the United

States made to us. We ask for you to do everything in your power to ensure that our Treaty rights are honored and that the salmon are restored to sustainable, harvestable populations. . . .

The restoration of the salmon and the honoring of our Treaty rights is just as important to the American people as it is to us. For us, it is a matter of our religion, culture and economy. For the citizens of the United States, it is a matter of honor. Right now, the integrity of the American people is being stripped away one salmon at a time, just as when the buffalo were slaughtered a century ago.

In implementing this policy, we will initiate actions to protect the salmon, the rivers, our religion, and our people. We are willing to work with others to minimize the impacts of these actions. We will, however, do everything in our power to restore salmon and their habitat, by any means necessary.

It is our vision and our hope that the Columbia Basin once again will be the largest salmon producer in the world. It is our vision that salmon once again will be a strong economic foundation in the Columbia Basin. We know that the existing economies of the Pacific Northwest can co-exist with salmon. We are going to make it happen.

Confederated Tribes of the Umatilla Indian Reservation, Columbia Basin Salmon Policy, March 8, 1995, www.umatilla.nsn.us/salmonpolicy.html, accessed May 1, 2007.

THE ROLE OF SALMON IN A FAMILY AND TRIBE
Marjorie Waheneka

Marjorie Waheneka, a curator at the Tamástslikt Cultural Institute, Pendleton, Oregon, has been involved in a number of community education projects aimed at introducing young people both on the Umatilla Reservation and in surrounding communities to the significance of salmon in the history and traditions of Columbia River Indians.

Salmon was the most important food source along the Columbia plateau. A lot of people think that all Indians were alike and that we all lived in buffalo-hide tepees and all the Indians ate buffalo, that's not necessarily true. Salmon was our most important food. The rivers were our transportation and our food source, and the rivers watered the ground to give us the roots and the berries, so fish was very important. I can remember crying sometimes because I was a girl and I wasn't allowed to go fishing; I had to stay with my grandma.

Salmon would come up in the springtime and one thing I remembered about the salmon my uncle told me: the cottonwood, you know when it blows and the cotton comes off the tree and it looks like it snowing, he'd say, "Well, better get my poles ready because that is a sign that they are coming back up river." And so the boys would get anxious; they would get ready on a Saturday and they would go out real early and they would spend all day on the river and you know back then the salmon were huge; they were like thirty or forty pounds, you know, they were big. And it wasn't just one or two, because we had to think about all the families.

So fresh fish was something that was really good, and boiled potatoes. My grandma's homemade bread, it was just like a feast. We also had to dry it [the salmon] and that is where the girls came in; we had to clean it and dry it and store it and take care of it for the winter for trade. My uncles and my grandpas knew every part of the river. They knew where the big ones were; they knew what ones were good; they knew what fish was running up the river. Like now, getting close to December, pretty soon we are going to start steelhead fishing and after steelhead we have whitefish; we have every type. Trout was another one that we used to consume a lot of. Fish was just our way of life, you know, just like deer and elk was just another source of meat. And the protein that we got and then our vitamins, and our vegetables came from the roots, the roots are very high in vitamin C; they have a lot of vitamins in them once they are boiled and cooked. There is a lot of vitamin C in the berries that we gather so they have a good diet, you know, the Indian people.

The fish, you know, every part of it was used. I remember the most delicate part was the fish head. I remember my grandmas and my grandpas—the older people—used to race for the fish heads because that was the part to eat; they didn't care about the other part. It was the fish head, and I can remember watching my grandmas and grandpas eating every part of it, you know, the eyes—everything; and then, you know, my grandma used to save the grease that came off of that and my grandpa told me there were times they used to use that for bows, to help it stick together, you know, the twine and stuff they used to make their bows.

Yes, the dam was already built. I was born in 1953 and the Dalles dam was inundated, the Celilo Falls, and everything, in 1957. And I remember going across the bridge and having to pay a toll and that toll money helped pay for the McNary dam. I also saw when the Three Mile Dam was put on the Umatilla River, and that is where we used to go collect the eels. I remember that put the eel supply out completely, so I've seen changes in my time.

Actually, I don't remember Celilo but my grandma says we used to go there a lot and trade and a lot of my family used to go there and fish, but I don't really remember it. I remember seeing pictures and actually seeing old movies of it; it must have been something to see.

Marjorie Waheneka, filmed interview by Sally Thompson, Tamástslikt Cultural Institute, Pendleton, Oregon, November 1, 2004.

CHAPTER TWENTY

Environmental Protection

The Nez Perce historian Otis Half Moon recalls that just before signing the 1855 treaty with the United States, a tribal elder asked, "Does the earth know what is happening to her? Does the earth know that these lines are being drawn across it? Who is going to speak for the earth?" The elder understood that tribal leaders were concerned about the impact of the new agreement on the immediate livelihood of community members, but he wondered who would be responsible for the long-term protection of the natural world that sustained the tribes gathered at the treaty grounds that day.

Eight years after the 1855 treaty was ratified the Nez Perces agreed to reduce the size of their reservation, but they never abandoned that elder's belief that they were responsible for the health and well-being of their original, much larger homeland. Today the tribe has developed aggressive environmental protection programs to carry out that responsibility. The tribe's Department of Natural Resources manages a wide array of programs, from wolf recovery to wildlife protection and forest management. A separate Fisheries Department operates a fish hatchery and is actively restoring watersheds to help the process of bringing salmon back to the Nez Perce country.

"Speaking for the earth," modern Nez Perce people generally avoid courtroom confrontations, relying instead in each case on a negotiated Memorandum of Understanding (MOU) with federal agencies. Such an agreement commits the tribe to manage specific resources according to federal guidelines. The tribe's MOUs apply to the entire 1855 treaty area, many times larger than the current Nez Perce reservation. As a consequence of these agreements, Nez

Perce tribal employees carry out environmental protection programs across a broad area that would otherwise have been managed by federal agencies.

INDIAN COMMISSIONER COLLIER ON THE
WHEELER-HOWARD ACT, 1934

After the Dawes Act of 1887, which aimed to assimilate Native Americans in American society, Indians lands were gradually swallowed up by American homesteaders and speculators. By 1932, two-thirds of the Natives' 138 million acres of reservation lands were gone. Reversing this trend became the goal of John Collier, commissioner of Indian affairs throughout the long presidency of Franklin Roosevelt. In 1934 Collier proposed that tribes be authorized to establish formal governments to manage their affairs. At the same time, the commissioner proposed to end the policy of land allotments. Collier's proposal also set aside funds for educational assistance and for the repurchasing of tribal lands to create economically viable tracts of community property.

John Collier's proposal became law in 1934. While filled with legislative compromises and silent on a number of crucial issues, this Indian Reorganization Act triggered a governmental revival among tribes across the United States. The Nez Perces provide a vivid example of this process. Their original territory had covered approximately 17 million acres across the modern states of Washington, Oregon, Idaho, Wyoming, and Montana. At the depths of the allotment era, the tribe controlled only 250,000 acres, or 1.47 percent of its traditional homeland. Under the auspices of its modern tribal government the Nez Perces are currently trying to buy back as much of the land lost over the last 150 years as possible. Their holdings in 2003 amounted to some 770,000 acres.

John Collier hoped for progress among all tribes when he reported on the Indian Reorganization Act in his annual report for 1934.

In the last paragraph of the Commissioner's annual report for 1933 it was stated:

> If we can relieve the Indian of the unrealistic and fatal allotment system, if we can provide him with land and the means to work the land; if, through group organization and tribal incorporation, we can give him a real share in the management of his own affairs, he can develop normally in his own natural environment. The Indian problem as it exists today, including the heaviest and most unproductive administration costs of public service, has largely grown out of the allotment system which has destroyed the economic

integrity of the Indian estate and deprived the Indians of normal economic and human activity.

The allotment system with its train of evil consequences was definitely abandoned as the backbone of the national Indian policy when Congress adopted and the President approved the Wheeler-Howard bill. The first section of this act in effect repeals the General Allotment Act of 1887. During numerous committee hearings, during several redrafts and modifications affecting every other part of the measure, this first section was never questioned or revised. It reached the President's desk in its original form without the change of a word or a comma, indicating that Congress was thoroughly convinced of the allotment system's complete failure and was eager to abandon it as the governing policy.

The Act's Twofold Aim

The Wheeler-Howard Act, the most important piece of Indian legislation since the [eighteen] eighties, not only ends the long, painful, futile effort to speed up the normal rate of Indian assimilation by individualizing tribal land and other capital assets, but it also endeavors to provide the means, statutory and financial, to repair as far as possible, the incalculable damage done by the allotment policy and its corollaries. Unfortunately, the beginning of the repair work had to be in large part postponed because the authorized appropriations could not be made by Congress after the passage of the act during the closing days of the session.

The repair work authorized by Congress under the terms of the act aims at both the economic and the spiritual rehabilitation of the Indian race. Congress and the President recognized that the cumulative loss of land brought about by the allotment system, a loss reaching 90,000,000 acres—two-thirds of the land heritage of the Indian race in 1887—had robbed the Indians in large part of the necessary basis for self-support. They clearly saw that this loss and the companion effort to break up all Indian tribal relations had condemned large numbers of Indians to become chronic recipients of charity; that the system of leasing individualized holdings had created many thousands of petty landlords unfitted to support themselves when their rental income vanished; that a major proportion of the red race was, therefore, ruined economically and pauperized spiritually.

Economic Rehabilitation

To meet this situation, the act authorized a maximum annual appropriation of $2,000,000 for the purchase of land for landless Indians. This maximum appropriation, even if continued over a term of years, will meet only the most pressing emergency—land needs of the Indians. It must be remembered that since 1887 the Indian race has lost the use of 90,000,000 acres, the cream of its land holding. With an annual appropriation of $2,000,000 and an average base price of $20 per acre, it would require 20 years to restore 2,000,000 acres for Indian use.

While Congress did not specifically direct the consolidation of Indian lands broken up and checkerboarded with white holdings in the allotment process, it authorized such consolidation and set up the machinery for it. Congress also authorized the establishment of new reservations for now completely landless and homeless Indians and directed that title to all newly purchased land should be taken in the name of the United States in trust for the Indian tribe or individual Indian, who will have the use and occupancy of the land. Thus the policy of common ownership of land enunciated in section 1 of the Wheeler-Howard Act is reaffirmed and implemented throughout the body of the statute.

Part of the effort at economic rehabilitation is the indefinite extension of all restrictions on the alienation of Indian trust lands as prescribed by section 2. However, this section merely locks the door out of which passed the valuable team of work horses, leaving the decrepit plug behind.

The Revolving Credit Fund

The sponsors of the General Allotment Act of 1887 believed that the division of the tribal land among the members of the tribe would create in the Indian the pride of individual ownership and induce him to make use of his own land for the support of his family. Overlooked entirely was the cold fact that capital in some form is needed to transform even a piece of the best raw land into a productive farm. Since the Indian's newly acquired private land could not legally be pledged as security for bank or private loans, it was the duty of the Federal Government to place at the disposal of its wards credit in sufficient volume to meet their need for operating capital.

This imperative duty the Federal Government never recognized. Instead, it chose the easier road. It rapidly relaxed its restrictions on leasing. Lacking equipment for farming, the average Indian family proceeded to lease its land to white farmers or stockmen for cash. The leasing system, demoralizing to the Indians and contributing to the surplus of commercial farm products, spread like the Russian thistle. To this day the Indians who rely on the shrinking volume of lease money for their main support far outnumber those who farm their own allotted land.

What was true 50 years ago is true today. Without a reasonable amount of capital for permanent improvements, livestock, seed, implements, etc., the Indian owner of a piece of land cannot hope to make his living from the cultivation of the soil. To meet this pressing need, the Wheeler-Howard Act authorizes a revolving credit fund of $10,000,000.

This fund is to supply the long-term and short-term credit requirements of some 250,000 persons. Much of it must be tied up in long-term loans for sawmills, homes, and other improvements. Yet there is a huge demand for short-term loans to finance seasonal farm operations. The new lands to be bought for landless Indians must be improved and fenced, homes must be built, implements and seed acquired for the settlers, almost solely out of the revolving credit fund. In all probability the demands of the forthcoming year will demonstrate that it is inadequate.

The Heirship Land Problem

In the natural course of events, privately owned Indian lands must on the death of the owner be divided among his heirs and, in turn, among the heirs of the heirs. This result of the allotment system brings about the forced sale of Indian heirship lands, usually to white buyers. If there are no buyers, the heirship land must be leased and the proceeds distributed among the numerous heirs at an expense out of all proportion to the size of the gross revenue.

The Wheeler-Howard Act is taking the first hesitant step toward the solution of this problem. The new law, while allowing Indian owners to leave or devise their restricted land to any member of the tribe or to their heirs regardless of tribal affiliations in accordance with applicable State or Federal laws, bars the owners or heirs from selling restricted Indian lands to anyone except the tribe or the tribal corporation in the jurisdiction of which the land is located.

Obviously this negative provision, inapplicable in Oklahoma and on the Klamath Reservation, does not solve the problem. Some 7,000,000 acres are now in the heirship status; the acreage is increasing every month. The tribes have not the money with which to purchase this land. At only $5 per acre, it would require $35,000,000 to reacquire this land; the maximum authorized appropriation for 17½ years would be needed to return the land now in the heirship status for tribal use.

If the problem is to be solved within a reasonable time, the cooperation of the allottees and heirs must be had. They must learn that for the sake of their race and of their children they should voluntarily transfer the title to their individual holdings to the tribe or to the tribal corporation, receiving in return the same rights as they enjoy now; namely, the right to use and occupy the land and its improvements, to receive the income from the land and to leave the same rights to their children, except that the children and other heirs could not cut up the land into small, unusable pieces.

Where the land in process of inheritance has already been so divided among numerous heirs, they will have the opportunity to return the small parcels to the tribe or tribal corporation, receiving interests in the corporate property in exchange. Thus the tribe would acquire title to now unusable land which, after consolidation, could be assigned for the use of interest-holders in tracts of usable size.

Spiritual Rehabilitation

Through 50 years of "individualization," coupled with an ever-increasing amount of arbitrary supervision over the affairs of individuals and tribes so long as these individuals and tribes had any assets left, the Indians have been robbed of initiative, their spirit has been broken, their health undermined, and their native pride ground into the dust. The efforts at economic rehabilitation cannot and will not be more than partially successful unless they are accompanied by a determined simultaneous effort to rebuild the shattered morale of a subjugated people that has been taught to believe in its racial inferiority.

The Wheeler-Howard Act provides the means of destroying this inferiority complex, through those features which authorize and legalize tribal organization and incorporation, which give these tribal organizations and corporations limited but real power, and authority over their own affairs, which broaden the educational opportunities for Indians, and which give Indians a better chance to enter the Indian Service.

Even before the passage of the Wheeler-Howard bill a great spiritual stirring had become noticeable throughout the Indian country. That awakening of the racial spirit must be sustained, if the rehabilitation of the Indian people is to be successfully carried through. It is necessary to face the fact that pauperization, as the result of a century of spoliation, suppression, and paternalism, has made deep inroads. Of necessity it will take time, patience, and intelligent, sympathetic help to rebuild the Indian character where it has been broken down.

The first step in this rebuilding process must be the reorganization of the tribes, authorized by the Wheeler-Howard Act. In the past they managed their own affairs effectively whenever there was no white interference for selfish ends. They can learn to do it again under present conditions with the aid of modern organization methods, once they realize that these organizations will be permanent and will not be subject to the whims of changing administrations. These organizations, both tribal and corporate, will make many initial mistakes; there will be many complaints against shouldering the load of responsibility that accompanies authority. The task of organizing and incorporating the tribes will be difficult and laborious, calling for the maximum amount of skill, tact, firmness, and understanding on the part of the organizers. But the result should be the development of Indian leadership capable of making the Indian tribal organizations and corporations function effectively with a minimum of governmental interference.

"Indian Commissioner Collier on the Wheeler-Howard Act, 1934," U.S. Statutes at Large, v. 48, 984–88.

A MODERN TRIBE STRUGGLES TO PROTECT THE ENVIRONMENT

Treaties: Nez Perce Perspectives *is a publication collectively written by the tribe to "commemorate and honor our ancestors." Intended as a guide to Nez Perce history and an introduction to the tribe's legal claims to sovereignty over its ancestral lands, the book provides both an overview of events and a brief description of tribal values. Many outsiders have written about the Nez Perces; this is the first publication produced by the tribe itself. "It is time" for such a publication, the book's authors declare. They hope it will help people understand "the time honored beliefs of the Nimiipuu" and the "strong resolve that we, as a tribe, have for meeting . . . events yet to unfold." The following is a sweeping assessment of Nez Perce responsibilities today, all in an effort to "speak for the earth."*

The Nez Perce Tribe plays a crucial role in the management and the preservation of cultural and natural resources, the operation of health and judicial systems, and the development of economies within our reservation boundaries. The Tribe still retains certain rights to resources within its ceded lands, which include the Columbia River and its tributaries in the states of Oregon, Montana, Idaho, and Washington.

The challenge facing the Nez Perce Tribe, the U.S. government, states, counties, and cities is finding a way to effectively reconcile the many principles of law that impact our government-to-government relationships.

Land Base

The land and its resources have provided the basis for the Nez Perce way of life for countless generations. The lessons we learn from nature and the environment about its conservation and care are carried forward to each generation. The land defines who we are, and we recognize the unity of the physical and spiritual universe. We still move with the seasons, managing their bounty and diversity with an explicit respect for maintaining a balance with our surroundings. We celebrate Mother Earth's annual rebirths and offer thanks for the first foods she provides to us in recognition of our promise with the Creator and with the land. We possess a land ethic based on use, reciprocity, and balance.

When Lewis and Clark first came into contact with the Nez Perce, our people controlled vast territories. These lands were not individually owned but collectively used for the benefit of our families and bands. This method of collective land ownership could not be accommodated by the European legal system at the time, and, since it had no label, the term "Indian title" was developed to describe aboriginal tribal ownership of real property. The legal significance of Indian title was that Indian title could only be extinguished by the United States, and this, of course, was done using a number of different techniques.

Typically, Indian treaties resulted in tribes surrendering vast areas of land to the United States. When that happened, the Indian title was extinguished. If a reservation, comprised of part of the land previously owned by the tribe, was set aside for tribal use, the land so reserved continued to be held by Indian title.

In later years, the term "trust land" evolved out of the relationship that had developed between the United States and Indian tribes. Through treaties and agreements Indian tribes became dependent upon the United States for protection and subject to plenary governmental power of Congress. Nevertheless, the United States, by those same treaties and agreements, obligated itself to provide tribes with education, medical care, and housing.

The Nez Perce Tribe holds beneficial title to trust land. This beneficial title allows the Tribe to use the land, to lease it, to build on it, and, essentially, do anything—except sell it. The Tribe cannot sell its trust land because it does not own the legal title. The United States owns that title, and it would require an act of Congress to sell tribal trust property. Consequently, trust land enjoys certain immunities from state or local taxation, zoning laws, and the like.

Tribal Government

In 1923 James Stuart, who had been an interpreter for Alice Fletcher during the allotment years, became the first president of the Nez Perce Home and Farm Association. This group formed the basis for a tribal council that was organized in 1927. In the 1930s federal Indian policy with regard to Indian affairs focused on providing assistance to Indian tribes in organizing representative forms of government. The Bureau of Indian Affairs provided assistance in drafting tribal constitutions and developing tribal governmental structures. The Nez Perce Tribe presently operates under a constitution and bylaws originally adopted in 1948 and which subsequently have been amended several times.

The Nez Perce Constitution delegates most governmental functions to the Nez Perce Tribal Executive Committee, which is comprised of nine tribal members from the reservation elected at large for three year terms. Three positions on the Executive Committee are elected each year by the General Council, all enrolled members of the Tribe over the age of 18. Executive Committee members can run for reelection and serve several terms. The General Council meets twice a year, in May and September, for the purpose of hearing reports from the Executive Committee. Internal Executive Committee elections, for the positions of Chairman, Vice-Chair, and other offices are held during the Committee's May meetings.

The Nez Perce Tribal Government, like many tribal governments, began on a very small scale. Today, the Nez Perce Tribe employs about 900 individuals and has an operating budget of approximately $18 million. (An organizational chart of the Nez Perce Tribe can be found at the back of the book. The chart describes our governmental departments as well as our tribal enterprises and tribally owned businesses that provide additional revenue to the Tribe). The Nez Perce Tribe also has an aggressive land acquisition program through which tribal lands inside and outside the current reservation boundaries, lost through the treaty and allotment process, are being reacquired.

Today, over 3,300 individuals are enrolled as members of the Nez Perce Tribe. Elected tribal leaders represent the Tribe on wide variety of issues in interactions with federal, state, and local governments, as well as other tribal governments. In 2001, the Nez Perce Tribe passed an amendment to the voting requirements that now allow tribal members living anywhere to come home and vote in the bi-annual General Council meetings. The Tribe regulates the exercise of treaty-reserved rights to hunt and to fish by tribal members within and outside of the Nez Perce Reservation. The Tribe also exercises broad criminal jurisdiction over Indians within the reservation and civil jurisdiction over non-Indians whose actions affect the political integrity, economic well-being, or the health and welfare of the Tribe.

It is the obligation, as well as the commitment, of the Nez Perce Tribal Executive Committee to ensure a viable future for the Tribe and its members. This means providing a full measure of governmental services to the tribal community, protecting and preserving treaty rights and tribal sovereignty, and continuing to create and to keep secure a sound economic base. . . .

The United States' trust obligation includes a substantive duty to consult with a tribe in decision making to avoid adverse impacts on treaty resources and a duty to protect tribal treaty-reserved rights "and the resources on which those rights depend" (Klamath Tribes v. U.S., 1996). The duty ensures that the United States conduct meaningful consultation "in advance with the decision maker or with intermediaries with clear authority to present tribal views to the . . . decision maker" (Lower Brule Sioux Tribe v. Deer, 1995).

Further, Executive Order 13175 provides that each "agency shall have an accountable process to ensure meaningful and timely input by tribal officials in the development of regulatory policies that have tribal implications." According to the President's April 29, 1994, Memorandum Regarding Government-to-Government Relations with Native American Tribal Governments, federal agencies "shall assess the impacts of Federal Government plans, projects, programs, and activities on tribal trust resources and assure that Tribal government rights and concerns are considered during the development of such plans, projects, programs, and activities." As a result, federal agencies must proactively protect tribal interests, including those interests associated with tribal culture, tribal religion, tribal subsistence, and tribal commerce. Meaningful consultation with the Nez Perce Tribe is a vital component of this process.

Consultation is the formal process of negotiation, cooperation, and mutual decision-making between two sovereigns: the Nez Perce Tribe (NPT) and the United States (including all federal agencies). Consultation is the process that ultimately leads to the development of a decision—not just a process or a means to an end. The most important component of consultation is the ultimate decision.

Consultation does not mean notifying the Tribe that an action will occur, requesting written comments on that prospective action, and then proceeding with the action. In this scenario the decision is not affected. "Dear Interested Party" letters are not consultation.

It is equally important to understand that as a sovereign government, the Tribe may elect not to conduct government-to-government consultation or may decide to limit the scope of their consultation as needed. The primary objectives of consultation are

1. to insure that the Nez Perce Tribal Executive Committee (NPTEC) understands the technical and legal issues necessary to make an informed policy decision

2. to insure federal compliance with treaty and trust obligations, as well as other applicable federal laws and policies impacting tribal culture, religion, subsistence, and commerce

3. to improve policy-level decision-making of both NPTEC and federal government

4. to facilitate bilateral decision-making between two sovereigns (co-management of resources)

5. to guarantee the protection of NPT resources, culture, religion, and economy

6. to insure compliance with tribal laws and policies

7. to develop and achieve mutual decisions through a complete understanding of technical and legal issues, and

8. to improve the integrity of federal/tribal decisions.

The Process of Consultation

Consultation works through both technical and policy-level meetings to distinguish between technical and policy issues. Consultation allows for proper technical-level staff consultation followed by policy-level consultation for those issues that remain unresolved (or for those issues that are clearly only capable of being resolved at the policy level). Consultation is the process of coming to common understanding of the technical and legal issues that affect (or are affected by) a decision, and then using this common understanding to formulate a decision.

Meaningful consultation requires that federal agencies and tribes understand their respective roles. Meaningful consultation requires that both sides have a basic understanding of the legal underpinnings of the government-to-government relationship, including the responsibility of the federal government under the Trust Doctrine. In addition, federal agencies will benefit from some understanding of tribal culture, tribal perspectives, tribal worldviews, and tribal treaty rights. Tribal governments must understand the policy decision-making authority of the federal agency. Tribal governments must understand the non-tribal politics of the federal agency decision that consultation will affect.

In these examples, it is critical to note that a tribal government cannot understand the politics of the federal agency decision without personal communications. Similarly, the federal agency cannot understand the Tribe's issues and concerns unless staff members of the federal agency meet with the Tribe to discuss those issues and concerns. Without communication, consultation is meaningless, and a mutual decision is difficult or impossible to reach.

The consultation process works like this:

1. Federal agency contacts NPTEC or its appointed point-of-contact to notify the Tribe of an impending project proposal or to conduct an activity that may or may not impact a tribal resource.

2. NPTEC responds that this issue is important and that it would like to initiate consultation. NPTEC requests that federal agency technical experts meet with tribal technical staff (or NPTEC requests a policy level meeting).

3. Consultation has been initiated. Technical staffs meet. Technical and legal issues are discussed; the result is that tribal staff members understand the proposal and federal agency staff members understand at the technical level why this proposed activity is of concern to the Tribe. Such a procedure allows respective technical staffs to brief respective policy entities and to provide informed opinions and recommendations.

4. Tribal staff briefs NPTEC. Consultation is initiated between policy level decision-makers from both the Tribe and the federal agency.

5. Additional meetings are held, if necessary, leading up to the decision.

6. The federal agency and the Tribe formulate a decision. Assurances are made that the decision is consistent with federal laws and tribal laws and policies. This means the decision is consistent with applicable natural and cultural resource laws and policies. For the Nez Perce Tribe specifically, it means the decision protects the resources to which the Nez Perce Tribe has specific treaty-reserved rights and enables continued practice of tribal religious, cultural, and subsistence activities.

These steps may be adapted to suit the needs of the decision-making process leading to the formulation of a decision.

Nez Perce Inter-governmental Relationships Today

The federal trust responsibility imposes an affirmative duty on federal agencies to safeguard treaty-reserved natural resources, which are of critical importance to tribal self-government and prosperity. Whenever a federal agency proposes an action that will impact those resources, the agency is obligated to engage in meaningful government-to-government consultation with the Nez Perce Tribe. Ideally, the consultation will be ongoing throughout the life of the project and result in mutual decision-making. The Nez Perce Tribe has adopted guidelines to aid in government-to-government consultations. These guidelines detail the process the Tribe would like to follow to insure effective communication, and to insure the full consideration of resource issues significant to the Tribe.

The Nez Perce Tribe has established working relationships with several government agencies including the National Park Service, the Bureau of Indian Affairs, Indian Health Service, the U.S. Department of the Interior, the U.S. Environmental Protection Agency, Washington State Department of Ecology, the Bonneville Power Agency, and the U.S. Department of Energy. A brief discussion of some of these working relationships that presently exist between the Tribe and these agencies follows below.

United States Forest Service

As a result of the Treaty of 1855, the Nez Perce Tribe ceded huge tracts of our aboriginal territory to the United States in exchange for such reserved treaty rights as "the exclusive right of taking fish in all the streams . . . running through or bordering" our reservation. We "further secured . . . the right of taking fish at all usual and accustomed places in common with citizens of the Territory; and or erecting temporary buildings for curing, together with the privilege of hunting, gathering roots and berries, and pasturing" our "horses and cattle upon open and unclaimed land."

Tribal members continue to exercise these treaty-reserved rights in areas that are today administered by the United States Forest Service (USFS). In January 1992, the Nez Perce Tribe entered into a unique Memorandum of Understanding (MOU) with five national forests: the Umatilla National Forest, the Clearwater National Forest, the Nez Perce National Forest, the Payette National

Forest, and the Wallowa-Whitman National Forest. The 1992 Memorandum enabled the creation of a USFS–Nez Perce tribal liaison position to strengthen communications between the Tribe and the USFS. Such a position has assisted the parties in "promoting" the furtherance of dialogue and coordination on contemporary natural resource issues not only of concern for the Nez Perce Tribe, but for all "American Indian Tribes."

The improved communication outlined in the MOU led to discussion between the parties about the need to allow tribal members to camp in National Forests while en route to a fishing, hunting, gathering, or grazing site—or while exercising a treaty right. These discussions led to another MOU signed (by tribal leaders, the Northern Region, Inter-mountain Region, and Pacific Region Foresters) in May of 1998. This MOU recognized the inherent right of tribal members to camp in areas where they have historically camped without paying USFS use fees and without length-of-stay obligations.

In addition to these agreements, the United States Forest Service and the Nez Perce Tribe participate in numerous collaborative land and resource management activities that benefit all public users, including fish and wildlife habitat improvement activities, cooperative law enforcement activities, cooperative fire management activities, cooperative watershed management activities, and forest and basin-wide planning. These efforts and others were made possible by visionary leaders who sincerely believed that mutually beneficial goals could be met by working closely and cooperatively together.

Bonneville Power Agency

The Nez Perce Tribe contracts with Bonneville Power Agency (BPA) to conduct various fisheries and wildlife projects related to impacts of the Columbia River power system. The Tribe's Department of Fisheries Resource Management has several projects underway funded by BPA. These projects include conservation enforcement and tributaries restoration. In particular, BPA has funded our habitat/watershed restoration activities in the Lochsa River, the South Fork of the Clearwater River, the Clearwater River tributaries, and (with the creation of the Nez Perce Tribal Hatchery) fall Chinook acclimation, the Northeast Oregon Hatchery, and many other research and monitoring projects of resident fish. These programs impact restoration for a variety of fish species, including Chinook salmon, coho salmon, rainbow trout, cutthroat trout, bull trout, and sturgeon.

The Conservation Resource Division works to provide optimum fish and wildlife conservation protection within the Nez Perce Reservation and Treaty of 1855 areas in order to enhance and sustain tribal fisheries, wildlife, and the natural ecosystem for the use of future generations.

The Habitat/Watershed Division focuses on protecting, restoring, and enhancing watersheds and all treaty resources. Our Production Division concentrates on using surplus adult fish and hatchery production to provide fish for natural spawning runs and to create harvest opportunities. Our Research Division provides information on population status, effectiveness of hatchery programs, smolt survival estimates, and fisheries management recommendations. Our Resident Fish Division attempts to conserve, restore, and recover native resident fish populations including sturgeon, Westslope Cutthroat trout, and bull trout.

The Nez Perce Tribe also has a Precious Lands program that is active in acquiring ceded lands in Idaho, Oregon, and Washington. In September of 1996 the Nez Perce Tribe signed a Memorandum of Agreement with the BPA. The resulting contract, known as the Northeast Oregon Wildlife Project, called for the purchase of approximately 16,500 acres of wildlife habitat. The general objective of the project is to purchase and manage canyon grasslands and their habitats to benefit wildlife as partial mitigation for construction of the four Lower Snake River Dams. An estimated 9,669 habitat units (HUs) protected under this contract will be credited to BPA for habitat permanently dedicated to wildlife and wildlife mitigation. At the time of this writing, the project contains 15,359 acres of low elevation habitat within and adjacent to the Joseph Creek watershed in northeastern Oregon. Approximately 14.6 miles of perennial streams are being managed to improve riparian habitat conditions to benefit wildlife and Endangered Species Act–listed Snake River steelhead.

United States Fish and Wildlife Service

In 1995, the United States Fish and Wildlife Service (USFWS) entered into a cooperative agreement with the Nez Perce Tribe to recover and manage wolves in Idaho. The Tribe completed, and the USFWS approved, the Nez Perce Tribal Gray Wolf Recovery and Management Plan for Idaho. This plan operates within the broad guidelines set forth in the Final Environmental Impact Statement and Final Rule. The plan is the umbrella document that directs recovery activities in Idaho.

The goal of the Wolf Recovery Program is to restore a self-sustaining population of gray wolves to Idaho by maintaining a minimum of 10 breeding pairs for three consecutive years, thereby contributing to the delisting of wolves throughout the northern Rocky Mountains. By integrating four key program elements (monitoring, management and control, information and education, and research), wolf recovery in Idaho employs an effective team approach: the Nez Perce Tribe, federal and state agencies, regional universities, local governments, private organizations, and individuals all work together toward a common goal.

The United States Fish and Wildlife Service and the Nez Perce Tribe also have a Memorandum of Agreement describing production of coho salmon by the Tribe at the USFWS Administration Facility, Dworshak National Fish Hatchery.

Evironmental Protection Agency

The Nez Perce Tribe works with the Environmental Protection Agency (EPA) in many different areas. We have applied for and received grants from this agency to conduct various kinds of work. One of our most notable activities is the Nez Perce Tribe's Air Quality Program. The Tribe currently administers two air quality projects. One project, begun in 1998, looks at air quality monitoring and data gathering, education and outreach, health effects, and capacity building. The other project is a cooperative agreement between EPA and the Tribe to run a pilot smoke management plan on the reservation for agricultural burning in coordination with the State of Idaho's smoke plan. We also work with the Coeur d'Alene Tribe on a project with the University of Idaho and regional growers on the two reservations to develop alternative Kentucky Bluegrass crop management systems that reduce or eliminate the need for burning.

The Nez Perce Tribe also works with EPA on several programs funded through the Clean Water Act. The Tribe's Water Resources Division, for example, uses EPA funding to monitor water quality at 48 sites on the Reservation for baseline data collection, long-term assessment, pollution detection, and total maximum daily load development.

The Nez Perce Tribe also works with EPA to implement the Non-Point Source Program to restore and improve watersheds. Through this program, the Tribe coordinates with various inter-tribal departments, other local land management agencies, and private landowners on restoration projects. Examples of successful restoration projects include riparian corridor plantings using native tree and shrub species, road stabilization, culvert replacement, campground nutrient management, horse barn cleanup, protective fencing, and soil stabilization. In addition, the Nez Perce Tribe works with the EPA and other federal agencies on various projects, including mine reclamations, point source discharge permits, confined animal feeding operations, and underground storage tanks.

The Nez Perce and the U.S. Department of Energy

The Nez Perce have a centuries-long history of resource utilization in the Columbia Basin, including use of the present-day Hanford Site. In the 1940s the Hanford Site hosted the original location of the Manhattan Project. The Manhattan Project was responsible for the first full-scale production of weapons-grade plutonium that was used to end World War II with the first use of atomic bombs.

Nez Perce Treaty rights extend to natural resources in the Hanford Reach of the Columbia River. That very special stretch of the Columbia River is one of the Tribe's "usual and accustomed" places as stipulated in the Treaty of 1855 and provides a basis for the Nez Perce Tribe's relationship with the United States Department of Energy.

The Environmental Restoration and Waste Management Program (ERWM) is a part of the Nez Perce Tribe's Department of Natural Resources. ERWM facilitates the Tribe's participation in and monitoring of all relevant activities at the U.S. Department of Energy (DOE) Hanford Site. Furthermore, ERWM is the only organization that represents the interests of Idaho at Hanford. ERWM's staff provides oversight and participation in the cleanup and restoration of the Hanford Site. ERWM's involvement at Hanford protects treaty rights as well as both cultural and natural resources.

The Nez Perce ERWM was formed in 1992 to review regulatory documents and to suggest remediation strategies in a number of areas. ERWM works with agencies such as the United States Environmental Protection Agency and Washington Department of Ecology on hazardous waste and on monitoring projects and health concerns that affect reserved treaty rights at usual and accustomed places and on the Nez Perce Reservation. ERWM is firmly committed to educating tribal members and the reservation community about its (and DOE's) activities at Hanford. This book is one way of doing that.

The ERWM monitors and participates in Hanford environmental restoration and waste management activities by reviewing and analyzing Hanford operations to identify the impacts such operations will have on the environment and upon Nez Perce Treaty rights. The program works to institutionalize Nez Perce involvement in DOE decision-making, in federal compliance with trust responsibility, in protection of treaty rights and privileges, in protection of cultural resources, and in implementation of the DOE Indian policy. ERWM's primary goal, however, is to stop further degradation of the Columbia River Ecosystem and native shrub-steppe habitat. Participation in environmental surveillance and oversight programs enables ERWM to protect treaty rights and to advise DOE and the Tribal public of the efficacy of such programs.

National Park Service

The Nez Perce Tribe has an active and ongoing relationship with the Nez Perce National Historical Park whose headquarters and visitor center are located on the reservation near Lapwai. The National Park Service preserves unimpaired the natural and cultural resources and values of the national park system for the enjoyment, education, and inspiration of this and future generations. The Park Service cooperates with partners to extend the benefits of natural and cultural resource conservation and outdoor recreation throughout this country and the world. The Park Service also works with the Nez Perce Tribe to host speakers and presentations. In 1996, the Nez Perce Historical Park presented a three-part seminar on the Nez Perce Treaties led by Professor Dennis Colson of the University of Idaho School of Law. This seminar was presented at a controversial and difficult time when the North Central Idaho Jurisdictional Alliance sought to dismantle tribal sovereignty.

The Park maintains an important photo archive and library often utilized by tribal members. The Park seeks to preserve many other treasures and resources of tangible and intangible nature. For example, the Park Service played a crucial role in acquiring the Spalding-Allen Collection of Nez Perce items for the Nez Perce Tribe. . . .

Nez Perce Tribe Strategic Plan

The Nez Perce Strategic Plan is a comprehensive plan that will allow departments to better integrate their priorities with those of the tribe's leadership. It is an opportunity for the tribe to restructure tribal programs based upon the priorities of the tribe.

The goal of the Nez Perce Strategic Plan is to effectively serve and to effectively protect the present and future interests of the Nez Perce People. It is a planning process for tribal leaders

1. to create a vision for the future
2. to identify obstacles and contradictions
3. to identify strategic directions and
4. to develop time-specific implementation steps.

The Nez Perce Strategic Plan was envisioned to give the Tribe a mechanism with which we can, in so far as possible, accurately gauge our development and growth in three primary areas: improving the Nez Perce way of life, exercising and protecting Nez Perce sovereignty, and developing and improving our governmental services. The planning process involves elected officials, top tribal management, and key representatives from tribal enterprises. Our mission statement will be integrated into the various tribal departments and will clarify the various roles within the organizational structure, teach and educate our staff and tribal members about programs, and improve our working relationships with each other.

Some of the values that we hold sacred are expressed in our Strategic Plan. Core values in the plan that are discussed below include treaty rights, culture, elders, family, education, empowerment, equality, life, language, and wellness.

Treaty Rights

The Nez Perce reserved, within our treaties, certain aboriginal rights that were and are crucial to our continued existence as a people. The treaties also provided a designation of our aboriginal territories. They provided us with the continuing right to choose our own leaders, the right to utilize our usual and accustomed fishing, hunting, and gathering places, the right to use the springs and fountains, the right to pasture animals. These are a few of the rights our people reserved within the Treaty of 1855. There are, of course, other aboriginal rights that we, as Nez Perce people, retain and maintain, rights that go unmentioned in the treaties: our right, for example, to follow the religion of our forefathers or our right to speak our own language. Again, we believe it worth repeating that the treaties did not grant us our rights. The treaties were, however, a reservation (and a kind of declaration) of rights that we, the Nez Perce people, already held sacred. We will continue to defend our right to preserve who we are and what we hold sacred.

Love for Children, Elders, and Family

The purpose of tradition is to ensure the Tribe's future through its children. By hearing our literature, our stories, our legends, our history, and by watching and dancing and singing and drumming, our children have always learned to honor and respect their proper relationships with other people and with their environment. Among many other things, they learned to be good listeners, careful and accurate and conscientious observers, and to develop and practice patience. Although fewer elders today still tell our traditional Coyote stories, all our elders nevertheless pass on their riches in the family stories they relate and through their extended family relationships, providing our young people with steady and continuing nourishment.

Many tribal families today continue to formally celebrate the achievements of our young people. These celebrations take various forms that include name giving, first kill, and first root-digging ceremonies held by families at special times throughout the year. We also hold community celebrations to honor achievements of our young people by welcoming new births, honoring educational achievements, accomplishments in sports, and other activities. These celebrations help to combine our historic culture with the contemporary world in which our youngsters must be able to excel. Tribal elders encourage positive and loving relationships between parents and their children. The whole Nez Perce community recognizes a child's growth and development. It is often extended family—aunts, uncles, cousins, nieces, and nephews—who assist in the child's development of particular gathering, hunting, or fishing skills.

Education, Empowerment, and Self-Sufficiency

The education of our people was important to those who negotiated the treaties in 1855 and 1863. Our elders understood the importance of education even prior to the treaties when the sons of various chiefs were sent to the Red River School at Fort Vancouver in the 1830s. Our valuing of education carries forward with each generation.

The Tribe earnestly endeavors to combine science and culture by instituting a circle of learning. We established this circle to provide students with contemporary scientific facts and contemporary knowledge while concurrently providing them with confirmation of the Nez Perce value system. Our goal of self-sufficiency and self-empowerment is tied to our continuing education.

Equality, Fairness, and Integrity

It is through respect that we value equality, fairness, and integrity. The Nez Perce way of life inevitably creates various roles and responsibilities for our people. We respect and value the equality of the roles within our families, our communities, and our leadership. Our native religion teaches us that all life is equal, all life is sacred. No one person and no one being is a "higher" member of creation than the other. Each has a specific purpose or role as envisioned by the Creator.

Today, we must strive long and hard to maintain equality, fairness, and integrity in our dealings with all other people wherever they are. Unfortunately, some segments of non-Indian society on the reservation view the Tribe and our government as less than equals. We, however, nevertheless maintain our status as equals and will continue to demonstrate our equality in our dealings with other governments.

The Gift of Life

Our young people learn that when the taking of a life is necessary, as in hunting, fishing, or food gathering, a special prayer is offered to thank the Creator for this life. In that prayer we promise the nourishment provided by that life will be put to good use. We value the sacrifice of that life so we can continue to exist. We are taught never to take more than we need and never to waste food that has been provided for our use.

Our elders remind us to make good use of this life we have on earth, and to live in a way that shows respect and honor for those whose lives we represent within our families and communities. This view, of course, is not unique to Nez Perce culture, but it is nonetheless an important and vital part of who we are as Nez Perce people.

Nez Perce Language

Through the perseverance of our elders, our language—once in real danger of being lost forever—has been preserved, and it is once more becoming increasingly important to the cultural identity of our people. Our language is a source of pride, a source of connection to our past, and a way of communicating that helps us understand and enlarge the meaning of the stories passed down to each generation through our oral (and now our written) traditions. Some of our Nez Perce words have no English equivalents and therefore no accurate translation. To understand the meaning of some of the lessons in our oral literature, including our legends and stories, we all need to learn our language. By learning our native tongue, we can unlock the doors of cultural knowledge that only our native language itself can fully explain.

Many of our place names are tied to characteristics of the physical site or to important events that took place there (or both). A thorough knowledge of our language is essential to a deeper understanding of our culture, our history, and our environment. We invite non-Indians to learn our language as well.

Wellness and Holistic Health

Long ago our ancestors understood the medicinal values of plants and how to use these plants to treat particular illnesses. This knowledge, still practiced by a few, was based on being in balance and harmony with oneself and the environment. Of course, our tribal healers could not cure the various epidemics and exotic diseases imported into our country by non-Indians. Suffering, panic, and fear of these diseases spread across our homeland. Because of the very real threats brought to us by introduced diseases, our ancestral tribal leaders expressly demanded the inclusion of a skilled and competent non-Indian physician and health care provider for our people if the treaties were to be signed and accepted.

The practice of what is now commonly referred to as "holistic health" was fundamental to our traditional religious beliefs in living in balance and harmony. The practice of holistic health treatment is now part of the tribal programs designed for the disease prevention and treatment of tribal members. Programs are now being designed that recognize the various roles of family members in building healthy families. Our treatment plans must look at the mental, spiritual, physical, and social aspects of an individual. This old "new" approach will increase our chances of healing our people and keeping them healthy.

During the treaty-making time, our leaders were also very concerned about keeping alcohol off the reservation. So great, in fact, was their concern for the problems associated with the misuse of alcohol and the additional problems it could create for our tribe that our leaders insisted that a written prohibition against alcohol be included as a part of the treaties of 1855 and 1863 and as a part of the 1893 Agreement.

American Armed Forces

Indian people served in the armed forces even before they were granted citizenship in 1924. In 1917 and 1918, over 10,000 American Indians enlisted in the armed services to serve in World War I. More than 44,000 American Indians served from 1941–1945 in both European and Pacific theaters of war. Nez Perce tribal members take their United States citizenship seriously and have a long history of supporting the government during its involvement in wars it has fought throughout the world. Well over 300 Nez Perce tribal members (both men and women) have served in the armed forces in World War I, World War II, Korean War, Vietnam War, and the Gulf War. Many tribal veterans have been paratroopers. Many tribal members today are also serving in various branches of the armed services. Each year the Tribe celebrates and honors those veterans who have represented the Tribe and their country.

Current Challenges for the Nez Perce Tribe Treaty Rights

Good relationships with federal agencies, state agencies, and local governments are a vital part of the Nez Perce Tribe's efforts to improve the lives of our people. Over the very short span of time that our Nez Perce governments and our people have interacted with newer governments, the Tribe has been subjected to countless misunderstandings, broken promises, and bad faith negotiations. Rebuilding relationships will serve all parties in a positive way. As our natural resources dwindle and our ecosystems continue to deteriorate and decline, it is especially important that good relationships grow even stronger and continue so that global assistance can be aimed at these growing problems.

Solid, mutually respectful relationships based on sovereignty are the foundation for the future. The Nez Perce Tribe will continue to bring our culture, our traditions, and our expertise to the table while addressing the challenging issues facing Indian people today, as well as those issues that may arise in the future. We have survived by adapting to change in our own way. As we look forward now, into the times that are yet to be, we therefore reflect back on the past to guide us on our journey.

In 1855, the Nez Perce Tribe reserved, for future generations, rights that were essential to the Tribe's culture, beliefs, economy, and way of life. Today, the Nez Perce Tribe has taken a leadership role in restoring the natural resources that are so critical to being Niimiipuu. The Tribe's [sic] undertook management of gray wolves in Idaho, and the Tribe's success is evident: gray wolves are close to being delisted under the federal Endangered Species Act. The Tribe's deep commitment to salmon recovery is evident in its habitat restoration and supplementation activities, as well as in its constant advocacy. The Tribe's positions on natural resource management continue to reaffirm that the Tribe has always been here and does not intend to go anywhere. Thus, in advocating for breaching the lower Snake River dams to rebuild salmon runs, the Tribe is also supporting investments in the local communities that would be affected by that decision. Despite the Tribe's leadership, many challenges remain to fulfill the rights that the Tribe reserved and that the United States secured to the Tribe.

Lewis and Clark, in passing through Nez Perce Country, recorded in their journals runs of salmon that they could only describe as "nearly inexhaustible." Yet today, every species of salmon and steelhead returning to the Tribe's usual and accustomed fishing places in Nez Perce Country is either extinct (Snake River coho), endangered (Snake River sockeye) or threatened (Snake River spring, summer, and fall chinook; Snake River steelhead). A recent report of tribal circumstances has documented the high status of unemployment, poverty, and other problems among the Nez Perce and other treaty tribes that are directly traceable to destruction of treaty-reserved assets.

The Tribe has long restricted its harvest in hopes that the United States and the States would take actions to restore these salmon runs. Today, much of the salmon is being harvested by the United States, through the operation of the Federal Columbia River Power System, timber, grazing and road construction on Forest Service and Bureau of Land Management lands. This leaves the Tribe's treaty fishermen in nearly the same place they were in the late 1960s—being placed at the end of the line after all other harvest had occurred and being asked to bear the conservation burden.

Will the United States ever honor the promises it made in the treaties? As the Tribe's trustee, will the United States ensure that the Tribe's rights are protected? Will the Nation reciprocate the generosity the Tribe demonstrated in rescuing the struggling Lewis and Clark party 200 years ago by assisting the Nez Perce in restoring resources that are icons of the Pacific Northwest? These are the questions that remain to be answered in the days ahead. It is the fervent hope of the Nez Perce that "great nations, like great men, keep their word."

"The Nez Perce Today," in *Treaties: Nez Perce Perspectives* (Lewiston, Idaho: Nez Perce Tribe and Confluence Press, 2003), 86–110.

CHAPTER TWENTY-ONE

Language Preservation

Throughout the Indian country, missionaries, government administrators, and schoolteachers participated in coordinated efforts to replace indigenous languages with English, stressing that Native Americans would not make any progress until ancient languages were abandoned. Resistance to this policy arose in many communities, but there was little opportunity to combat it in a systematic way until after World War II. Beginning in the 1950s and 1960s, the rise of bilingual education and the emergence of a critical mass of Native American educators produced an atmosphere in which tribal leaders could effectively combat the Indian Office's traditional "English only" policy in tribal schools. Over the past generation, this movement has grown. Today a great many communities have devised strategies for preserving and passing on their indigenous languages. Few are as effective as the Blackfeet language immersion school in Browning, Montana.

Nizipuhwasin ("Real Speak") Center opened in 1995. The center was founded by men and women who believed that the Blackfeet language is more than a means of communication. Today Nizipuhwasin offers children from kindergarten to grade eight a complete curriculum in Blackfeet. Its goal, like the goal of other tribal language programs in the Indian country, is to provide students with an anchor in their communities' culture as well as to prepare them for an advanced education.

WHY TEACH AN ANCIENT LANGUAGE?
Darrell Robes Kipp

When it opened its doors, the Nizipuhwasin Center set out to reverse a widely held belief that the education of Native American children required that they master the English language. Many educators had admired the beauty and complexity of tribal languages, but they assumed the death of these ancient tongues was an inevitable consequence of American Indian progress.

Nizipuhwasin was founded on a different assumption. Educational researchers now argue that multilingual children are better learners, but the school's director, Darrell Robes Kipp, takes that idea a step further. He insists that Blackfeet is more than a means of communication. "The language made us healthy and allowed us to survive for thousands of years," Kipp has declared. "It is not something to be overcome; it is an integral part of who we are."

Nizipuhwasin encourages families to participate in language learning and advocates greater public understanding of Blackfeet culture through conferences and outreach programs. Nizipuhwasin is a vital part of the ongoing process of revitilization of Indian culture as a whole.

How I Became Involved with the Blackfeet Language

I grew up in the community in the 1960s in a one-room school on the Blackfeet reservation. My father dropped me off and walked away (there was no orientation like there is today). One friend was the toughest kid I knew, girl or boy. She would beat us up; I often kid her about it now. The one-room schools were a good place to learn. Ironically, they were closed down, and a less-effective districtwide system was implemented. But I remain an advocate of one-room schools and small classrooms—even though I was glad to graduate in one piece.

After leaving that school, I went to college at Eastern Montana College. I showed up with no dorm assignment, and there were no Indians there. We slept on the floor in the basement until they could get rooms organized for me and the other kids from the farms (who were also a bit clueless about the fact that we were supposed to have registered for rooms).

Finally, I got my roommate. He was an Italian from New Jersey who, I was told, was very afraid of me. (I got the feeling when he just looked at me, said nothing, and walked out. What, he should be afraid of me? I should have been afraid of him!) And after testing the waters, he and I grew to be very close and are still close today. In addition, I had not purchased a meal ticket since, again, I didn't know I had to; so throughout my time there, I worked in the kitchen ("kitchen dogs," we affectionately called ourselves).

I was given a test for English, but as an Indian, it was assumed that I would fail, and I was assigned to "bonehead English." Ironically, I eventually majored in English and got an MFA in writing from Goddard College, which later became Vermont College. After that, in the mid-1970s, I got drafted (June 28 I graduated and was out of college, and July 6 I went to the army induction center). After serving in the army, I went to Harvard. I got a master's degree at Harvard University in 1975, studying social change and institutional change. My career kept me very active; I lived in Boston and other places. I consulted with a lot of tribes in the country, and I traveled extensively. But in the 1980s, it was time to go home.

As Indian people, we are always drawn home.

"You Are the First Indians That Have Ever Come Here"

We were told as kids that only failures stayed on the reserve. That notion is reinforced even today by some of my professional colleagues. But in 1983–84, Dr. Dorothy Still Smoking and I (she and I have very similar backgrounds) asked ourselves, "What will we do on this reserve to make a change?" We wanted to develop our education, our experience, and our vision to create new opportunities. (Of course, in the process my own tribe fired me three times—primarily because funded programs would come to a close. It might also have been that I was perceived as a bit of an agitator, a little different.) We did a lot of work developing the community college but never found our real place there.

In 1984, I was teaching advanced writing techniques, and Dorothy was teaching advanced Native American studies. We organized a joint field trip to the Glenbow Museum up in Canada. The Glenbow Museum, it turns out, had volumes of papers, history, and documents on the Blackfeet Tribe. A little old curator who was standing there kept saying over and over, "But who are you?" (to our incredible annoyance). We gently reminded him that we had sent a letter from the community college, that we had permission to visit. That wasn't what he wanted. "Who are you?" he kept saying. Finally, when we stopped to have a dialogue with him, after a while, he responded, "You are the first Indians that have ever come here."

Since 1910, researchers have done a thousand studies on us. One study even measured our noses. It was all there. A very special thing happened on that trip. A young girl had a stack of photos, and as she looked through them, she announced, "Look at this! There is a picture of me." She had an elk tooth dress on. It really looked exactly like her, but in fact, it was her grandmother in 1890. It was a dumbfounding experience. Good things stay the same—yet we were the first in our tribe to know this or to see any of this.

We went into a frenzy. We asked for anything and everything on language. We asked for dictionaries. They pulled out a cart with fifty dictionaries on the tribe's language, written by priests, by linguists, some handwritten dictionaries. The first day, all the kids wanted to go to the mall. By the last day, no one would leave. We spent the entire $2,000 we had raised from the taco feed on copying charges. When we came back to the Canadian border, they asked, "What is all this?" We boldly (I was more brash in those days) stated that we were not paying anything in duties (we didn't have the money). We had finally retrieved what was ours. The officials just backed off. What a success!

So we really started in 1984–85. We were knocked out. We finally understood, we finally realized that the real key factor is knowledge of yourself, of your tribe. This concept was new to us. We had been taught to study Egypt and France, and to learn Spanish. No one ever said, "Study yourself." This was a big revelation. It was unique. It was five times more interesting than was anything we had studied before. Those original students formed our first study group, our first commitment.

Don't Set Up a Bilingual Program

Community colleges don't cover immersion language programming or language like they should. In 1982, Dorothy wrote a proposal for a bilingual program grant, which is fine, but you don't want to get into bilingual programs.

We all speak English too well. Bilingual programs are designed to teach English, not your tribal language. We aren't against English, but we want to add our own language and give it equal status. We don't allow slang or shortcuts; we teach the heritage language forms. Our immersion-school children speak high-standard, high-caliber Blackfeet. You can accomplish that through immersion only, not through bilingual education. Bilingual education typically teaches the language fifteen minutes a day. Kids who study with bilingual techniques will end up saying, "I can understand the language but can't speak it." Teach the children to speak the language. There are no other rules.

You will never have enough of anything. But if we had to, we could teach in a tent. We don't have enough computers. No computers will save the language. No CD-ROM will do anything. Don't hire linguists. *They* can speak the language, but the kids won't, and in bilingual education, they still can't. Nothing against linguists; they can talk the language, but they don't act like us. They are not us; they are recorders. CD-ROMs don't learn language like children do. At the community college, the bilingual grant eventually died out. (They always do.) It might have become too successful; too many people wanted to take the language. It became an annoyance for the college. Increased registrations would have meant more work for the administration.

In 1987, we were into the language ourselves, when the college defunded us. I did not want to go back to teaching college English. We were dreaming in our language, we would hear our language in our dreams, and we became tuned in, back in touch with our language community. In 1987, when no one else would take the language program and when it was not even supported by the tribal council (in council-speak, "I'm with you, but the council won't go for it"), we took it upon ourselves.

Rule 1: Never Ask Permission, Never Beg to Save the Language

Never beg to save the language. *Never beg.* Tell them you could use some help and explain to them clearly what is needed, but don't beg. We tell the council all the time (not that it helps much). They gave $10,000 so they can have a basketball tournament for people shorter than six feet. They gave $10,000 for a rodeo (give an Indian a hat and he becomes a cowboy). They gave $30,000 for this and for that, but only last year did they finally give us $5,000. One year, they gave us $100.

Hey, what about $10,000 for language? "Darrell, don't misunderstand me, I'm all for it, all for it, all for it. But we have a deficit, we have these other programs, but . . . but . . . but . . ." This year though, they showed up for the school community dinner. "Here, Mr. Chair, you can talk first. By the way, where is the money?" The same thing will happen to you.

We Are All Relearners

We are all relearners. We grew up in homes where grandmothers couldn't speak English. "Goll darn you," was all my grandmother could say, and when she did, you'd better watch it! My mother was a Catholic mission school kid, and my dad went to the third grade in government schools. When we researched, we understood why we didn't learn the language. We are good old grad students. We used all the academic skills that we possess to seek the reason we could not speak our language despite our home life. The truth we found is that they didn't teach us the language because they didn't want us to be abused like they were in school. We too have been using our educational skills for assimilation programming like everyone else. Now we use them in our own way, and now we understand some very profound truths.

Education, for Native Americans, was a journey to lead us away from who we really are. It's no wonder that none of us who had a college education knew our language. It's obvious that in order to get through the educational system, to make it to college, to get through college, to be recognized for our work, we had to leave many things behind. Language relearning is a journey back home. But this time you have the tools. I am sure that many people are suspicious of your motivations. In the morning, people would call us, "You white people from Boston and Concordia, you don't know anything about us." Bemused, we would listen. Of course, we are all Blackfeet people. No one was born in a mansion on the hill. They would go away. Then in the afternoon, another bunch of people would come in and say, "Look at you, we sent you to Concordia and Harvard, and now here you are doing nothing but looking at the language. You are just a bunch of full bloods."

We are an oppressed people. We have been so colonized that we can now, easily, perpetuate it ourselves.

Our Self-Definition—Never Use the Word Culture

When we lose the ability to define ourselves, to define us, then other people can define us. The priest defines the percentage of us who go to mass as Christians. The social worker or the statistician tells us that eight or nine of us in a group of ten are alcoholics. We are told that four or five are this, eight or nine are that. We take what other people tell us. In a single room, we can get fifteen different definitions of us.

Unless we free our minds, we cannot get a definition of our own. These Blackfeet children *will* define us. These are our children, our relatives; they are ultimately our definition.

Who we are comes from the language, not from the Indian culture. What is culture? That Indian culture could be construed as beat-up old pickup trucks, buckskin jackets, and powwows. Sure, in fact, that is contemporary Indian culture today —we are living it. We are not using the word *culture*. *Culture* is too vague, too consuming, and too volatile. Never use the word. It's meaning-less. It's debatable, a loaded word. Use the word *language*. The culture comes from the language.

If you want to study culture, go to the museum. At Glenbow Museum, after they got to know us, they showed us their entire collection: buttons, Indian gloves (in a drawer), thousands, every glove from every tribe in the nation. What are you doing with these gloves? No wonder all Indians are wearing jersey gloves. Dresses, tons of women's dresses. These are dresses our women wore to special times; no wonder our sisters are wearing blue jeans. The museums have all the dresses.

They did everything to take the language. But when you bring it back, the little kids will make new dresses. The little kids will make new gloves and new shoes. And the next time they come to take away the dresses and the gloves, the kids will not give them up.

You Save Your Strength

You do not ask permission to use your language, to work with it, to revitalize it. You do not ask permission. You don't go to the school board and ask for fifteen minutes to plead your case. You don't change the entire community. You save your strength; you find the ones who want it. You look for the young couples; you work with the people who want you to work with them. You hone your skills, talent, and time. And these are precious. Take care of yourselves.

You don't go to the tribal council and grovel, "Would it be okay if you gave us an old condemned BIA building to teach the language?" This is our language, and it deserves a beautiful place to be. An old condemned church? That's an irony, isn't it? All the old mission school buildings look like de-cayed buildings now. And, ironically, many are now alcohol treatment centers. Don't go near those places and other abandoned, broken-down places for your language programs. Bad vibes. Build new buildings and bless them in your language.

Get Your Supporting Data

We did a survey based on empirical survey methodology. It was a random sample. We did it right. We hired college students trained in statistical analysis and trained them as interviewers. We did the survey door to door. We asked, do they have language in the house, sweetgrass, a drum, and books on Black-feet? Do they have pictures on the wall about Indians? Do they have pictures of their family displayed or pictures of Michael Jordan and John Wayne? We then selected people in age groups to get information. We tried to interview every person over the age of ninety, then eighty, then seventy, and now we are doing every person over sixty. We are compiling the data. Don't listen to hearsay or gossip. Learn the truth about your community, and use the data for your purposes.

We had the best news. An honor student from our tribe whom we allowed to test the kids in our preschools did testing for two years. Our kids score above all the standards. The WITS test, which measures language articulateness, is not a good indicator for how Indian communities use the English language and our Indian children don't typically do well on the test. But our kids scored above the national averages, even though the test was in English. We are building language acquisition skills. We allowed the children to build their skills and, guess what, they scored in the top percentile. We want, and we have developed, high-level language acquisition skills in our children.

We asked the fluent-speaking elders of our language: Did you remain happy people all your years? What was the price, what were the struggles that you endured to use your language? What were the prices you faced?

For the most part, the people responded that they had to stay self-employed. They had no access to the best jobs. But they also realized they were the happiest and most centered in the community.

Our staff has produced academic achievement. Laurie Falcon, one of our immersion teachers, produced her thesis, "Immersion School as a New Paradigm in Native Education," from Vermont College. Dr. Dorothy Still Smoking, one of the founders, did her doctoral thesis on the interviews of the elders, and Billi Jo Kipp will get her doctoral degree in psychology with honors from the University of Montana next spring based on her work in our language schools.

We produce papers, scholarship, and high-quality investigative studies. We produce optimal learning in our students (our goal is 100 percent recall). We have produced films, videos, and articles. The film *Transitions: Death of a Mother Tongue* won a lot of awards. In 1997, we produced limited editions of *A Special Study of the Blackfoot Language: 1932–1997* for our schools, community, and patrons. Today, we use the book as the foundation of our language learning in our schools. Everyone—babies, parents, students, and staff—use the same book.

Parents Did Not Teach the Language Out of Love

Here's a story: Parents did not teach the language because they loved us and they didn't want us to suffer, to be abused, or to have a tough life. Because our parents loved us and our grandparents loved us, they tried to protect us from the humiliation and suffering that they went through. If you truly love your parents and grandparents, you can reconcile that. Because we live in an enlightened age today, opportunities are available to us that simply were not available to our parents.

Some of you will live a life first as a little girl, then as a young lady, as a mother, and then as a grandmother or great-grandmother. Some of you will live a life as a little boy, a young man, a father, and a grandfather or a great-grandfather. If we all live the good life, we get to be all those things.

If mission, government, or public institutions took the language from your mother or your father, you can replace that at some point during your own journey through life. As a young girl, you can put that continuum back. You can grow to be a mom, a grandmother, and a great-grandmother. You can pass your relearned knowledge to your daughters and sons and encourage them to pass it to theirs. This is what we should be doing as responsible Indian people. That is reconciliation with our parents and grandparents and our ways. Quit blaming them. Quit blaming the past. Take it upon yourself to do courageous acts, and just do it. As our parents loved us and protected us by shielding us from the humiliation brought on our languages, from all the horror that they had suffered because they spoke the language, it is now your turn to reconcile what was done in the name of love. You can now demonstrate your love for them by protecting and shielding the language in a different way. You can begin to embrace it, to use it, to foster it, to renew it, to teach it to your daughters, to teach it to your sons.

Immersion School: How We Got Started

In 1994, we went to a bilingual conference. We didn't want to do bilingual education. We wanted to start an immersion program. But there were no resources. There was this bilingual conference, so we went. And when we were there, we saw these most beautiful people, good-looking people, all speaking their language, and we said, "Hey, they look like us. Let's go sit with them." So we did. They were Native Hawaiians, and they were down to less than a thousand native speakers. So, they started the language nests called *Punana Leo* in their language and taught their children their language. They were the first people we ever met who knew what we were seeking, and they shared everything they knew with us. Today, we are the best of friends and would not be where we are except for their friendship. They showed us how to get started. They were mentors, our support, and our guides. They even paid for us to go to Hawaii. And today, they have twenty-eight schools. Last year, they graduated their first class of Native Hawaiian kids who had been in immersion school since preschool. Those Native Hawaiians would sit for hours with us in their homes and schools. They would show us everything, and now we can share the secrets of successful immersion with others, like you today, for instance.

And the Biggest Secret Is, Don't Ask Permission

Don't ask permission. Go ahead and get started, don't wait even five minutes. Don't wait for a grant. Don't wait, even if you can't speak the language. Even if you have only ten words. Get started. Teach those ten words to someone who knows another ten words. In the beginning, I knew thirty words, then fifty, then sixty. One day I woke up and realized I was dreaming in Blackfeet.

Don't let the bias and the prejudice of others dictate your approach, your message, or your program. Examine the bias of every public school teacher and those steeped in their ways of teaching. Their bias is that a dictionary of the English language, if complete, would be three feet deep and that the dictionary of the Blackfeet language would be less than an inch. This is false; in fact, it is probably just the opposite. Blackfeet and your tribal language are not secondary languages, are not inferior languages, and are not to be discounted. Don't let them tell you this.

In 1994, we took sixty-five of our tribal members to this big world retreat in Hawaii. We took many Blackfeet from Canada with us, and now they have many immersion schools on their reserves. We are all meat-eaters (we don't eat fish; it is taboo). We had some challenges when we were there. They very generously gave us all this fish, crab legs, squid, shrimp. We starved. We gave it to the Salish from the Columbia River basin and other fish-eaters who live near the water. We'd run to Henry's hamburgers every night to eat. It was a slight discomfort to us, but on the last day, all the children from their immersion schools, the parents, and grandparents got on stage and spoke in their language to us. One founder of Punana Leo named Koanao Karmana spoke to us and told us to go home and *just do it,* so we started our program as soon as we got home, and we engaged our community in the work.

Rule 2: Don't Debate the Issues

Don't debate the issues. Don't let anyone debate you. Don't let them start in on you. Don't let them even start. They will say, "What good is your language in Duluth?" They will sucker you to defend your work. They want to de-energize you. They want to bring doubt into your mind. They want to raise hell with you.

This is about us. We don't need their permission. Tell them, "I am not going to debate you. Go play bingo, go gamble, go somewhere elsewhere. We don't allow any debate about the language." Never bring your language into any arguments. If someone argues about the language, move away from him or her and do not participate. Leave the language out of it. Never disgrace our language with debate. You can't do it. We will not allow you to do it. You will feel physically flogged if you do, and it will take time to recover. It will de-energize you.

They will come around to you. But debate them, and you will get doubts in your mind. You need all of your strength to do this work. You have to go to bed and go to sleep.

The language is powerful. It will handle many things for you if you trust it. With thirty-seven dollars in the bank and payroll on Thursday, go to bed and sleep well. You cannot have doubts about your work. Go sleep like a rock.

Rule 3: Be Very Action-Oriented; Just Act

You have to be very action-oriented. Just act. "But we don't have land," you might think. Then go buy land. You buy the land—lock, stock, and barrel. You figure it out. Buy it, then figure out how to put the deal together to do it. But putting the school off trying to figure out how to get money is debating. Don't debate.

Everyone else is a horse trader, but we are not. We stand firm. Teaching the language is our only goal. We will give you anything you want for the land, for the cost of construction, for the supplies. You say, "You tell me what you want for what I need, and I will give it to you." We will not argue. We are not bargaining. We are not entrepreneurs. What you have in hand is what you work with. We went up to a lady and asked how much for the land. She told us, and we told her we would come back the next day with the money. We did. We figured it out ourselves. We got the money and said, "Give us the deed," and now it's ours. Find your friends.

I have a friend who helped us contact Jane Fonda, who wrote a $100,000 check to finish our school building on Moccasin Flat. Then representatives from a family foundation visited and gave money for this building here for the Lost Children School (the name comes from our Blackfeet stories). Within five years, we bought these plots of land that you see. The woman who owned this land worked in the post office. Believe me, it's hard to find land. You see it everywhere, but it's trust land. She owned this land in her name. She said, "This is all that I have. I have been saving. I bought this land through my savings deduction plan at work." When I asked her to tell how much she wanted, she said, "Everyone just laughs when I tell them because they say it is too high a price." Again we said, "We will bring the check." She sold us the land on the spot. We did not debate her. She said, "I will do it because of my grandmother who spoke our language. I will sell it for the language school in honor of my grandmother." And so, she gave up her land she had worked hard for in honor of her grandmother.

Last year, we went to the next-door neighbor when we saw that we had to expand. We told her that we needed to build on to the school. She was not interested in selling. She said, "No, my daughter lives there." And we asked her how much she wanted, and she said $100,000 (which is more than we had). So, we left her alone. But three months later, she called and said, "Here's what I want" (it was far more reasonable—half that, $50,000), and so we said okay. She then sold all the land, including her house, in honor of the language and her family. It will come to you.

Get an architect and say; "We want skylights. We want the walls open, and once a year on the equinox, we want the sun to come streaming through the door." Build it so that the sun follows you around throughout the day. Use the language to design the building.

Use the Language to Design the Building

People ask why there is no furniture in this spacious classroom. You see chairs and desks around, but they are stacked neatly or pushed against the wall. We learn through physical movement. We tell the children, "Go touch the door. Stand up. Sit down. Now turn around. Now jump." We need room. Don't let other people define your room, your needs, how you do things. Don't model your program on a traditional public school classroom where the tables and desks and chairs restrict movement, restrict vitality, restrict ideas. Don't debate. Your language will show you the way.

Rule 4: Show, Don't Tell

Show, don't tell. Don't talk about what you will do. Do it and show it. This is what they are ultimately going to listen to—not your words, but to the abilities of the children.

When a baby talks our language, the older women say, "Ohhh, let me have that kid." People will come to visit. Our pipe holders, our women will come and see the children talking in their language and say, "Ohhh, let us have that kid." Concentrate on the children. You teach the children, and they will show your success, and the others will say, "Ohhh, let me have that kid." Children who speak our language—everyone wants one.

Put Status Back in the Language

You have to put status back in the language, so you have to do status checks. You need to pay 10 percent more than any school in the vicinity so that your teachers feel proud to be there. You are cultivating a professional status with a salary and all benefits. Create a status for the language.

Then, give them a chance to improve themselves. Let them write master's and doctoral theses. Tell everyone that this is an environment to study the language. Tell them, "We are writing books about ourselves. Finally, we are empowering the language." The original children from that museum trip in 1984 were the ones who brought their children here. These students worked with us. They know us, support us. This is their vision, too.

If you bring one child here, you can bring brothers and sisters. Every two years you have new students. However, once a child leaves, they cannot come back if their parents doubt the program's effectiveness. If they leave for good reason on a temporary basis, they can come back. I know that if parents lose faith in the program, it is because someone is debating them and bringing doubt into their minds. This is not a dropout program. This is not a remedial program. We are a private Blackfeet language immersion school. You give your child to our care. The responsibility for teaching the language is up to us as teachers. We have no administrators here. Dr. Still Smoking and I are volunteers. Until very recently, neither of us had ever worked here. We are not building a school for the administrators or for the staff or for the parents. It is the home of our language and the children who learn it. And the pride in our goal and the clarity of the goal help create the language status. The top priority is the language. First, that's all this school exists for; it's only for the language and the children. The parents, the teachers, finally the administrators follow suit.

HONORING NATIVE LANGUAGES, DEFEATING THE SHAME
Marjane Ambler

Historians have yet to write the history of the struggle to save and preserve tribal languages, but dedicated journalists like Marjane Ambler have produced the "first draft" of the story. In her view, erasing the stigma to speaking in native tongues was the key to beginning this process of cultural reconstruction.

> Elohe mai ia makou, I ka ÿolelo kupa o ka ÿaina. . . .
> (Hear us as we speak the Native language of the land.)
> Na makou, na pua lei o Hawaiÿi. . . .
> (This is what we are doing, little children who are like the flowers
>   of Hawaii's lei garlands.)

The children's faces warmed the room as they sang, embraced in their parents' and teachers' arms. Their song was part of a language workshop at the World Indigenous Peoples Conference on Education in Hilo, Hawaii, which many tribal college representatives attended in 1999. The children's immersion school in Hilo is taught entirely in Hawaiian until the fifth grade, when English is introduced an hour a day. Listening to their voices, one felt they could accomplish anything, and standardized tests have proven that indeed they can; immersion school students equaled their peers in most areas and received even higher scores in mathematics. They were proud to be Hawaiian. Their pride and their potential filled the room like tropical sunshine.

Across the nation, many Native communities are striving to restore and preserve their languages, and tribal colleges and universities are leading these efforts in their communities. For some of the tribal colleges, the success of the Hawaiian language restoration has been an important model. Through their efforts, language advocates hope to also improve academic performance, family and community interactions, and even physical health.

Many forces have colluded to weaken and destroy Native languages, but the most effective has been humiliation. The U.S. government forbade use of "barbarous dialects" in the schools in the late 1800s, and education continued to be a tool of assimilation for many decades. Language advocates encounter the scars of such policies in their communities constantly today. Albert White Hat's older sister opposed his participation in cultural activities on the Rosebud Reservation, saying, "Dancing will send you to hell!" Kenneth Ryan visited a cousin on the Fort Peck Reservation who ranted and raved against his language work. Later, she tearfully explained that as a child, she had been caned for using the Assiniboine language, and she wanted to protect him. Lakota language advocate Cecilia Fire Thunder uses healing ceremonies to free the tongues of people too ashamed to "remember" their Native language. In many cases, these feelings toward the language have led to hating their own skin color.

When the schools punished students for using their Native languages, they also created a deep distrust of education, which persists today in many communities. Doris Leader Charge, who has taught the Lakota language and culture at Sinte Gleska University in South Dakota for 27 years, once felt this way. As a girl, she was punished at school when she tried to help the younger, Lakota-speaking students understand the teacher's instructions. "I thought that was what education was—punishment," she said.

Offering a Safe Place

How do the colleges fight the shame? How do they create an atmosphere where children and adults want to converse in their Native language? The tribal colleges utilize various approaches, as described in this issue. The successful programs all share a common characteristic with the immersion schools in Hawaii: They offer a safe place where children and adults are honored for using the Native language, not shamed.

This is not easy in the United States where the airwaves constantly bombard us with English. When northern Europeans turn on their television sets, they hear programs in Danish, Swedish, German, and English on different channels. Young and old understand the importance of knowing several languages there. In the United States a century ago, tribal statesmen often spoke three or more different languages, including Spanish or English. However, English has always been the language of power in this country. Language knowledge is no longer honored; many mainstream public schools have stopped requiring any foreign languages. Anyone in the world who does not know English is considered ignorant by many Americans.

During World War II, the United States military recognized the value of diversity. We utilized soldiers who spoke Navajo, Lakota, or Comanche, and the German and Japanese intelligence forces were not able to break their code. At the same time that R. C. Gorman (the Navajo artist) was being punished for speaking Navajo at school, his father, Carl Gorman, was serving as a Navajo codetalker in the Marines.

Knowing diverse languages is important to the country, to the tribes, and to the individuals. Without the language, ceremonies cannot continue; children cannot communicate with their grandparents; and adults cannot voice their prayers. Some attribute their tribes' social disintegration to the loss of their language and culture. "Our moral imperatives are in the language," said Alan Caldwell, director of the College of the Menominee Nation Culture Institute in Wisconsin. On the Blackfeet Reservation in Montana, teachers at the Head Start have noticed that children with behavioral problems have been transformed by their experiences in immersion school. By connecting them with their language, the Head Start instructors link the children with their traditional values. The Winnebago Tribal Diabetes Project Director believes that Little Priest Tribal College's language classes help improve physical and mental health. Native languages differ from English not just in the words used but also in the concepts conveyed. The common Navajo greeting, Yá'át'ééh, is much more than "Hello, how are you?" To the Diné people, it means, "Everything is good between us," according to Frank Morgan of Diné College. Many common expressions have spiritual connotations, according to Blackfeet Community College language instructor Marvin Weatherwax, as discussed by Paul Boyer in this issue.

Reconstructing a Culture

In groundbreaking research, Blackfoot language scholars at Red Crow Community College in Alberta are using words and phrases to reconstruct their culture. In the process, they are healing themselves, according to Duane Mistaken Chief's article in this issue. For example, by studying the word Ainna'kowa (to show respect), they learned Ainna'kohsit!—to respect themselves.

Tribal colleges and universities have been exploring different approaches for decades; teaching Native languages is part of their central mission. On the Blackfeet Reservation, a stunning 450 people are exposed to the language each year through classes and camps. Fort Peck has two immersion Montessori schools (see *Tribal College Journal* 9, no. 4). Little Priest Tribal College involves both parents and children in immersion classes one weekend per month in Nebraska. In Michigan, Bay Mills Community College provides a three-year summer program for Anishnabe instructors, who take their talents back to the communities throughout the Great Lakes region. The College of the Menominee Nation provides an apprenticeship program to train language teachers (*Tribal College Journal* 10, no. 4).

In most cases, the tribal colleges must create their own curriculum materials. Sinte Gleska University instructor Albert White Hat wrote a book on the Lakota language (*Tribal College Journal* 11, no. 1); Bay Mills students are creating instructors' manuals; and Salish Kootenai College puts its language materials on its website. Little Big Horn College instructor Dale Old Crow has created a 10-chapter ethnography on Crow songs, accompanied by recordings, to be used in his class, "Music and Dance of the Crow Indian." These publications provide a lasting legacy.

As Dr. Richard Little Bear points out in his article, good intentions are not enough to save the languages. Not all teaching methods work, and teachers must revise their methods accordingly. Speakers sometimes humiliate the learners, adding more shame to the many obstacles.

While Native communities must do the language restoration work themselves, outsiders must provide resources to help support their efforts—and avoid creating artificial barriers, such as English-only laws. To test the effectiveness of their teaching methods, they need consistent financial support over many years, not small, two-year grants. While many government agencies and foundations encourage math and science programs, few support Native languages. The tribal colleges need both. The W. K. Kellogg Foundation provided a generous, four-year grant of $850,000 to support language efforts at seven tribal college communities in Montana, but the grant period will be over soon.

Gradually tribal colleges are creating places where languages are safe. A place where the language is honored is a place that education, too, becomes honored. By recognizing Native languages, they recognize Native people, leading to self-esteem and academic success.

Marjane Ambler, "Honoring Native Languages, Defeating the Shame," *Tribal College Journal* 11, no. 3 (Spring 2000), 10–12. Reprinted with permission from *Tribal College Journal*, a quarterly magazine published at P.O. Box 720, Mancos, Colo. 81328. For information call (888) 899–6693, e-mail info@tribalcollegejournal.org, or see the Web site at www.tribalcollegejournal.org.

Darrell Robes Kipp

Darrell Robes Kipp, the director of the Piegan Institute, described the process by which he became persuaded that the most significant educational contribution he could make to his home community was to work toward the restoration of the Blackfeet language.

In 1980 when I returned home to the reservation, to this community, several of us met and discussed our various adventurous treks since we were teenagers. Now that we were all home, we realized that we were home because we were all homesick to be here. And one of the things we wanted to do was to relearn our language, and consequently that was the very first awakenings we had, was the early attempts to relearn the language. And consequently others joined us, particularly young college-aged students joined us. And a lot of people began to study the language, not as linguists, not as anthropologists, not as academics, but just simply as Blackfeet people wanting to relearn something about themselves.

Everybody thinks there's a mystic quality to everything, you know, but in a way it was. I recall very clearly having studied the language for, oh, I don't know, three or four months, five months with some speakers. And one night having a dream, and in this dream it was nothing particularly significant about the dream except the people, including myself, in the dream were speaking Blackfoot. And that really had a profound impact on me, and when I woke up I always say, "Wow, why do I feel so good?" You know I felt very, ah, comfortable and protected and happy. I went to the mirror, and went, "Wow, I feel so good I don't even think I'll wash my face today. I'm not even going to comb my hair." And I believe that that was indicative, not only to me personally, as a personal experience, but also with children and others, members of this tribe, find when they find out something, the language, and how the language can impact on us.

And I always say the language has secrets, and these are the secrets that allow us then to partake in. And it's a world apart from studying about ourselves in English. I think if you really wanted to get to the quintessential self, the essential being of who Blackfeet, Pikuni people were, you have to do it in the language. Because the language then embraces you, and brings you into the paradigm of the language itself. And we know that the language, and most, almost all Native American languages, had a very different structure, and a very different paradigm, and a very different way of describing the world around us. And consequently you take languages such as ours that relies, very limited reliance on gender.

A majority of the language is based on verbs, on action or description; nothing in the language is dead, it's simply inanimate, or animated. So these are radical departures from how English works and consequently I believe people are intrigued by that and attracted by that. And that it fits well into their essential self.

I recall back in the 1980s our institute put on a series of seminars, and the first seminar was about who remembered our words, who recorded our stories, and we had writers that came in that had written books about us. And I remember that seminar was extremely well attended. Then [another seminar was about] who had recorded our images, and I remember that seminar was so well attended we had to move it to a large hotel in East Glacier Park. And the featured speaker at that time was Dr. John Ewers, who was the ethnographer that had spent a lot of time with the Blackfeet and had recorded on film and slides all the clothing and the material cultures. And the crowd, it was huge there.

The last seminar ironically was [about] who had recorded our voice and this was about our language, and nobody showed up. Maybe at tops fifteen people came, and it was rather disappointing. But it struck us again, I guess, maybe as academics, or as members of this tribe, and it struck us, why is that? Why did nobody show up for that? And we then began to study tribal language. All these other things had been well recorded, and they had been well documented—our art and our dance and our music—but our language (even though it had been well recorded, at least, in our count at least fifteen major grammar and dictionaries written about the Blackfoot language) did not generate much interest. We concluded that it was not because people didn't study Blackfeet, it's just a result of the actions from 1900 on when the language was suppressed. Schools thought the language was not to be used. That conditioning was handed down from generation to generation and so consequently even members of the tribe who did not speak the language at all still had that conditioning in their viewpoints.

Not long after the seminar we conducted a reservation-wide survey, and we set it up, again, very scientifically, and we hired college-aged students from the community college, who went out and interviewed all over the reservation. And they knocked on the doors, went in, and said, well, there's also a series of other questions that went with it. Do you have a drum in your house? Do you have sweet grass? Do you have books of the Blackfeet? Do you have pictures on your wall of your old people? And do you have any speakers in your house, and do your children speak? Do you think the language is important? And when we got back the results, the outstanding result and finding we found was that all of the fluent speakers (and this was in 1985) were over the age of fifty years old. And no teenagers and children, or people in their early twenties could speak the language.

So consequently, that again was another incentive for us to take another look at it. Well, why does that happen, how did this come to be? In 1994, a colleague of mine and I went to Native American voices television workshop, that was sponsored by Montana State University. We wrote the first treatment of a documentary film called *Transitions: Death of a Mother Tongue*. We subsequently came home, ran the cameras ourselves, and did the interviews. We interviewed people who had gone to the Holy Family Mission, where the greatest impact on our language took place. From about 1896 to 1934, this mission was in operation. Almost all of our parents, grandparents, aunts, and uncles came through that mission or had contact with it. So every family on this reservation has stories that come from that mission, that were told around the table by their parents, but the stories hadn't crystallized into action.

We made the film in the summer of '94, when we actually took people to the mission, sat there with them, and they recorded their recollections. That film went on to win many awards. It's still in wide distribution today; people tend to find it very poignant, very interesting, because it's really told from the heart, by the people that actually experienced it.

I think largely from that film and other efforts people began to change their perspective. They began to say, yes, the language is important, we didn't give it up on purpose, it was taken from us, or it was denied us. And now again, you have the right to speak it. This probably culminated in 1991, I believe, '90, '91, when President Bush then, the elder, signed the Native American language bill, which then essentially made it legal for Indian people to speak their language. . . .

In 1994 a group in Hawaii wanted to put their own children in a school that would be able to teach the Hawaiian language on a daily basis. They had started an immersion school. It was simply a small school, no English allowed; all the instruction was conducted in the Native language from the moment they walk in the door, to the moment they walk out.

In 1995 we came back from Hawaii and we began to build our first school. We didn't start it until November, in the middle of winter, and one of our first benefactors was the actress Jane Fonda, who we contacted through a friend of ours who had been a friend of hers. She was very generous and provided money that helped get the program started. We built the first school, it opened in 1995, in what was called Mossy Flat, which is one of the oldest community sections of this town. We took three-year-old children, by '97, '98, some kids were arriving in the first grade, so parents again from the community and our board said, let's build a first-grade room; so we came down here in '97, and this building and this school was built.

One of the big benefactors of this school was the Violet Foundation of Santa Fe, New Mexico. It's a family-based foundation as well as one of the larger foundations that I know is helping people help themselves. And so this school was built in '98, and in 1999, we completed the upper addition, or the grades five through eight. We've ranged from as many as fifty plus, but we've been more comfortable around the high-thirties range, that seems to work best for us. We have about sixty children in each category, about sixteen children K-4, the same around [grades] 5-8. We've had five graduates from the eighth grade; they went to four different high schools—all of them are honor students, extremely talented kids doing extremely well in high school.

So that really supports our notion, our inner feeling, our intuitive notion, that bringing the language back to our children produces healthy children, and we believe that healthy children then have choices, and healthy children with choices can achieve anything in a society. They do not have to carry the negative baggage or be obsessed with the obstacles in front of them, or consider their heritage a hindrance. Or their language. They can utilize these things in positive ways to become successful adults.

A lot of people ask us how we get the kids to come here. Well, the first kids that came here were the children of adult language students. They sent their children here. And then we'd take their brothers and sisters. So we have families; we have as many as three kids here from the same family. And they go home, and they interact in their house. They get their family to speak their language because their parents say, well, our kids come home and they speak the language, and they think and they want to learn, and then they want us to participate.

We're not out of the woods here; I mean, we're not safe yet. This effort has been successful as it can, and people would have said we've been fortunate, we've had good luck, and we've had good support, but we're not there yet. We've still got a long ways to go; we have to get more support, people have to start financially supporting it. This program was developed without public funding, without institutional funding. The most successful immersions programs are ones that don't have government funding in that they are allowed to develop on their own, through their own creative efforts; they are allowed to produce what they need.

Darrell Robes Kipp, filmed interview by Sally Thompson, Piegan Institute, Browning, Montana, September 9, 2004.

CHAPTER TWENTY-TWO

Education and Cultural Preservation

The Fort Berthold Indian Reservation is the modern home of the three-thousand-member Mandan, Hidatsa, and Arikara tribes. The community there has experienced many disruptions since the Corps of Discovery arrived in the fall of 1805. Fur traders, missionaries, and schoolteachers have each played a role in the disruption of traditional lifeways. And after World War II, the U.S. Army Corps of Engineers embarked on an ambitious flood control and hydroelectric project on the Missouri River, erecting a series of massive dams that inundated the fertile bottomlands the Native people had cultivated for centuries. The reservation's traditional villages were replaced by New Town, an administrative center, and other new settlements.

In the 1960s and 1970s the Three Affiliated Tribes struggled to rebuild their communities and identify strategies for sustaining their traditions. New businesses, from construction and woodworking to a modern casino and lodge, now sustain the local economy. Just as important has been the task of preserving tribal cultural traditions. Fort Berthold Community College, founded in 1973, has taken primary responsibility for that effort, offering courses, encouraging local artists and writers, and providing a solid institutional home for the work of cultural preservation.

Thirty-three tribal colleges exist in Indian communities across the United States. Together they serve over thirty thousand students. Authorized by Congress and chartered by local reservation governments, these colleges offer a wide variety of degree programs but share a common commitment to the preservation of tribal cultures and histories. They receive modest federal support as well as subsidies from local tribal governments and private foundations.

A PROFILE OF A TRIBALLY CHARTERED COLLEGE
Dorreen Yellow Bird

Today one in five American Indian students of higher education is enrolled in a tribal college. Community leaders hope these colleges will provide a degree of higher learning and ensure the survival of tribal culture and history. Native American institutions of higher learning provide benefits beyond a degree. Based in tribal communities, they contribute to the local economy and inspire a sense of community empowerment.

When Fort Berthold Community College opened, twenty students walked into the four condemned trailers that made up the campus. Thirty years and over three hundred graduates later, the campus is housed in a new building with state-of-the-art classrooms overlooking the Missouri River. The school currently enrolls more than three hundred students. This profile of the school was prepared in 1998 by Dorreen Yellow Bird, a columnist for the Grand Forks (North Dakota) Herald.

Fort Berthold Community College just passed a significant milestone—25 years as a college. After a celebration and a deep breath, they are ready to tackle the next 25 years. The college is one of the proud accomplishments of the Mandan, Hidatsa, and Arikara people of the Three Affiliated Tribes. It is one of the few educational institutions located in this isolated part of the state. Because the closest colleges and universities are 100 to 250 miles away, the tribal college fills an important niche by providing degree programs for the reservation and the rural farming community.

Twenty-five years ago, only a handful of people believed the college would succeed. Even these supporters had some doubt that the new college would be the vision it is today. "We came from very humble beginnings," says Deloris Wilkinson, dean of students. "Our success is because there was a certain camaraderie. We were almost like a family," she says. Wilkinson, an Arikara from White Shield, attributes that success and team effort to past president, Phyllis Howard.

The tribal college started as a college center in 1973 with Howard as the coordinator. Howard, a Hidatsa tribal member, said the college was part of a Title III higher education institutional development grant of the University of Mary in Bismarck. This grant program began to increase the number of Black colleges in the United States and was expanded to include other minorities.

Fort Berthold was among several colleges organized at that time on reservations throughout North Dakota and the nation. The idea for tribal colleges was a brainstorm of people who worked with student services such as TRIO (Talent Search, Upward Bound, Student Support Services) and other programs, says Carol Davis, a member of the Turtle Mountain Band of Chippewa and vice president of the Turtle Mountain Community College (Belcourt, N.D.). They discussed ways to make the colleges become a reality. She met Howard during those meetings, and the two have been friends for some 25 years.

During the first year, Howard tackled very basic tasks, such as finding an office and classrooms for their budding college. The staff included only Howard and a part-time secretary during those early years. "We had to go out and practically pull the students in. In that first year we had only about 20 students," compared with the current enrollment of 301. Initially, they offered extension courses from the state's universities and junior colleges. They also offered classes needed by the community, such as tribal government and early childhood education, and culturally appropriate classes, such as Arikara, Hidatsa, and Mandan languages.

Wilkinson says the early childhood education classes were needed for the tribal members who were teaching in the Head Start programs. Those classes were important so tribal people could earn degrees and then become qualified staff of the local program. One of the original graduates, Martha Lone Bear, a Hidatsa tribal member, started as a teacher and then became the director. She is still with the Head Start program. Without the college, Head Start would have been administered by non-Indian teachers, she says. The children need Native American teachers because they can relate to them, and these Native American teachers are role models.

By 1983 there were 180 students, but the college was still struggling for funds. "We would wring every dollar dry. There was no waste. We really disciplined ourselves to stay within the budget," Wilkinson says. Throughout those early years funding was their biggest problem, Howard says. When Congress passed the Tribally Controlled Community College Assistance Act of 1978, it meant some stable funding for the tribal college.

Then Howard decided to reach for the stars. She began to plan for a new campus to replace the deteriorating one. The college had moved from condemned trailers at the Four Bears village across the Missouri River to several rental buildings in New Town, N.D. Some of the old buildings at Four Bears were so cold during the winter that the students would practically freeze, she says. During those years, they would gather to talk about a new college. They wondered if they could really do it. She asked, "Why not?"

"It was a major undertaking," she says. They had to tap every source possible, including their own pockets and the purses of the community. Today the brand-new tribal community college building in New Town overlooks the Missouri River on the western plains of North Dakota. Since accreditation in 1985, the college has graduated over 300 students.

"We want to make classes culturally relevant to the tribe," says Elizabeth Demaray, Arikara tribal member and current president of the college. The curriculum incorporates the culture of the people and includes language studies of the three tribes. Demaray is putting together an elder advisory committee to work with the college, which will be important in maintaining the culture and promoting the languages. Through the IVN (Interactive Video Network) system they are able to hook up with all the districts on the reservation as well as other colleges and universities in the state.

The goal for the community college is to become a four-year institution. An innovative elementary teacher education project that is mentored and supported by University of North Dakota (UND) in Grand Forks, N.D., will help the tribal college to graduate their first four-year students. The students will receive their degrees from UND, but they will take their classes and do their student teaching in reservation community schools. The project is managed and taught by Dr. Clarice Big Back, a Hidatsa tribal member and UND professor.

The scene has changed since the years Howard struggled to find Native American professionals to fill the positions at the college. Currently there are many professionals in several different fields on the reservation. Unlike the freezing cold trailers of earlier years, the college enjoys a modern building with state-of-the-art technology. The mission, however, remains the same: serving the Mandan, Hidatsa, and Arikara people in their own community.

Dorreen Yellow Bird, "Fort Berthold Community College Celebrates Twenty-Five Years of Growth," *Tribal College Journal* 10, no. 1 (Fall 1998): 26–27, 44.

TRIBAL MUSEUMS JOIN THE TASK OF PRESERVING COMMUNITY TRADITIONS

Carolyn Casey

Fewer in number than tribal colleges and without any common source of support, tribal museums are frequently overlooked as institutions supporting cultural preservation in Indian communities. Nevertheless tribal museums, like museums in other American communities, are a vital element in that effort. Today fewer than a dozen fully developed tribal museums exist, but they stretch across the United States, from the Hopi Reservation in Arizona to the glittering Mashantucket Pequot complex in southern Connecticut and the Tamástslikt Cultural Institute on the Umatilla Reservation in eastern Oregon.

When the Osage Tribal Museum in Oklahoma opened in 1938, it was the first of its kind. A museum dedicated to the story of one tribe. That is, unless you include the many informal museums that were strung across the country in people's basements and sheds. Tribal museums face challenges and share opportunities not encountered by non-native museums. They are a recent phenomena, a product of American Indian activism in the 60's and 70's when the question, Why is someone else displaying my ancestors' bones? was tackled. The recovery of artifacts continues today, and estimates now run between 100–200 tribal museums in America. The challenges have grown with them.

Tribal museums may store some of the same artifacts found in non-Native museums. They may take the precautions to protect and preserve their collections. And they may even follow standard research techniques. But they have more differences than similarities. For tribal museums such as the Makah Cultural and Research Center in Neah Bay, Wash., their collections are not dead relics from the past. Instead they are living pieces of their culture and a link with modern Native society. Makah youth come to the nationally recognized Makah center to learn their language and their history. Elders come to refresh their memories and share their understanding with tribal researchers.

Other museums often house Native baskets under glass or in storage, never allowing human hands to soil these treasures. Janine Bowechop believes the baskets should be used to keep weaving skills alive.

"Part of our mission is to protect and preserve cultural and archeological resources," says Bowechop, acting director of the Makah center. "If letting our weavers handle the baskets preserves certain techniques and skills, then we don't consider it destructive. We've been told it may shorten the life of the baskets, but we believe it will add immeasurably to the life of basket weaving among our people."

Finding Money

Tribal museums face constant financial struggle to cope with dwindling federal support and fluctuating tribal support. Few have the resources of many urban museums with rich docents who host tea parties to raise money and donate time.

Even gift shops, which can supplement the budgets of urban museums, offer little assistance in much of Indian Country, well off the typical tourist's path. "Our funding has been schizophrenic," Bowechop says. Started as a vision of the Makah Tribal Council in the 1970s, the center went without council money for eight years in the 1980s. Now the council supports it again. The center also relies upon an intricate web of support from public and private institutions.

The constant grant writing and soliciting have paid off. In 1993 the Makah center added a $1.6 million storage facility of 8,100 square feet. The Administration for Native Americans recently funded their Makah Mentor/Apprentice Language Proficiency Project. The new facility allowed curators to finally house the artifacts in a manner reflecting current Makah values. Close attention is paid to cultural and gender restrictions that apply to certain objects, Bowechop says. Breaking from standard European cataloguing and storage techniques, the Makah curators grouped items together based upon family ownership. They used the Makah language to label and organize the vast collection.

Physically storing and labeling the archeological artifacts according to Makah language encourages analysis of the cultural meanings in the collection and provides insights into the Makah language and thought, Bowechop says.

Very few groups will give money for ongoing operating costs, so Bowechop says she especially values the grants from the Institute of Museum Services (IMS) in Washington, D.C. The only federal source of operating support for many museums, IMS [now IMLS, Institute of Museum and Library Services] has suffered recently from congressional budget cuts. With federal money less available, Makah staff has worked to strengthen relationships with private foundations. Although the center includes a craft shop and charges admission to visitors, these two sources of revenue cannot support the growing facility, which employs 13 tribal members.

The Ned A. Hatathli Museum at Navajo Community College in Tsaile, Ariz., is funded through the college. It was created to foster traditional language, culture, and arts, says museum director Harry Walters. The money for the museum was part of a congressional bill that created the college. Grants and contributions added to the museum's start-up money. Because nearly all of the people who attend this museum are local Navajos, a gift shop can't supply much revenue. Money always is in short supply, Walters says.

Non-tribal museums have trouble dealing with Native philosophies of interacting with their artifacts, Walters says. When a traveling Smithsonian exhibit of historic Navajo weavings came to his museum, he had a difficult time convincing Smithsonian staff that the Navajo weavers who attended would need to touch the exhibit fabrics. He nearly had to cancel the exhibit after learning how expensive it would be to meet Smithsonian security standards. "It would have taken our whole year's exhibit budget just for security," he says.

Forming Collections

Despite great competition for the grant money available to tribal museums, more and more tribes are considering opening their own museums or cultural centers. Experts predict in the next five years the number of tribal museums will double. Part of the reason for the growth is the long-overdue enforcement of the Native American Graves Protection and Repatriation Act (NAGPRA). Because of the forced return of sacred items, more museums are returning other items beyond the requirements, says James Nason (Comanche), head of the repatriation committee at the Burke Museum at the University of Washington in Seattle.

The Hatathli Museum began its collection by asking museums and individual collectors for donations. They had a good response because collectors gained tax write-offs from the donations, Walters says. Today the collection includes mainly Navajo material including sacred paraphernalia, paintings, basketry, pottery, and jewelry.

Unlike many tribes, the Makah didn't have to rely on NAGPRA to get its artifacts back. They have more than 55,000 well-preserved artifacts recovered from a nearby archeological dig where a mudslide destroyed a Makah winter village about 300 years ago. Although the dig began in the 1960s, it wasn't until the 1980s that the tribe got a court ruling saying all of the artifacts belonged to the tribe, not the university overseeing the dig.

Nason and his staff have assisted numerous tribes, including the Makah, to plan their museums. Nason says museum training can be offered flexibly to meet whatever time and financial constraints exist, but they should meet professional standards.

Tribes will have the greatest success, he says, if they: define and meet the goals of their community; commit to giving ongoing tribal financial support; and foster the support of the tribal elders. "If you don't have the support of your elders, you really are up a creek," Nason says. "This is essential."

Walters echoed the importance of the support and help from elders. "All of our exhibits reflect the traditional Navajo viewpoint," Walters says. "We always get input from our medicine people on our new exhibits. We take their advice."

Getting Trained

Tribes must balance their need for professional museum staffs with the cost of educating them. The Smithsonian Institution has an ongoing program of free regional tribal museum training and internships at the main Smithsonian museums. Regional Smithsonian trainings are offered twice a year to groups of 35 people.

The Smithsonian pays the cost of attendees' travel and lodging, says Susan Secakuku (Hopi), a training assistant at the Smithsonian's National Museum of the American Indian. The Smithsonian will also be training staffs at the tribal college log museums. At the regional training, Native experts teach about repatriation, research, and curation. The institution also offers several short-term paid internships and one year-long internship. "I think training of Native people in museum studies is increasing," Secakuku says. "But there still is so much to be done. There is a great need. Unfortunately, it always comes down to money." Bowechop says the Makah center relies on training offered by the Smithsonian, the University of Washington, and the National Park Service.

Several museum directors say staff hesitate to attend distant training that requires being apart from their families for months at a time. "Our families come first," Bowechop says. "I think you find that all over Indian Country. You cannot ask someone to forget about family for a year-long training."

Walters echoed this viewpoint, saying tribal museum studies and work-shops must be more accessible to those in need of training. He welcomed the idea of tribal colleges taking a more active role in providing training for tribal museums.

"I think that there are Native studies in other colleges, but they are from the viewpoint of how the higher, dominant European culture views Native people—a lot is lost," Walters says. "I think tribal colleges are now at the point where they can explain to the world the true Native culture and world view. What better way to do this than through our own museums?" Chuck Dailey, interim director of the Institute of American Indian Arts Museum (IAIA), agrees with Walters. In 1971 IAIA began a formal museum studies program. It offers an accredited two-year museum studies degree, including training in museum management and operation, exhibition, collections, and research. This January a new course dedicated exclusively to repatriation will be offered, pending funding. The new director of the museum will be Fred Nahwooksy (Comanche). All of the classes are geared toward tribal needs and beliefs, Dailey says. In addition, the staff and students will travel to help train tribal museum staff and help launch museums, only charging tribes the cost of their transportation and lodging. IAIA maintains an extensive collection of videotapes and written materials, including tapes about museum management and repatriation, which are available for tribal use at no charge.

The institute, which is funded almost entirely with federal money, began in 1962 and sporadically operated a small gallery showing student and faculty work for about nine years. The 24,000-square-foot museum in downtown Santa Fe is the only museum in the world dedicated to the collection and exhibition of contemporary American Indian and Alaskan Native art, according to Dailey.

In addition to offering low-cost consultations and workshops, this fall IAIA will launch a collection of traveling exhibits for tribal museums, many available at low cost without requiring expensive cases or security. "Most tribal museums don't have big insurance policies to cover works of art. This is a reality we have to accept," Dailey says.

Carolyn Casey, "Tribal Museums Keep Exhibits, Culture Alive," *Tribal College Journal* 8, no. 2 (Fall 1996): 12–15.

VOICES OF THE NEXT GENERATION

One measure of cultural preservation in any community is the presence of a new generation whose members are eager to continue that community's traditions into the future. These writings from students at Fort Berthold Community College, New Town, North Dakota, were published in Tribal College Journal, *the quarterly publication of the American Indian Higher Education Consortium. They demonstrate that reflection, imagination, and optimism are very much in evidence in contemporary Native American communities.*

Since 1989 Tribal College Journal *has served the nation's tribally chartered institutions by facilitating communication among administrators and faculty members and providing a publishing outlet for exceptional work by some of their students.*

Growing Up
Twyla Baker

Growing up on an Indian reservation is not unlike growing up anywhere else. You get in the same scrapes as a kid, argue with your parents as a teen, and have hopes and dreams for yourself, just like anyone else. The only differences is that on the "res," as we who live there call it, you grow up with a constant awareness of the color barrier. When I was young, growing up in my hometown of New Town, North Dakota, on the Fort Berthold Indian Reservation, color didn't matter much. Children have little use for color distinctions when what one really needs is a good, hard push on the swings. Take, for example, my best friend in kindergarten.

Her name was JoLynn, and she had the most beautiful, long, wavy, blonde hair and sparkling blue eyes; a stark contrast to my own thick, straight, dark locks and chocolate brown eyes. She had a fair complexion that burned easily whenever we spent a little too much time playing outside, whereas my own copper skin merely turned a deeper shade. Ironically, she was also Indian, from my very same tribe, only her mother was white, and both my parents were Indians. I never really thought about this much. She was simply my friend and playmate. But all good things come to an end, and I realized our differences in a fairly brusque manner.

I planned to take Jo to a pow-wow with my family. Pow-wows were a regular event for me, but Jo had only been to a few. My mother packed us up and bundled us off to the pow-wow grounds, and as soon as we got there, Jo and I ran off to see if we could find any more of our friends.

We'd been running around for some time when I bumped into one of my aunts, Colette. She and a friend of hers were carrying lawn chairs to the arena where they could watch the dancers. In my culture, there is no difference between the role of aunts and mothers. Aunts are expected to treat their nieces and nephews as they would their own children. Such was the relationship between me and my aunt Colette.

She greeted me with a smile and a hug and asked, "Where's your mom?"

"Prob'ly sittin' down," I said pointing to the arena. Then I looked up at her friend. She had a somewhat condescending, impatient look on her face and didn't seem like the type to have any children of her own, nor to care. She didn't seem at all the nice kind of lady my aunt was. But, I smiled anyway. Colette introduced me to her as "Cerese's little girl." I beamed up at the lady when my aunt mentioned my mother's name. She looked at me critically, half-smiling.

Then she asked, "So who is your little maꞋshee friend?" My eyes widened, and my mouth dropped in surprise. Then I turned to Jo. She stared back innocently, not aware of what had just been said. I felt anger welling up inside me, and I lashed back.

"She's not a maꞋshee!" I spit back at her. The two women looked at each other. The lady began to laugh, and my aunt shushed her. Then my aunt looked at me with concern in her eyes. "Honey, do you know what 'maʔshee' means?" she asked me.

"Yeah!" I blurted back indignantly. "Well . . . no," I added sheepishly.

"It just means *white*." I stood puzzled for some time. Never before had it entered my mind to categorize any of my friends as being black, white, Indian, green, blue, or any other color, especially Jo. She was my best friend. Why would this lady choose to call her white and not call my other friends Indian? So I answered the only thing I could think of in our defense. "She's not white. She's my friend."

The incident at the pow-wow was only my first taste of prejudice. I soon found that its ugliness can appear anywhere and from anyone. It can find its way into even the most innocent of settings; for example, the State Fair.

For an eight-year-old kid, a trip to the State Fair is a pretty big deal, and I was as excited as I could be. Even the hot, sticky weather couldn't dampen my spirits. I had waited for this trip practically all summer. Then, the day finally arrived.

The sight and sound of the Midway reached me before I could get through the gate. My older brother Scott and I raced each other to the admission booth and paid our way with the money our mother had given us. Then we ran to the nearest ticket booth and paid for the bracelets that allowed us all-day admission on the rides. When we'd gotten them, we grabbed each other's hands and walked off into the wonderland of the Fair.

The rest of the day flew by in a blur of colors, lights, smells, and roaring sound. Along the way we met two of our cousins, Marlon and Christy, who were our same ages.

Around four o'clock in the afternoon, the initial excitement had worn off, and the four of us had been on each ride at least twice. I was tired, of course, but being a little kid, I would never have admitted it. With my fatigue came a cranky attitude. I know I must have been annoying others with my smart comments, but no more than any other child would have under those circumstances. I was uncomfortably hot, dirty, tired, and I had eaten far too much junk food that day. We all trudged along, determined to have as much fun as possible. We got into yet another line for a ride that hadn't particularly appealed to me the first three times we'd been on it. Christy and I got more and more obnoxious as we waited. We punched each other around and got into mock fights, "accidentally" knocking each other into other people. Scott and Marlon merely laughed once in a while and occasionally told us both to shut-up. Then Scott did something that surprised me.

He'd been watching the ticket-taker at the front of the line when he turned to us and said: "Hey you guys, knock it off." We paid him no mind and continued our horseplay. Scott cast another wary eye at the man in front. He was of average build and height, with long, greasy, blonde hair. By the look of him, one could assume that he'd been working this ride all day long. His hands were brown and leathery and jammed halfway into his oil-stained jeans. Sweat ran down his temples and into his tired, blood-shot blue eyes as he glared at us, showing his obvious annoyance.

"Hey, I mean it, you guys. *Knock it off.*" Scott's tone quieted our laughter. My silly grin was replaced by an indignant frown. I was about to snap back at him when I heard the ticket man yell from the front of the line. "Whyncha' knock it off back there, you fucking little *prairie niggers!*"

I froze. I could feel my stomach falling sickeningly and my mouth dropping open. I felt as if the wind had been kicked out of me. Then a hundred different emotions flooded into my chest all at once. Anger, fear, defiance, and other feelings formed a knot in the pit of my stomach. Then the man grumbled under his breath: "*Squaws.*"

This last terrible insult finally broke through my shock. How *dare* he? He didn't even know what it *meant.* I spun around and gave him the most defiant look I could muster, and finally found my tongue. "Sh-SHUT-UP!" I managed feebly as hot, angry tears stung my eyes and rolled down my cheeks. My outburst roused the others from their silence. Scott gripped my wrist and Chris's too. "Come on!" he said and hurried us away. Marlon followed, shouting expletives back at the man the entire time.

Soon I found myself in the coolness of the park with my mother's arms around Chris and me, comforting and shushing us.

I tried to babble through tears what had happened. "He was mean, and I heard him, he said . . . he said I was . . . a prairie . . . a prairie . . . and then, and then . . ." And then I buried my face in my mother's arm and let Scott finish the story.

"Shh, honey, quiet now." My mother calmed me as she stroked my hair. Then I heard my father's strained voice. "Where?" was all he asked when Scott and Marlon finished their story. I looked up at him and could tell by the expression on his face that he was incredibly angry. Scott pointed, and then the three of them walked off in the direction of the Midway. I was utterly exhausted by the roller-coaster ride of emotions I'd experienced and simply dropped off to sleep with my cousin Christy on one side of me and the protective presence of my mother on the other side.

Afterwards, as my brother tells me, my father and the ticket man "had words." Everything ended with the man being reported and dismissed from his job and my learning a harsh lesson. On reflection I often think that he was let off easier. He only lost a seasonal job. I lost my innocence.

I run into prejudice and hypocrisy a lot more now that I'm older, off the reservation, and have learned to recognize it. Only now it's much more subtle. I pay it less mind than I used to. Most of the time I'm too busy getting on with my life and have no time to worry about what a stranger thinks of me. This upsets a lot of my friends. For some reason, they all feel that they have to defend me since I don't really do it myself.

Later on, I figured out that dealing with ignorance was something new to most of my friends. I'd learned at an early age what it was like to be confronted with ignorance and that it's not limited to one race. I also learned, as I grew, how I was going to deal with it. At first, I let it get to me. It ate at my insides, like a disease. It was bitter, sour, like acid, and it made me bitter too. Then as I grew, I realized that if I hate back, then I am no better than those people who choose to hate me. Those are not the people I want to be like. I want to be different. Smarter.

Sometimes the injustice of it all still gets to me but only rarely. I fight it. Only now, I fight it in a different way. On my terms. Many of my friends think that I should get angry, scream, and lash out. What they don't know is that it's ten times harder not to. Most of the time, when someone provokes you, a reaction is exactly what they want. So why give them that? I can't change these people's minds. They've already made their judgments, and if it's their wish to shut me out, then so be it. But along with me, they also shut out a whole world of beautiful, unique colors.

In a strange way, I'm glad I learned early on what prejudice is. It's given me time to adjust, get ready for a battle I'll be waging for the rest of my life. Sure, others may fight this battle violently, voicing loud opinions. As for me, I think I'll just keep fighting it my own way, winning one quiet victory after another.

Twyla Baker (Hidatsa), "Growing Up," *Tribal College Journal* 3, no. 1 (Spring/Summer 1997): 14–16.

Chief Coyote
Veronica Serdahl

There was a man walking down the road, and far away in the distance he could hear drumbeats, and he saw an earth lodge. He stopped to listen. There was a dance at the lodge. He walked over and saw everyone was having a great time, and so he wanted to join in with the dancing but he did not have an outfit. As he was pondering about his dilemma, a porcupine came along and offered his quills for a headdress, and then a rabbit came along and offered his fur for leggings, and so Chief Coyote had an outfit to dance.

Chief Coyote wished he could see himself in his finery. Since there were no mirrors to see himself in, he improvised by using his shadow to check to be sure that everything was in place. Satisfied that everything was okay, he walked down to the earth lodge with his head held high, proud of his outfit. At the doorway of the lodge he once again checked his shadow out, and everything being fine, he entered proudly, head high. The people began to yell, "Oh, here comes Chief Coyote!" and started running in all directions. Chief Coyote realized that the people in the lodge were ants and that there were many of them, and they made much noise dancing.

When Chief Coyote raised his head up he was wearing a buffalo skull—the earth lodge was the buffalo skull, so Chief Coyote said, "Oh! My brothers are playing a trick on me." Chief Coyote took off the skull and undressed, giving back the fur to the rabbit and the quills to the porcupine.

This is how we got the animals to help us with our outfits, and Chief Coyote was the originator of the Indian outfit.

Veronica Serdahl (Mandan/Hidatsa), "Chief Coyote," *Tribal College Journal* 12, no. 2 (Fall 2000): S15. Serdahl was a grandmother and a student at Fort Berthold Community College when she wrote this story.

Who Am I?
Roger D. White Owl

> Who am I?
> Am I the person of my past
> Am I the person who is lost
> Who am I?
> I hear tales of my ancestors

I feel my chest fill with pride
Knowing where I am from
But . . .
I can never live as they did
So my past is my past
Who am I?
I search for an identity
I look to my television
I find gangster rap stars
And Latin gangs
Catch my eye
But . . .
I am proud of my past
And where I come from
So I put those ideas to the side
And I again wonder
Who am I?
When I have tried to be traditional
People not only in their words
But in their looks say to me
"Just who do you think you're trying to be!"
These words and looks rip through my soul
And make me feel like I was stabbed
Many times with a double-edged knife
All I can do is wonder
Who am I?

Roger D. White Owl (Mandan/Hidatsa), "Who Am I?"
Tribal College Journal 10, no. 4 (Summer 1999): S11.

CHAPTER TWENTY-THREE

The Meaning of the Lewis and Clark
Bicentennial for Native Americans

American Indians have occupied their homelands for more than ten thousand years. By the time the Corps of Discovery traveled up the Missouri two centuries ago, four hundred generations of Native people had already made their lives in this beautiful country. Aspects of the Indian country live on today. Deeply held community beliefs regarding treaties, the environment, tribal languages, and tribal traditions offer compelling proof that the cardinal values of ancient Native Americans—respect for creation, an ethic of generosity, and loyalty to community life—have endured through decades of change.

This persistence of the Indian country calls students of the expedition to view the Lewis and Clark journey in a new light. It helps make clear that, two hundred years ago, the members of the Corps of Discovery were successful because they learned from the many new communities they encountered. And they failed when the friendships and promises made on that expedition and afterward—the ties forged between people from different cultures—were forgotten, ignored, or broken. The next hundred years will determine how much of the promise of the Corps of Discovery's journey we can fulfill.

FIVE NATIVE AMERICAN EDUCATORS REFLECT ON THE LEWIS AND CLARK EXPEDITION AND ITS AFTERMATH

The exhibit Lewis and Clark and the Indian Country came to life because of the collaboration of a non-Indian historian and five Native American educators. The educators brought years of experience and a wary eye for fluffy rhetoric to the project;

their contributions gave the exhibit its distinct voice and vision. It is appropriate then, to conclude this documentary collection based on the exhibit with excerpts from five interviews with these educators.

Darrell Robes Kipp (Blackfeet)

In the 1980s, Darrell Robes Kipp founded the Piegan Institute, a reservation-based center for curriculum and professional development. The institute has developed a national reputation for innovative programming, and its success inspired Kipp and his colleagues to launch Nizipuhwasin ("Real Speak") School, a Blackfeet language immersion school for children in kindergarten through eighth grade.

When I first was on the state Lewis and Clark Bicentennial Commission many native people viewed that as somewhat of a turncoat type of appointment. Why would you want to be a part of that? But the other Native Americans that were on that commission with me, even today, we felt it was our chance, our opportunity and our obligation and our responsibility to participate. We wanted to be sure that someone would be telling the Native American perspective on Lewis and Clark even though it didn't necessarily jive with the, you know, the atmosphere, of the discovery.

So that was the first thing Native Americans said, "Okay you can knock that word out, you know, let's quit using 'discovery.' Lewis and Clark didn't discover anybody." And the second thing was "celebration." "Oh, this celebration of the—oh, wait a minute, let's get, you know, celebration, for the Native Americans didn't necessarily consider it a celebration." My fellow Native American commissioners and I tried to really speak loud and clear about what we expected to come out of our participation at the state of Montana's commemorative event. And as a result, one of the signature events of the Montana State Lewis and Clark Commission was a major symposium held at the University of Montana in May 2003, where Native American students, young people, were given the perfect opportunity to voice their reaction, the contemporary, modern-day reactions to this expedition. So we began to infuse the Native American perspective into what Lewis and Clark was about.

We want new words to describe our presence; we don't want to be considered the "Vanishing American" or the invisible American. We are Americans; we are part of this country. We don't want to be considered backward because we speak our language, or because we know our traditional ways. Inferring that we're remnants of a primordial day. We are modernists, people who speak their tribal language, know their ways, are well versed in society in general, that are contributing to American society, are good citizens to their own tribal societies. These are modernists. These are what Native American people want to be. We don't want to be always listening to the rap that we're the poorest, that we're the most oppressed, that we're the drunkest, that we're saturated with nothing but problems. Because we did not create those problems; those problems were handed to us, were imposed upon us. And so I think the new approach to Native Americans is not to continue to discuss our problems, but to begin to discuss our solutions, and our involvement and our inclusion in everything that goes on in America. And that includes the Lewis and Clark commemorative.

Darrell Robes Kipp, filmed interview by Sally Thompson, Piegan Institute, Browning, Montana, July 30, 2005.

Otis Half Moon (Nez Perce)

The son of Richard Half Moon, the former Nez Perce tribal chairman, Otis Half Moon grew up amid the plateaus and river valleys of his community's Idaho homeland and is a native speaker of the Nez Perce language. After service in the U.S. Army, Half Moon joined the National Park Service. Over the past two decades he has worked as an interpreter, park historian, unit administrator, and liaison officer with indigenous peoples across the western states.

The whole idea of the Lewis and Clark bicentennial came into play several years ago in my community and people started talking about the thousands, millions of people that were going to follow this trail, trying to discover this country again. If you have been to my country up in Lolo Trail and seen that area, you can see the birds, you can hear the insects, you can see the moose and elk and deer and everything; the huckleberries, smell the pine, the wind going through the trees. It is so beautiful, and unfortunately that is the same route the Corps of Discovery came in 1805. And I was thinking, even if 1 percent of those people went on that trail, what is it going to do to that resource? That is something that we really have to think about. We have to work as a partnership not only with the National Park Service, but also the U.S. Forest Service, Bureau of Land Management, and Army Corps of Engineers to help protect this resource.

We used to joke around about catch-and-release tourism. You know, you go for the people who come by, you know you'll get them and shake out their money, and then you'll release them and hope they don't come back. I don't know.

In some places near us there is not a positive feeling toward Indians and there is a lot of racism that can go on. But you realize the same thing hit them at the same time: these tourists. So now all of a sudden they ask endorsements from the Nez Perce tribe to help them endorse this or that to help control this. Then a few years before that the football team came into Lapwai for a game one time and they had turkey feathers tied on their helmets to mock us, just a few years before that. I remember that, when they did that. And now all of sudden they want us to do these things, have us help them.

Now they are upset about this whole Lewis and Clark bicentennial as well, where they are mandated by executive order by the president of the United States to consult with the tribes. The irony is all of these years trying to work with the Forest Service on forest plans or timber cuts or whatever, the tribes always want to be involved with these things. Tribes will talk to the Forest Service here in Idaho, they'll listen to us but they won't take no advice from us. They'll deny that today but I know for a fact they won't listen to us, and then all of a sudden now an executive order comes down and now they have to work with us.

One time I was in a meeting in Portland, Oregon, and I made that comment to all of these federal officials, I made the comment to them: "Boy, it is sure funny it took two lost white guys to make you talk to us. You guys know you have to consult with us." They didn't say anything. They all didn't want to say nothing at all because they knew I was right. It took two lost white guys to get that going. So maybe it's the legacy we can look at as far as consultation with federal entities and working with communities near the reservation during this Lewis and Clark bicentennial.

Otis Half Moon, filmed interview by Sally Thompson, Pendleton, Oregon, November 1, 2004.

Frederick Baker (Mandan/Hidatsa)

In 1991, Frederick Baker returned to his home community of Fort Berthold, North Dakota, after forty years as a Bureau of Indian Affairs administrator and health official. Having grown up speaking the Hidatsa language on land his ancestors had occupied for centuries, Fred is determined to preserve the heritage of Fort Berthold's three tribes—the Mandans, Hidatsa, and Arikaras—for the next generation. He is executive director of the Mandan, Hidatsa, and Arikara Board of Directors of the Three Affiliated Tribes Museum, and treasurer of the Fort Berthold Community College Board of Directors.

Who is the modern Hidatsa? What kinds of things do we need to do to be Hidatsa? There is no question that we have to have an education; we have to have decent training; we have to have a job; we have to have a way of making a living that allows our children to be comfortable, at least decent things that they need in order to be successful, self-esteem, and all those types of things. So I think it's incumbent upon us—when I say "us" I mean people in my age group—we need to sit down and to think seriously to come up with the answers to some of these questions. Who are we? What is our role? What can we bring back that is going to fit with this generation? Because basically culture is a living thing, and the concept of living things, is that they evolve.

Frederick Baker, filmed interview by Sally Thompson, Newberry Library, Chicago, Illinois, April 18, 2005.

Pat Courtney Gold (Wasco)

Raised on Oregon's Warm Springs Reservation, Pat Courtney Gold earned a degree in mathematics at Whitman College and pursued a career in computer science before turning to basket making. Gold has described herself as a basket holding information about her Wasco community's artistic traditions. Her work has led her to explore both the aesthetic and material aspects of basketry. Inspired by using local plant materials in her baseket making, she has also become an outspoken advocate for the preservation of natural plant habitats.

Basketry is real important to all cultures along the Columbia River. And so that is my contribution to keep the culture going for the next seven generations; that's my vision. My parents used to make this four-hour drive from Warm Springs to the Mary Hill Museum. My mother would take us to the museum and they had one of the best Native American basket collections, and they still do. And when my mother would take us through she would point out the Wasco baskets, and we didn't have any back home. She didn't make any, my grandparents didn't make any; in our extended family I don't know of anyone who made Wasco baskets. When our mother took all of us kids through the collections she would point out the Wasco baskets with their geometric figures and she would say (and I could hear the pride in her voice)—our people made these. And they were just gorgeous; they were just beautiful.

So when my sister called me to tell me about this opportunity to make baskets it never dawned on me that I would have this opportunity to learn how to make these baskets, so I said, "I gotta go, I'll be there." So the Wasco women that were taking this class were my sister, myself, and my friend Arlene. We worked with Mary Slick, who is a curator here at the Mary Hill Museum and an author. She is also non-Indian but we all think of her as Indian and she has lived in this area for most of our lives. . . . So she went from reservation to reservation and the elders accepted her and she learned all about Native American leatherwork and basketry. She has learned all the cultures, the songs, the ceremonies; she learned all that, so we just naturally think of her as Native American. So in all of her travels to reservations she pieced together how to weave the Wasco baskets and she gave this class. So we learned from her. The . . . thing about learning basket weaving from Mary is that she invited elders to come. Some of the elders knew how to weave and some elders forgot how to do the top or maybe did the bottom a little bit differently, but the elders were very important in sharing their knowledge and their experiences with us. Mary also had contacts with different museums so she took us not only to Mary Hill but the High Desert Museum in Bend. They have a very nice Native American collection. So we got to look at the older baskets and get ideas and inspiration and the feel of our ancestors, the connection to our ancestors through study at different museums. That was sort of an inspirational part, not just this technique, but also being aware of our connection to the past. . . .

When I contrast the 10,000-year history of the Wasco people with the 230-some-odd years of the United States, it is really difficult to get the concept across of how our history defines who I am. My history defines who I am. My history reflects a continuity of a language, a continuity of a culture, a continuity of the makeup of our community: the extended families, the rules and regulations of extended families. They are not written down, we are taught at a very early age. We are taught how to behave and how not to behave. It is really difficult to get this concept across to someone from a culture that is so young. When I talk to Chinese and Japanese people it is much easier for me to express the concepts because they grasp them. For example, when I talk to Americans and I talk about our culture, they ask, "How many years ago did your people come across the land bridge?" Well, first of all I disagree with the concept of a land bridge, and second of all, they are looking at a long period of time and they are trying to press it into a period they understand. They

understand their ancestors were immigrants from Europe and they are trying to project that concept and their idea of where we came from. To me it is
totally mismatched and tells me that there is no understanding of our culture.
I don't know how to get that concept across. . . .

We were pretty much forced to move to the Warm Springs reservation [in
the nineteenth century]. Our ancestors learned a lot from moving in the late
1870s. During that move I think a lot happened to the ancestors. First of all
there was, physically, a real shock. You have to imagine what it would be like for
you to be forced to leave and be moved out of your house and your community
into an area you didn't know well. And we were known for our trade, for our
salmon fishing, the food was always with us; and we were moved south to a
semi-arid area, totally isolated, and there were no people to trade with. I think
what happened was our ancestors were focused just on surviving. They didn't
have the time to carry on the tradition of basket weaving; they didn't have the
time or energy to carry on the tradition of carving the horn bowls—I know of
no one who carved those horn bowls. So it was a very difficult period, and I
think it took two generations of people to adjust to living under those conditions. We were not allowed to go back to the Columbia River, our ancestors,
so I think it was a very difficult time and a crucial part in our history. When
I think back on that, I am really amazed that we kept our language, that our
language was preserved. I am amazed and impressed that our ancestors kept
that for us. It is a real sad part of our history.

About ten years ago we formed the Northwest Native American Bas-
ketweavers Association (NNABA), that provides a number of functions besides helping us be an entity that federal agencies will recognize. They are
working with us now. We identify to those agencies the areas where we go
to harvest plants and we don't want it sprayed at certain times and they are
working with us, which is really nice. . . . We just had our ninth gathering; we
are nine years old and it is important we have our elders come and meet with
us. When we first started we had no idea how extensive basketry was in this
area but we wanted to make contact with as many basket weavers as we could,
especially elders. I was just amazed at how many elders we had available that
I wasn't aware of. It is important we have our elders with us. That was one
good thing, bringing together our elders; the other was being aware of who
all the weavers were because we didn't know who the other weavers were. So
forming this organization tied it all together. That is what we do every year:
we have one big gathering, between two hundred and three hundred weavers,
and it is an opportunity to share weaving techniques and to share plant fibers.

I needed some big pieces of cedar to do a two-dimensional wall hanging and at this last gathering I met some cedar weavers, so I am trading some of my baskets for the cedar that I need. That is another nice thing about having a basket organization. Another important thing is that we are keeping all of our weaving techniques; we are mentoring; we are teaching; we are keeping this for the next generation.

When Lewis and Clark came down the river they came down in October; there were no roots then and people had just come back from berry picking. They were also salmon fishing. But anyway I mention the berries because when Lewis and Clark collected the 1805 Wasco Sally Bag it was a gift to them and it had dried huckleberries—dried berries—in it; that is in the journal. When they were coming up in April everything was ready to be harvested up on the hill above the Columbia River. The first plant that we harvest is the balsan plant; we pick it and eat the stem, we eat it just like celery. When you look at it, it looks just like celery. It has the stringy fiber and you peel it off and then you eat it. That is a very important fiber in the early spring because you have gone all winter eating dried food so you really need fresh vegetables, vitamin C and vitamin E. That is the perfect way to get it. It always amazed me that Lewis and Clark would observe all of this and record it in their journals and it was as if plants were poison to them and they would not eat it. Here they were having all of these dysentery problems, constipation problems, boils, they were having all kinds of health problems yet they would not ever venture out of eating meat.

So the other plants that were out in April and May were the bitterroot, and they grow all around the Columbia River. Well, it is a big plant; it is a bulb—there are a number of different bulbs, they are the brashite family. So you can harvest them or eat them fresh and quite often we would pound them and make a meal out of them. Lewis and Clark mentioned in their journals they were trading for kous and that is what this bulb was. You would pound it and you mash it when it is still damp and you form a little biscuit. Or you can just pat it—it is crumbly—and that we add to a soup or a stew. Then there is what we call weepam [?]. It is like a celery plant but it is a little different than salt and it has a real strong flavor. We harvest that for the stem and eat the stem, and that you just eat fresh; then later on we'll harvest the seeds because that have a strong celery scent. We use that in soups also. So there are a lot of food crops and bulbs that we were harvesting in April and May and we still do; we still carry on those traditions. These are gifts from the earth and they are pure; they haven't been sprayed, they haven't been in contaminated soil, and they have been handed down to us from the Creator and it is up to us to take care of it. And that is what we do.

When I've gone to all of the museums that I have gone to, all the Wasco baskets are different. They are woven the same way, the technique is the same, but there are variations of material: from the early ones that were plant material, to the gradual plant material plus wool for wool blankets, to plant material with a mixture of hop twine when our people used to go to the valley and harvest hops, to 100 percent hops, because now a lot of the contemporary weavers are starting to use colored yarn because they like to emphasize the designs using patterns. So it really reflects the change in all of the weavers through time.

This is a super contemporary basket; I call it the urban yuppie Indian couple. On the earth line I wanted to demonstrate what the year 2000 is like so I put images of traffic—cars, trucks, SUVs, and I also put a train, the little train down here. I wanted to demonstrate a yuppie couple so I modified the traditional geometric design. These images, we call them x-ray images, they represent our ancestors, and in this couple the woman is pregnant and this is symbolic of the next generation. Then I also put a little heart in to show how nurturing women are and that is what the traditional design is based on; I modified that design for my contemporary urban couple. I put a suit on the man and correlated his socks and his handkerchief and his tie and his hat. And then with the women these are texture lines; it is a micro fiber that was really hard to work with. Then I had to have matching heels and jewelry; all women have to have jewelry. But on this one, to experiment, I wanted to show the wealth of the couple, so I wanted him to have a potbelly. So I pulled on the fibers when I was weaving to make sure they popped out and he got his little potbelly, so he is a little corporate executive there. Historically, if you look at the little baskets they had, on the baskets the images were a mountain goat and a frog, and then I just put in a ship because on the Columbia River now it doesn't have mountain goats on the Cascades but it does have ships going up and down the Columbia. And also on the Columbia we used to have condors; the Wascos even raised condor chicks but they are extinct now—they were all shot out by the early 1900s—so what we have in place of the condors are airplanes. And on this one again I tried to pouf out the airplane; I wanted it more three-dimensional and I'm not sure I like it. I might redo that part. So anyway, that is a contemporary basket that I did this year.

When you think about our culture, it is ten thousand years old, and I think it reflects stability for literally thousands of years. The stability in language, the stability in how we fish and process our food. The real change in our people came probably in the 1800s with the meeting of Europeans along the coast and the meeting of Americans from the East. Suddenly there was just tremendous change, there was just an accelerated change. It just amazes me that we've maintained so much of our culture.

I am really curious as to what the baskets are going to look like thirty, forty, even fifty years from now. My two-dimensional wall hangings, I'm basing them on cedar mats, tule mats, and cattail mats but I am doing my own variations. I am doing open weaves and adding different fibers and I am doing different interpretations. It is sort of a mat; it's not a wall hanging. And I've done weaving based on the mats using plastic, so I have basic plastic-bag background and I have colored plastic bags to emphasize colors. And I use wire because I like the texture, and I've thought, "What can I do with wire?" I think our culture is dynamic; it is not static. It'll be here; it is here now and it'll be here in the future.

Pat Courtney Gold, filmed interview by Sally Thompson, Skapoose, Washington, March 7, 2005.

Marjorie Waheneka (Umatilla)

Raised by her maternal grandparents on the Umatilla Indian reservation, Marjorie Waheneka has devoted herself to passing the wisdom of tribal elders on to young people. In 1987 she became the first Native American ranger at the Whitman Mission National Historic Site in Walla Walla, Washington. In 1999, after many years of building bridges between the park service and local tribes, she became assistant director of the Confederated Tribes of the Umatilla Reservation's Tamástslikt Cultural Institute, a tribally chartered museum near Pendleton, Oregon. She is now the institute's exhibits manager.

The Lewis and Clark bicentennial was important because we got to stress the importance of the interaction with the non-Indians when they came through our country. Lewis and Clark were like tourists; they didn't realize they were walking on foods and on medicines, that food was plentiful.

This exhibit is supposed to teach or inform the visitors, as they go through, how important the Indian people were to Lewis and Clark because it was the Indian people that they interacted with. It was the Indian people that they got food and horses as transportation from. There were groups that showed them how to make canoes; they also showed them how to navigate the rivers. They warned them which country was more fierce than the next and they really tried to show them what it was like to live in this country. They showed them the foods and how to survive out here because they didn't have any idea. That's what we want people to know: that the Indians played a very big part in the Lewis and Clark expedition. We are at a point now where we have a chance to do that.

Well, it has always been Indian custom—one of the things I always hear our people on the Umatilla say—that the Indian people were very hospitable people and whenever anybody came in you always sat them down, brought them in and sat them down, and always offered food and drink to them, no matter if it was just a piece of bread and water. They at least got that from you and then they stated why they were there—you know, they needed a place to stay—it was just something common courtesy on our part. That is just how we were.

Marjorie Waheneka, filmed interview by Sally Thompson, Tamástslikt Cultural Institute, Pendleton, Oregon, November 1, 2004.

CONCLUSION

———◆·◆·◆———

Lewis and Clark Reconsidered:
Some Sober Second Thoughts
James P. Ronda

September 2006 marked the end of the official Lewis and Clark bicentennial. I don't think anyone doubts that the bicentennial grew to become a traveling sideshow, a movable feast that made its way from Monticello and Philadelphia to the Columbia River and the Pacific Ocean. For three years Jefferson's expedition was part of a great cultural and historical wallow. William Clark once called the journey he made with Meriwether Lewis "so vast an enterprise." And the bicentennial was certainly an enterprise of nearly biblical (or at least continental) dimensions. The bicentennial yielded hundreds of Lewis and Clark books—everything from Gary Moulton's magnificent multivolume edition of the expedition's journals to cookbooks, coloring books, and trail guides. A Monticello gift shop catalog from those years contained the following items: a stuffed, plush Newfoundland dog; a bison doll described as "cute and cuddly"; an expedition cross-stitch kit; a life-size prairie dog doll that is—and here I quote—"furry and huggable, with a cute, curious expression typical of the species and its head swivels 360 degrees"; and my personal favorite, stuffed versions of Lewis, Clark, Sekakawea, and York in a canoe, "with detailed removable clothing." The only thing left to the imagination is: are these dolls anatomically correct? There were Corps of Discovery videos, television documentaries, a big-screen movie, and Internet Web sites beyond counting.

The bicentennial calendar was crowded with Lewis and Clark conferences, museum exhibitions, and trail rides. One enterprising merchant offered a vial of Missouri River sand from a place near where the expedition made camp. Never mind that the river had changed course many times since 1804. Audiences from St. Louis and Louisville to Denver and Portland were treated to more than their fair share of overblown scholarship and gassy pomposity, to say nothing of self-righteous patriotism and cultural arrogance on all sides of the cultural divide. In summer 2004 more than fifty thousand Nebraskans and fellow travelers attended the Nebraska State Lewis and Clark signature event. This was, of course, on a non-football weekend, perhaps suggesting that those folks really didn't have enough to do.

Now, I would be the last person to splash cold water on all of this. Much of the bicentennial stuff—and I do mean "stuff"—was good, clean, family fun. It was sometimes informative and almost always entertaining, depending on your definition of entertainment. Whether the bicentennial was billed as a celebration or a commemoration there was the ever-present risk of missing the central meanings in the Lewis and Clark story. Even more important, there were missed chances to connect Lewis and Clark to the larger, richer, deeper stories in our past and our present.

We could be skeptical here—something I encourage—and say that the Lewis and Clark bicentennial was one more example of our remarkable ability to make the past a product and then sell it in a marketplace where everything has a price and no one knows the value of anything. I am reminded of Richard White's observation that "Americans have never had much use for history, but we do love anniversaries." Wasn't the bicentennial just heritage tourism run amuck? It used to be George Washington slept here. Now the slogan became "Lewis and Clark camped here"—or at least somewhere nearby. And "nearby" was sometimes a parking lot, or alongside a grain elevator, or even under water.

Before we drown in all of this it might be a good idea to pause and ask some irreverent, even heretical questions. Having spent so much time preaching the Lewis and Clark gospel, I now find heresy remarkably appealing.

In so many ways we should ask: Lewis and Clark—so what, who cares, why bother? Isn't this just the Rover Boys out West, yet another male adventure story filled with high-energy testosterone and not really meaning very much? Swept along by bicentennial enthusiasm, it still remains easy to claim too much for this one brief moment in the long history of the West. I am reminded of one self-important American historian who confidently told an unsuspecting British audience that the Lewis and Clark expedition was the single most important event in American history. Somehow he conveniently forgot the American Revolution, the Louisiana Purchase, the Mexican War, the Civil War, and even World War II. After all, Lewis and Clark were not the first white men to cross the continent from Atlantic to Pacific north of Mexico—as if that really means very much. And they went no place not already seen and often mapped by generations of Native people. And it is not inappropriate to say bluntly that Lewis and Clark began the American invasion of the West, an invasion aimed at making the West safe for cows, corn, and capital. That meant cows in and bison out; that meant hybrid corn in and prairie grasses out; that meant capital investment in and those peoples and cultures that didn't fit the capitalist agenda out. There is a global story here. That story is all about the emergence of the United States as a world power, and, as Henry Adams reminded us a century ago, in many ways that began with Lewis and Clark and the Louisiana Purchase. If we wanted to be hard-edged about it, we could say that the Lewis and Clark story is part of the same old shelf-worn narrative—the one that glorifies and justifies the steamroller of conquest and dispossession. Unless we can answer the "who cares" and "why bother" questions, we should relegate Lewis and Clark to one short paragraph in a long history textbook.

But I think there are answers—answers that expand and enrich the traditional expedition story and then connect it to larger North American, and even global, stories. We can go at this by thinking about the legitimate attractions of the Lewis and Clark story. What is it about this story that can make it part of our usable, meaningful past? It seems to me that there are at least four reasons why we might begin to pay attention to an enlarged Lewis and Clark story, Lewis and Clark beyond the bicentennial.

It is a story, or rather a series of stories, told by many actors and narrators. Human beings are storytellers. We explain our lives to ourselves and to others in story form. We do that as individuals, in families and communities, and as a nation. Even when life is in bits and pieces, we stitch the fragments together and make a story. There is no more magic line to fall on human ears and hearts than "once upon a time." Think about the American West as the historian William Cronon once described it—as a storied place, a place of many narrative stories, and of countless layers of meaning and experience like the stories in some grand building. Some of us are uncomfortable with words like "story" and "storyteller." The slang expression "what's your story" tells it all. "Story" has become another word for alibi, something that hovers uncomfortably between truth and falsehood. We do not expect stories to ponder and then reveal the many faces of truth. Stories are for bedtime; they are moments of fantasy, escape, and happy endings. We sometimes dismiss Homer's *Odyssey* or the exodus of Moses and the Jews from Egypt as "just stories" belonging to a realm of meaning remote from real life. But in recent times writers like Barry Lopez, Sherman Alexie, Mary Clearman Blew, and William Kittredge have rediscovered the power of stories as narrative and explanation. As Kittredge says in a compelling essay on narrative and the West, stories are "maps or paradigms in which we see our purposes defined." And he goes on to say that when the stories we inhabit no longer work, and we stick with them anyway, they become nightmares. This is surely a cautionary tale for Lewis and Clark storytellers determined to spin out narratives of male adventure and undaunted courage in the land of the Big Empty.

What happened to Thomas Jefferson's Corps of Discovery is a great story, with lots of energy and forward motion. It has wonderful settings, memorable action, and a remarkable cast of characters speaking with many voices and in many languages. It has drama, adventure, struggle, failure, disappointment, and an enduring set of consequences. So it is a tellable story. As the distinguished psychiatrist and author Robert Coles says, we are "called by stories." Stories call out to us and then expect us to respond. Good stories prompt us to consider our own stories and then share them with others, as they share theirs with us.

And it is exactly at this point—when talking about stories—that we need to ask why Native American tribes and nations should continue pay any attention to the Lewis and Clark story. At the height of the bicentennial I saw a bumper sticker that not so politely said: Lewis and Clark Go Home! The obvious answer along the expedition's trail is tourism and the money generated by those Americans bent on driving the trail. But I think there is a more compelling reason for Native people to remain engaged in the life and times of Jefferson's captains. The point is stories. Native people have important stories to tell, stories about the past, the present, and the future. Catching the public's ear with Lewis and Clark is a good way to begin to talk about other stories—stories about land and water, endangered languages and threatened sacred places.

This is no ordinary story. There are American stories beyond counting. As they used to say on 1950s television, there are a "million stories in the Naked City." Why pay any special attention to this one? As my friends in the English Department would say, aren't we just privileging this one and making it a master narrative that continues to oppress Native people and silence women? Again, why pay special attention to this one? Perhaps it is because this is a story about a journey. If we are a storytelling people, then we are also a nation of journey makers. Some of the oldest Native American stories are about journeys. Coyote was always going somewhere. Journeys brought Africans and Europeans to eastern North America. Journeys took Americans west by way of the Oregon Trail and the transcontinental railroad. Journeys across the Pacific took Chinese women and men from places like Shanghai and Guangdong Province to California, Idaho, and Wyoming. Journeys took—and continue to take—Spanish-speaking men and women to a place they properly call El Norte. And in the twentieth century the journeys of African Americans from the rural South to the urban, industrial North remade the racial, cultural, and political map of the United States. So we are a people on the road, whether the road is the Trail of Tears, Route 66, or the Interstate Highway System. From Jack Kerouac's *On the Road* to Willie Nelson's "On the Road Again," we talk about "Home, Sweet Home" but it is the lure of the road and the promise of the journey that still holds us. Lewis and Clark gave us our first national road story. Willa Cather once said that there are only two or three great human stories, and we keep repeating them over and over again. One of those stories is the journey story. In song and story it had always been what Woody Guthrie called "hard travelin'" on the long, lonesome road. Lewis and Clark remind us of all the journey stories that have shaped North American history, time out of mind. Telling the Lewis and Clark journey story clears a space so that we can share our own journey stories with others.

We are rightly drawn to Lewis and Clark because their experiences tell a story about a compelling human journey. But there is surely more. If you are making mental notes, here is yet another reason. Some folks imagine the Lewis and Clark expedition as a white man's army rolling west, something right out of *Apocalypse Now*. Think again. We might consider the expedition as a human community, a community as diverse as any in America today. Look at this community closely. Here are men of many different racial, ethnic, cultural, and social backgrounds. Consider York, William Clark's slave and fellow adventurer. Consider Pierre Cruzatte, the one-eyed, fiddle-playing engagé. He was French (however that is defined) and Omaha. Here is the expedition member Private John Potts, born in Germany, a miller by trade, a soldier perhaps by necessity, a man heading for a violent death at the hands of the Blackfeet in 1808. Do the simple categories of red, white, and black really make any sense in so diverse a community? Here is Sekakawea, a Shoshone woman who spent formative years with the Hidatsas. And here is Jean Baptiste Charbonneau, son of Toussaint Charbonneau and Sekakawea. But there is more here than a handful of examples. With Lewis and Clark we always think about western landscapes. Rarely do we consider the soundscapes of the past. Pause and listen to what that community sounded like: William Clark's Virginia-Kentucky accent, Sergeant John Ordway's New Hampshire inflections, George Drouillard's Shawnee-flavored French, and the cries and first words from a child brought up in a linguistic Tower of Babel. What could be more American than this? This is the crazy quilt that was and is America. The Lewis and Clark story puts us on a journey with a distinctively American community.

About now some alert reader should be asking, "distinctively American community? You must be joking." For all the revisions, reinterpretations, and renegotiations in telling this story, isn't it just one more example of a male story, with one woman hanging out on the fringes? Isn't this just one more verse of "Oh Beautiful for Spacious Guys?" But a close reading of the expedition records and associated materials reveals a very different story, one in which women are part of the journey every step of the way. They didn't make the journey; they made it possible and were involved in its outcome. Consider the following: the Philadelphia seamstress Matilda Chapman, who sewed shirts for the expedition; Priscilla Logan, a Philadelphia merchant who sold Meriwether Lewis several canisters of hyson tea; the women who did laundry and sold provisions to the expedition during its winter outside St. Louis; Arikara, Mandan, and Hidatsa women who were a constant part of expedition life up the Missouri; Lemhi Shoshone women who carried expedition baggage over the Continental Divide; the Nez Perce woman Watkuweis, whose previous experience with white traders was crucial in the friendly relations between the Americans and the Nez Perces; Yellow Corn, wife of Sheheke-Shot, who joined him on the delegation bound for Washington organized by Lewis and Clark and became perhaps the first Native American woman from west of the Mississippi to explore the nation's capital. And the list goes on. The point here is that a reading of this story as white- and male-centered simply does not pay adequate attention to the surviving record. In fact, it does that record considerable violence.

Then we see that expedition community moving through the lands and lives of other communities. Lewis and Clark's West was not an empty place. William Clark knew that. On the day before leaving St. Louis, he wrote that the expedition's "road across the continent" would take the Corps of Discovery through "a multitude of Indians." These are not generic Indians straight from Hollywood's central casting. We can name the names: the Mandan chief

Black Cat, the Lemhi Shoshone headman Cameahwait, and the Clatsop village leader Coboway. These are not cardboard cutouts, pasteboard figures present just to add some color to what is really a white man's adventure. Native people are at the center of the Lewis and Clark journey. Without them this is a much-diminished story. On the road with Lewis and Clark the journey story is always about encounters—encounters with many peoples and places.

This is a remarkably accessible story. This is what the great novelist Henry James called "the visitable past." We can still float part of the Upper Missouri and look on Lewis's "seens of visionary inchantment." We can still stand at Lemhi Pass and see the distant Bitterroots. We can still hike parts of the Lolo Trail. We can still walk the beach at the edge of the Pacific and hear the roar of what Clark called those "emence Seas and waves." But there is a dangerous fantasy at work here, one that has been aided and abetted by well-intentioned bicentennial and heritage tourism planners. If you get behind the wheel of your SUV in St. Louis and drive the trail to Fort Clatsop you will not have experienced the Lewis and Clark West. What you will have done is make a diverting, educational, and probably memorable American vacation—hopefully without Chevy Chase along for the ride. The hard, irreducible truth is this: a great deal—maybe most—of the Lewis and Clark West is either gone or profoundly transformed. We've dammed the rivers, plowed the Plains, and laced the sky with high-tension wires. We need to face facts here. All too often we think about the West as a changeless place, something that belongs only in a museum. But Lewis and Clark found a West filled with environmental change; the one sure thing in the West is change. It was true then; it's true now. How should we measure that change; how should we understand it? Lewis and Clark give us a yardstick, a baseline for appreciating two centuries of human activity in the West. What was it like at the beginning of the nineteenth century; what is it like at the beginning of the twenty-first? But it is not just the physical West that has changed. We modern Americans see and understand the landscape differently than did Lewis and Clark. We look at the Rockies and, thanks to the artists Albert Bierstadt and Thomas Moran, we wonder at their beauty. Sergeant Patrick Gass looked at the same mountains and called them a desert.

When I suggest that the Lewis and Clark story is an accessible one I mean that it involves more than a day trip to Fort Mandan or a college alumni adventure in the Bitterroot Mountains. The distinguished exploration scholar Donald Jackson once said that Lewis and Clark were the "writingest" explorers in American history. The expedition diarists—all seven if we count Robert

Frazer, author of a still-missing journal—wrote page after page about everything from bison to thunderstorms, from tribal politics to river currents, from mountain ranges to prairie plants. Some of that writing is dull, plodding stuff recording miles traveled and campsites set up. But there are also passages of the most marvelous, flashing prose in which the West comes alive, leaps the abyss of time, and dances for us across the page. And all of it, whether dull or delightful, is written in a language we can understand. The expedition journals are not jargon-encrusted scientific reports written for a few technocrats. We can read Lewis and Clark. They are part of our literary patrimony. And if we have sufficient imagination we can in some way march with them on their way into the West. And what is even more compelling, we can sometimes get off the boats, get on the bank, and join Native people as the travelers come to us. Perhaps nothing is more rewarding than changing the angle of vision.

Reconsidering Lewis and Clark we are compelled to think again about the largest, most complex themes and experiences in North American history. Invasion, conquest, empire building, resistance, survival, and persistence—all are present in the Lewis and Clark stories. As I reconsider expedition stories, I am reminded of a favorite Jack Nicholson movie—*Five Easy Pieces*. These are my sober second thoughts, my Five Easy Pieces.

First: all good stories are complicated ones. In fact, the Lewis and Clark story is not one story but many overlapping and sometimes contradictory ones. One of the best things we can do in reconsidering this particular moment in American history is to acknowledge contradiction and accept ambiguity. I know that teachers and scholars are in love with ambiguity and that we bestowed sainthood on Woody Allen when he reportedly said, "Give me ambiguity or give me something else." But having spent most of my professional life writing about the life and times of this one emblematic journey, I can tell you that it seems ever more slippery and elusive to me. I am angered by those who seek to reduce this story to a simpleminded tale of undaunted courage and nationalist triumph—something like the first chapter of Teddy Roosevelt's *The Winning of the West*. And I am especially dismayed by those intent on making Lewis and Clark bear all the burdens for what happened in the West in the two centuries after their journey. Perhaps the lesson here is that neither the apologists nor the bashers do us any favors. Lewis and Clark and all the Native people they saw along the way lived in complex times. It is especially important to say that Native North America was not a pristine wilderness, some Garden of Eden removed from time and remote from the hand of change. What Lewis and Clark saw was a world as complex and as confusing as ours. And I'd suggest that their struggles with complexity and ambiguity can teach us that we are not the only humans to confront such mazes and life passages.

Second: America was and always will be a diverse place. This may be obvious to many but it is a gospel message sometimes unknown and often unwelcome. Lewis and Clark usher us into a West of remarkable cultural and biological diversity. It was a crazy quilt then; it is now; and it always will be. What appear to be rigid lines of race and culture were and remain semi-permeable membranes. Into what racial or ethnic box would we dare to put Pierre Cruzatte or Jean Baptiste Charbonneau? Recognizing that the peoples of North America come in many shapes, sizes, genders, classes, and colors is a fundamental lesson from all our journeys.

Third: every story in our past and our present is not one but many—and with many points of view. I am not suggesting that every story and every storyteller can bear up under modern critical scrutiny. French boatmen told Meriwether Lewis that the booming sound he heard along the Missouri River near present-day Helena, Montana, came from mountains bursting with silver. No one would expect that story to have geological truth—but it does reveal intriguing folk ideas about mountains. Every story is worthy of our attention and respect. Here I am reminded of that wonderful line from Henry David Thoreau: "The universe is wider than our views of it."

Fourth: The Lewis and Clark journey stories call us to reconsider our complicated, often troubled relationship with nature. When we follow Lewis and Clark we are brought into the presence of the real "wild" West. Paul Schullery makes this point with great grace and force in a book with a memorable title—*Lewis and Clark among the Grizzlies*. Thomas Jefferson commanded Lewis and Clark to describe what he called "the face of the country." And what the expedition diarists gave us are remarkable life portraits of bison and salmon, prairie dogs and grizzly bears. But there is more here. The Lewis and Clark journey prompts us to ask: where in the world are we? Where do human beings fit in the created order of things? Are we above nature, pulling the strings like some latter-day Wizards of Oz? Are we alongside nature, living parallel lives in air-conditioned cocoons, all the while pretending that nature is for someone else to worry about? Or are we in nature, inextricably bound up in the destiny of bison, butterflies, and the Big Bluestem grass? What did Lewis and Clark think about this? What did the Arikara chief Arketarnarshar think when he told Clark stories about turtles, snakes, and rocks that could tell the future? What do we think about the home place we've inherited from all those who have gone before?

Fifth, and finally: there is the whole matter of journey. We journey through life; we are on the pilgrim's way. We live in a world shaped by journeys. We inherit and repeat journey stories. And we like to think that we have some role to play in the journeys made by friends and family. The Lewis and Clark expedition is one of the great American road stories. To recount that story in all its richness and diversity, with a full cast of characters fully engaged in the drama, is to touch the fundamentals in the American experience. If we are thoughtful, if we look carefully and listen patiently, the Lewis and Clark stories offer us two grand rewards: the promise of expanding the imagination and the experience of meeting strangeness. On the road with Lewis and Clark, or standing alongside the trail as they pass by, we meet ourselves. More important, we encounter people who are not us. This is, I think, the most important thing. On this journey we meet strangeness, just as Black Cat, Cameahwait, and Coboway met strangeness. And that is what I fear we lost in a bicentennial spasm of self-congratulation and overblown self-importance. All too often the bicentennial became an endless round of shaking hands with ourselves. On too many occasions the bicentennial offered the Little Jack Horner version of American history. We stick in our thumbs, pull out plums, and repeat endlessly what good, bright boys and girls we've been. We do not learn and grow by shaking hands with ourselves. In his book *Where Dead Voices Gather,* the novelist and music historian Nick Tosches writes: "True history seeks, it does not answer; for the deeper we seek, the deeper we descend from knowledge to mystery, which is the only place where wisdom abides." The Lewis and Clark journey can take us into those American mysteries—the fundamental mysteries of how we live together and how we live in the place we all call home. And in those mysteries we might at last find what Henry David Thoreau once called "the only true America." Then indeed there will be life after Lewis and Clark.

INDEX

Page numbers in italics refer to maps.

fur traders: as biosphere people, 203–4; exploitation of, 202, 204; imperial expansion, as agents of, 116; motivations of, 196; and robe production, 206n40

Gass, Patrick, 349; Blackfeet, encounter with, 176–78
Gattacka (Kiowa-Apache), 23
gender: gifts of, as complementary, 77
General Allotment Act (1887), 272, 273
generosity: community life, as element of, 56
Gilman, Carolyn, 232
Glenbow Museum, 296
Goes-to-next-timber, 74, 75, 75
Goetzmann, W. H., 195, 196, 198
Gold, Pat Courtney, 335
gold rush, 181, 207, 229; in Black Hills, 226; Nez Perce lands, map of, 224–25
Goodbird, 233, 234, 238
Gorman, Carl, 309
Gorman, R. C., 309
gratitude, 56
Great Britain: border dispute with, 181; United States, treaty with, 207
Great Plains: Europeans to, 115, 116; farmer-Indians on, 71; Village Indians of, 71; and white travelers, 115
Greenwood, Caleb, 198
Grinnell, Calvin, 127
Grinnell, George Bird, 178, 179
Griswold, Gillett, 164
Gros Ventres, 88, 112
Guthrie, Woody, 347

Hafen, LeRoy R., 198
Haines, Francis, 21, 22
Half Moon, Otis, 98, 228, 270, 333
Half Moon, Richard, 227, 228, 333
Hanford Site, 286
Hawaii, 303, 307, 308, 313
Head Start, 309, 318
Hendry, Anthony, 25, 84–85
Henry, Alexander (the elder), 25, 88
Henry, Alexander (the younger), 26, 88
Hidatsas, 31, 34, 49, 71, 73, 81, 117, 127, 128,

203, 316, 334; Americans, partnership with, 111; and Arikaras, 123; and cattle, 232, 233, 234, 235, 236, 237, 238; Crow, separation from, 28; landscape, view of, 119; and Mandans, 123; as modern, 335; and Plains Village Tradition, 72; subgroups of, 72; and white traders, 30
Hidatsa villages, 27, 28; agriculture of, 70; horses, diffusion of in, 30; and trade, 121; visitors to, 116, 120
Holy Family Mission, 313
Homer, 5
homesteaders, 182, 229, 231; and Indian lands, 271
Hopi Reservation, 319
Horse Culture period, 19
horse frontier: expansion of, 25
horses, 99; diffusion of, 30, 31, 35; diffusion, trade routes of, 27, 28, 31; and firearms, 34; importance of, 29; nomadic, and horticultural peoples, trade between, 31; and Plains Indians, 20, 21, 22, 23; scarcity of, 24; slaves, exchange of, 23; spread of, 23, 24, 26, 27; and theft, 35; trading of, 25, 31, 35; trading of, as profitable, 34
horticultural tribes, 30; nomadic tribes, trading with, 34
Howard, General, 141
Howard, Phyllis, 317, 318
Hudson's Bay Company, 30, 88, 116, 184–85, 189, 193, 194, 199, 200; and Columbia River, 190; and Northwest Company, 190
Hunt, W. P., 189

Icaʼiwikec, 73. See also Corn Sucker
Idaho, 143, 181, 241, 271, 277, 347; smoke plan of, 285; wolf recovery in, 284, 285, 292
Indian country, 6, 14, 259; and alcoholism, 80; American settlement in, 207, 214, 231; and disease, 39; and fur trade, 188; and generosity, 56; and gratitude, 56; intermarriage in, 39; lands of, taking of, 271; language preservation in, 294; as little known, 105, 106; loyalty in, 39; moral code of, 39; schools in, 239–40; songs in,

39; stories of creation in, 39; and trade, 83; undermining of, 182; well-being of, 70; West, as new name of, 182

Indian Health Service, 282

Indian Reorganization Act: and allotment system, 271–72

Indian schools: and day schools, 239, 240; and mission schools, 239; and off-reservation boarding schools, 239, 240, 243; and on-reservation boarding schools, 239, 240, 243

Indian School Service, 239; agents of, 242–46; cook of, 250; laundress of, 250; manual training teachers of, 249; matron of, 249–50; physician of, 248–49; reservation school superintendents, 246–48; rules for, 240; superintendent of, 240–41; supervisors of, 241–42

Indian treaties: and alcohol, 291; land, surrendering of, 277

Innis, Harold, 197

Institute of American Indian Arts Museum (IAIA), 323, 324

Institute of Museum Services (IMS), 321

Interactive Video Network (IVN), 319

Iowa, 198

Iron Eyes, 57

Jackson, David E., 197

Jackson, Donald, 349

James, Henry, 349

Jefferson, Thomas, 1, 5, 6, 8, 103, 105, 351; on buffalo, 106, 107, 108; exploration, as inquiry, 122; and fur trade, 197, 198; on Native Americans, 109, 110; West, interest in, 101

Jones, W. A., 240

Joseph, Chief, 229

journey, 352

journey story, 347, 352; and encounters, 349. *See also* expedition story; road story; stories

Jusseaume, René, 116, 124

Kakawita, 119

Kalispel tribe, 27

Kansas, 241

Kansa tribe, 24

Karmana, Koanao, 303

Kerouac, Jack, 347

Kiowa, 23, 27, 29, 31; and horse trading, 30

Kiowa-Apache, 29, 31; and horse trading, 30

Kipp, Darrell Robes, 255, 295, 311, 332

Kittredge, William, 346

Klamath, 166

Klamath Reservation, 274

Klamath Trail, 166

Klikitat, 167

Koolkooltom, Jr., 141

Koolkooltom, Sr., 141

Kurz, Rudolph, 206n36

La Harpe, Bernard de, 24

land: Native American, and Europeans, differences among, 227; life, as source of, 227; as property, 227

Lander, F. W., 215

Larocque, François, 28

La Salle, Robert de, 23, 24, 25

La Vérendrye, P. G. V., 24, 25, 33

Leader Charge, Doris, 308

Le Borgne, 88, 90, 91, 92, 93, 94, 96, 97, 98, 120; Lewis, meeting with, 126

Lemhi Shoshone: and horses, 26–27

Leonard, Zenas, 196

Leopold, Aldo, 202

Lewis, Meriwether, 1, 5, 9, 101, 105, 116, 152, 163, 343, 348, 349, 351; Blackfeet, encounter with, 168–76, 175, 179; on Clatsops, 150–52; and Fort Clatsop, 148; Le Borgne, meeting with, 126; plan of, 123; Shoshones, negotiation with, 103; and trading, 166–67

Lewis and Clark, 88, 99, 127, 139, 141, 163, 189, 226, 259, 277, 332, 338, 351; American sovereignty, proclaiming of, 123; and Columbia River system, 164; diplomatic agenda of, 118, 123; intentions of, as mystery, 117, 122; intertribal alliance, against Sioux, 123; intertribal peace, preaching of, 121; as intruders, 118; Native hospitality, dependence on, 102; and salmon,

McClintock, Walter, 40
McKay, William C., 209
McMullin, Fayette, 215
McWhorter, Lucullus, 138
Meek, Joe, 199
Meldrum, Robert, 28
Merk, F., 199
Mexican-American War, 207, 345
Mexico, 99, *184–85,* 207
Michigan, 310
military frontiers, 200, 201
miners, 231; in Nez Perce, disputes between, 223
mining, 182
Minnesota, 198, 241
Minthorn, Armand, 54
Minthorn, Philip, 66
missionaries, 201; Americanization efforts of, 182; assimilation campaign of, 239; and fur trade, 200; and Indians, 200
Mississippi River, 182, 198
Missoula floods, 55
Missouri, 198
Missouri tribe, 24, 28, 91
Mistaken Chief, Duane, 309
Modoc, 166
Monroe, James, 194
Montana, 144, 145, 168, 181, 200, 241, 256, 271, 277, 310
Montana State Lewis and Clark Commission, 332
Montreal (Quebec), 7
Moon, 41, 42, 44
Moran, Thomas, 349
Morgan, Frank, 309
Morgan, Lewis Henry, 28
Morning Star, 40, 41, 42, 44, 45
Morrow, J. A., 232
Moulton, Gary, 9, 343
Mrs. Good Bear, 60

Nahwooksy, Fred, 323
Naouadiché, 24
Napoleon, 101
National Bicentennial Exhibition, 5–6; and Native Americans, 6

National Forest Management Act, 266
National Park Service, 282, 333
Native American Graves Protection and Repatriation Act (NAGPRA), 322
Native Americans, 6; alcohol, effects on, 203, 213; balance, seeking of, 119; and cattle, 232; and common good, 17; and Corps of Discovery, 114; earth, respect for, 17; as ecosystem people, 203; and fur traders, 203; and missionaries, 239; social ethic of, 17; and stories, 346, 347; two nations, as belonging to, 259; whites, power of, 116
Native American stories, 346; and journeys, 347
Native American women: and buffalo-calling ceremony, 125; Lewis and Clark expedition, relations among, 124–25
Native Hawaiians, 302, 303; language restoration of, as role model, 307
Navaho, 99
Nebraska, 241, 310
Ned A. Hatathli Museum, 321, 322
Nelson, Willie, 347
Nevada, 181, 241
Newell, Robert, 199
New England, 200
New Mexico, 28, 33, 181, 198, 241; Spaniards in, 23
New Mexico Territory, 241
Nez Perce (alternately, Nez Percé), 9, 14, 27, 69, 141–42n2, 152, 161, 168, 208, 229, 230; and alcohol, 291; in American armed forces, 292; annual cycle of, 144–45; and Appaloosa, 99; calendar year of, 65–66; and William Clark, 136–38; William Clark, hospitality toward, 8; and community celebrations, 289; constitution of, 278; and Corps of Discovery, 103, 141–42n2, 142, 168; and Coyote stories, 289; creation story of, 46–49; and Crow, 98–99; and education, 289; and Department of Natural Resources, 270, 286; Environmental Restoration and Waste Management Program (ERWM) of, 286, 287; and first horses, 27, 99; fish hatchery of,

FREDERICK E. HOXIE is the Swanlund Professor in the Department of History at the University of Illinois. His publications include *Parading through History: The Making of the Crow Nation in America, 1805–1935; The Encyclopedia of North American Indians;* and *Talking Back to Civilization: Indian Voices from the Progressive Era.* Professor Hoxie was a founding trustee of the Smithsonian Institution's National Museum of the American Indian.

JAY T. NELSON is a program assistant at the D'Arcy McNickle Center for American Indian History at the Newberry Library and an adjunct faculty member of the Department of History at DePaul University.

The University of Illinois Press
is a founding member of the
Association of American University Presses.

Composed in 11/14 Bulmer
by Jim Proefrock
at the University of Illinois Press
Designed by Paula Newcomb
Manufactured by Sheridan Books, Inc.

University of Illinois Press
1325 South Oak Street
Champaign, IL 61820-6903
www.press.uillinois.edu